Our *not-so* Lonely Planet
Travel Guide
• •

2

MONE SORAI

Itinerary

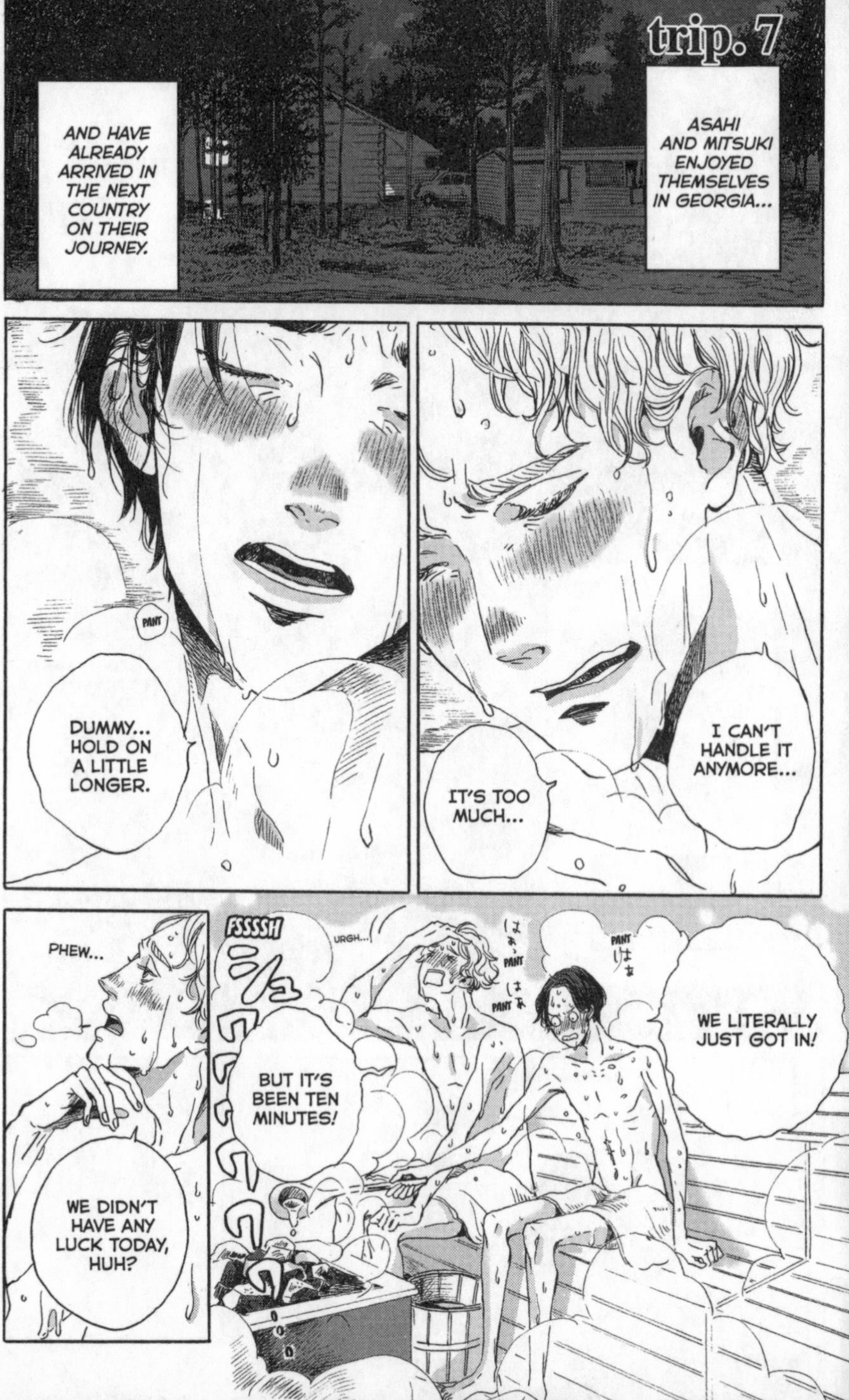
trip. 7
ASAHI AND MITSUKI ENJOYED THEMSELVES IN GEORGIA...
AND HAVE ALREADY ARRIVED IN THE NEXT COUNTRY ON THEIR JOURNEY.
I CAN'T HANDLE IT ANYMORE...
IT'S TOO MUCH...
PANT
DUMMY... HOLD ON A LITTLE LONGER.
WE LITERALLY JUST GOT IN!
PANT
PANT
PANT
URGH...
FSSSSH
BUT IT'S BEEN TEN MINUTES!
PHEW...
WE DIDN'T HAVE ANY LUCK TODAY, HUH?

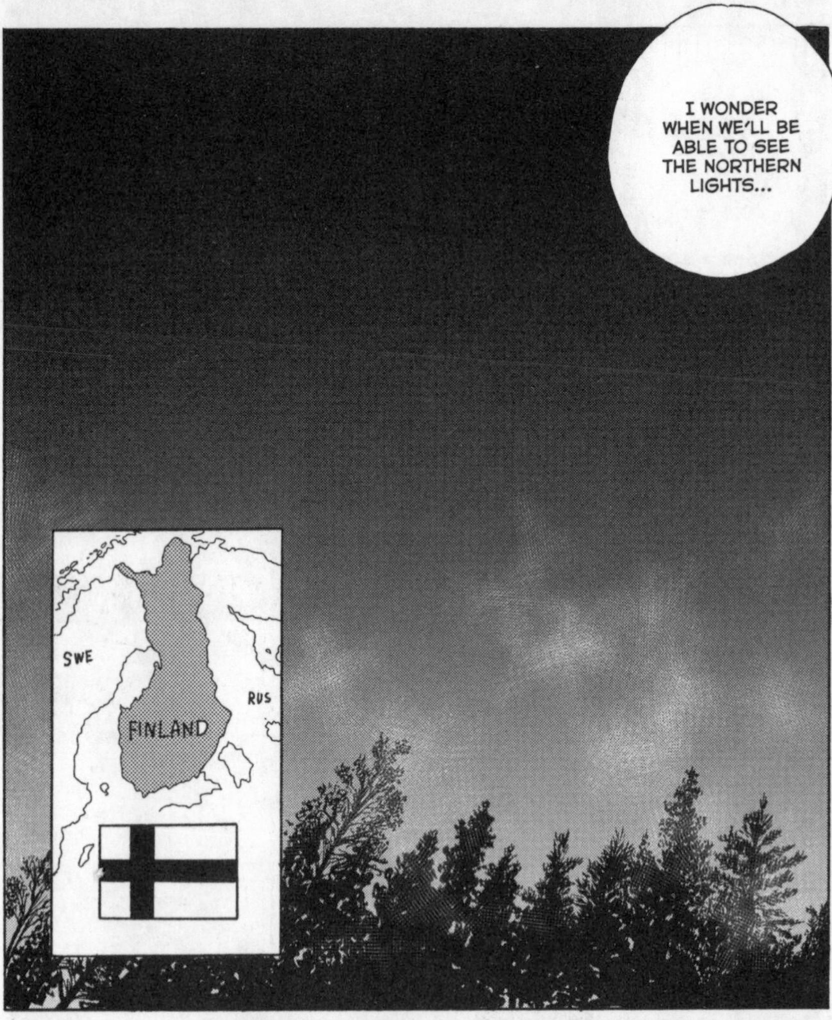
I WONDER WHEN WE'LL BE ABLE TO SEE THE NORTHERN LIGHTS...
SWE
RUS
FINLAND
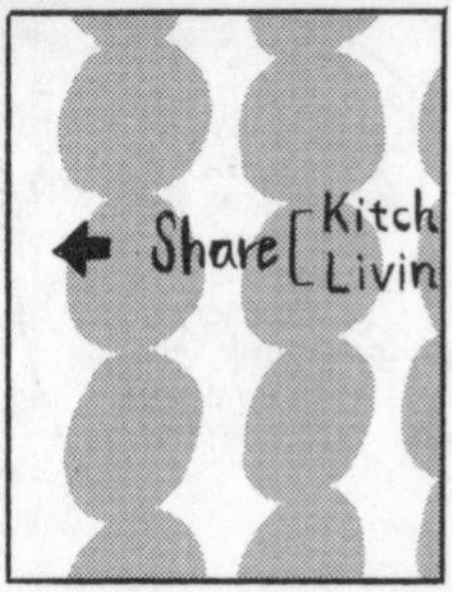
Share
Kitch
Livin
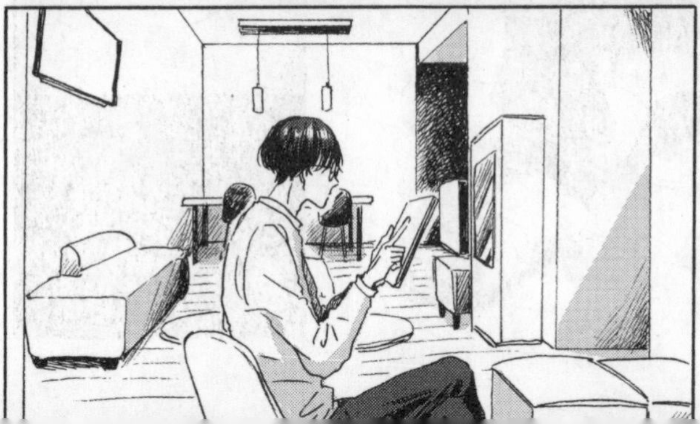

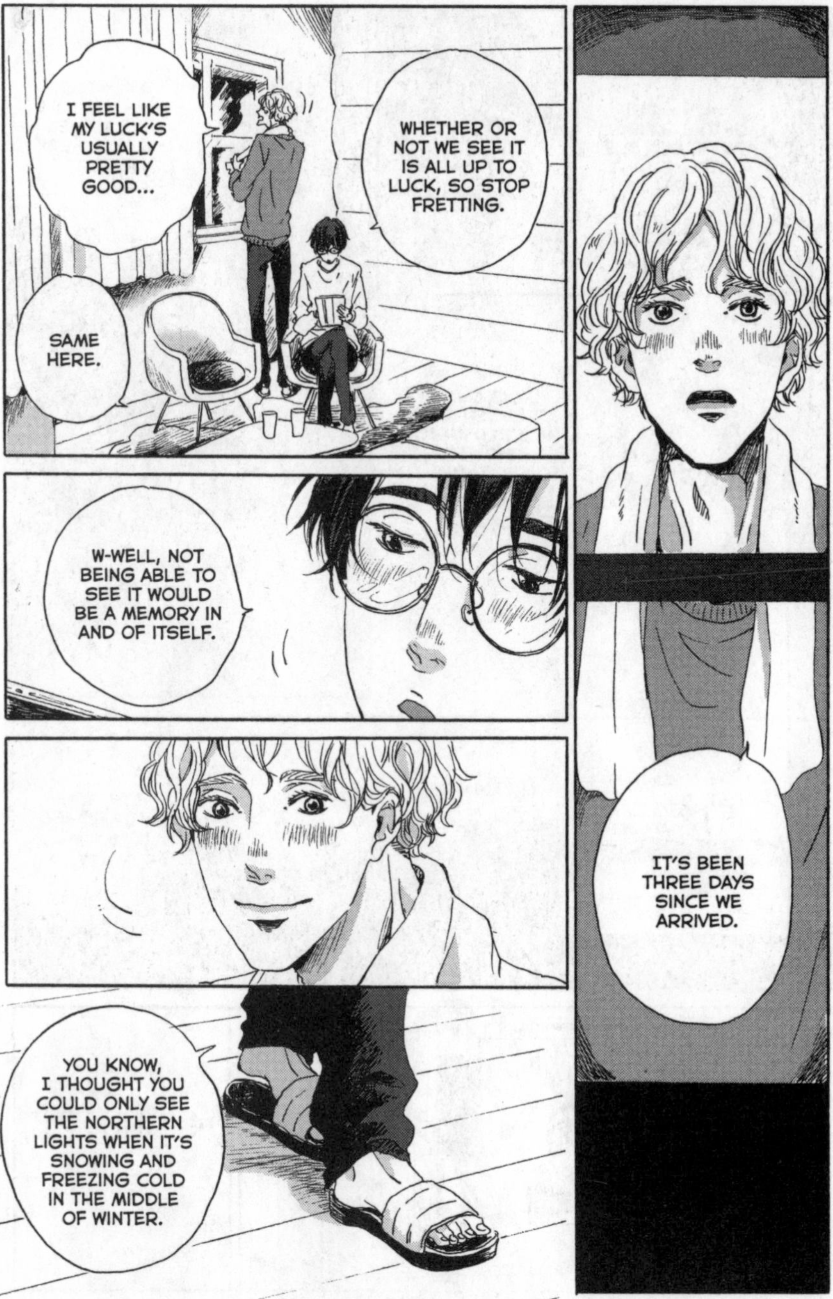
IT'S BEEN THREE DAYS SINCE WE ARRIVED.
WHETHER OR NOT WE SEE IT IS ALL UP TO LUCK, SO STOP FRETTING.
I FEEL LIKE MY LUCK'S USUALLY PRETTY GOOD...
SAME HERE.
W-WELL, NOT BEING ABLE TO SEE IT WOULD BE A MEMORY IN AND OF ITSELF.
YOU KNOW, I THOUGHT YOU COULD ONLY SEE THE NORTHERN LIGHTS WHEN IT'S SNOWING AND FREEZING COLD IN THE MIDDLE OF WINTER.

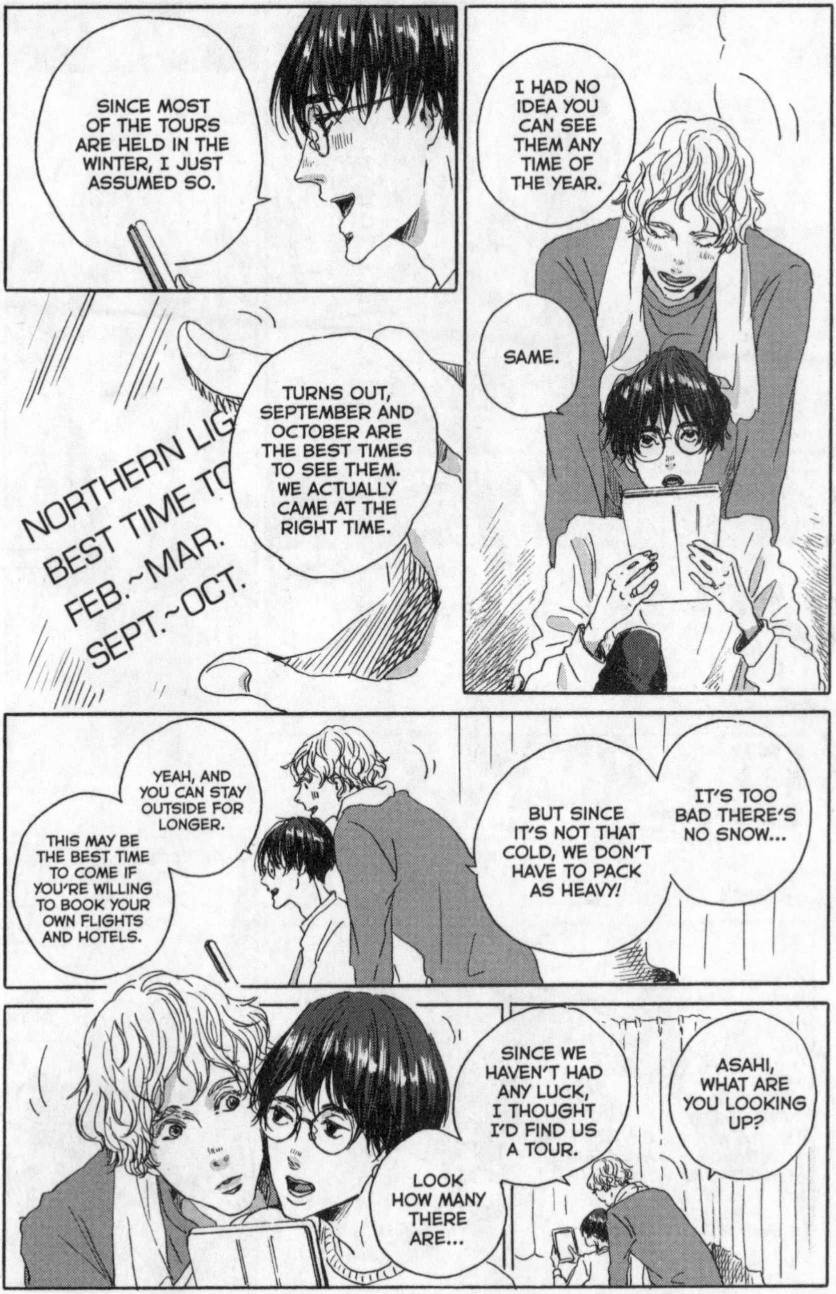
I HAD NO IDEA YOU CAN SEE THEM ANY TIME OF THE YEAR.
SAME.
SINCE MOST OF THE TOURS ARE HELD IN THE WINTER, I JUST ASSUMED SO.
TURNS OUT, SEPTEMBER AND OCTOBER ARE THE BEST TIMES TO SEE THEM. WE ACTUALLY CAME AT THE RIGHT TIME.
NORTHERN LIG
BEST TIME TO
FEB.~MAR.
SEPT.~OCT.
IT'S TOO BAD THERE'S NO SNOW...
BUT SINCE IT'S NOT THAT COLD, WE DON'T HAVE TO PACK AS HEAVY!
YEAH, AND YOU CAN STAY OUTSIDE FOR LONGER.
THIS MAY BE THE BEST TIME TO COME IF YOU'RE WILLING TO BOOK YOUR OWN FLIGHTS AND HOTELS.
ASAHI, WHAT ARE YOU LOOKING UP?
SINCE WE HAVEN'T HAD ANY LUCK, I THOUGHT I'D FIND US A TOUR.
LOOK HOW MANY THERE ARE...

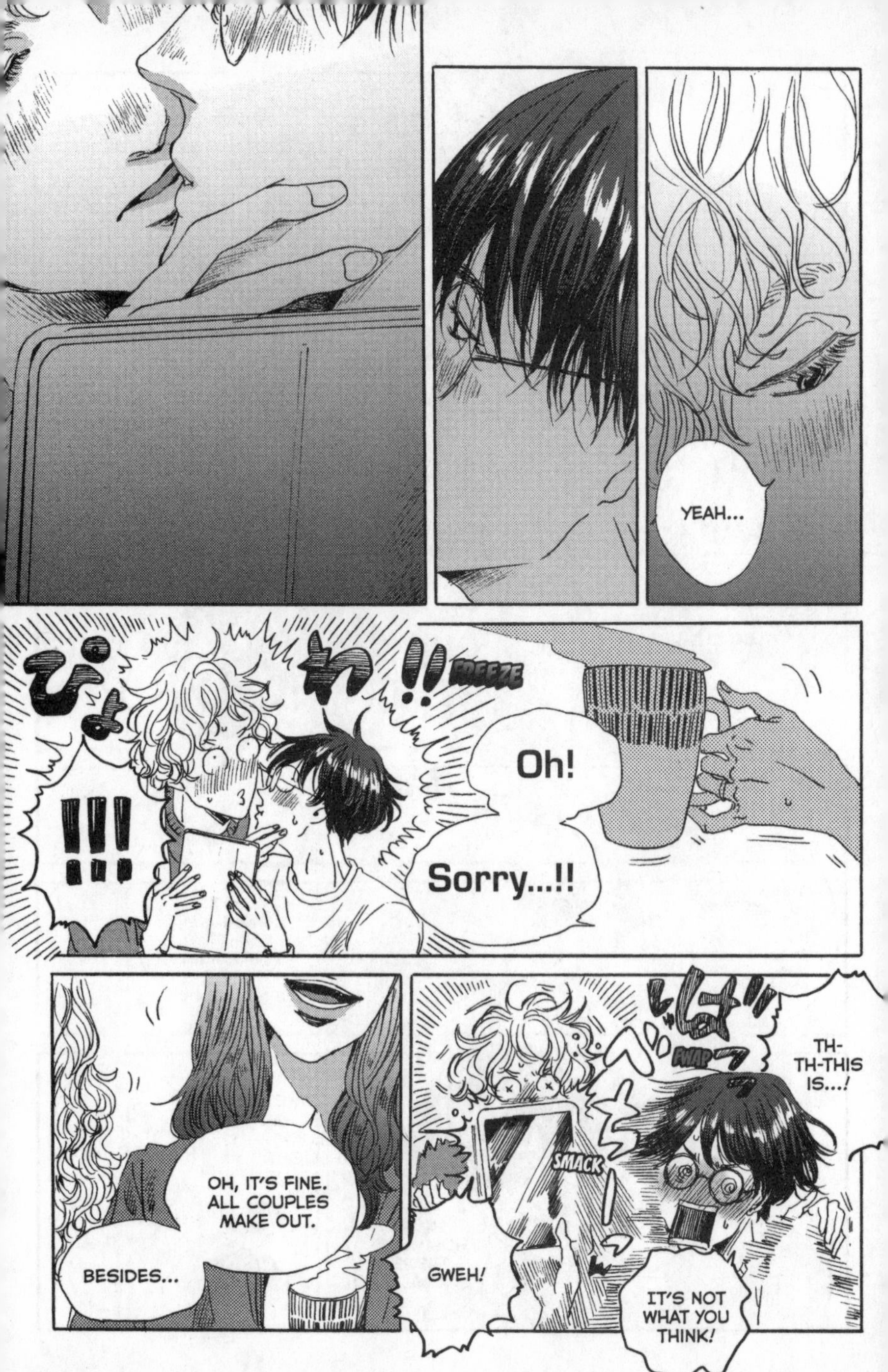
YEAH...
Oh!
Sorry...!!
FREEZE
!!!
TH-TH-THIS IS...!
SWAP
SMACK
GWEH!
IT'S NOT WHAT YOU THINK!
OH, IT'S FINE. ALL COUPLES MAKE OUT.
BESIDES...

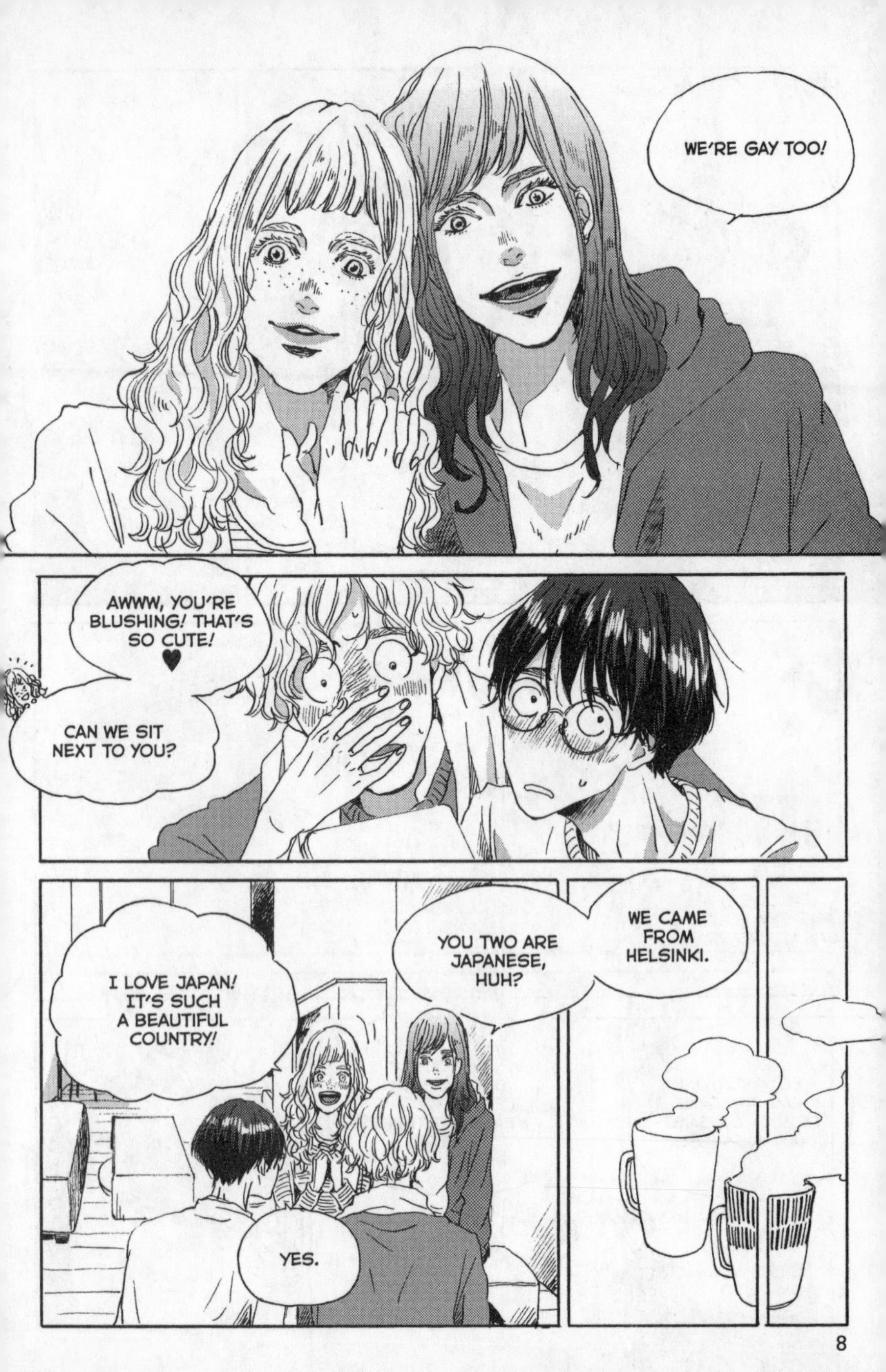
WE'RE GAY TOO!
AWWW, YOU'RE BLUSHING! THAT'S SO CUTE! ♥
CAN WE SIT NEXT TO YOU?
WE CAME FROM HELSINKI.
YOU TWO ARE JAPANESE, HUH?
I LOVE JAPAN! IT'S SUCH A BEAUTIFUL COUNTRY!
YES.

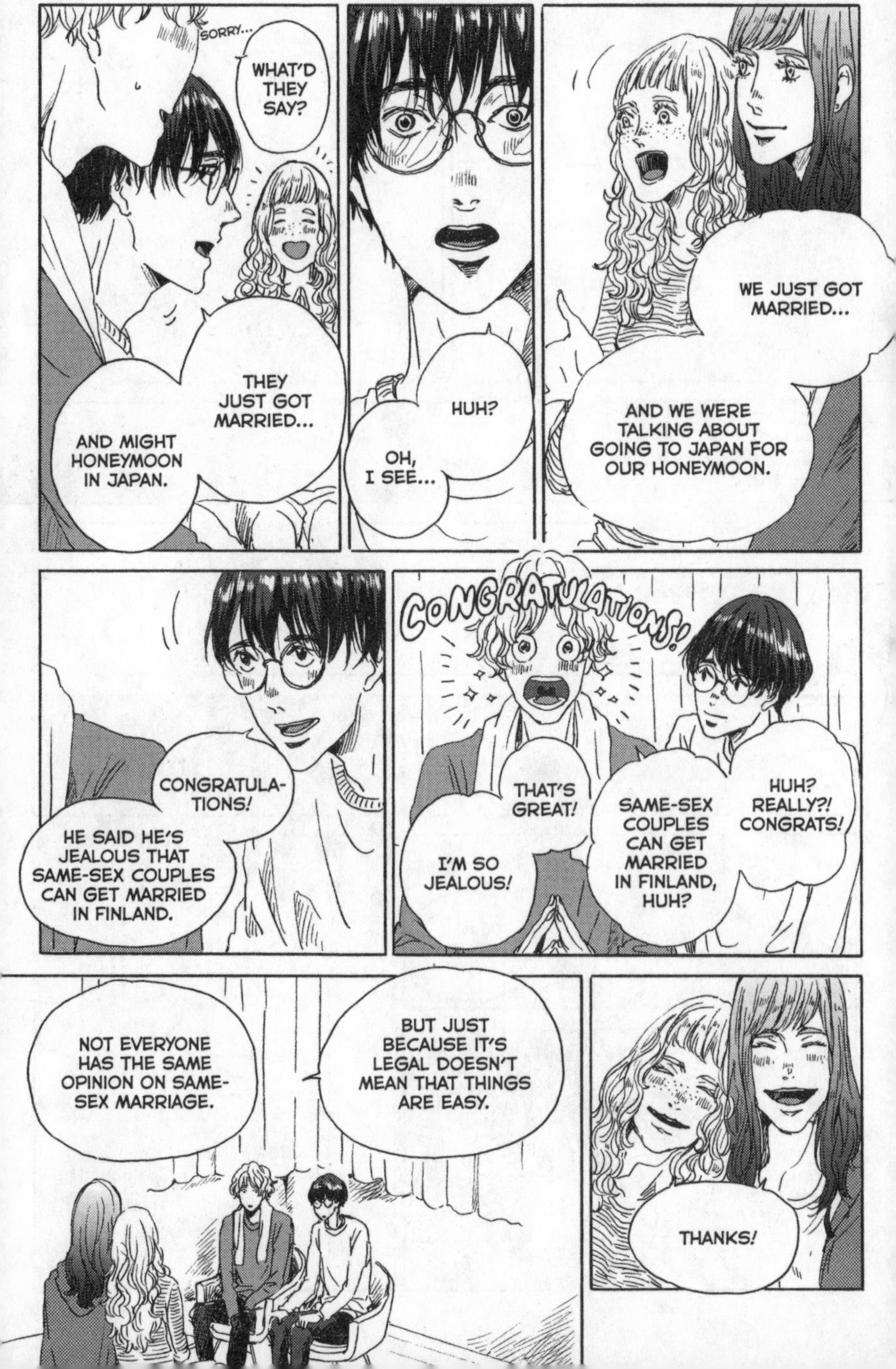
WE JUST GOT MARRIED...
AND WE WERE TALKING ABOUT GOING TO JAPAN FOR OUR HONEYMOON.
HUH?
OH, I SEE...
SORRY...
WHAT'D THEY SAY?
THEY JUST GOT MARRIED...
AND MIGHT HONEYMOON IN JAPAN.
CONGRATULATIONS!
HUH? REALLY?! CONGRATS!
SAME-SEX COUPLES CAN GET MARRIED IN FINLAND, HUH?
THAT'S GREAT!
I'M SO JEALOUS!
CONGRATULA-TIONS!
HE SAID HE'S JEALOUS THAT SAME-SEX COUPLES CAN GET MARRIED IN FINLAND.
THANKS!
BUT JUST BECAUSE IT'S LEGAL DOESN'T MEAN THAT THINGS ARE EASY.
NOT EVERYONE HAS THE SAME OPINION ON SAME-SEX MARRIAGE.

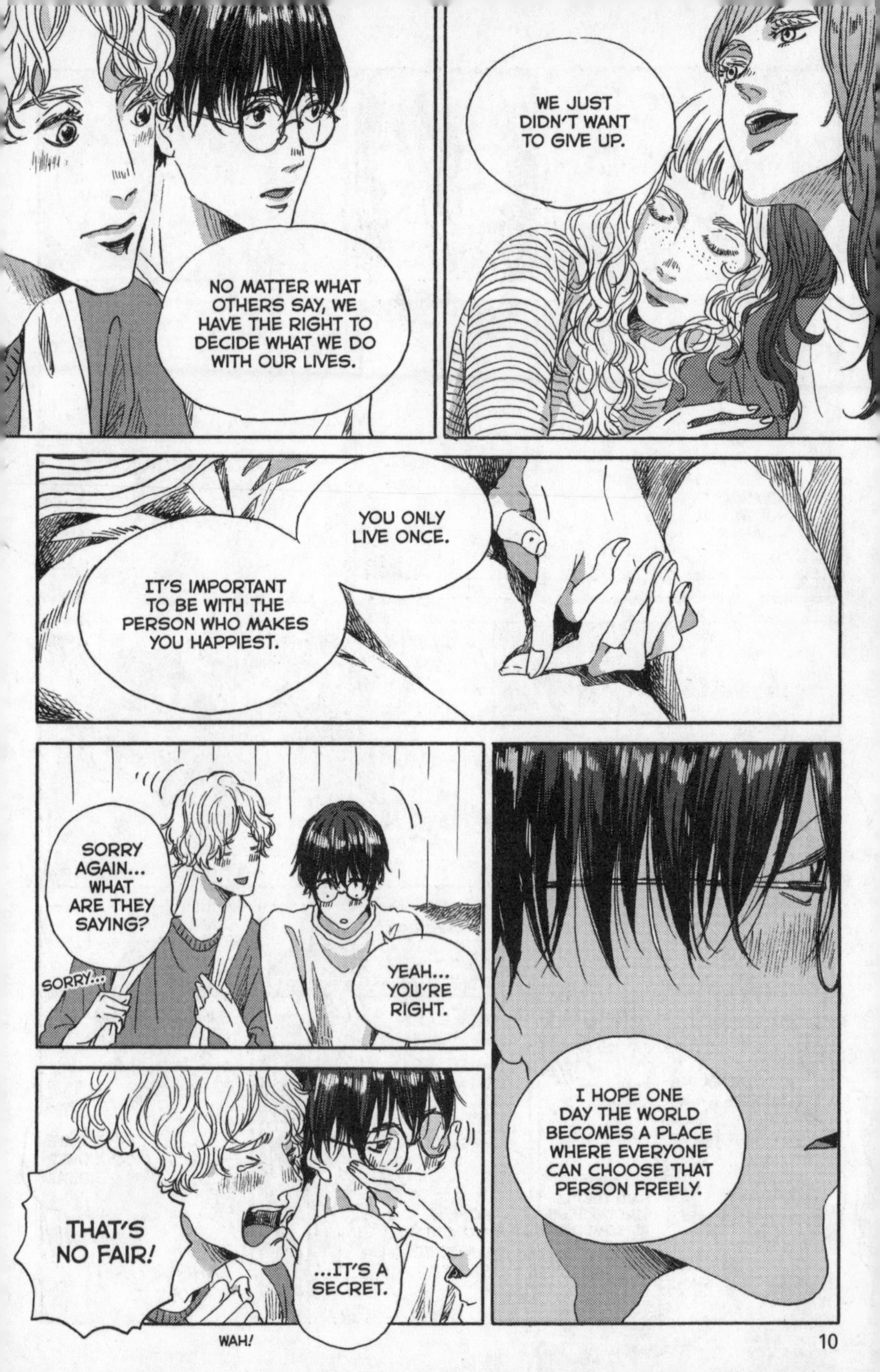
WE JUST DIDN'T WANT TO GIVE UP.
NO MATTER WHAT OTHERS SAY, WE HAVE THE RIGHT TO DECIDE WHAT WE DO WITH OUR LIVES.
YOU ONLY LIVE ONCE.
IT'S IMPORTANT TO BE WITH THE PERSON WHO MAKES YOU HAPPIEST.
I HOPE ONE DAY THE WORLD BECOMES A PLACE WHERE EVERYONE CAN CHOOSE THAT PERSON FREELY.
SORRY AGAIN... WHAT ARE THEY SAYING?
YEAH... YOU'RE RIGHT.
SORRY...
...IT'S A SECRET.
THAT'S NO FAIR!
WAH!

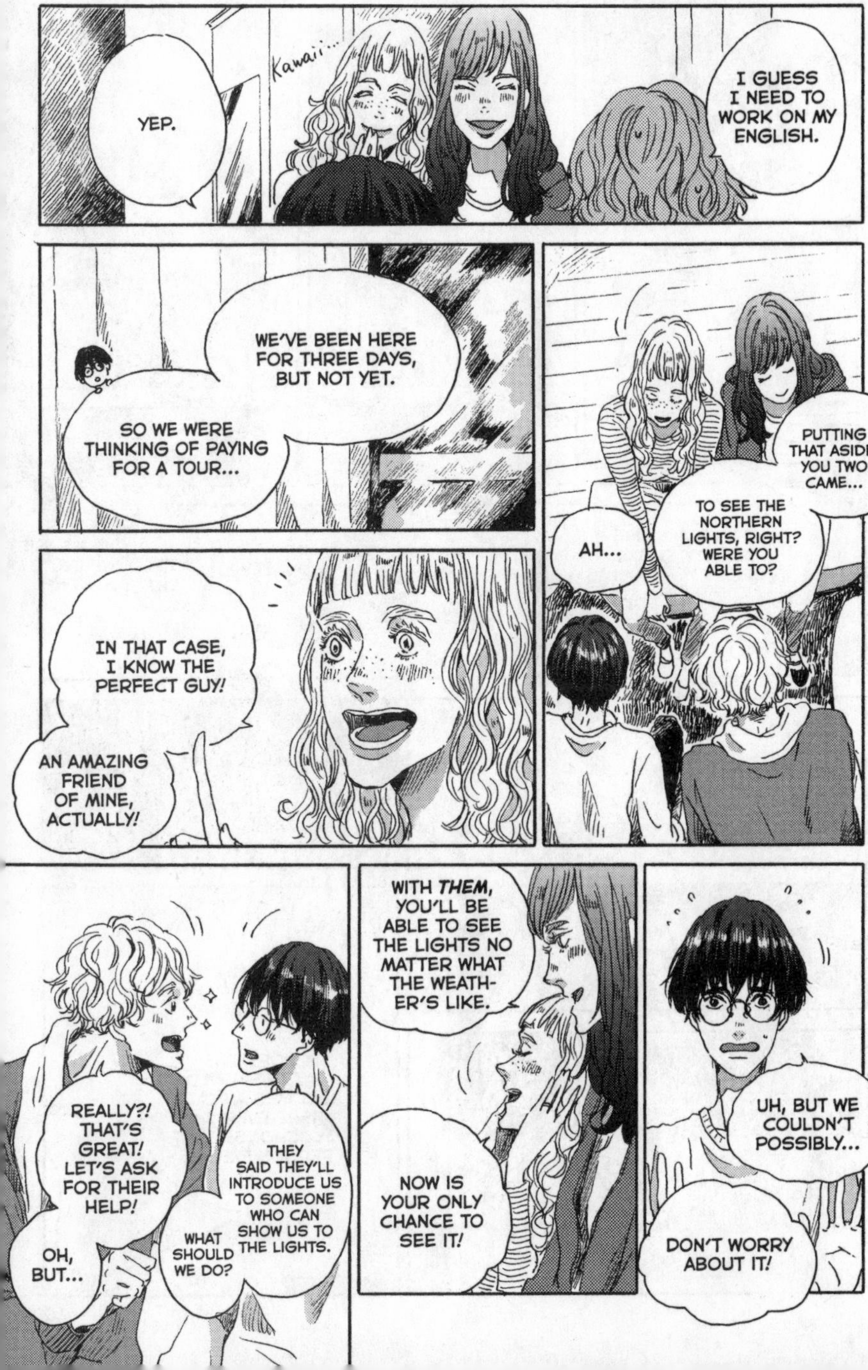
I GUESS I NEED TO WORK ON MY ENGLISH.
Kawaii...
YEP.
PUTTING THAT ASIDE, YOU TWO CAME...
TO SEE THE NORTHERN LIGHTS, RIGHT? WERE YOU ABLE TO?
AH...
WE'VE BEEN HERE FOR THREE DAYS, BUT NOT YET.
SO WE WERE THINKING OF PAYING FOR A TOUR...
IN THAT CASE, I KNOW THE PERFECT GUY!
AN AMAZING FRIEND OF MINE, ACTUALLY!
UH, BUT WE COULDN'T POSSIBLY...
DON'T WORRY ABOUT IT!
WITH *THEM*, YOU'LL BE ABLE TO SEE THE LIGHTS NO MATTER WHAT THE WEATHER'S LIKE.
NOW IS YOUR ONLY CHANCE TO SEE IT!
THEY SAID THEY'LL INTRODUCE US TO SOMEONE WHO CAN SHOW US TO THE LIGHTS.
WHAT SHOULD WE DO?
REALLY?! THAT'S GREAT! LET'S ASK FOR THEIR HELP!
OH, BUT...

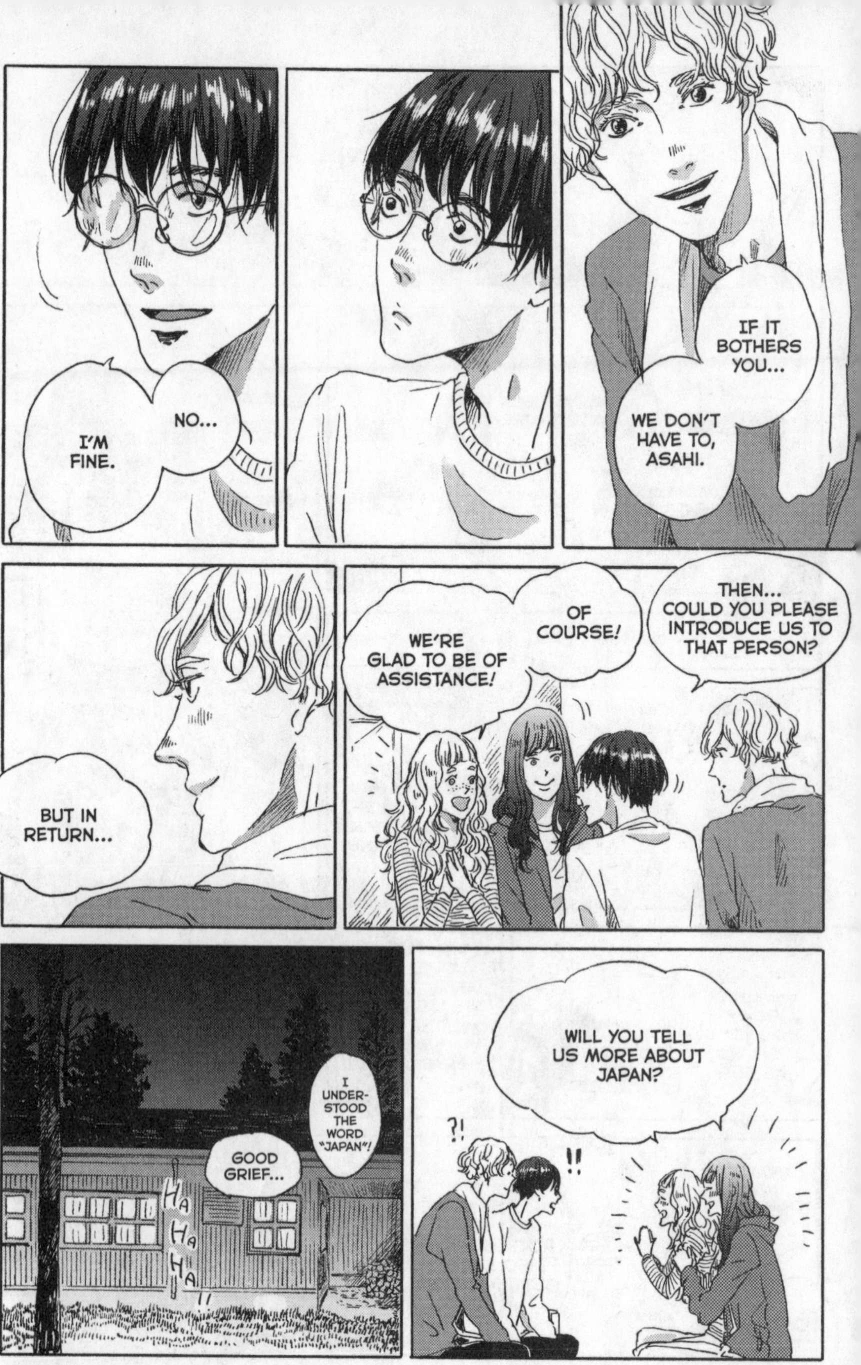
IF IT BOTHERS YOU...
WE DON'T HAVE TO, ASAHI.
NO...
I'M FINE.
THEN... COULD YOU PLEASE INTRODUCE US TO THAT PERSON?
OF COURSE!
WE'RE GLAD TO BE OF ASSISTANCE!
BUT IN RETURN...
WILL YOU TELL US MORE ABOUT JAPAN?
?!
!!
I UNDERSTOOD THE WORD "JAPAN"!
GOOD GRIEF...
HA HA HA

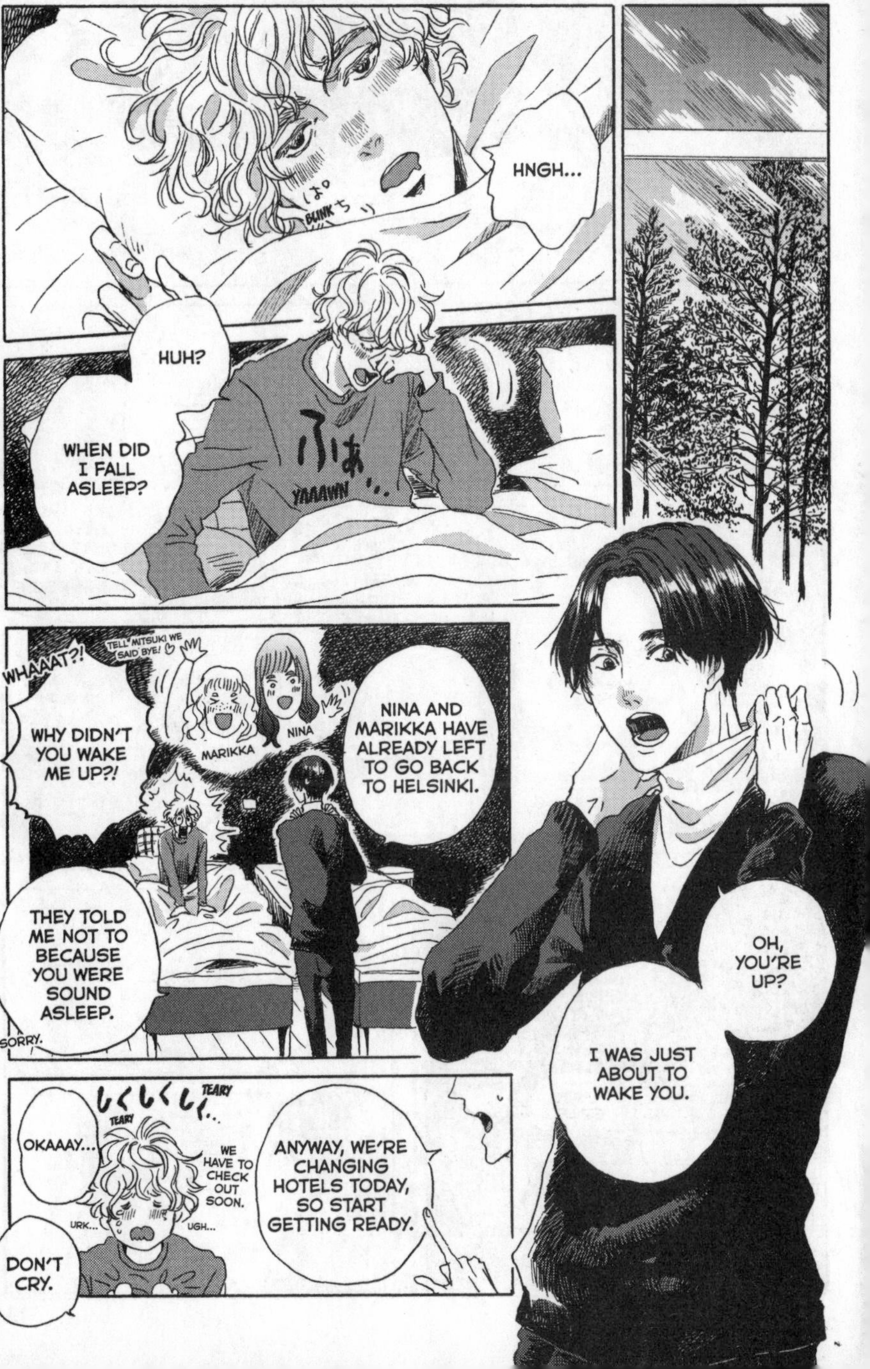
HNGH...
ぱちり
BLINK
HUH?
WHEN DID I FALL ASLEEP?
ふぁ...
YAAAWN
OH, YOU'RE UP?
I WAS JUST ABOUT TO WAKE YOU.
NINA AND MARIKKA HAVE ALREADY LEFT TO GO BACK TO HELSINKI.
TELL MITSUKI WE SAID BYE!
NINA
MARIKKA
WHAAAT?!
WHY DIDN'T YOU WAKE ME UP?!
THEY TOLD ME NOT TO BECAUSE YOU WERE SOUND ASLEEP.
SORRY.
ANYWAY, WE'RE CHANGING HOTELS TODAY, SO START GETTING READY.
WE HAVE TO CHECK OUT SOON.
しくしくしく...
TEARY
TEARY
OKAAAY...
UGH...
URK...
DON'T CRY.

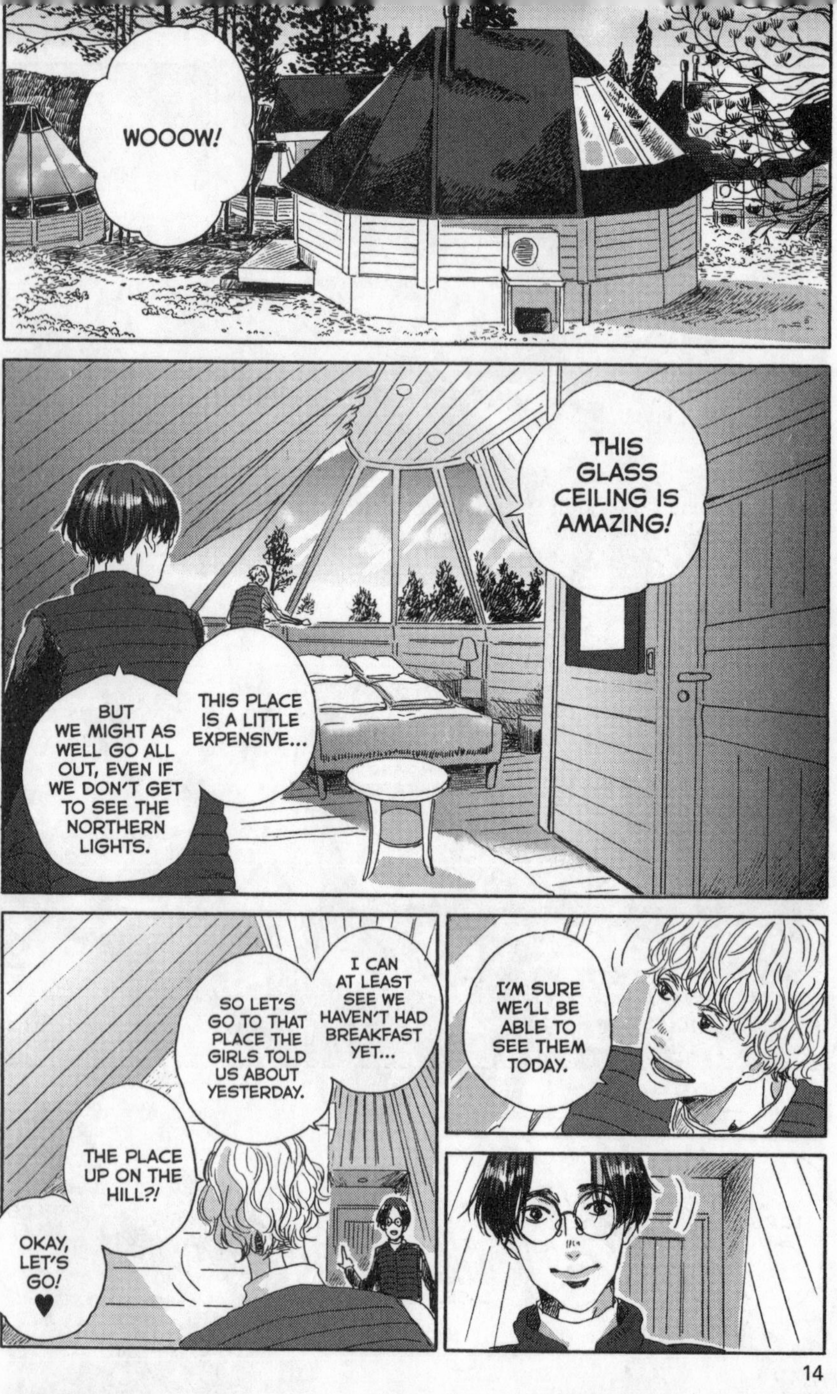
WOOOW!
THIS GLASS CEILING IS AMAZING!
THIS PLACE IS A LITTLE EXPENSIVE...
BUT WE MIGHT AS WELL GO ALL OUT, EVEN IF WE DON'T GET TO SEE THE NORTHERN LIGHTS.
I'M SURE WE'LL BE ABLE TO SEE THEM TODAY.
I CAN AT LEAST SEE WE HAVEN'T HAD BREAKFAST YET...
SO LET'S GO TO THAT PLACE THE GIRLS TOLD US ABOUT YESTERDAY.
THE PLACE UP ON THE HILL?!
OKAY, LET'S GO! ♥

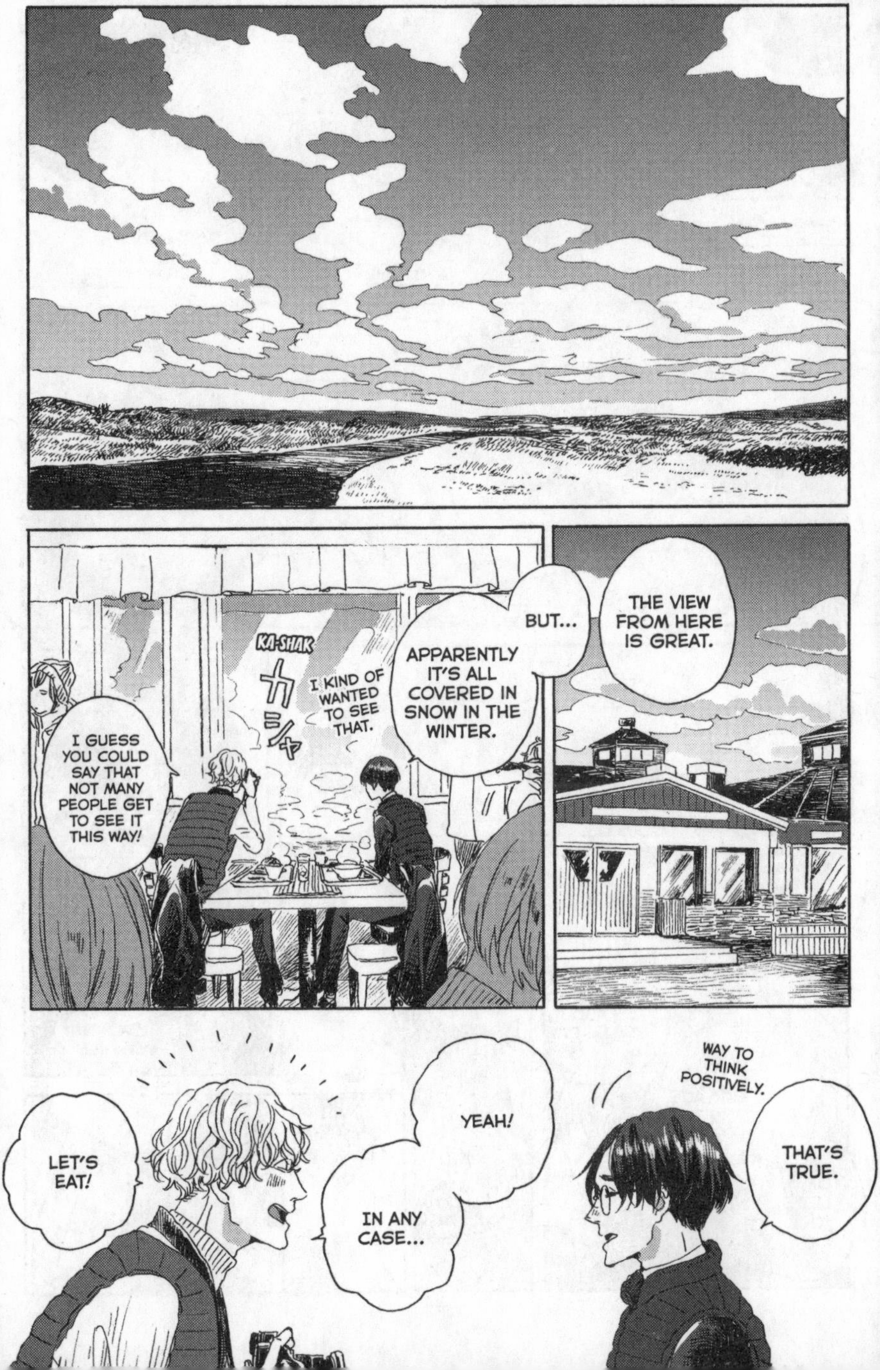
THE VIEW FROM HERE IS GREAT.
BUT...
APPARENTLY IT'S ALL COVERED IN SNOW IN THE WINTER.
I KIND OF WANTED TO SEE THAT.
KA-SHAK
カシャ
I GUESS YOU COULD SAY THAT NOT MANY PEOPLE GET TO SEE IT THIS WAY!
THAT'S TRUE.
WAY TO THINK POSITIVELY.
YEAH!
IN ANY CASE...
LET'S EAT!

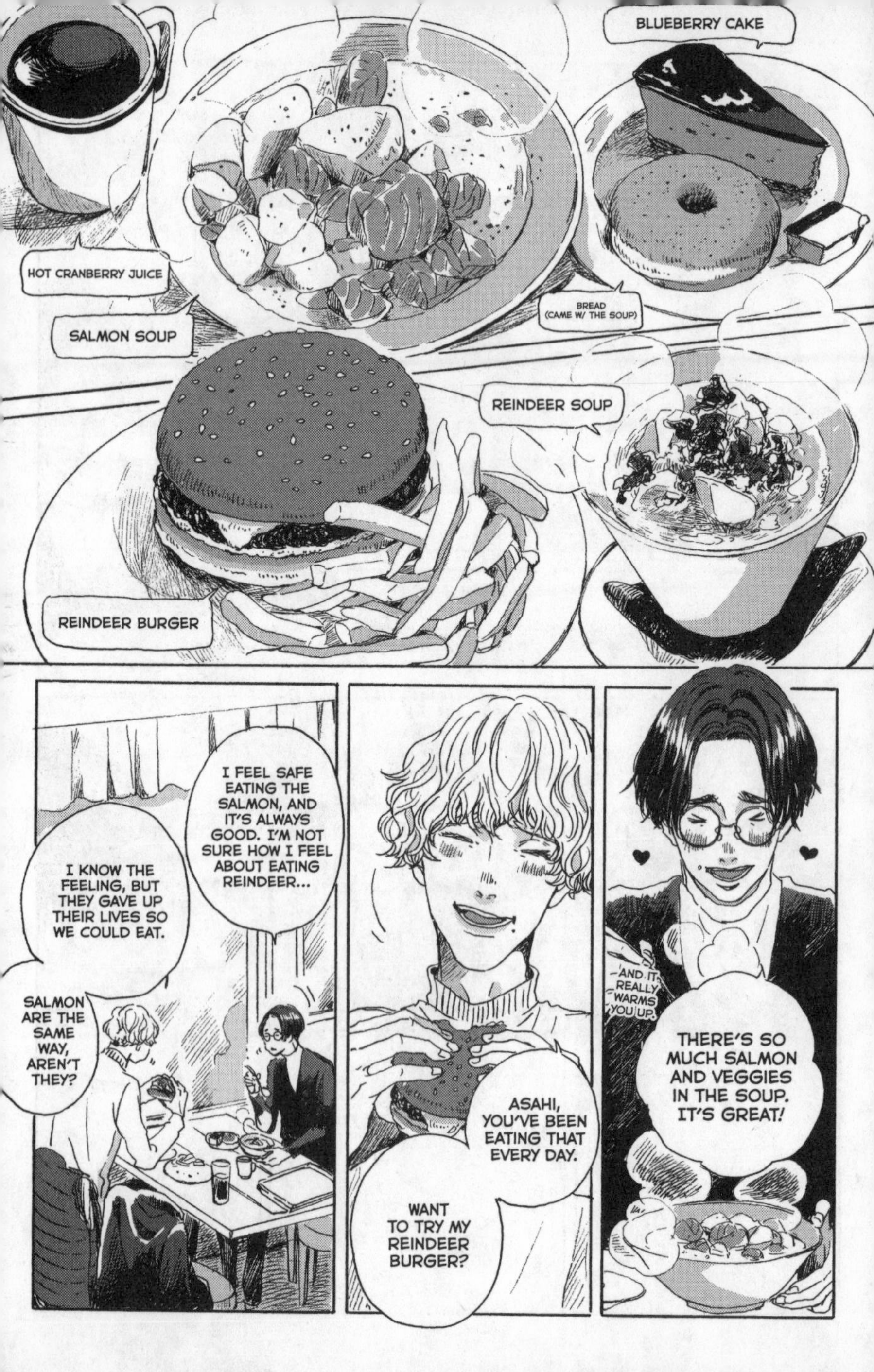
BLUEBERRY CAKE
BREAD (CAME W/ THE SOUP)
HOT CRANBERRY JUICE
SALMON SOUP
REINDEER SOUP
REINDEER BURGER
THERE'S SO MUCH SALMON AND VEGGIES IN THE SOUP. IT'S GREAT!
AND IT REALLY WARMS YOU UP.
ASAHI, YOU'VE BEEN EATING THAT EVERY DAY.
WANT TO TRY MY REINDEER BURGER?
I FEEL SAFE EATING THE SALMON, AND IT'S ALWAYS GOOD. I'M NOT SURE HOW I FEEL ABOUT EATING REINDEER...
I KNOW THE FEELING, BUT THEY GAVE UP THEIR LIVES SO WE COULD EAT.
SALMON ARE THE SAME WAY, AREN'T THEY?

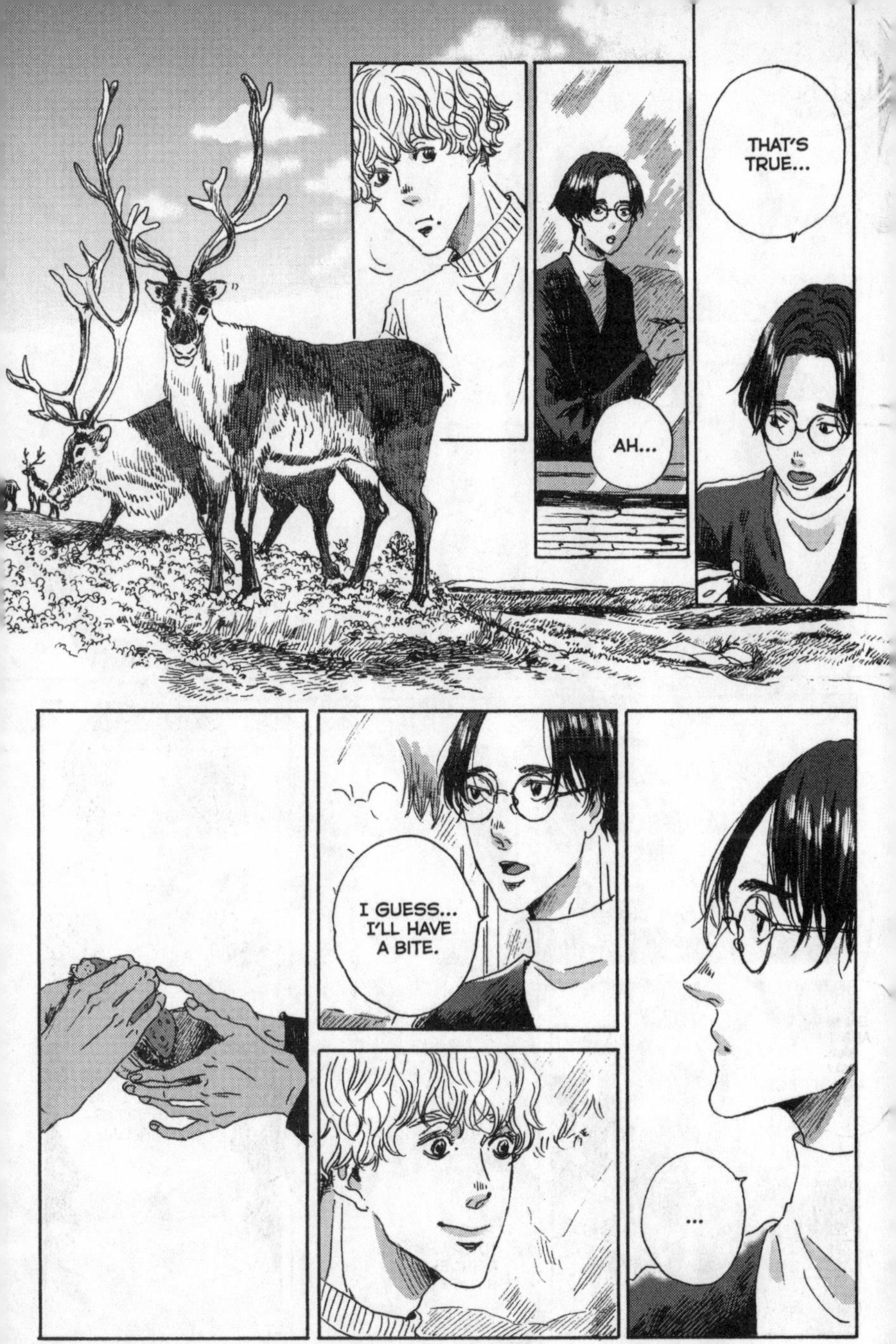
THAT'S TRUE...
AH...
...
I GUESS... I'LL HAVE A BITE.

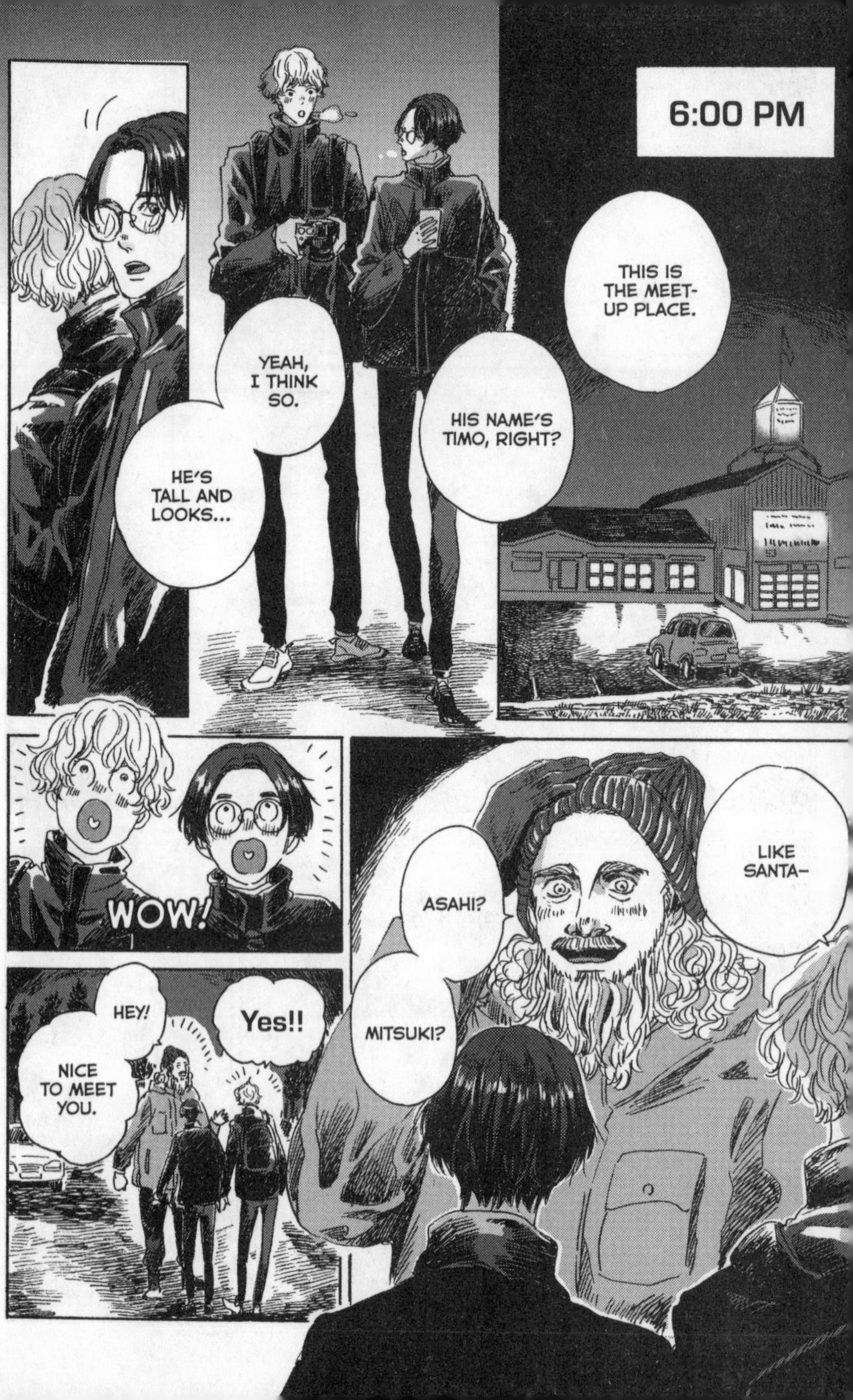
6:00 PM
THIS IS THE MEET-UP PLACE.
HIS NAME'S TIMO, RIGHT?
YEAH, I THINK SO.
HE'S TALL AND LOOKS...
LIKE SANTA-
ASAHI?
MITSUKI?
WOW!
Yes!!
HEY!
NICE TO MEET YOU.

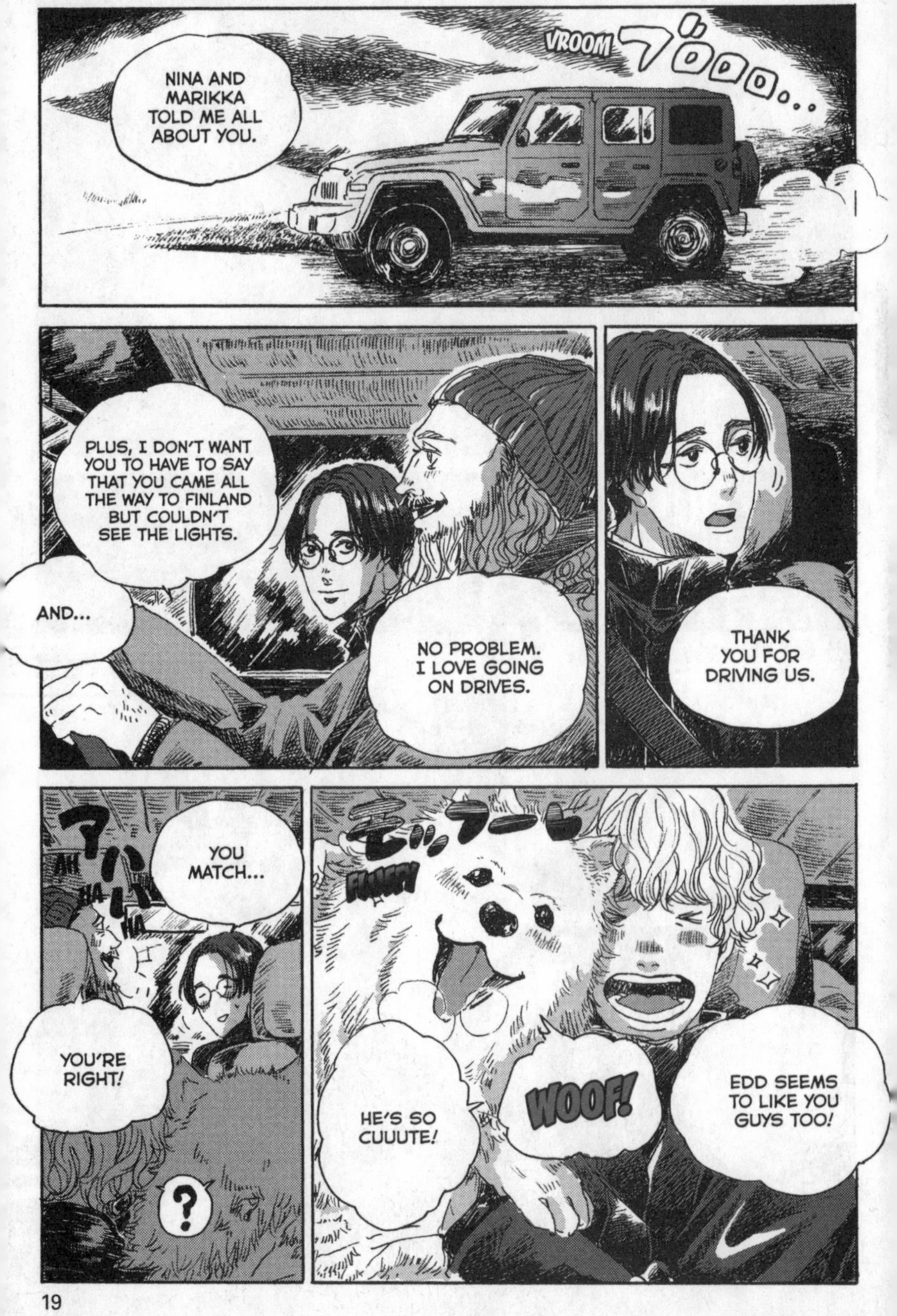
VROOM
NINA AND MARIKKA TOLD ME ALL ABOUT YOU.
THANK YOU FOR DRIVING US.
NO PROBLEM. I LOVE GOING ON DRIVES.
PLUS, I DON'T WANT YOU TO HAVE TO SAY THAT YOU CAME ALL THE WAY TO FINLAND BUT COULDN'T SEE THE LIGHTS.
AND...
FLUFFY
EDD SEEMS TO LIKE YOU GUYS TOO!
WOOF!
HE'S SO CUUUTE!
AH HA HA HA
YOU MATCH...
YOU'RE RIGHT!
?

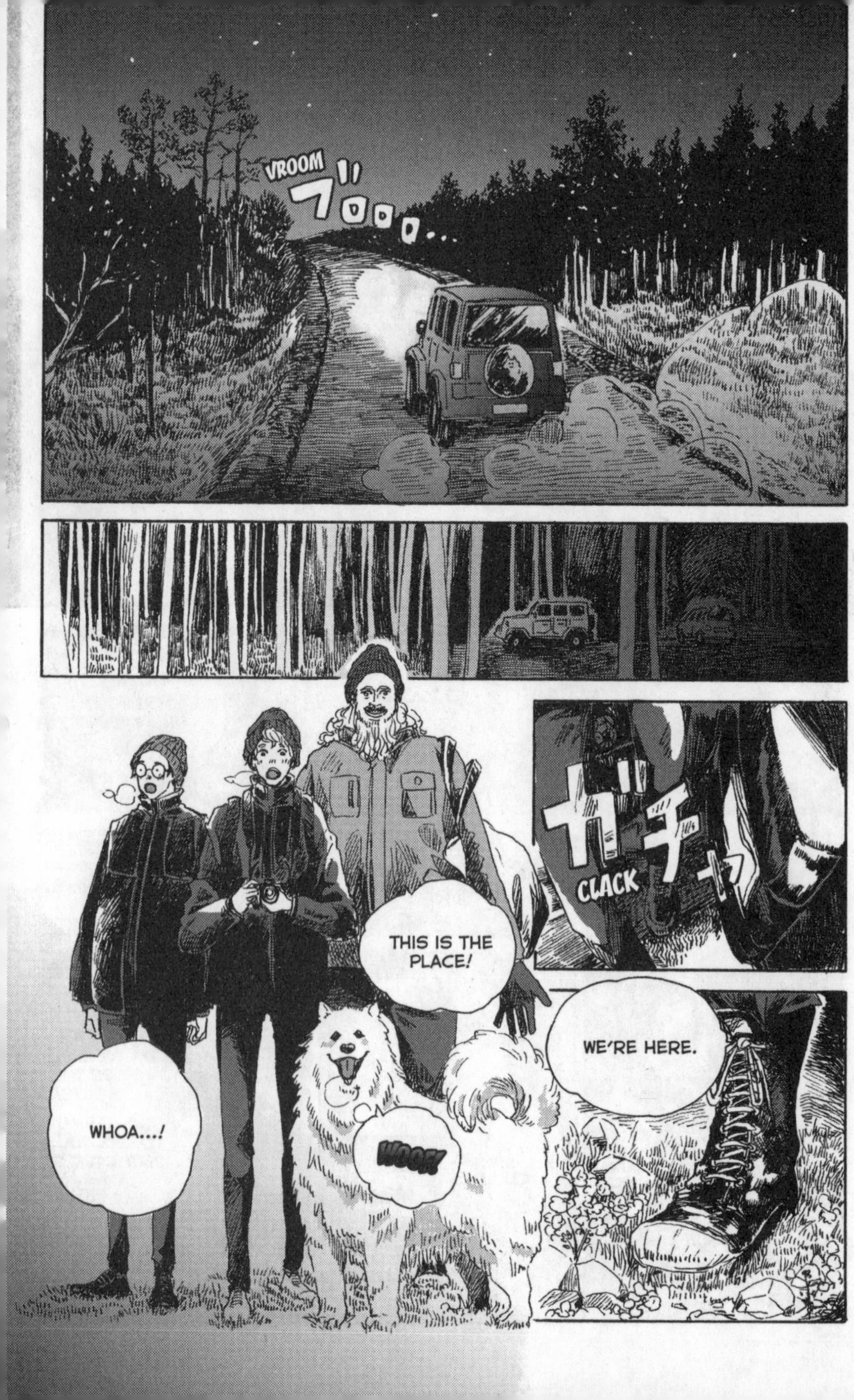
VROOM
ブロロロ...
ガチャ
CLACK
WE'RE HERE.
THIS IS THE PLACE!
WOOF!
WHOA...!

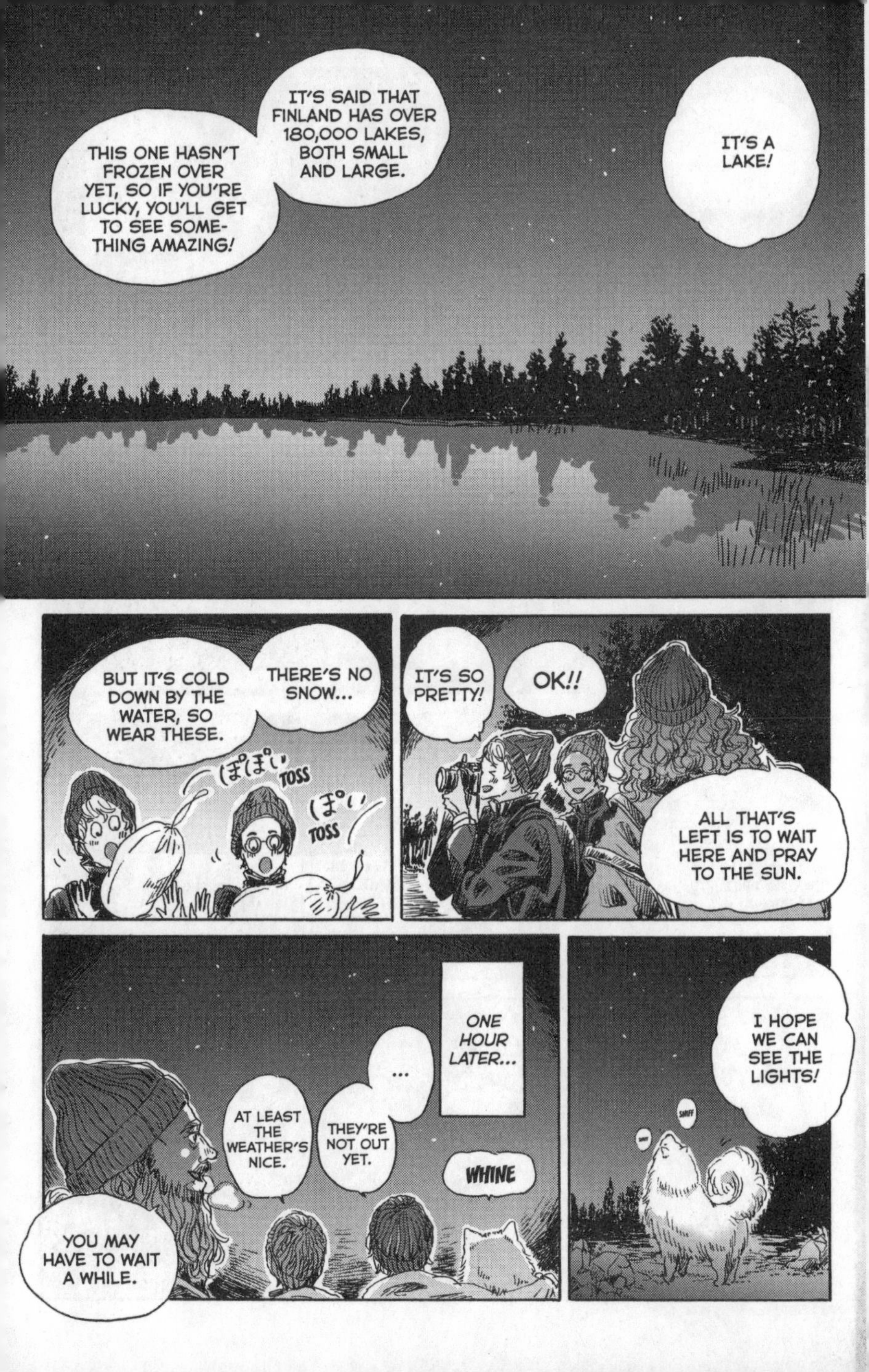
IT'S A LAKE!
IT'S SAID THAT FINLAND HAS OVER 180,000 LAKES, BOTH SMALL AND LARGE.
THIS ONE HASN'T FROZEN OVER YET, SO IF YOU'RE LUCKY, YOU'LL GET TO SEE SOME-THING AMAZING!
OK!!
IT'S SO PRETTY!
ALL THAT'S LEFT IS TO WAIT HERE AND PRAY TO THE SUN.
THERE'S NO SNOW...
BUT IT'S COLD DOWN BY THE WATER, SO WEAR THESE.
ぽぽい TOSS
ぽい TOSS
I HOPE WE CAN SEE THE LIGHTS!
SNIFF
ONE HOUR LATER...
...
THEY'RE NOT OUT YET.
AT LEAST THE WEATHER'S NICE.
WHINE
YOU MAY HAVE TO WAIT A WHILE.

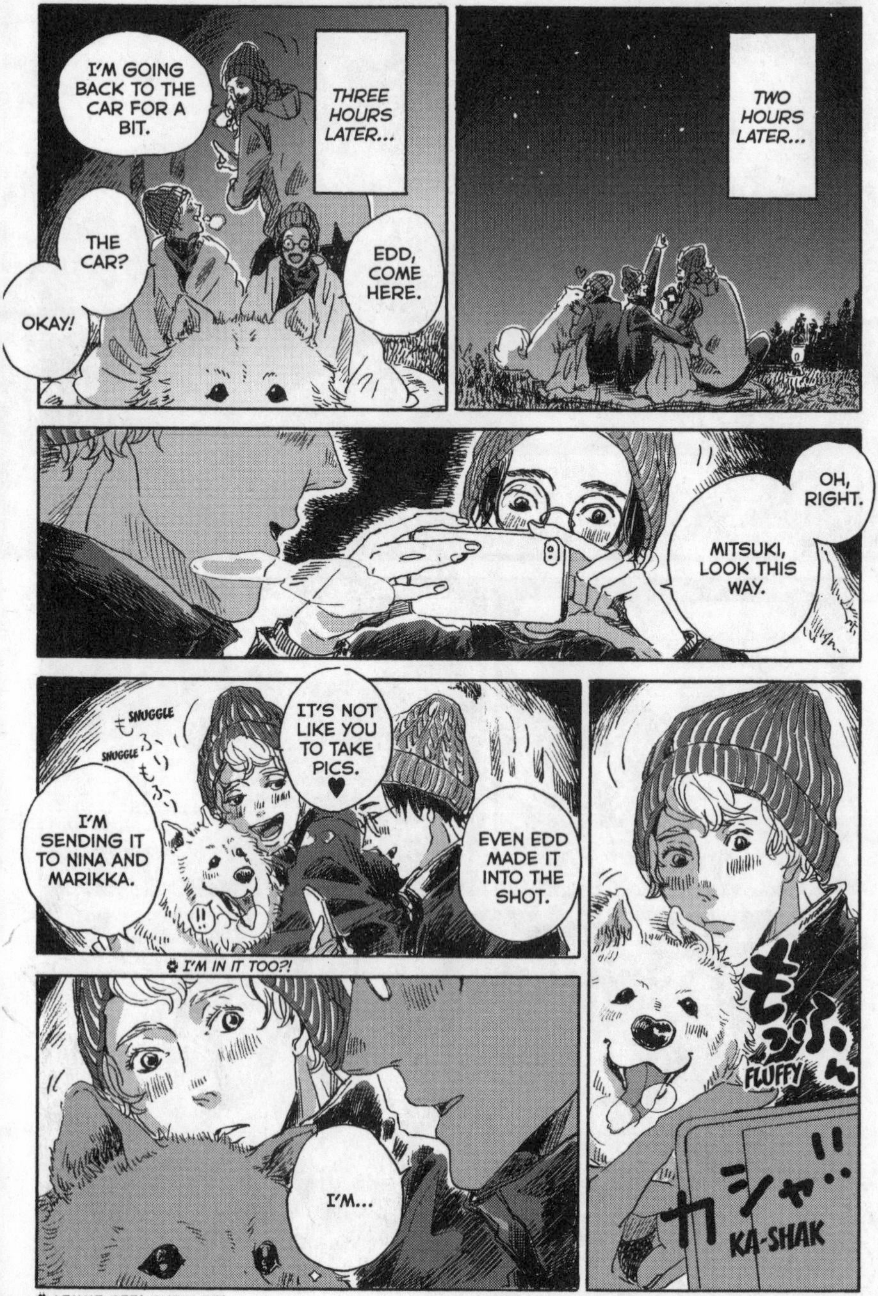
TWO HOURS LATER...
THREE HOURS LATER...
I'M GOING BACK TO THE CAR FOR A BIT.
EDD, COME HERE.
THE CAR?
OKAY!
OH, RIGHT.
MITSUKI, LOOK THIS WAY.
FLUFFY
KA-SHAK
IT'S NOT LIKE YOU TO TAKE PICS. ♥
EVEN EDD MADE IT INTO THE SHOT.
SNUGGLE
SNUGGLE
I'M SENDING IT TO NINA AND MARIKKA.
✿ I'M IN IT TOO?!
I'M...
✿ LEMME SEE! SHOW ME!

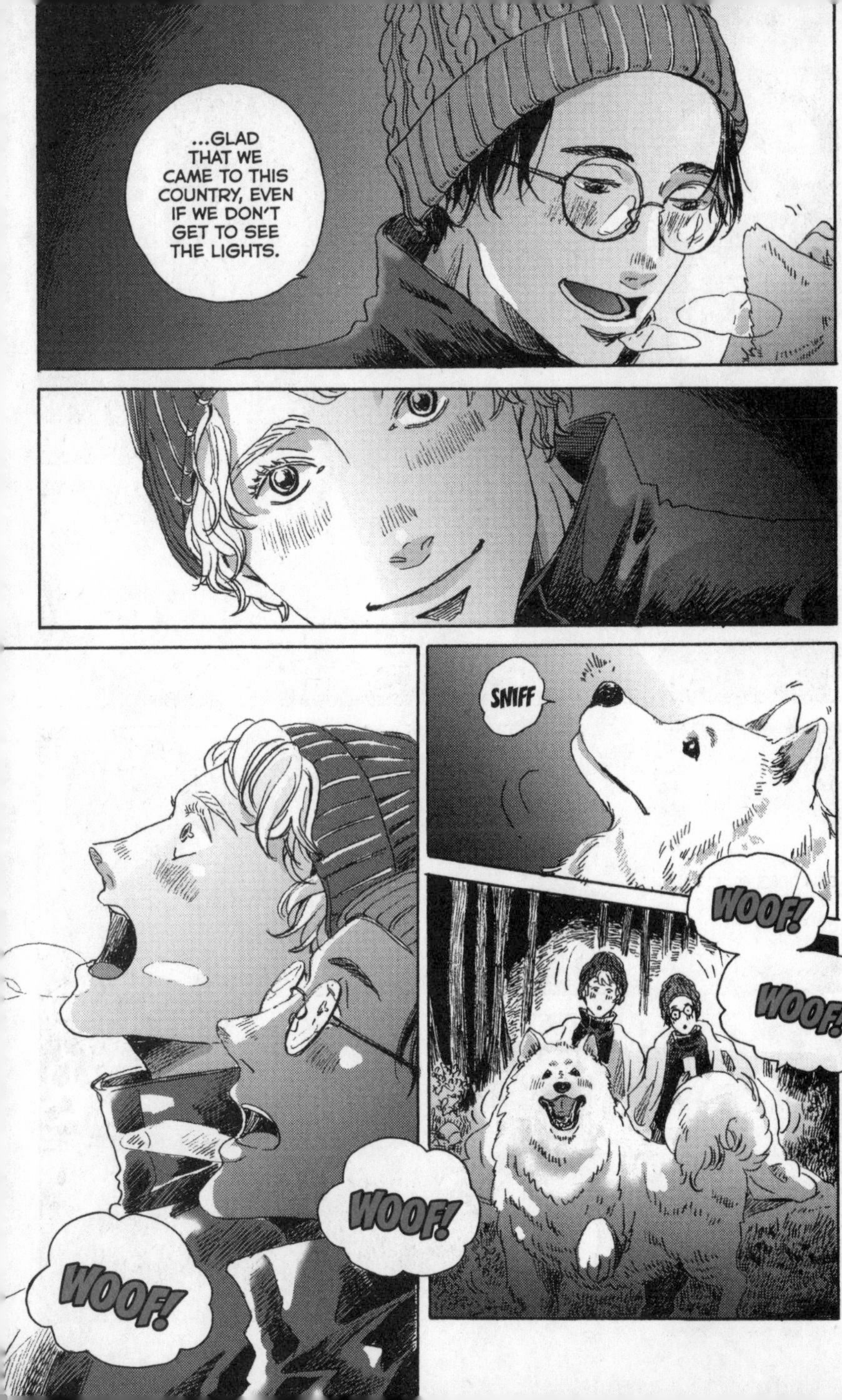
...GLAD THAT WE CAME TO THIS COUNTRY, EVEN IF WE DON'T GET TO SEE THE LIGHTS.
SNIFF
WOOF!
WOOF!
WOOF!
WOOF!

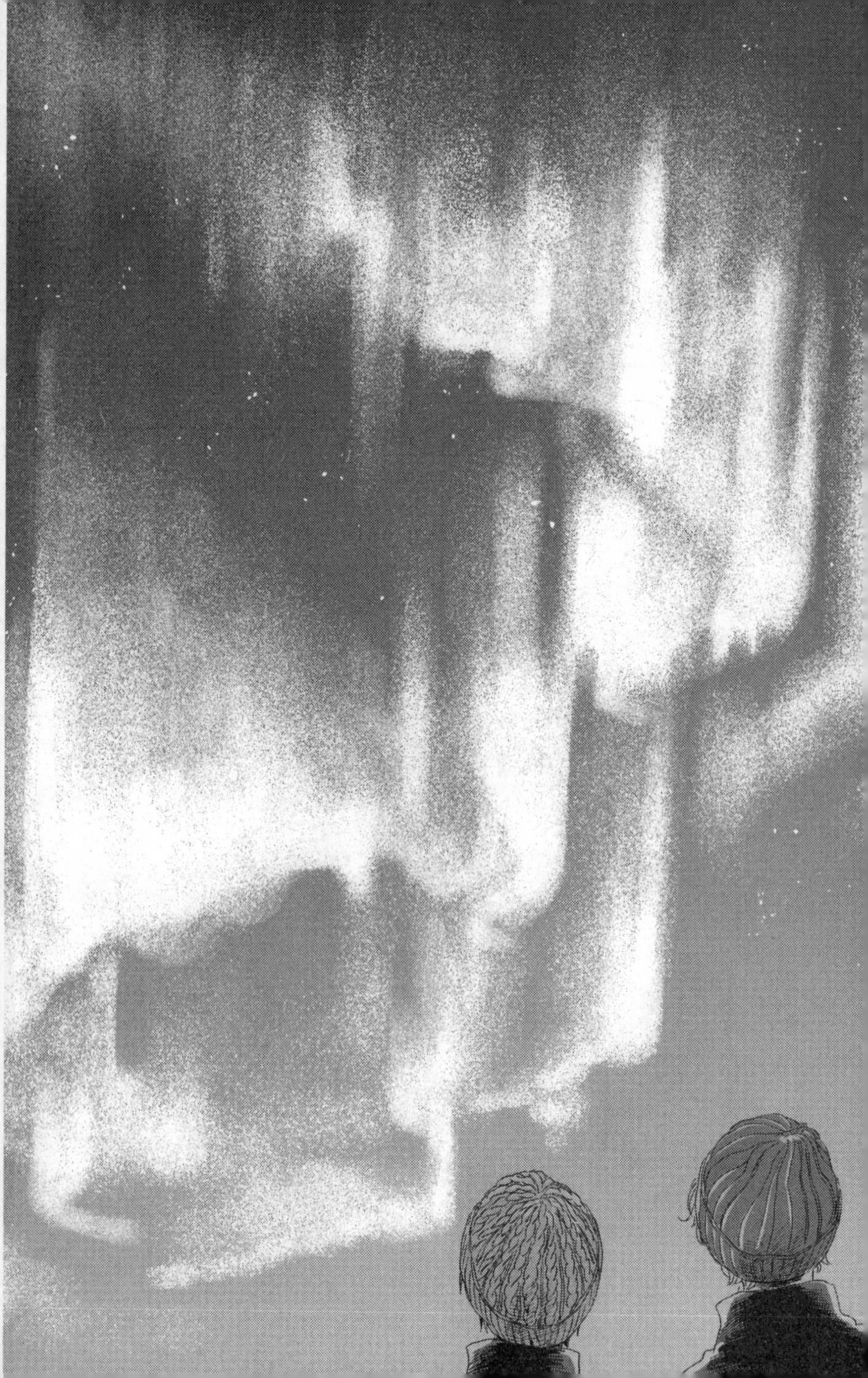

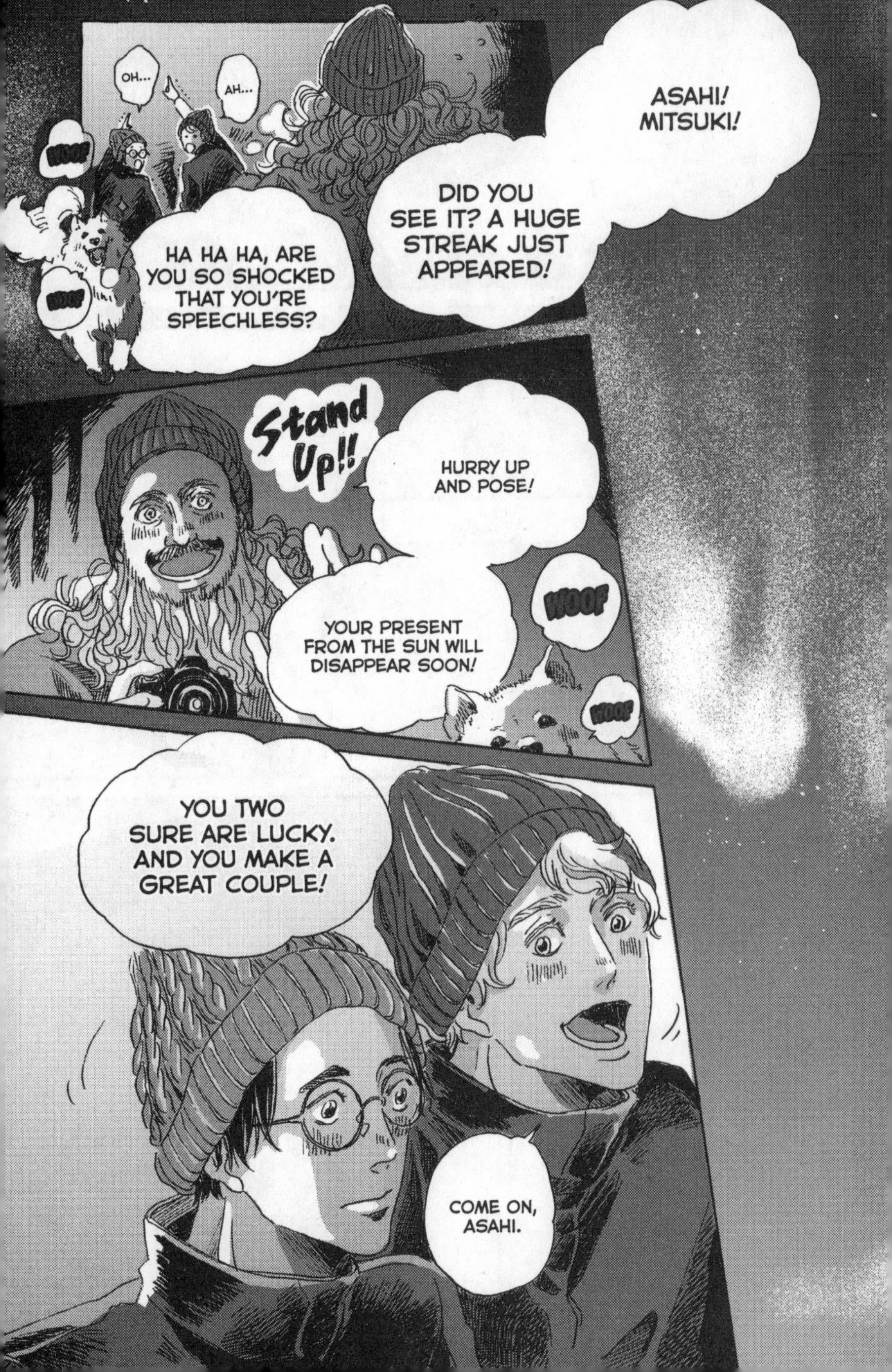
ASAHI! MITSUKI!
DID YOU SEE IT? A HUGE STREAK JUST APPEARED!
AH...
OH...
WOOF
HA HA HA, ARE YOU SO SHOCKED THAT YOU'RE SPEECHLESS?
WOOF
HURRY UP AND POSE!
Stand Up!!
WOOF
YOUR PRESENT FROM THE SUN WILL DISAPPEAR SOON!
WOOF
YOU TWO SURE ARE LUCKY. AND YOU MAKE A GREAT COUPLE!
COME ON, ASAHI.

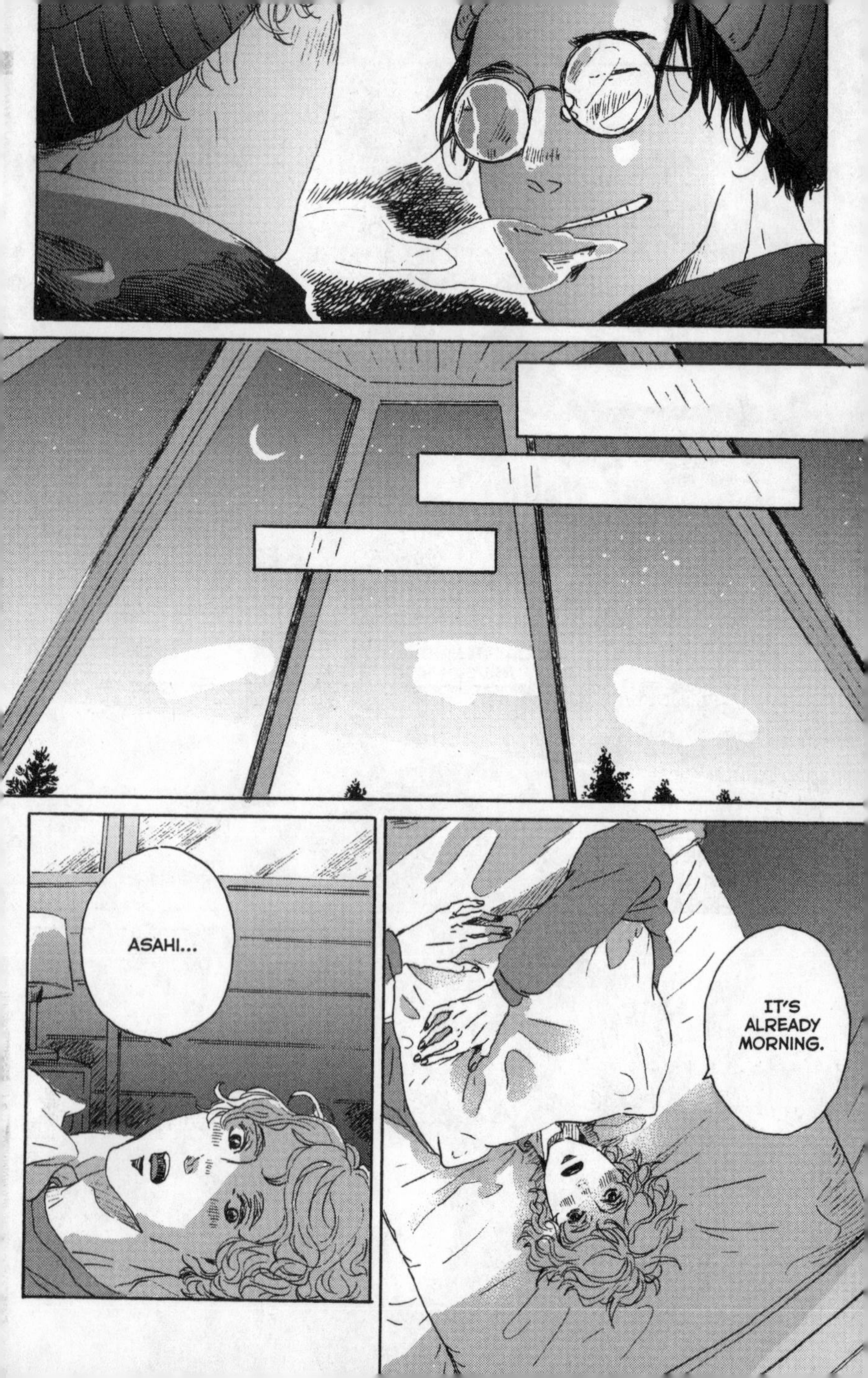
IT'S ALREADY MORNING.
ASAHI...

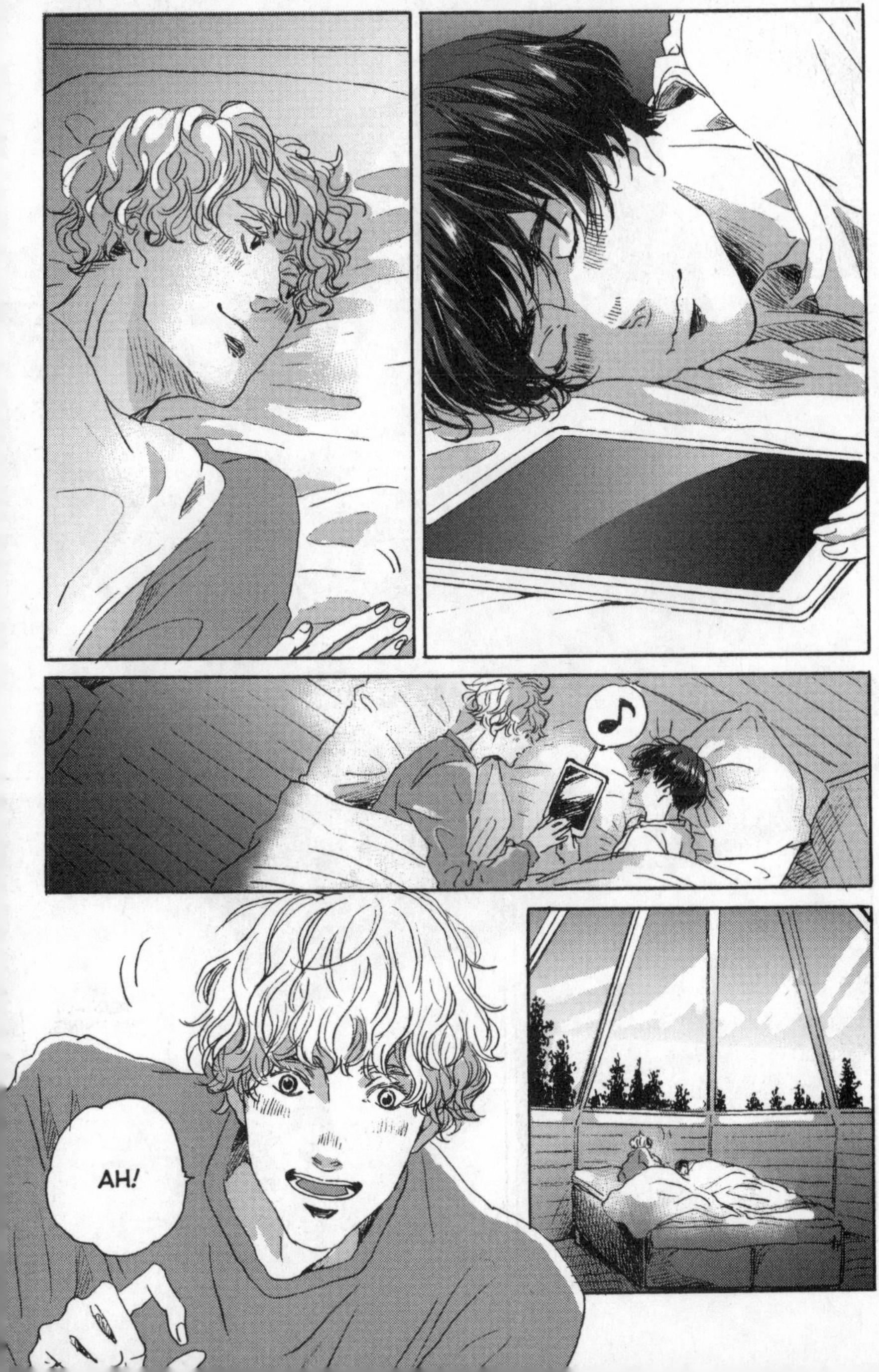
AH!

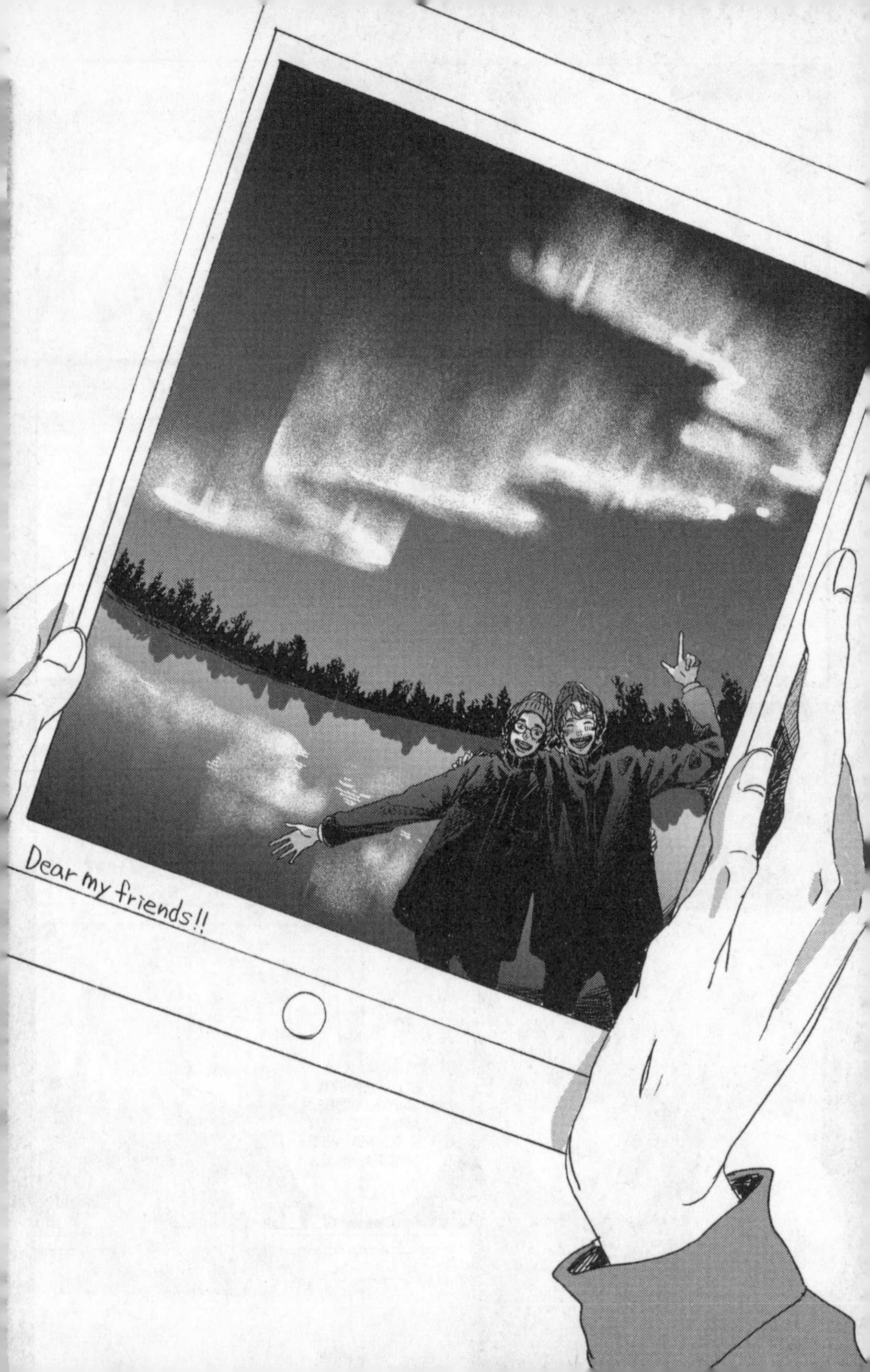
Dear my friends!!

trip. 8

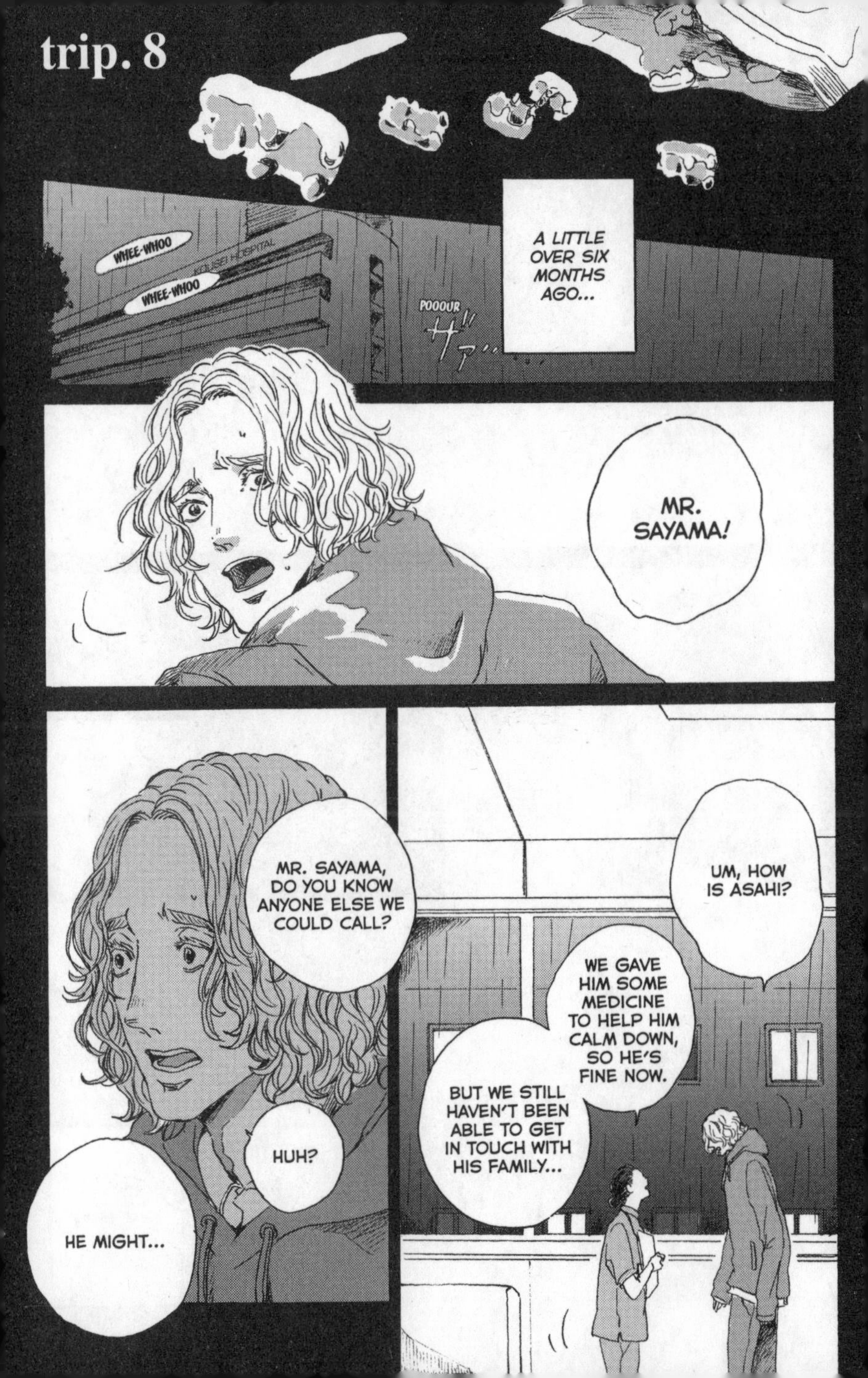
A LITTLE OVER SIX MONTHS AGO...
POOOUR
ザァ‥
WHEE-WHOO
KOUSEI HOSPITAL
WHEE-WHOO
MR. SAYAMA!
UM, HOW IS ASAHI?
WE GAVE HIM SOME MEDICINE TO HELP HIM CALM DOWN, SO HE'S FINE NOW.
BUT WE STILL HAVEN'T BEEN ABLE TO GET IN TOUCH WITH HIS FAMILY...
MR. SAYAMA, DO YOU KNOW ANYONE ELSE WE COULD CALL?
HUH?
HE MIGHT...

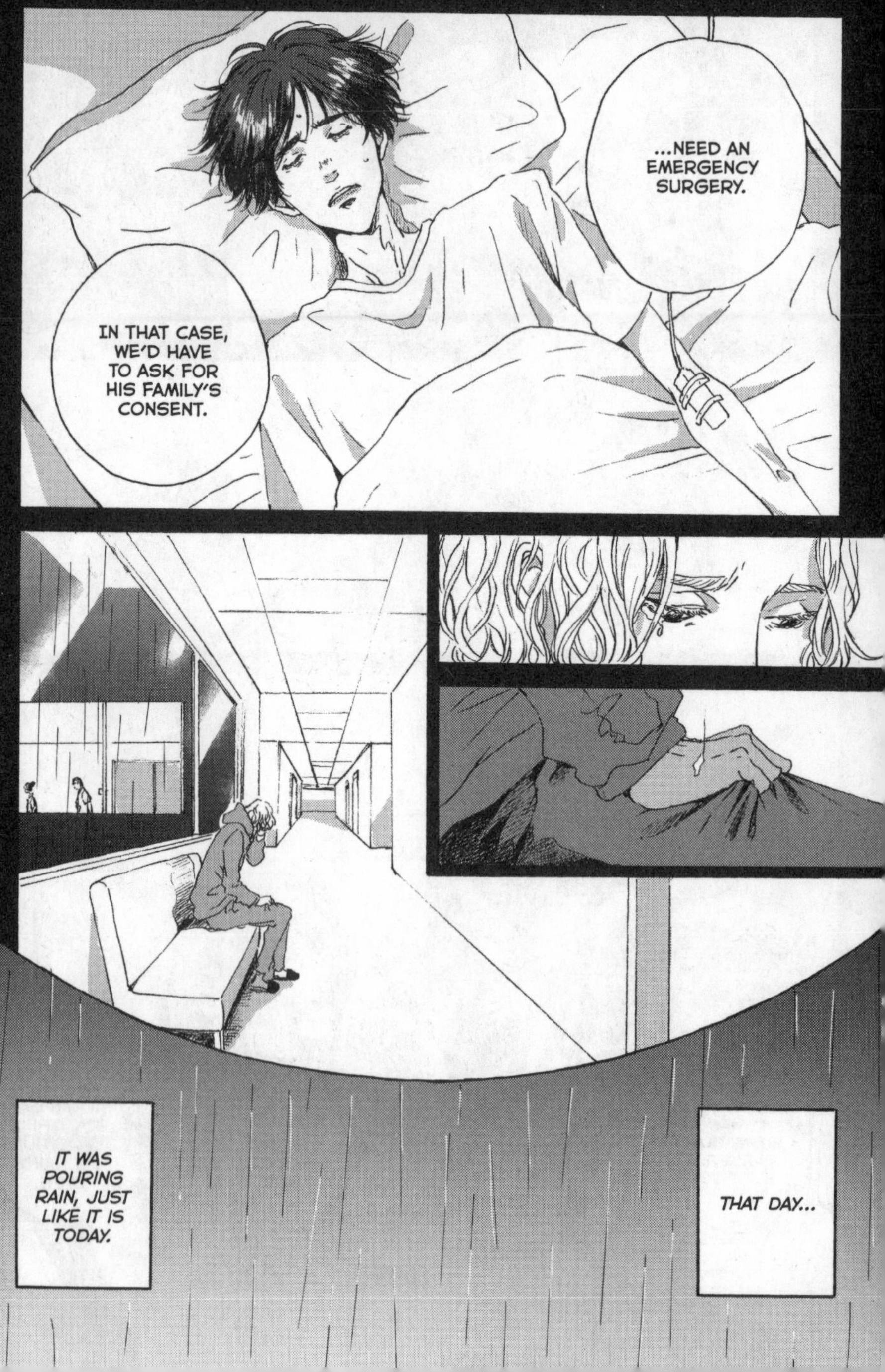
...NEED AN EMERGENCY SURGERY.
IN THAT CASE, WE'D HAVE TO ASK FOR HIS FAMILY'S CONSENT.
THAT DAY...
IT WAS POURING RAIN, JUST LIKE IT IS TODAY.

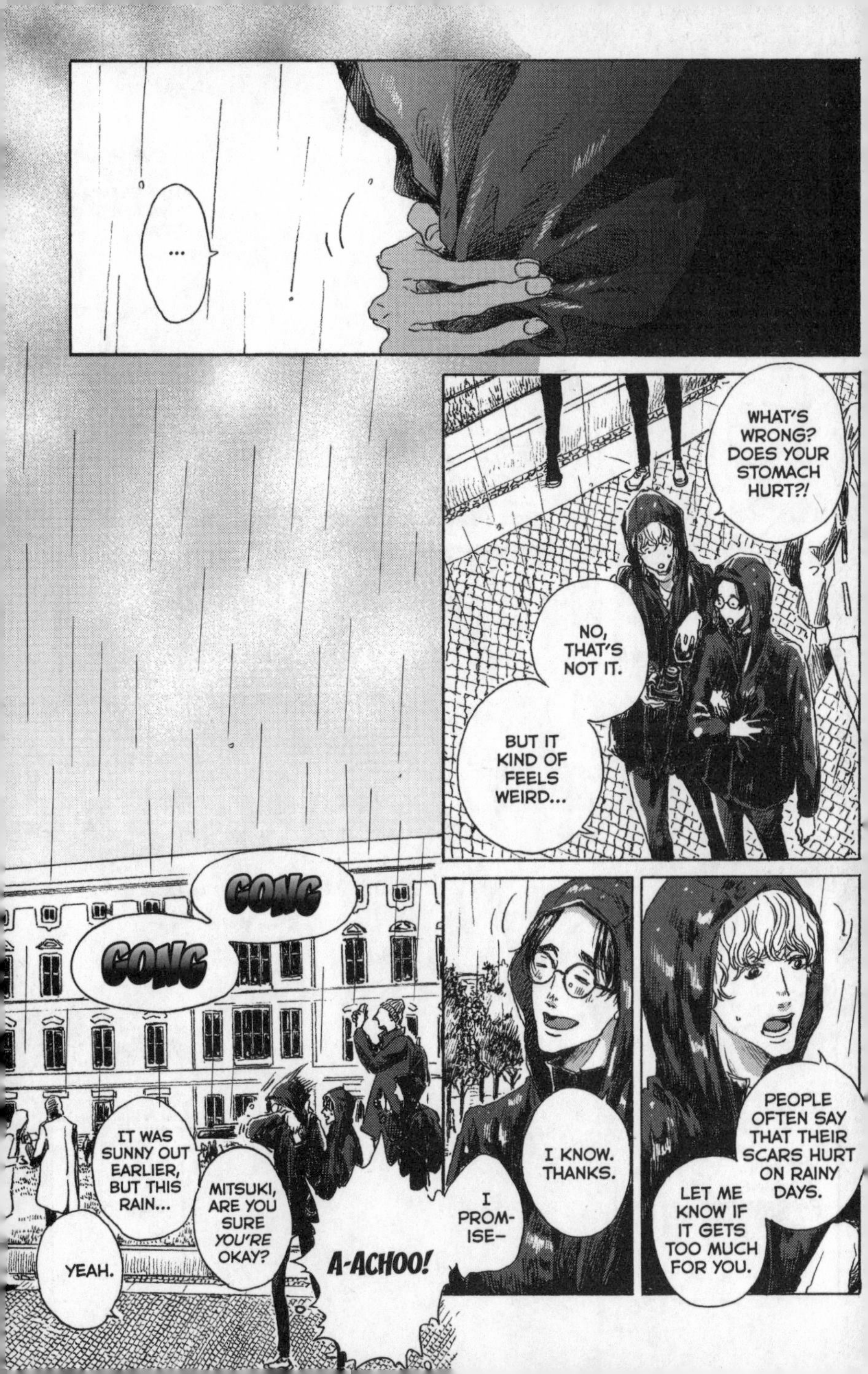
...
WHAT'S WRONG? DOES YOUR STOMACH HURT?!
NO, THAT'S NOT IT.
BUT IT KIND OF FEELS WEIRD...
PEOPLE OFTEN SAY THAT THEIR SCARS HURT ON RAINY DAYS.
LET ME KNOW IF IT GETS TOO MUCH FOR YOU.
I KNOW. THANKS.
I PROM-ISE-
A-ACHOO!
GONG
GONG
IT WAS SUNNY OUT EARLIER, BUT THIS RAIN...
MITSUKI, ARE YOU SURE *YOU'RE* OKAY?
YEAH.

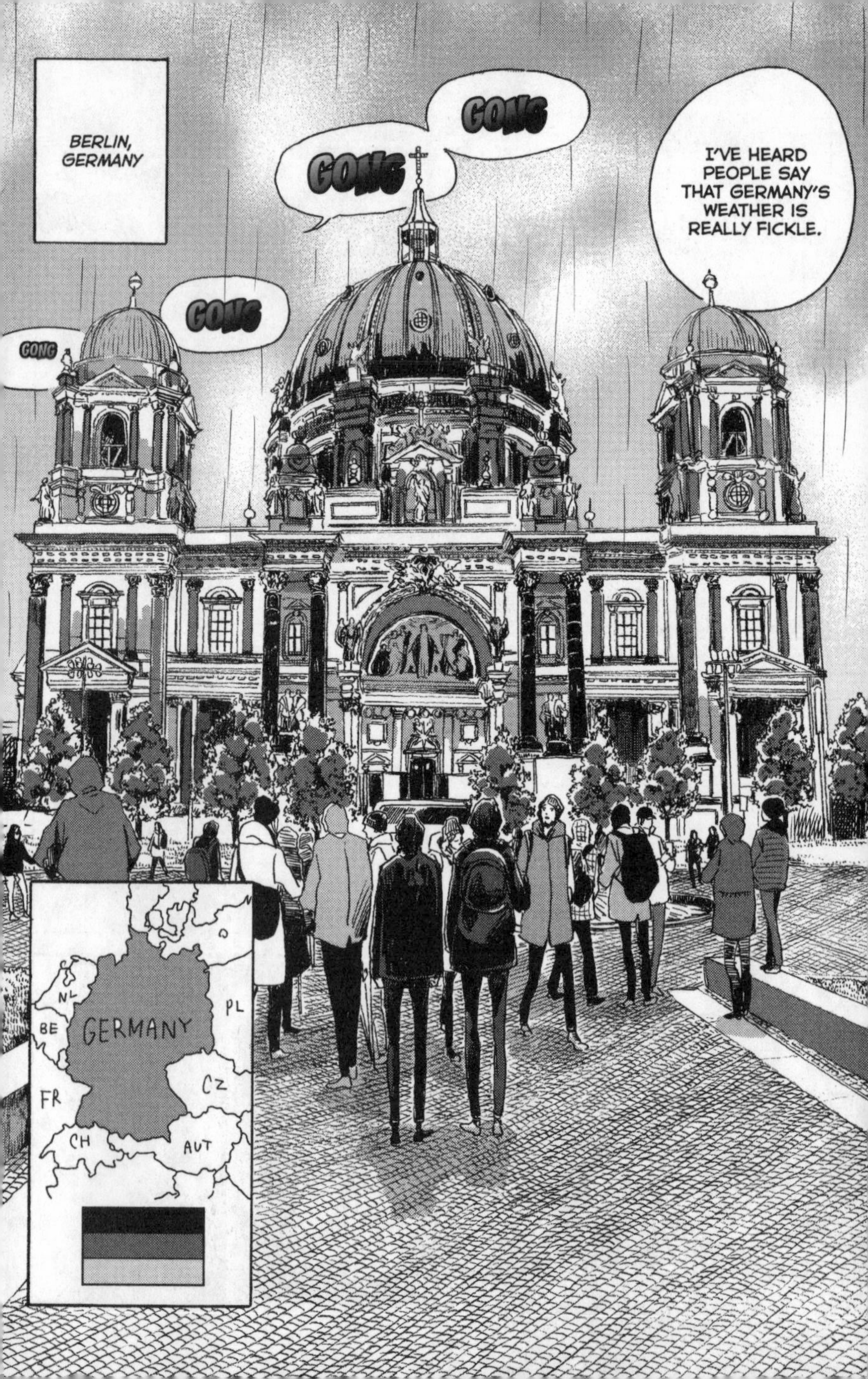
I'VE HEARD PEOPLE SAY THAT GERMANY'S WEATHER IS REALLY FICKLE.
GONG
GONG
BERLIN, GERMANY
GONG
GONG
PL
NL
GERMANY
BE
CZ
FR
AUT
CH

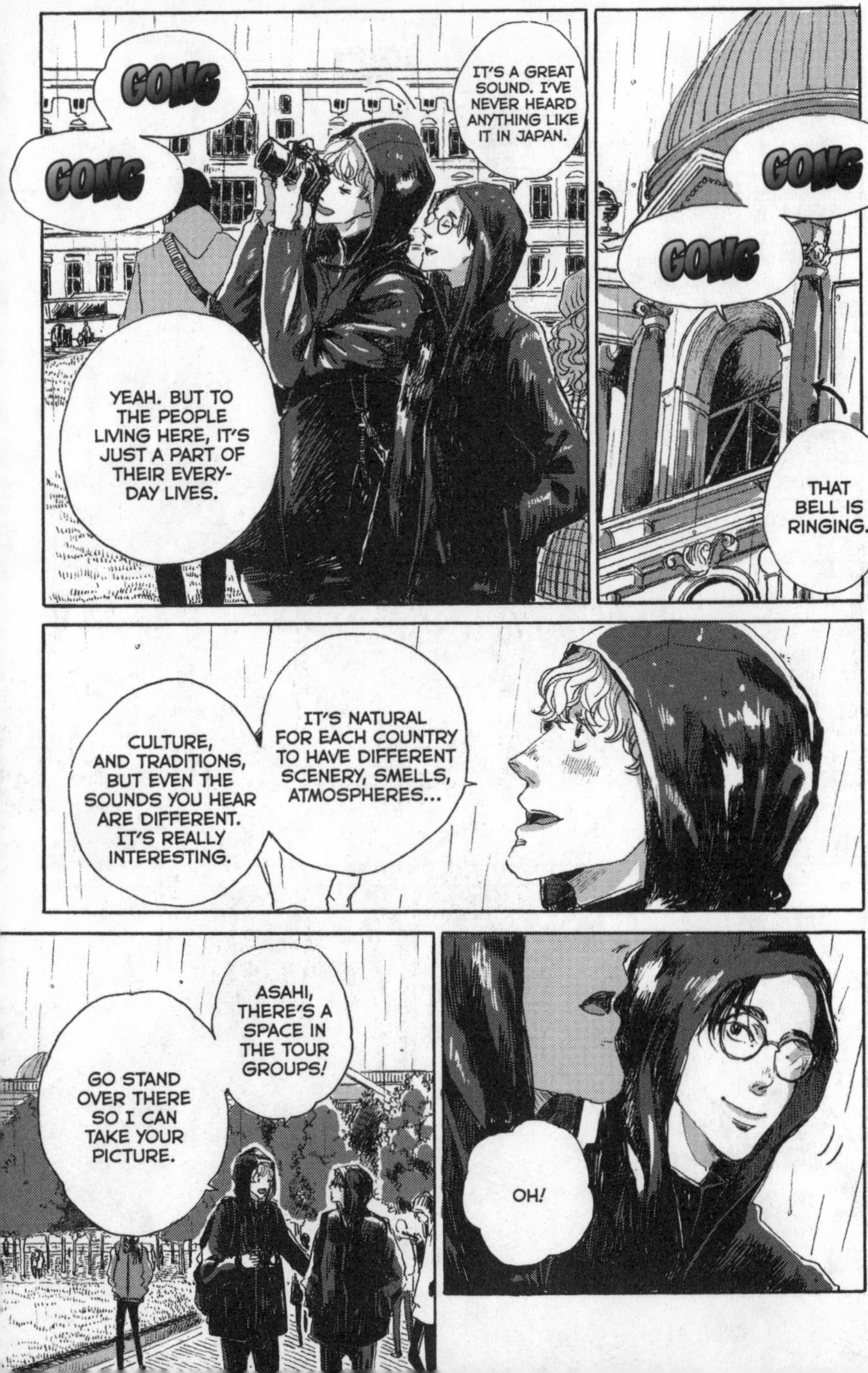
GONG
GONG
THAT BELL IS RINGING.
IT'S A GREAT SOUND. I'VE NEVER HEARD ANYTHING LIKE IT IN JAPAN.
GONG
GONG
YEAH. BUT TO THE PEOPLE LIVING HERE, IT'S JUST A PART OF THEIR EVERY-DAY LIVES.
IT'S NATURAL FOR EACH COUNTRY TO HAVE DIFFERENT SCENERY, SMELLS, ATMOSPHERES...
CULTURE, AND TRADITIONS, BUT EVEN THE SOUNDS YOU HEAR ARE DIFFERENT. IT'S REALLY INTERESTING.
OH!
ASAHI, THERE'S A SPACE IN THE TOUR GROUPS!
GO STAND OVER THERE SO I CAN TAKE YOUR PICTURE.

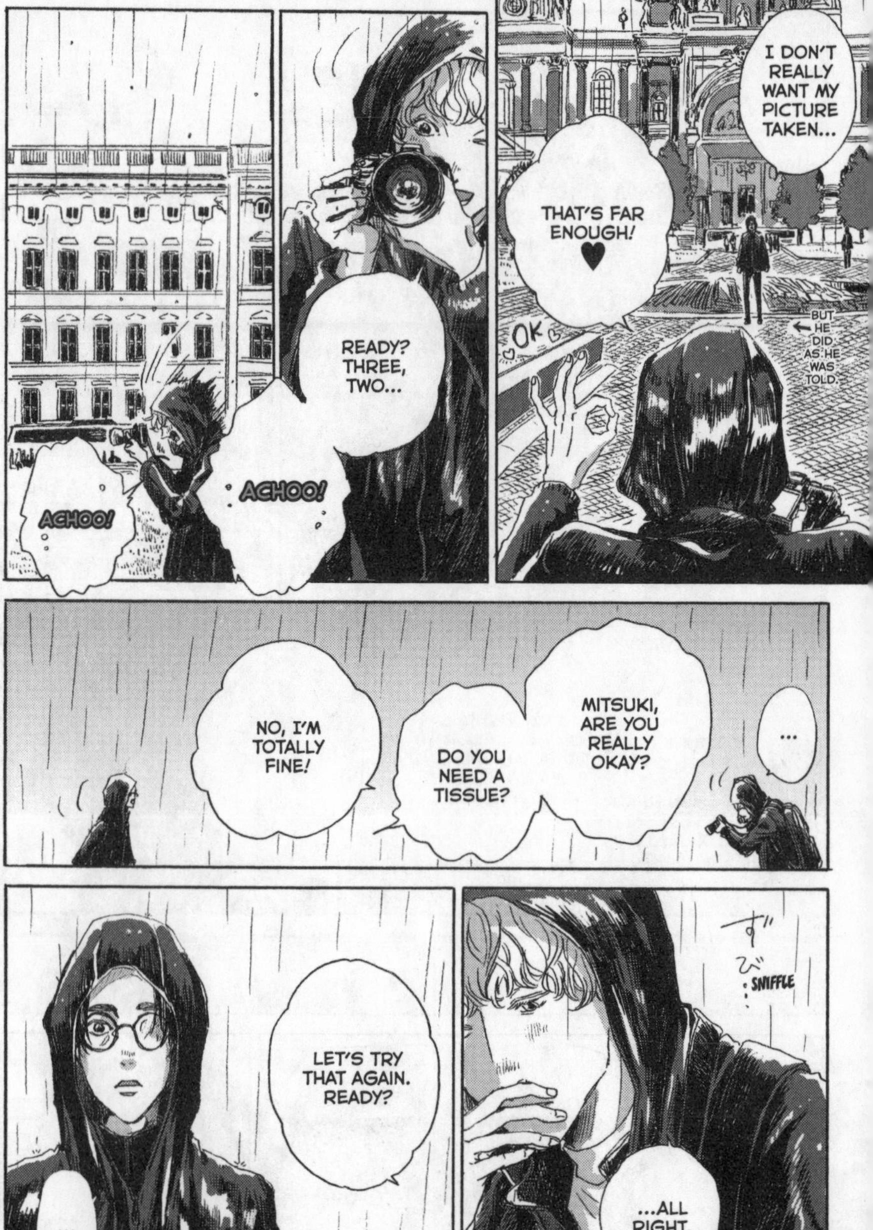
I DON'T REALLY WANT MY PICTURE TAKEN...
THAT'S FAR ENOUGH! ♥
OK
BUT HE DID AS HE WAS TOLD.
READY? THREE, TWO...
ACHOO!
ACHOO!
...
MITSUKI, ARE YOU REALLY OKAY?
DO YOU NEED A TISSUE?
NO, I'M TOTALLY FINE!
ずび
SNIFFLE
...ALL RIGHT.
LET'S TRY THAT AGAIN. READY?
...

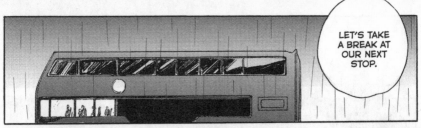

LET'S TAKE A BREAK AT OUR NEXT STOP.

ONE HOT LATTE AND AN AMERICANO.

BOTH TALLS, PLEASE.

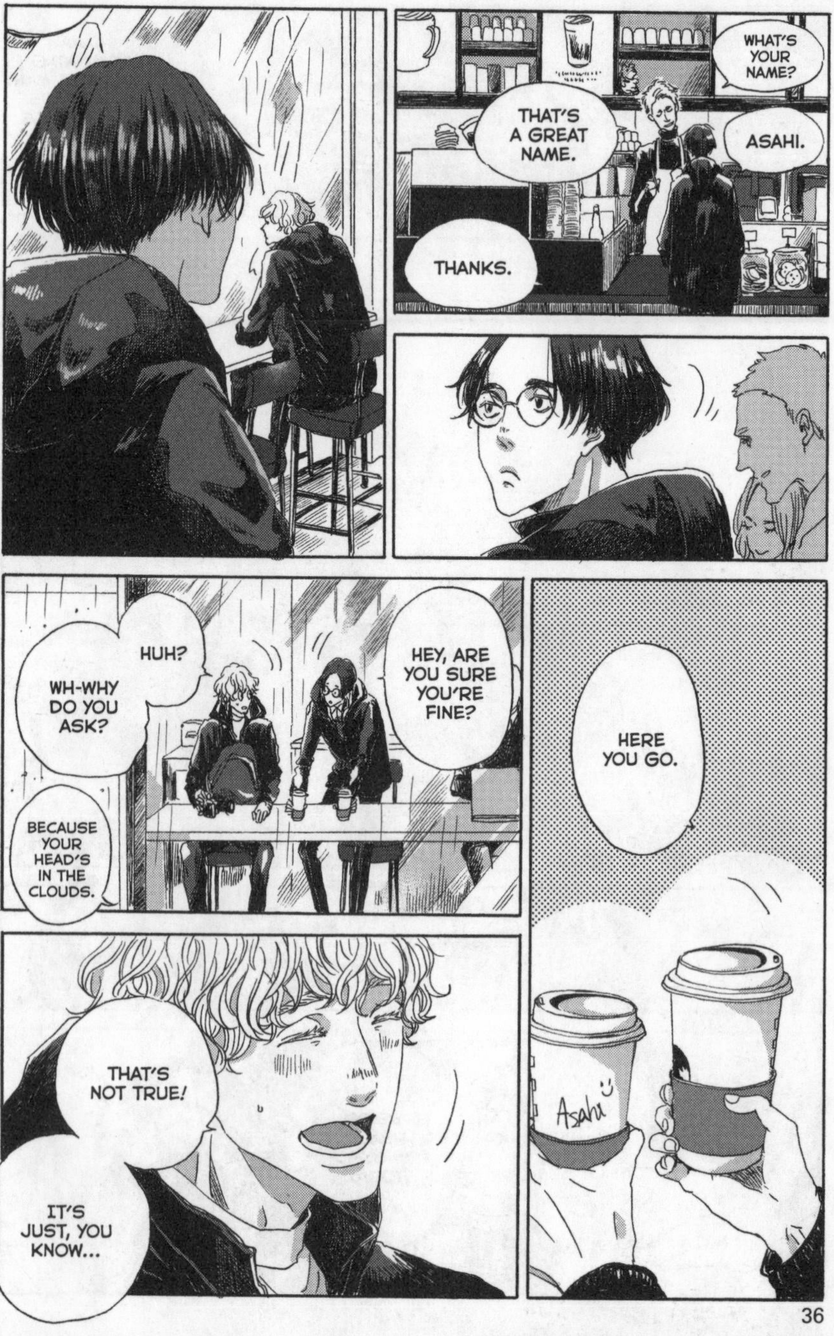
WHAT'S YOUR NAME?
ASAHI.
THAT'S A GREAT NAME.
THANKS.
HERE YOU GO.
Asahi
HEY, ARE YOU SURE YOU'RE FINE?
HUH?
WH-WHY DO YOU ASK?
BECAUSE YOUR HEAD'S IN THE CLOUDS.
THAT'S NOT TRUE!
IT'S JUST, YOU KNOW...

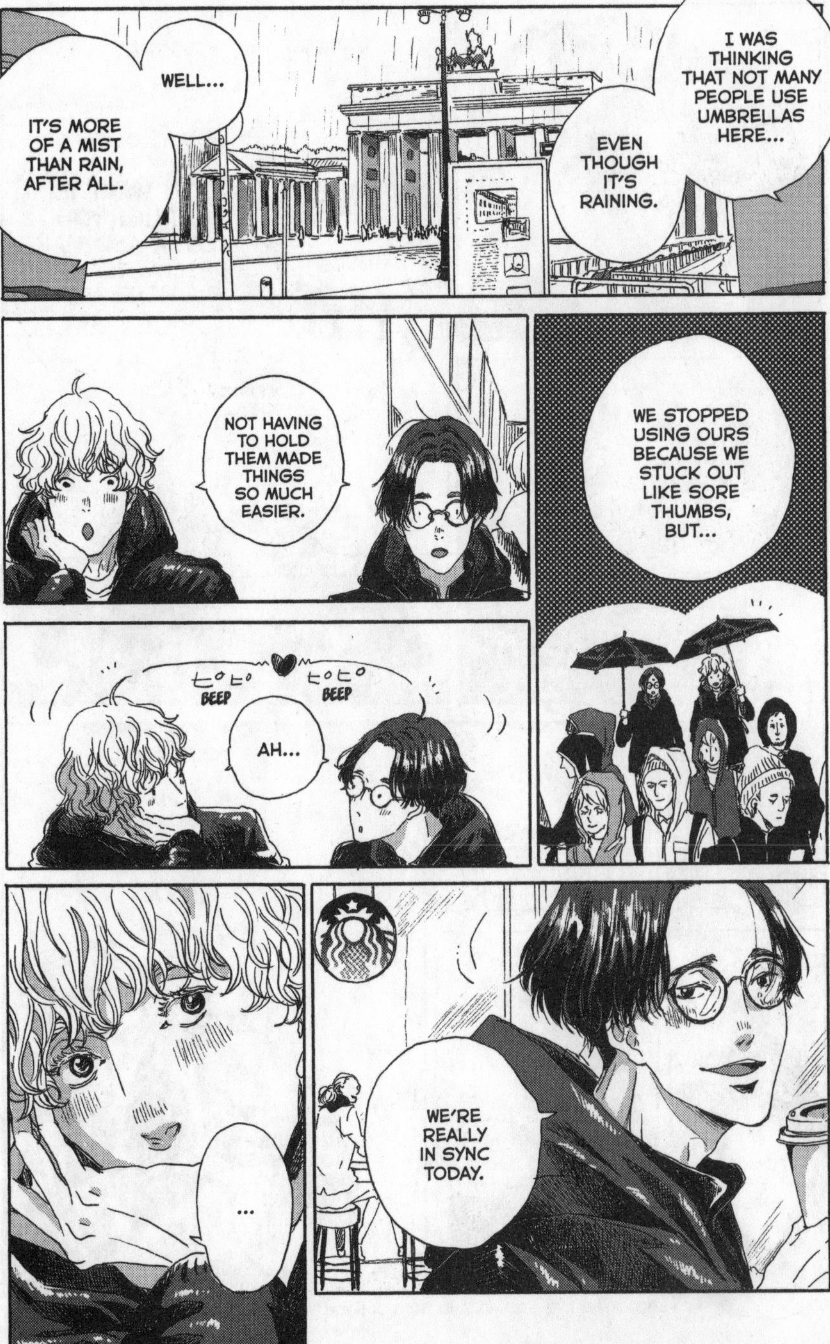
I WAS THINKING THAT NOT MANY PEOPLE USE UMBRELLAS HERE...
EVEN THOUGH IT'S RAINING.
WELL...
IT'S MORE OF A MIST THAN RAIN, AFTER ALL.
WE STOPPED USING OURS BECAUSE WE STUCK OUT LIKE SORE THUMBS, BUT...
NOT HAVING TO HOLD THEM MADE THINGS SO MUCH EASIER.
BEEP
BEEP
AH...
WE'RE REALLY IN SYNC TODAY.
...

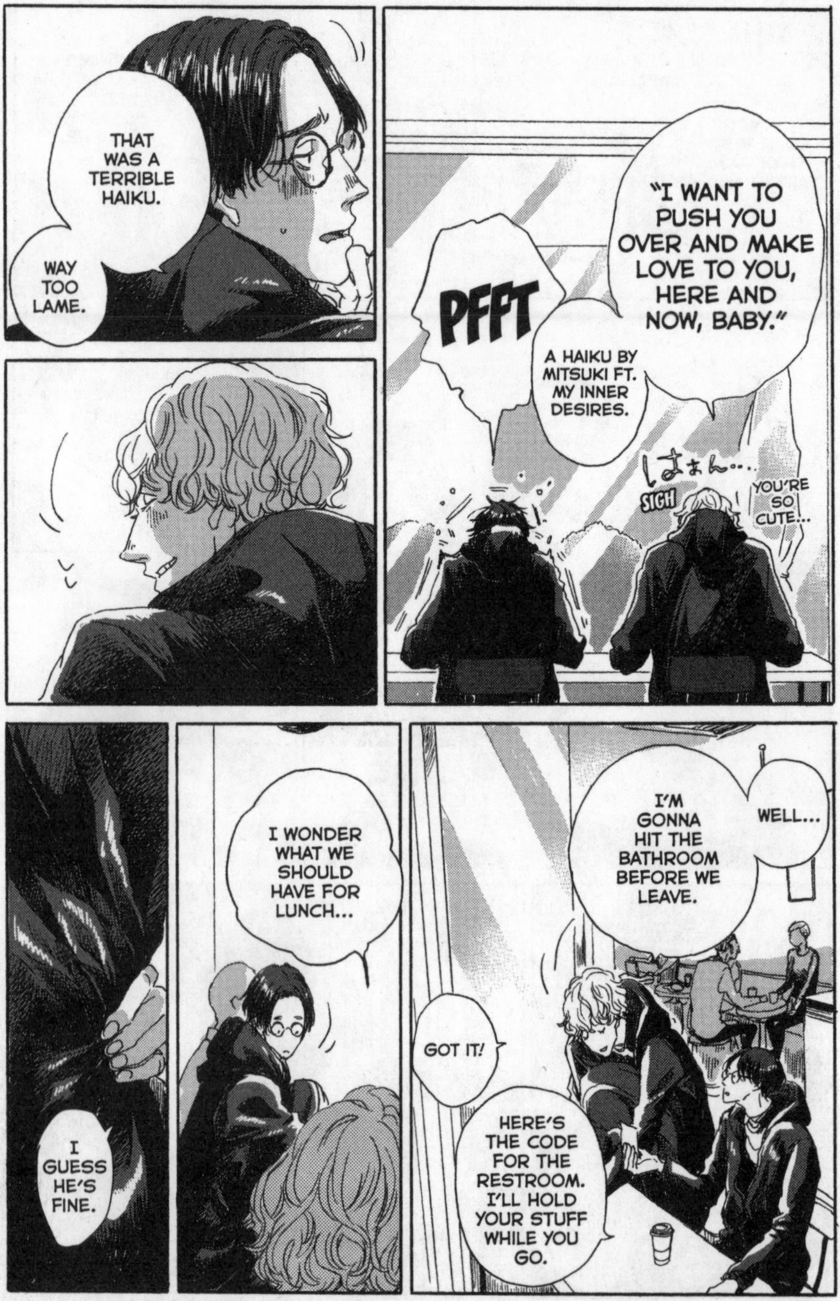
"I WANT TO PUSH YOU OVER AND MAKE LOVE TO YOU, HERE AND NOW, BABY."
PFFT
A HAIKU BY MITSUKI FT. MY INNER DESIRES.
YOU'RE SO CUTE...
SIGH
THAT WAS A TERRIBLE HAIKU.
WAY TOO LAME.
WELL...
I'M GONNA HIT THE BATHROOM BEFORE WE LEAVE.
GOT IT!
HERE'S THE CODE FOR THE RESTROOM. I'LL HOLD YOUR STUFF WHILE YOU GO.
I WONDER WHAT WE SHOULD HAVE FOR LUNCH...
I GUESS HE'S FINE.

THE RESTROOMS ARE LOCKED, AND THE CODE WRITTEN ON THE RECEIPT CHANGES EACH DAY.

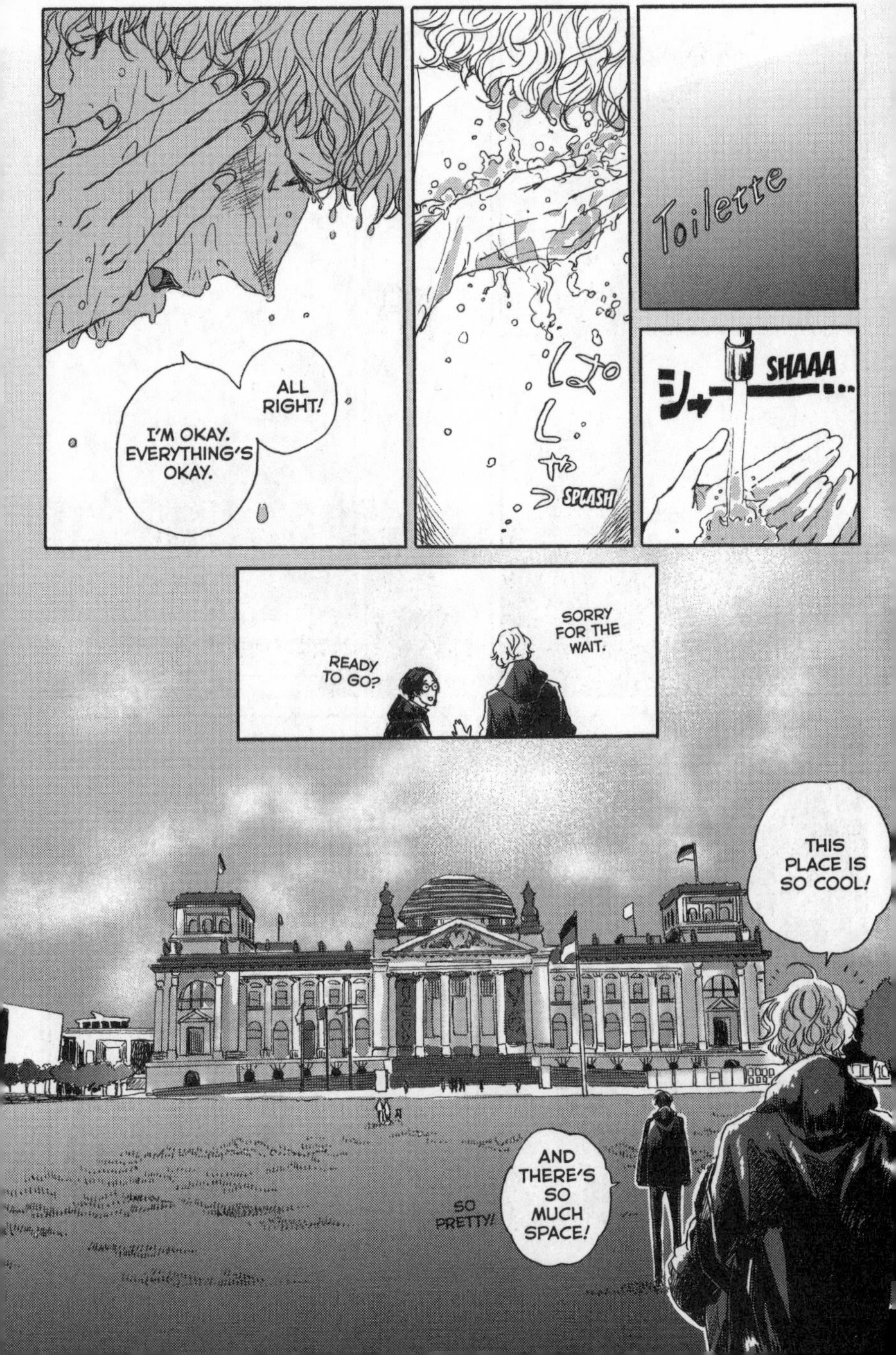
Toilette
シャー
SHAAA...
ばしゃっ
SPLASH
ALL RIGHT!
I'M OKAY. EVERYTHING'S OKAY.
SORRY FOR THE WAIT.
READY TO GO?
THIS PLACE IS SO COOL!
AND THERE'S SO MUCH SPACE!
SO PRETTY!

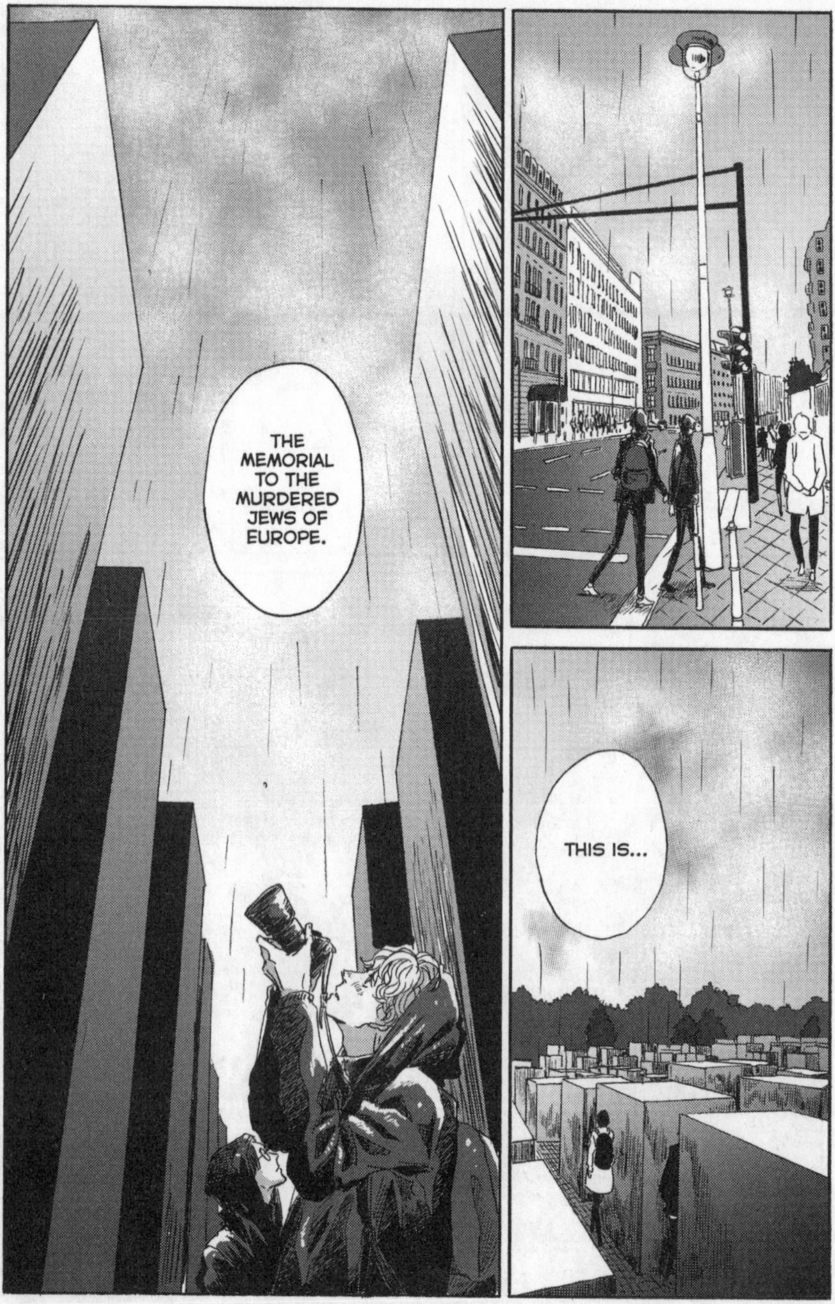
THIS IS...
THE MEMORIAL TO THE MURDERED JEWS OF EUROPE.

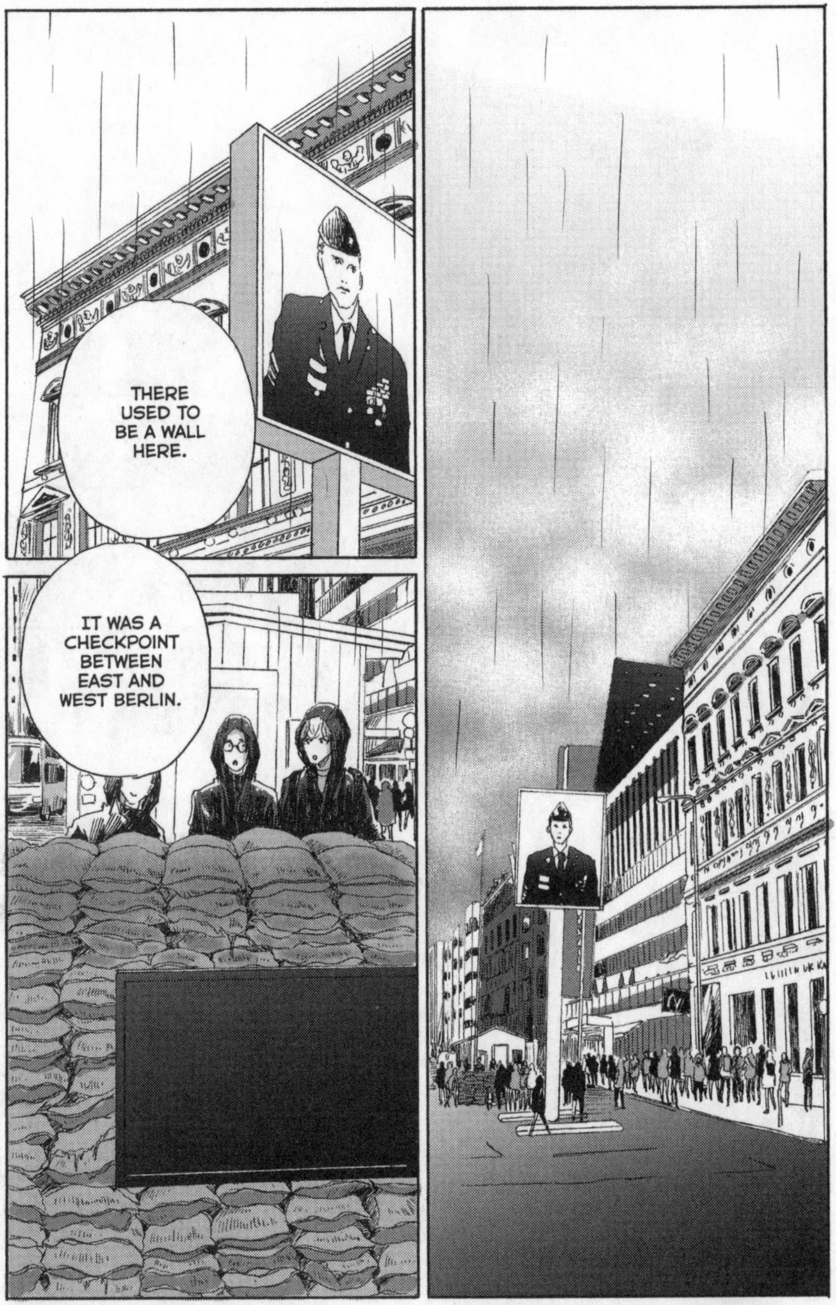
THERE USED TO BE A WALL HERE.
IT WAS A CHECKPOINT BETWEEN EAST AND WEST BERLIN.

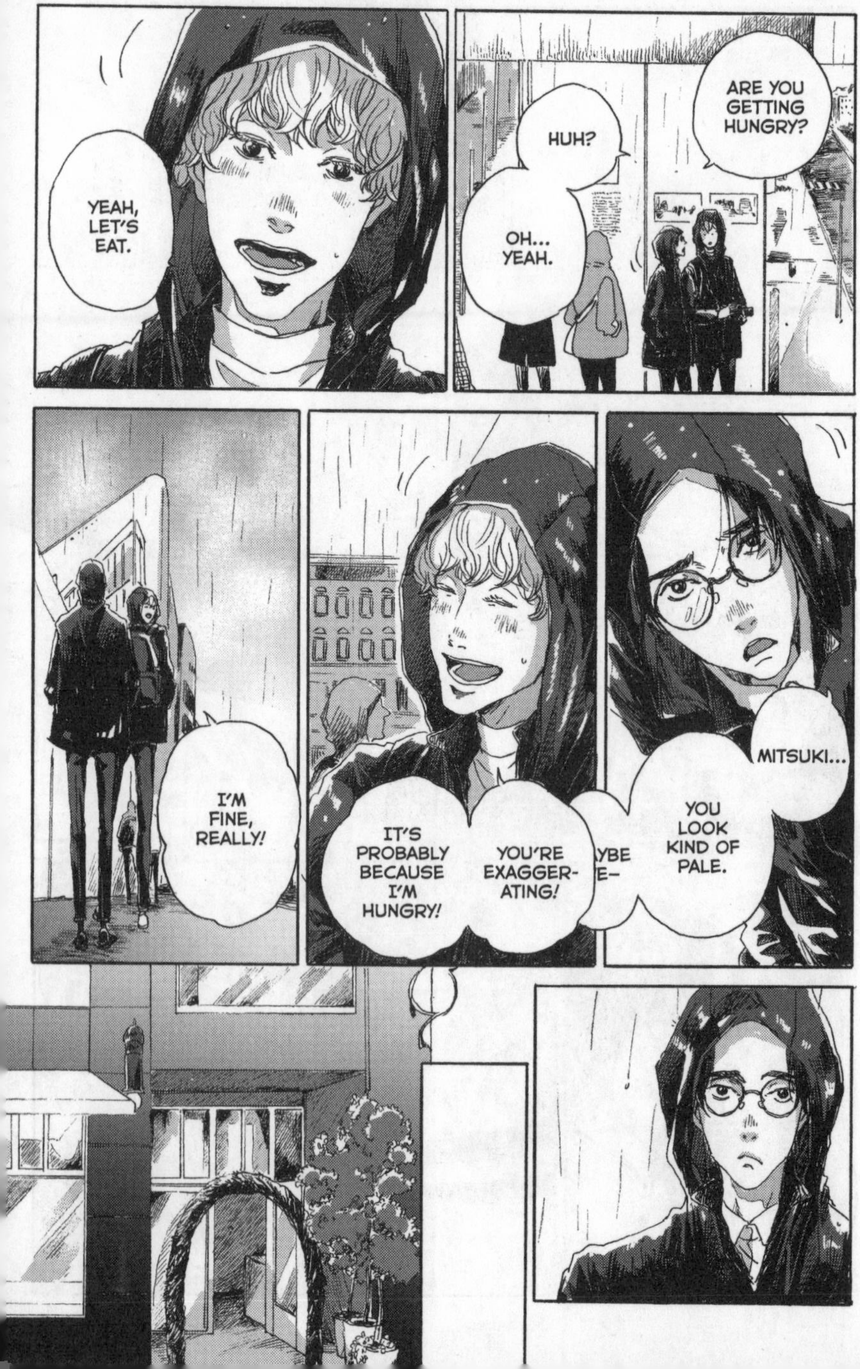
ARE YOU GETTING HUNGRY?
HUH?
OH... YEAH.
YEAH, LET'S EAT.
MITSUKI...
YOU LOOK KIND OF PALE.
AYBE E–
YOU'RE EXAGGERATING!
IT'S PROBABLY BECAUSE I'M HUNGRY!
I'M FINE, REALLY!

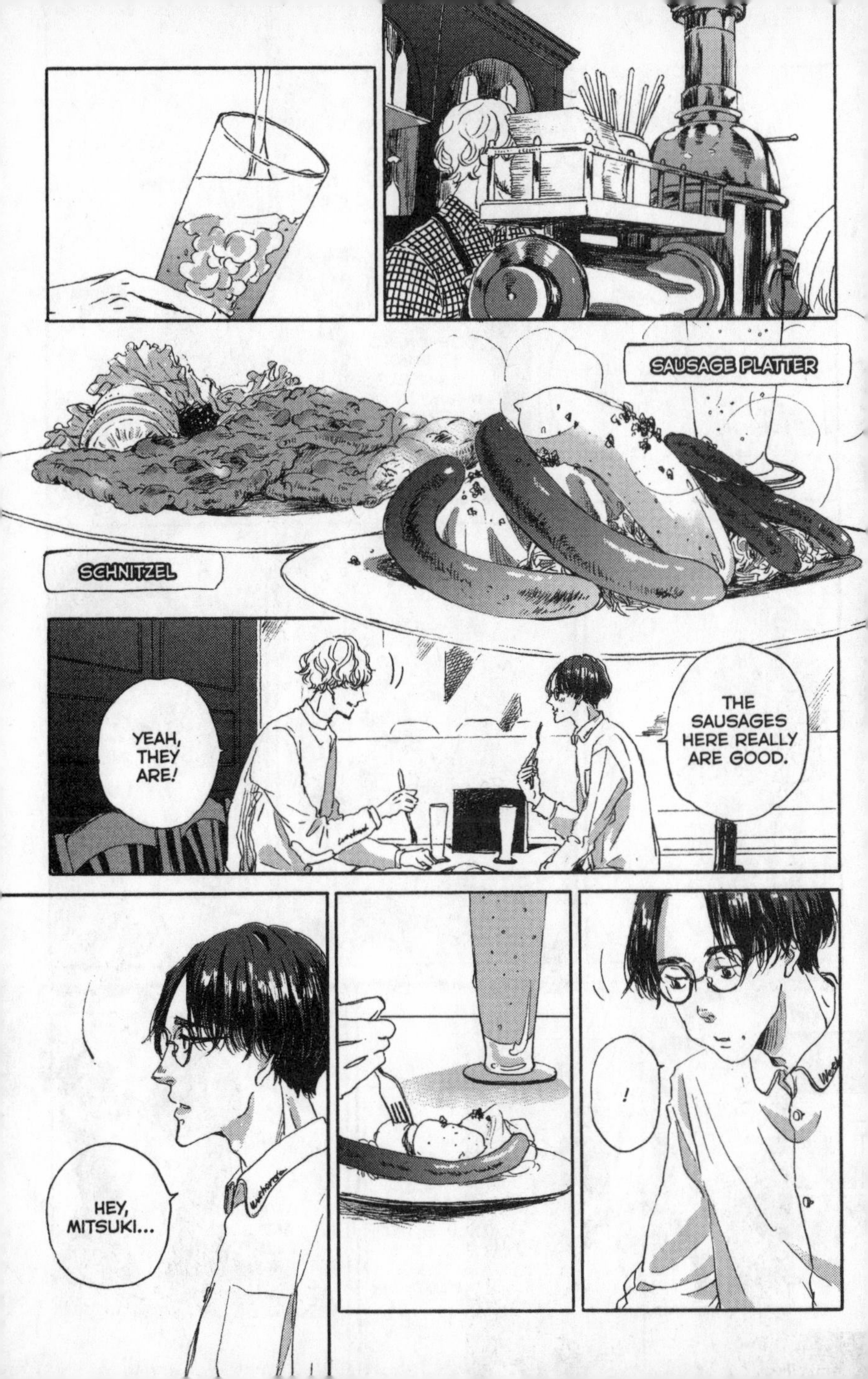
SAUSAGE PLATTER
SCHNITZEL
THE SAUSAGES HERE REALLY ARE GOOD.
YEAH, THEY ARE!
!
HEY, MITSUKI...

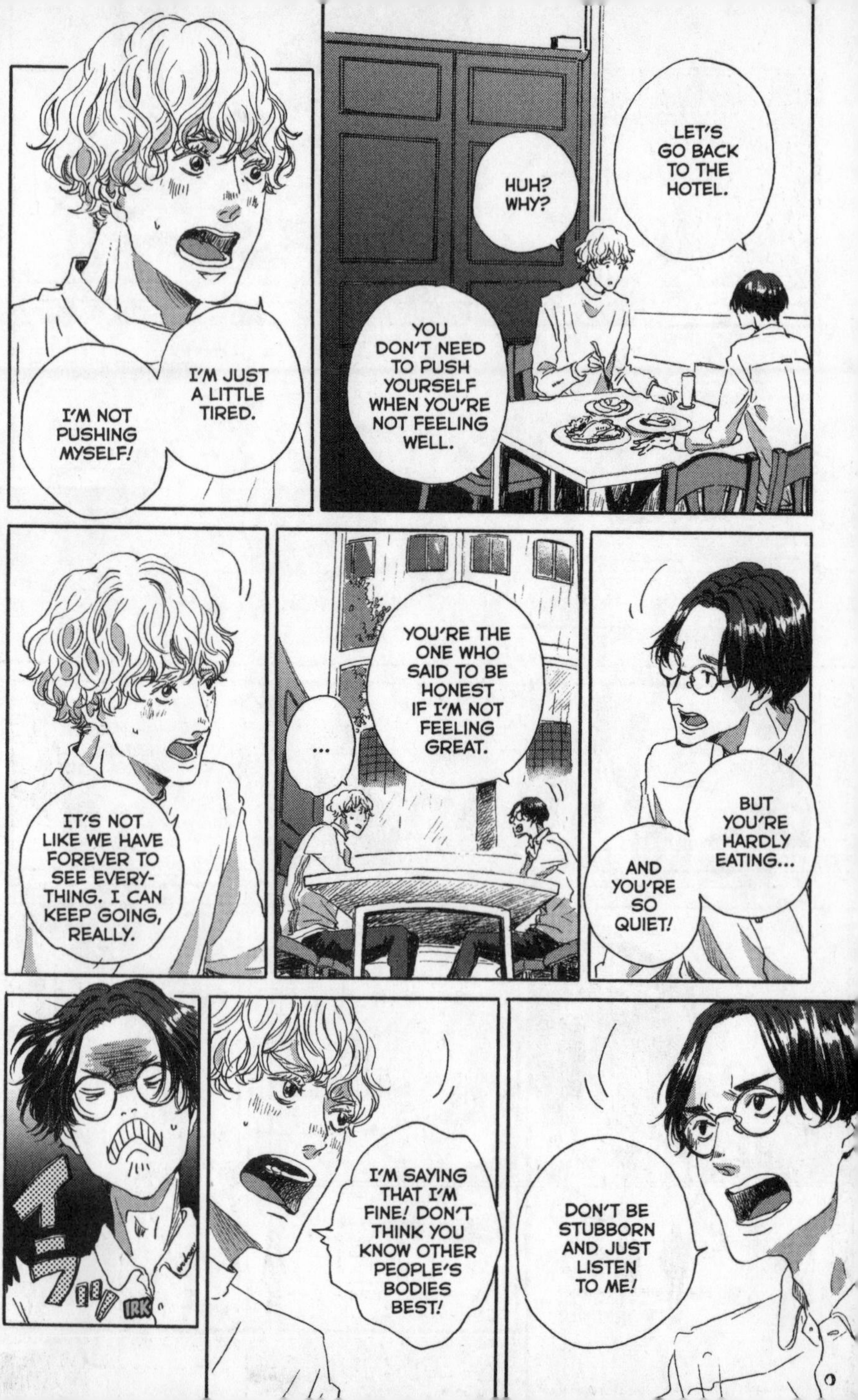
LET'S GO BACK TO THE HOTEL.
HUH? WHY?
YOU DON'T NEED TO PUSH YOURSELF WHEN YOU'RE NOT FEELING WELL.
I'M JUST A LITTLE TIRED.
I'M NOT PUSHING MYSELF!
BUT YOU'RE HARDLY EATING...
AND YOU'RE SO QUIET!
YOU'RE THE ONE WHO SAID TO BE HONEST IF I'M NOT FEELING GREAT.
...
IT'S NOT LIKE WE HAVE FOREVER TO SEE EVERY-THING. I CAN KEEP GOING, REALLY.
DON'T BE STUBBORN AND JUST LISTEN TO ME!
I'M SAYING THAT I'M FINE! DON'T THINK YOU KNOW OTHER PEOPLE'S BODIES BEST!
IRK

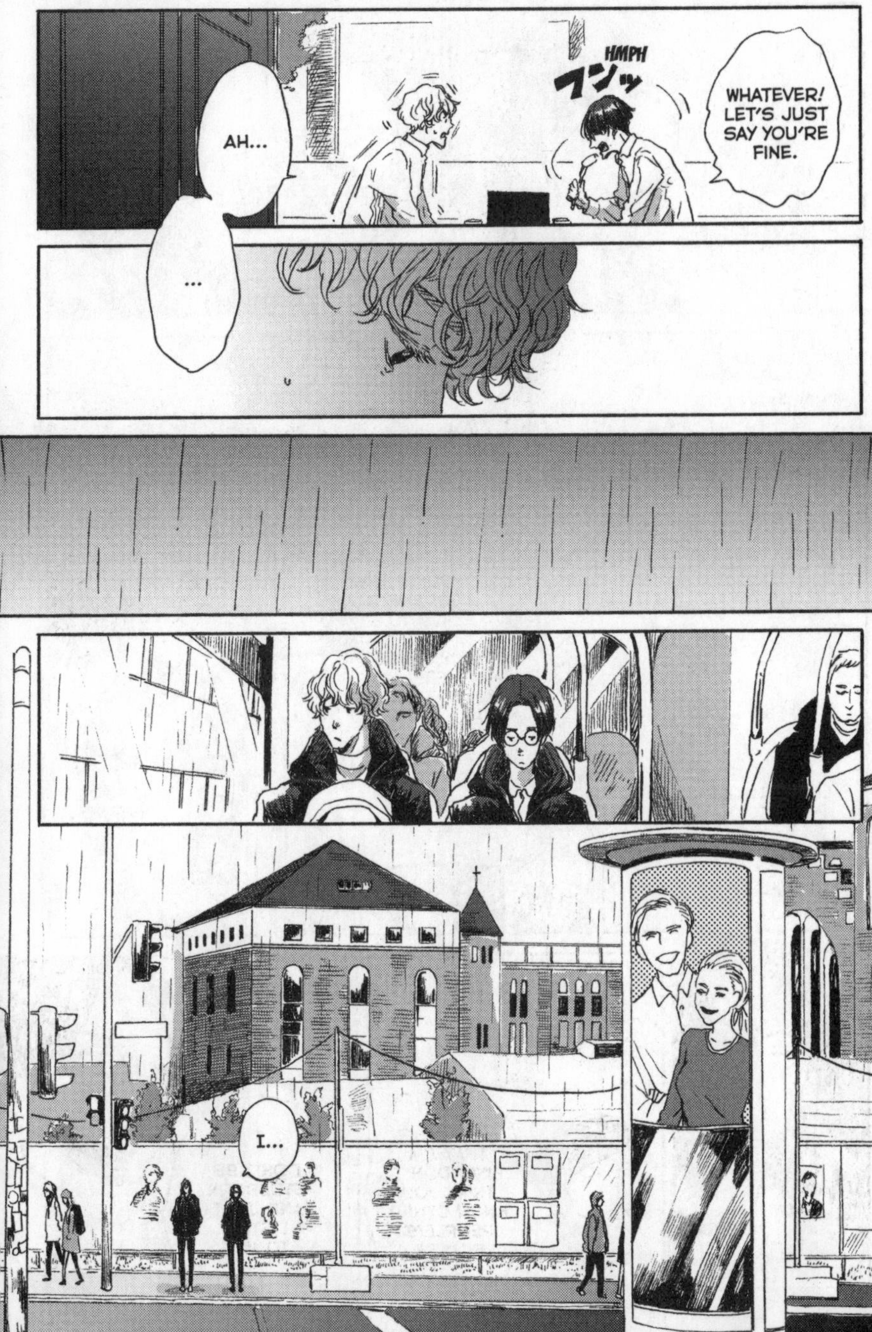
WHATEVER! LET'S JUST SAY YOU'RE FINE.
HMPH
フンッ
AH...
...
I...

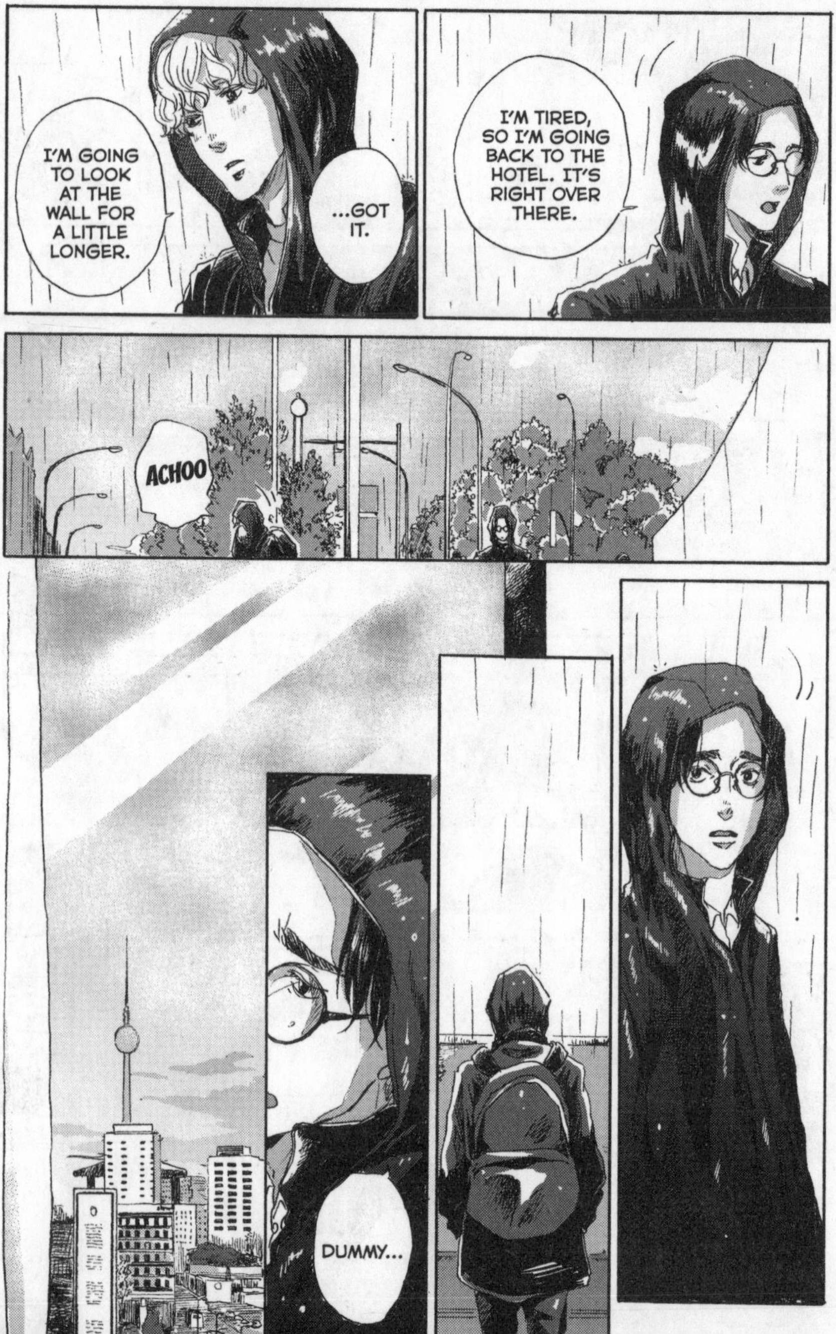
I'M TIRED, SO I'M GOING BACK TO THE HOTEL. IT'S RIGHT OVER THERE.
I'M GOING TO LOOK AT THE WALL FOR A LITTLE LONGER.
...GOT IT.
ACHOO
DUMMY...

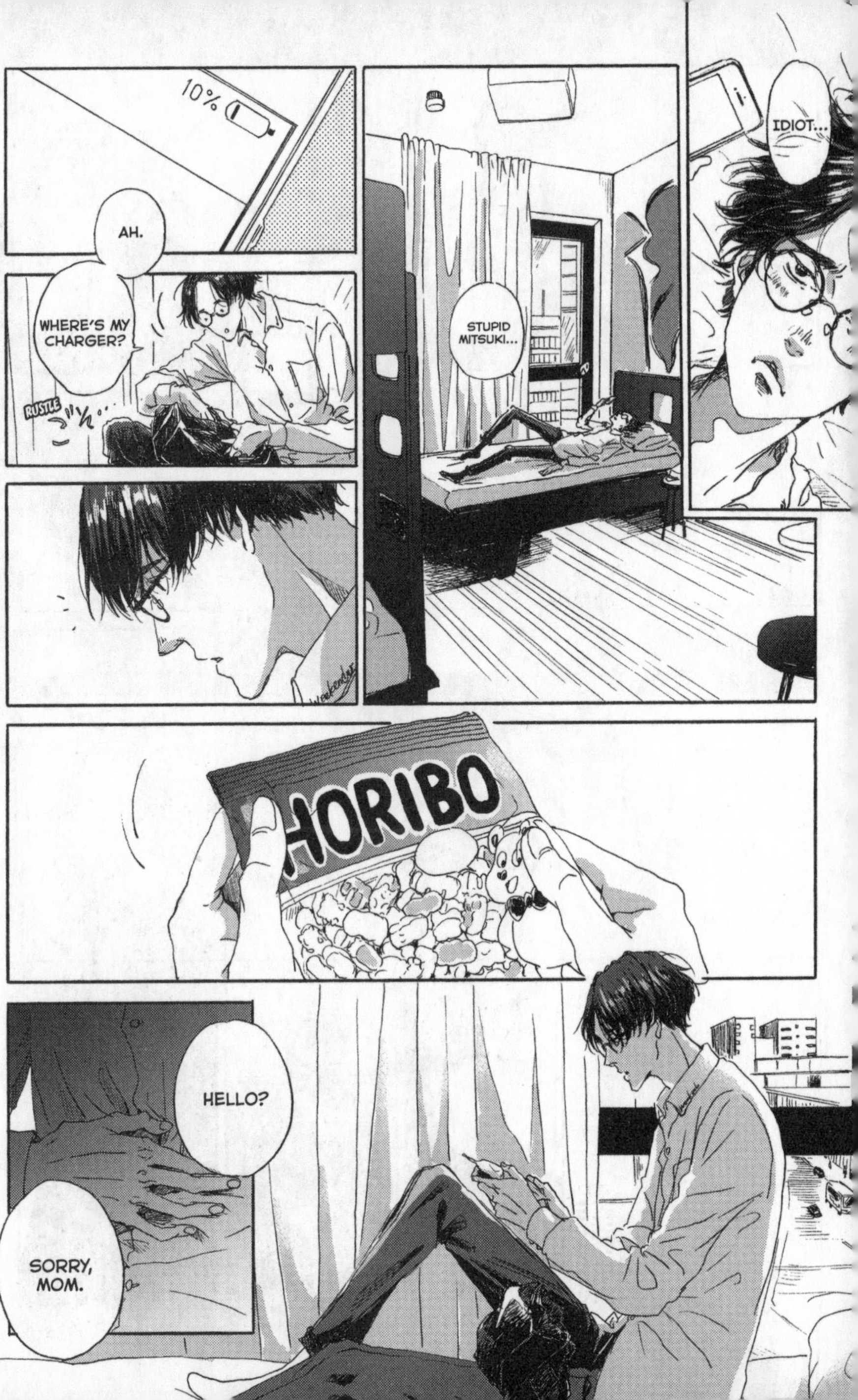
IDIOT...
STUPID MITSUKI...
10%
AH.
WHERE'S MY CHARGER?
RUSTLE
HORIBO
HELLO?
SORRY, MOM.

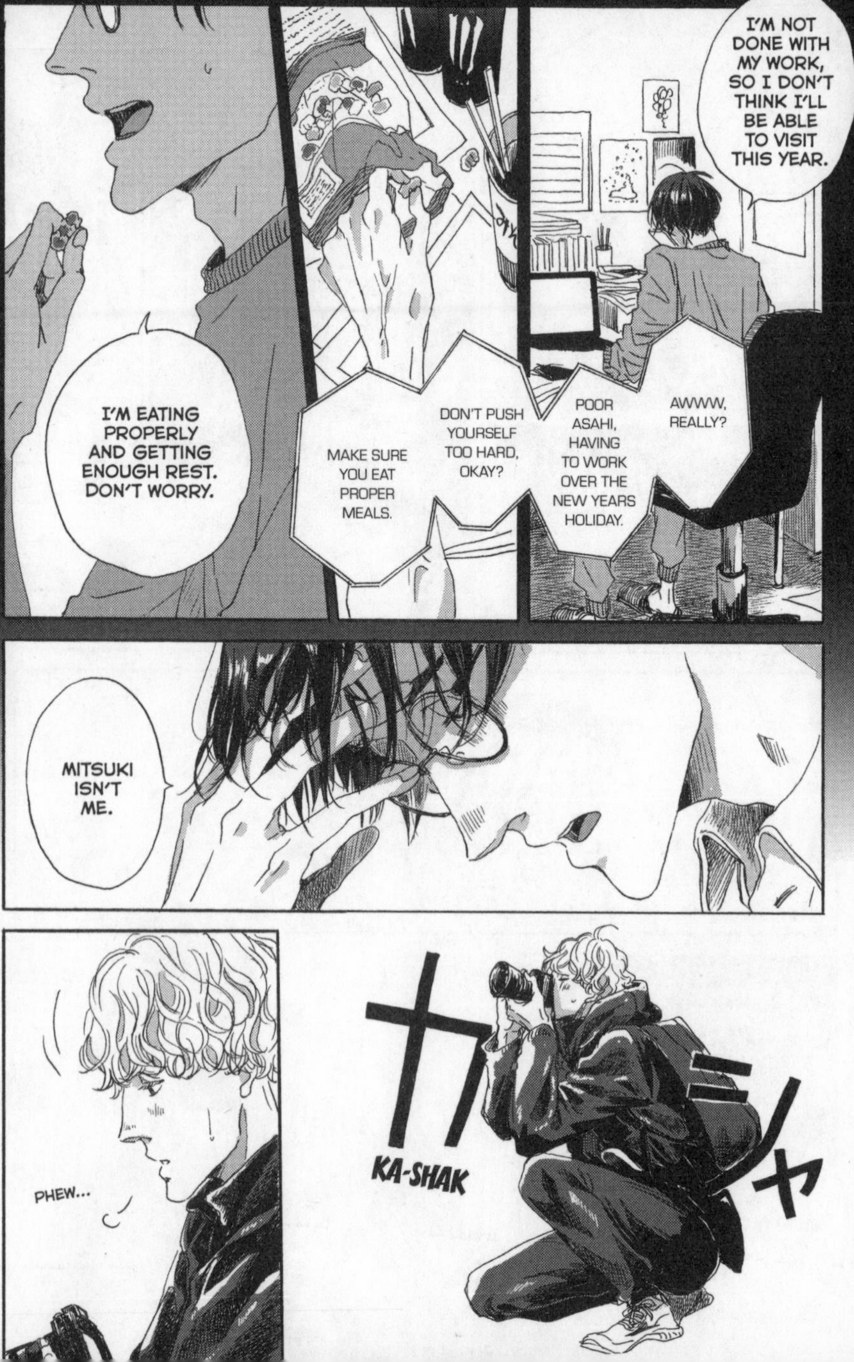
I'M NOT DONE WITH MY WORK, SO I DON'T THINK I'LL BE ABLE TO VISIT THIS YEAR.
AWWW, REALLY?
POOR ASAHI, HAVING TO WORK OVER THE NEW YEARS HOLIDAY.
DON'T PUSH YOURSELF TOO HARD, OKAY?
MAKE SURE YOU EAT PROPER MEALS.
I'M EATING PROPERLY AND GETTING ENOUGH REST. DON'T WORRY.
MITSUKI ISN'T ME.
カシャ
KA-SHAK
PHEW...

SORRY ABOUT EARLIER.
I WAS TOO WORRIED

CAN I JOIN YOU?

IT LOOKS LIKE IT
STOPPED RAINING

DAAAASH

WHAT'S
WITH THIS
STICKER?

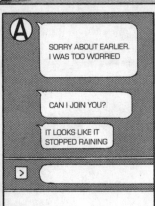

I'M SORRY TOO!

COME JOIN ME

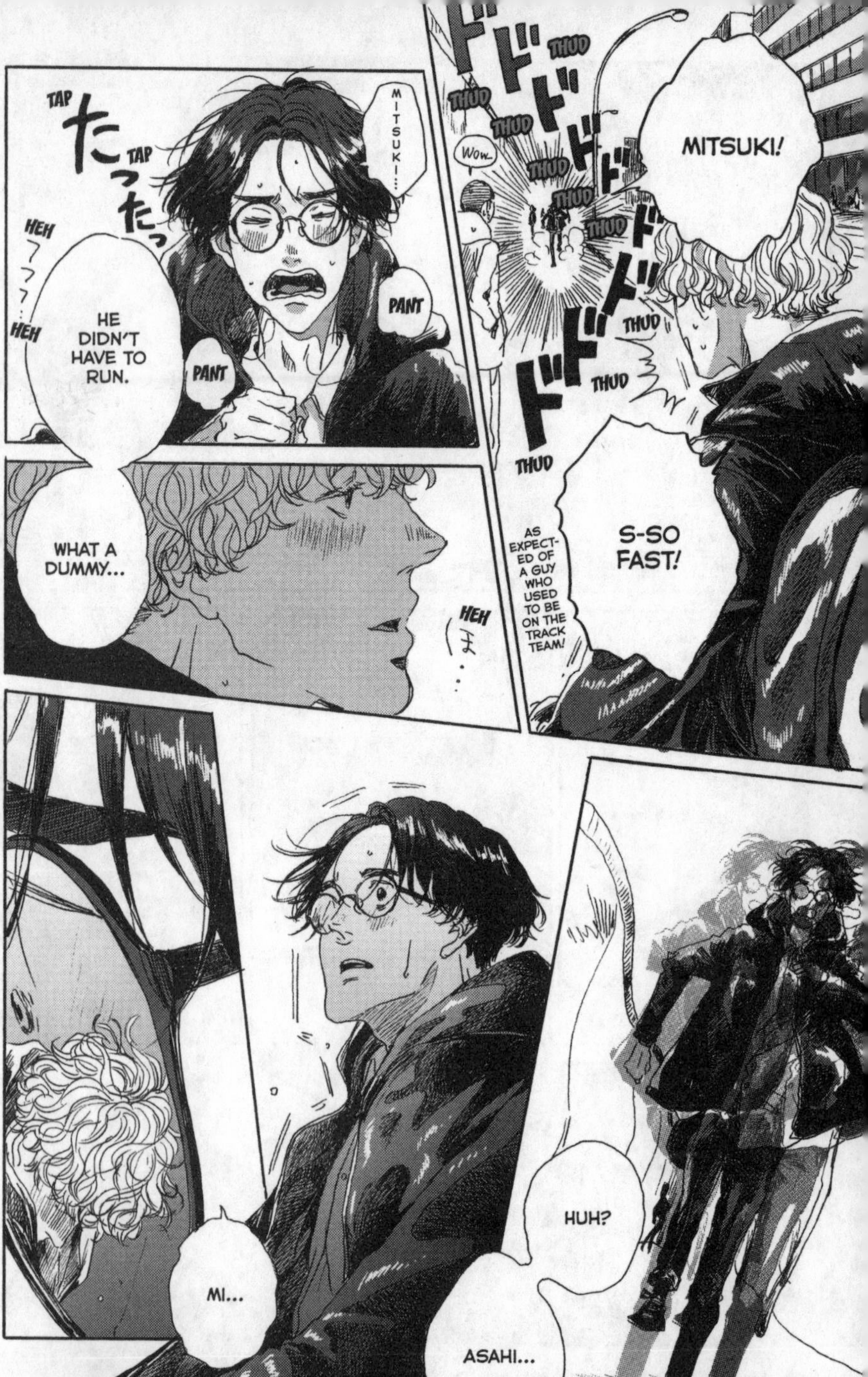
MITSUKI!
THUD
THUD
THUD
THUD
THUD
THUD
THUD
THUD
THUD
WOW...
S-SO FAST!
AS EXPECTED OF A GUY WHO USED TO BE ON THE TRACK TEAM!
TAP
TAP
MITSUKI...
HEH
HEH
HE DIDN'T HAVE TO RUN.
PANT
PANT
WHAT A DUMMY...
HEH
HUH?
ASAHI...
MI...

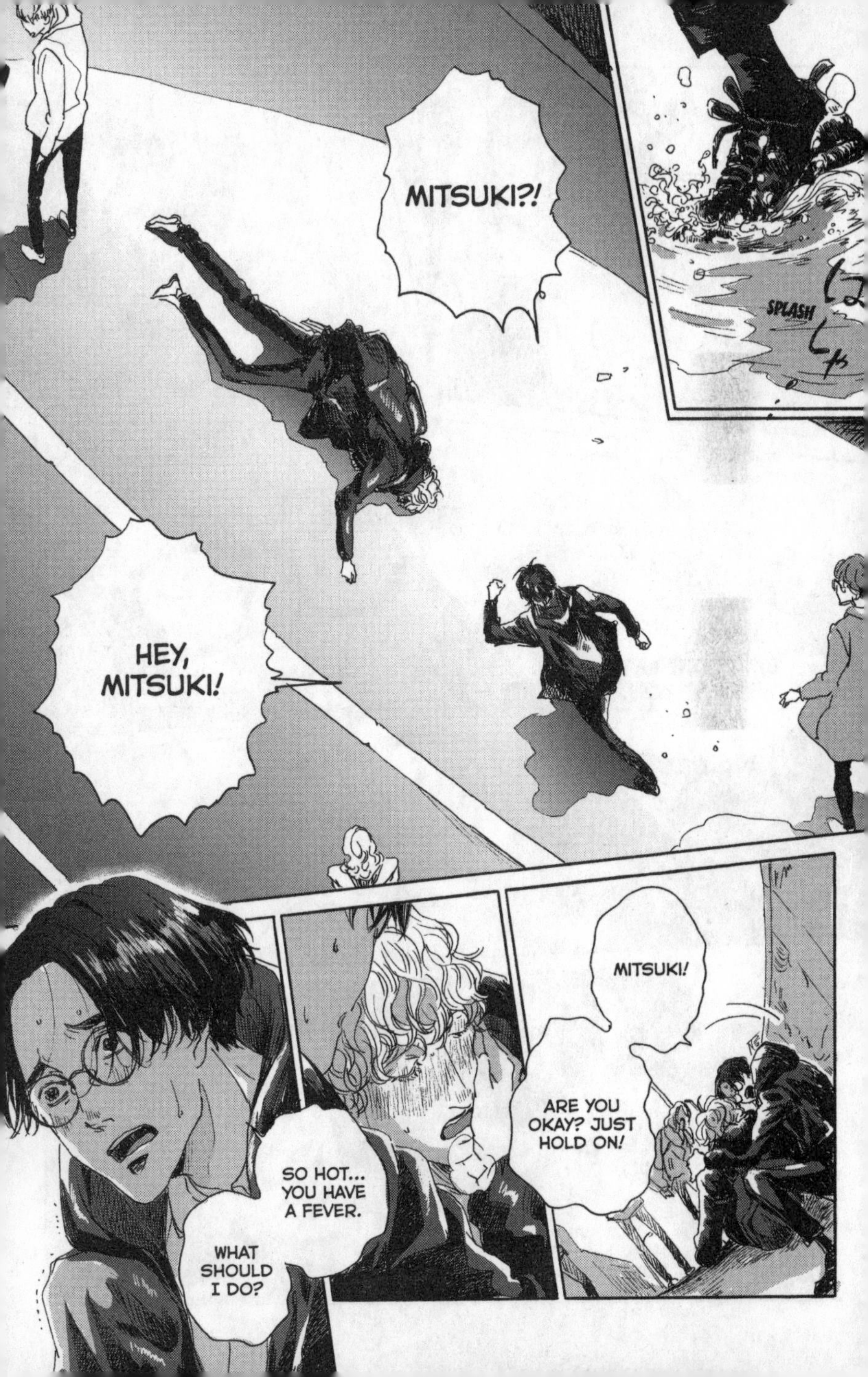
SPLASH
MITSUKI?!
HEY, MITSUKI!
MITSUKI!
ARE YOU OKAY? JUST HOLD ON!
SO HOT... YOU HAVE A FEVER.
WHAT SHOULD I DO?

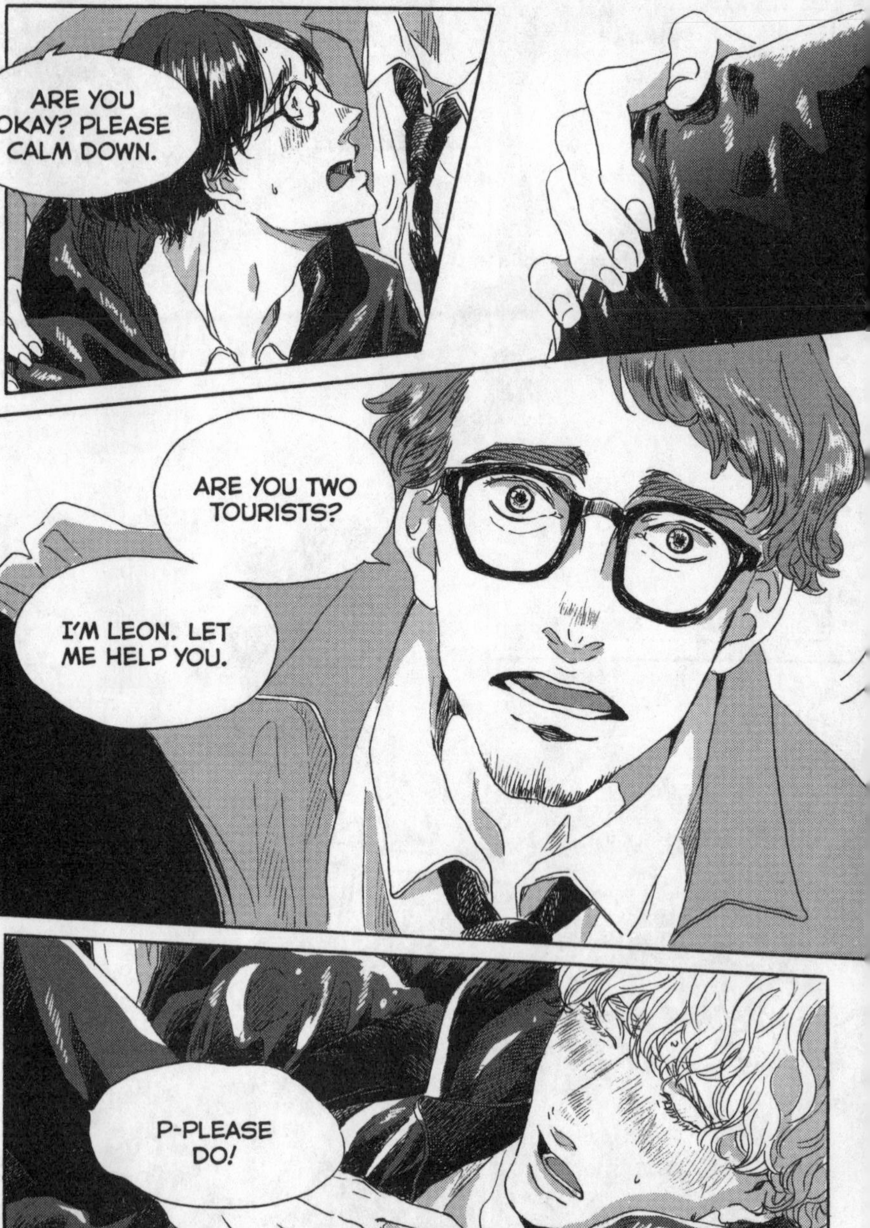
ARE YOU OKAY? PLEASE CALM DOWN.
ARE YOU TWO TOURISTS?
I'M LEON. LET ME HELP YOU.
P-PLEASE DO!

trip. 9

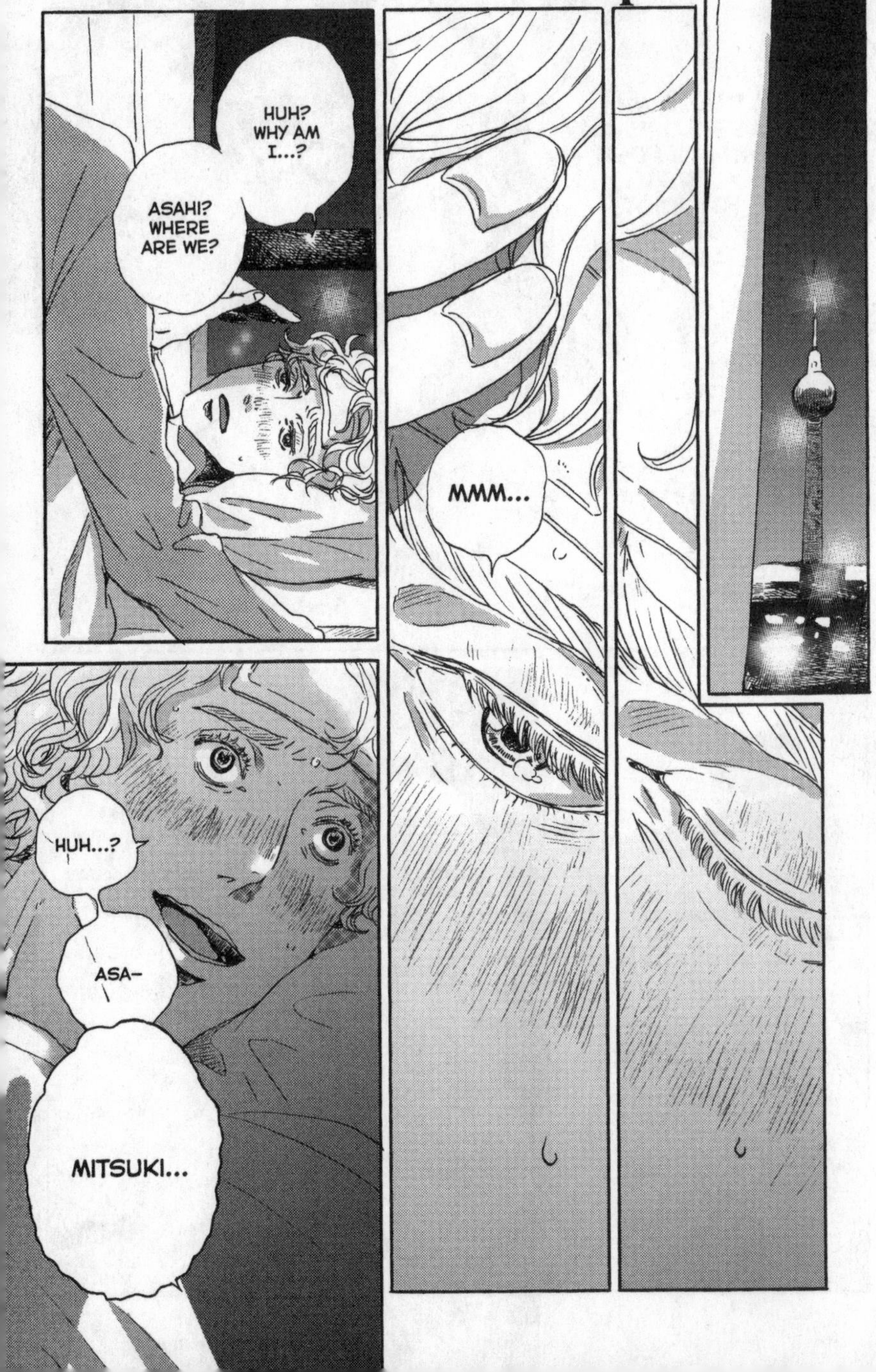
MMM...
HUH? WHY AM I...?
ASAHI? WHERE ARE WE?
HUH...?
ASA-
MITSUKI...

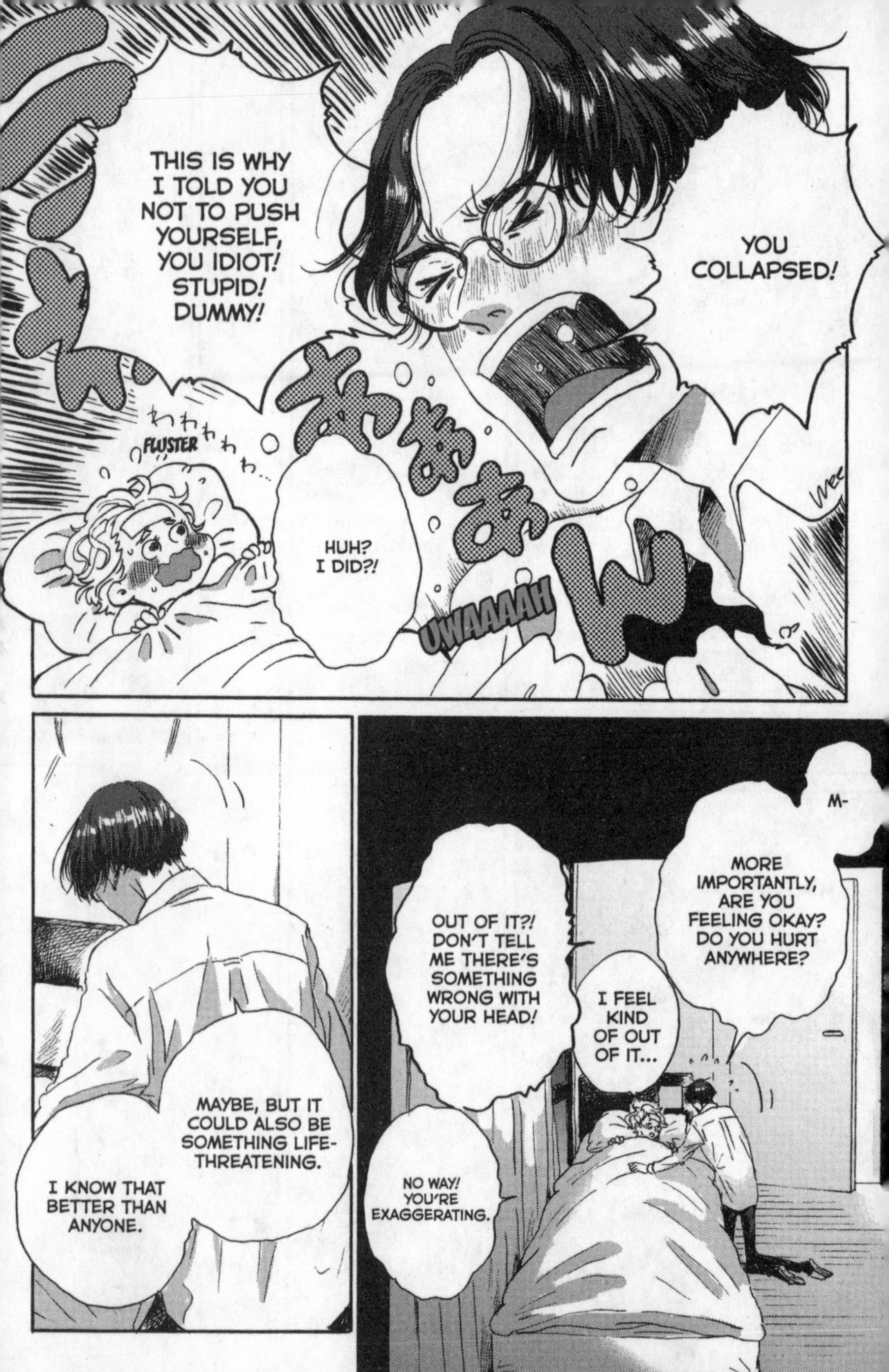
YOU COLLAPSED!
THIS IS WHY I TOLD YOU NOT TO PUSH YOURSELF, YOU IDIOT! STUPID! DUMMY!
UWAAAAH
HUH? I DID?!
わわわわわ…
FLUSTER
M-
MORE IMPORTANTLY, ARE YOU FEELING OKAY? DO YOU HURT ANYWHERE?
I FEEL KIND OF OUT OF IT...
OUT OF IT?! DON'T TELL ME THERE'S SOMETHING WRONG WITH YOUR HEAD!
NO WAY! YOU'RE EXAGGERATING.
MAYBE, BUT IT COULD ALSO BE SOMETHING LIFE-THREATENING.
I KNOW THAT BETTER THAN ANYONE.

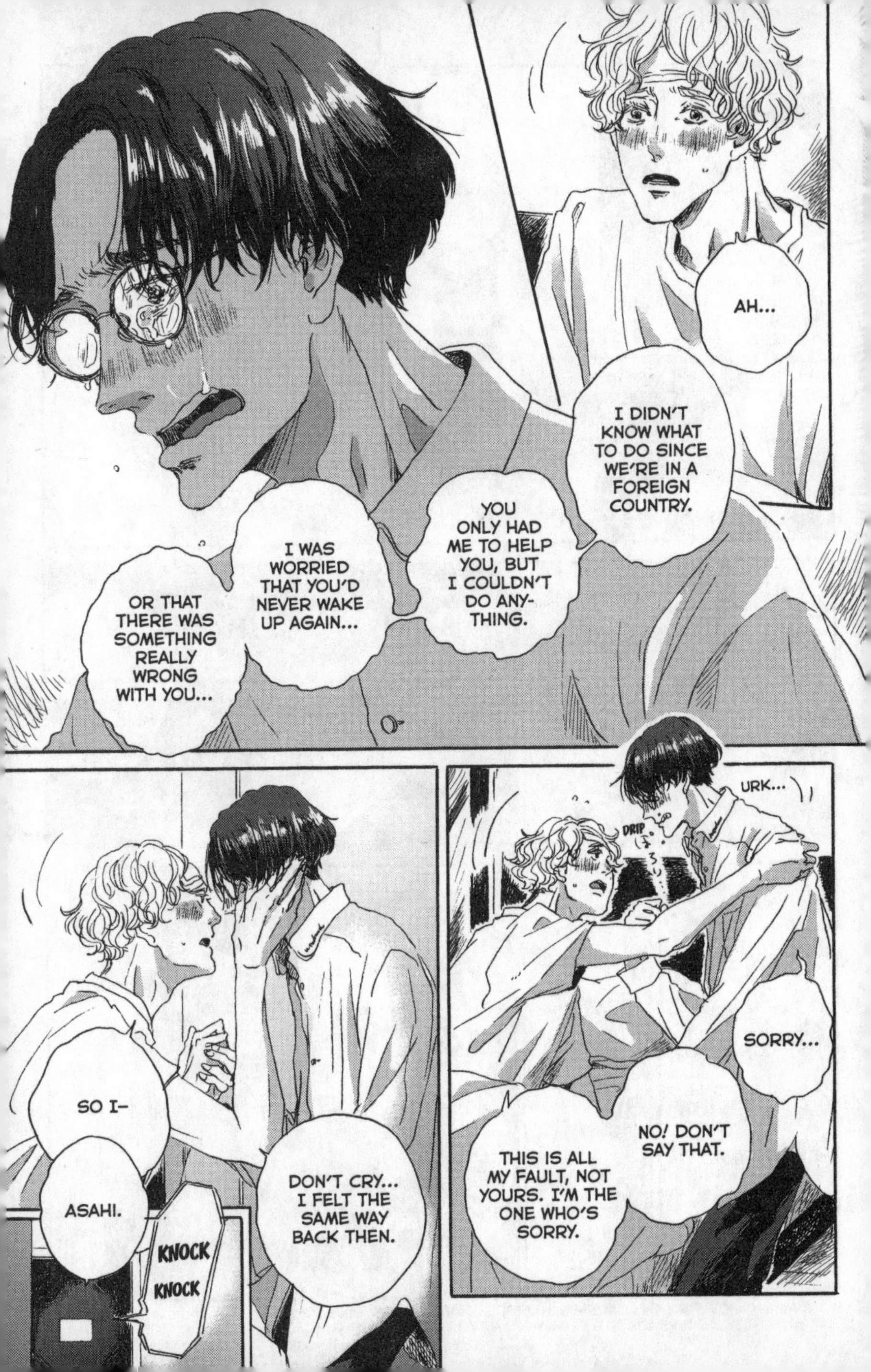
AH...
I DIDN'T KNOW WHAT TO DO SINCE WE'RE IN A FOREIGN COUNTRY.
YOU ONLY HAD ME TO HELP YOU, BUT I COULDN'T DO ANY-THING.
I WAS WORRIED THAT YOU'D NEVER WAKE UP AGAIN...
OR THAT THERE WAS SOMETHING REALLY WRONG WITH YOU...
URK...
DRIP
SORRY...
NO! DON'T SAY THAT.
THIS IS ALL MY FAULT, NOT YOURS. I'M THE ONE WHO'S SORRY.
SO I-
ASAHI.
DON'T CRY... I FELT THE SAME WAY BACK THEN.
KNOCK
KNOCK

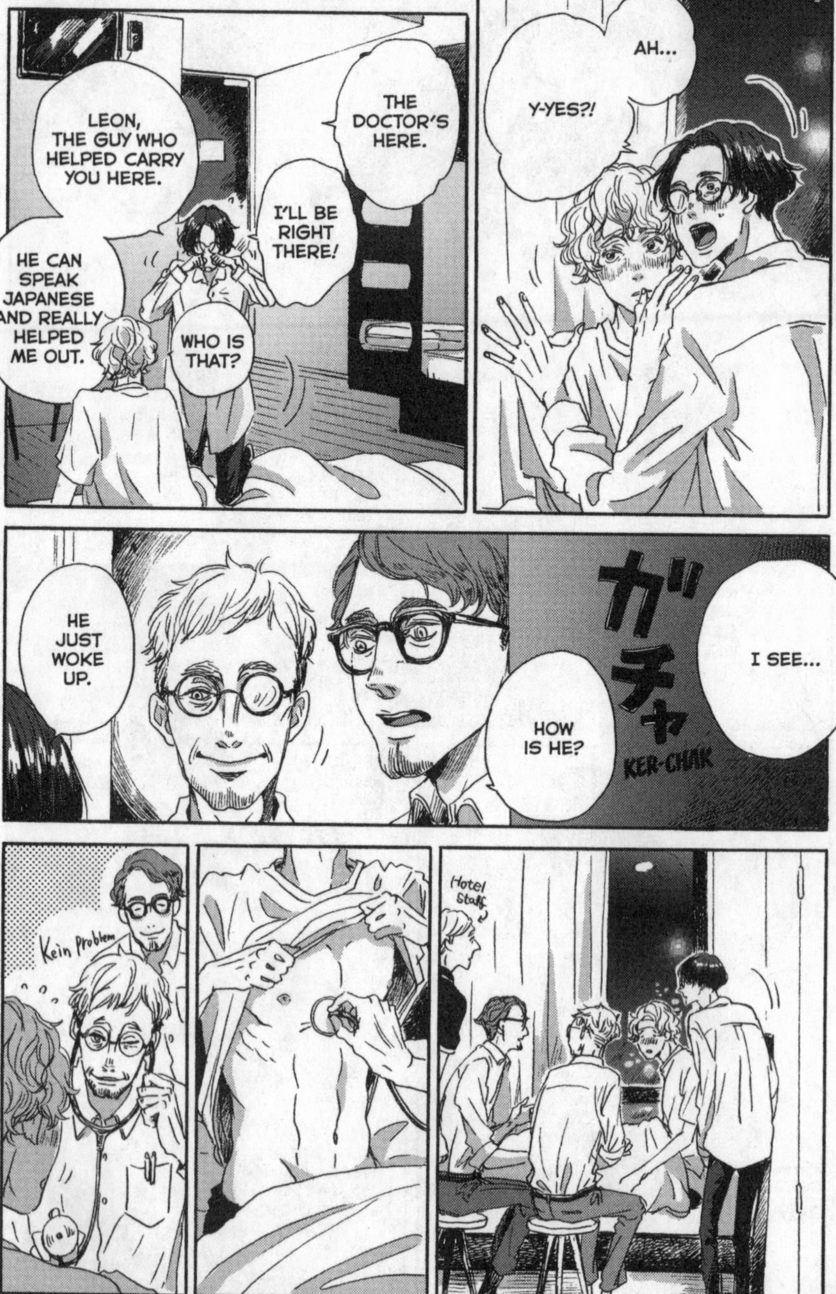
AH...
Y-YES?!
THE DOCTOR'S HERE.
I'LL BE RIGHT THERE!
WHO IS THAT?
LEON, THE GUY WHO HELPED CARRY YOU HERE.
HE CAN SPEAK JAPANESE AND REALLY HELPED ME OUT.
I SEE...
ガチャ
KER-CHAK
HOW IS HE?
HE JUST WOKE UP.
Hotel Staff
Kein Problem

* TREATMENT FOR SUDDEN ILLNESSES MAY BE DIFFERENT DEPENDING ON THE COUNTRY/HOTEL YOU'RE STAYING IN, AS WELL AS YOUR TRAVEL INSURANCE.

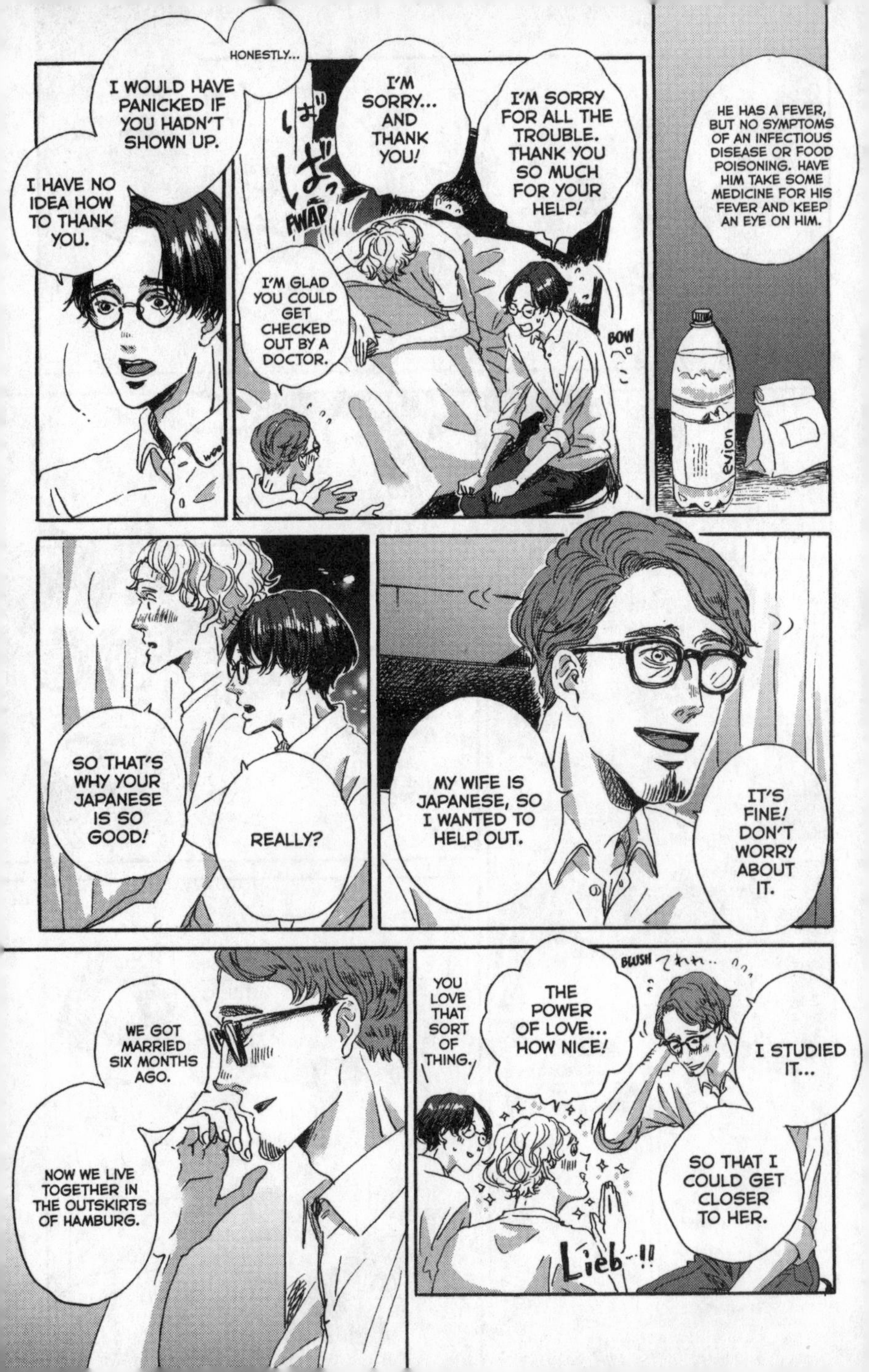
HE HAS A FEVER, BUT NO SYMPTOMS OF AN INFECTIOUS DISEASE OR FOOD POISONING. HAVE HIM TAKE SOME MEDICINE FOR HIS FEVER AND KEEP AN EYE ON HIM.
I'M SORRY FOR ALL THE TROUBLE. THANK YOU SO MUCH FOR YOUR HELP!
I'M SORRY... AND THANK YOU!
FWAP
BOW
I'M GLAD YOU COULD GET CHECKED OUT BY A DOCTOR.
HONESTLY...
I WOULD HAVE PANICKED IF YOU HADN'T SHOWN UP.
I HAVE NO IDEA HOW TO THANK YOU.
IT'S FINE! DON'T WORRY ABOUT IT.
MY WIFE IS JAPANESE, SO I WANTED TO HELP OUT.
REALLY?
SO THAT'S WHY YOUR JAPANESE IS SO GOOD!
I STUDIED IT...
SO THAT I COULD GET CLOSER TO HER.
BLUSH
THE POWER OF LOVE... HOW NICE!
YOU LOVE THAT SORT OF THING.
Lieb~!!
WE GOT MARRIED SIX MONTHS AGO.
NOW WE LIVE TOGETHER IN THE OUTSKIRTS OF HAMBURG.

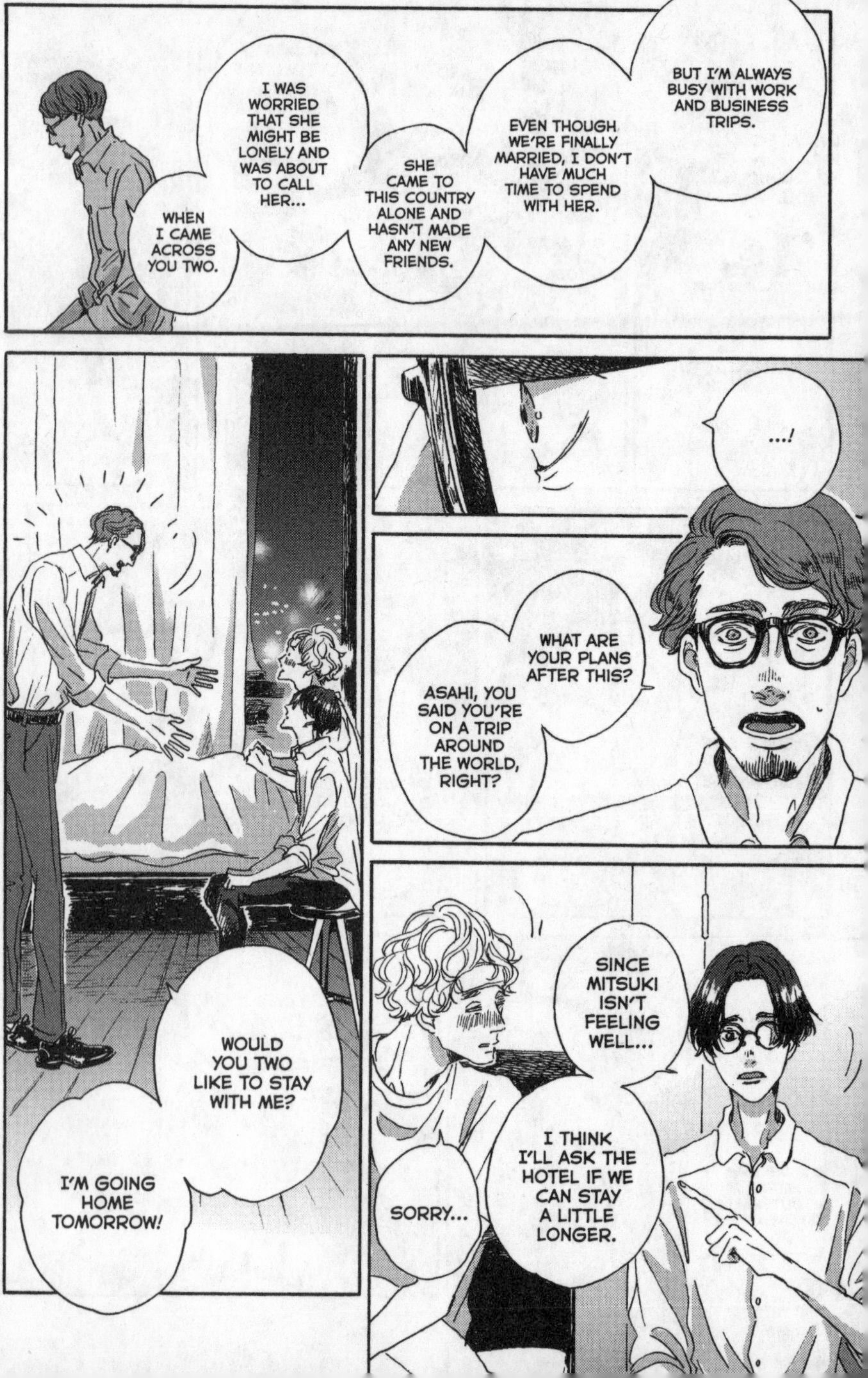
BUT I'M ALWAYS BUSY WITH WORK AND BUSINESS TRIPS.
EVEN THOUGH WE'RE FINALLY MARRIED, I DON'T HAVE MUCH TIME TO SPEND WITH HER.
SHE CAME TO THIS COUNTRY ALONE AND HASN'T MADE ANY NEW FRIENDS.
I WAS WORRIED THAT SHE MIGHT BE LONELY AND WAS ABOUT TO CALL HER...
WHEN I CAME ACROSS YOU TWO.
...!
WHAT ARE YOUR PLANS AFTER THIS?
ASAHI, YOU SAID YOU'RE ON A TRIP AROUND THE WORLD, RIGHT?
SINCE MITSUKI ISN'T FEELING WELL...
I THINK I'LL ASK THE HOTEL IF WE CAN STAY A LITTLE LONGER.
SORRY...
WOULD YOU TWO LIKE TO STAY WITH ME?
I'M GOING HOME TOMORROW!

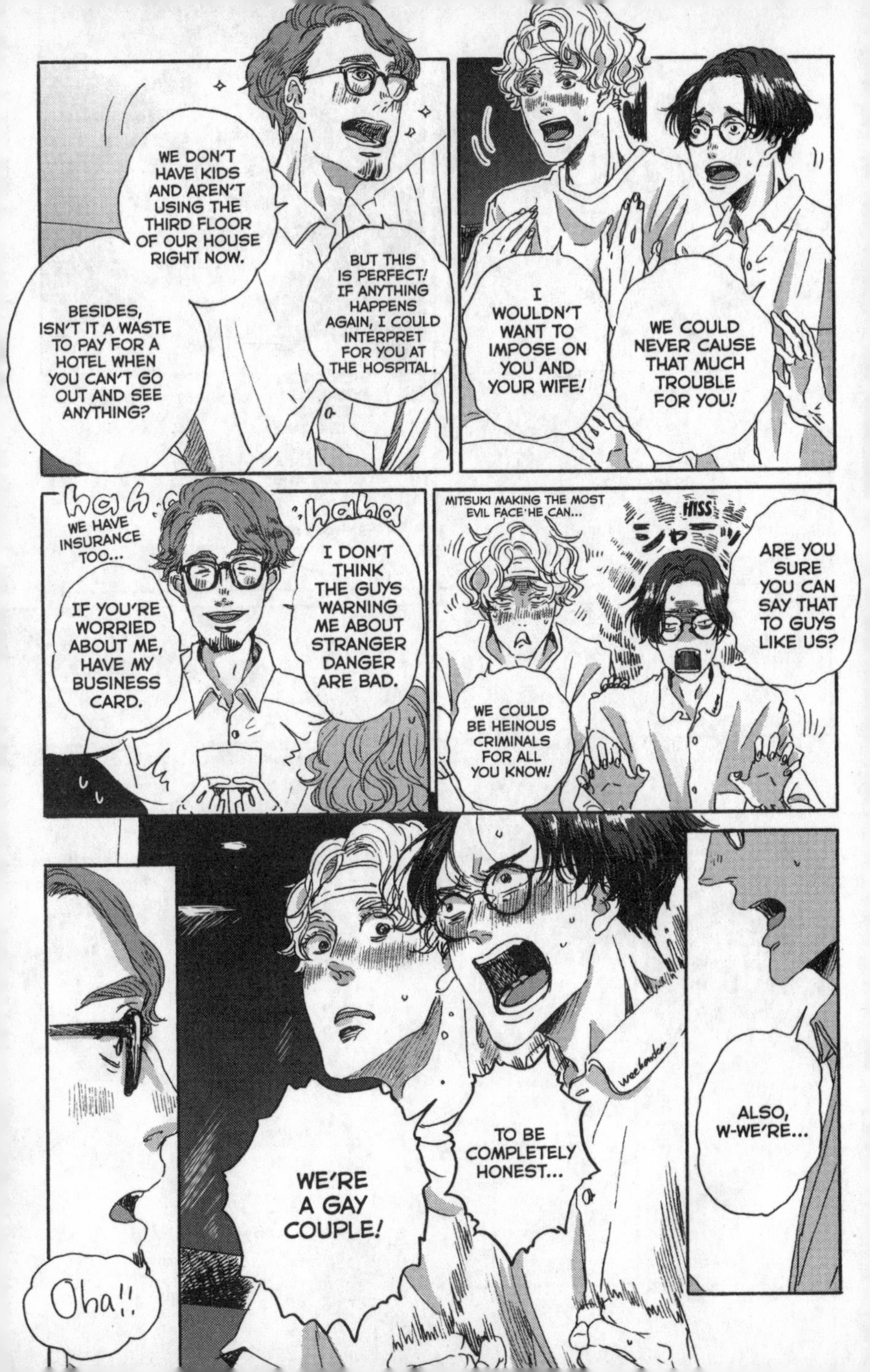

WE COULD NEVER CAUSE THAT MUCH TROUBLE FOR YOU!
I WOULDN'T WANT TO IMPOSE ON YOU AND YOUR WIFE!
WE DON'T HAVE KIDS AND AREN'T USING THE THIRD FLOOR OF OUR HOUSE RIGHT NOW.
BUT THIS IS PERFECT! IF ANYTHING HAPPENS AGAIN, I COULD INTERPRET FOR YOU AT THE HOSPITAL.
BESIDES, ISN'T IT A WASTE TO PAY FOR A HOTEL WHEN YOU CAN'T GO OUT AND SEE ANYTHING?
ARE YOU SURE YOU CAN SAY THAT TO GUYS LIKE US?
HISS
シャーッ
MITSUKI MAKING THE MOST EVIL FACE HE CAN...
WE COULD BE HEINOUS CRIMINALS FOR ALL YOU KNOW!
haha
I DON'T THINK THE GUYS WARNING ME ABOUT STRANGER DANGER ARE BAD.
haha
WE HAVE INSURANCE TOO...
IF YOU'RE WORRIED ABOUT ME, HAVE MY BUSINESS CARD.
ALSO, W-WE'RE...
weekender
TO BE COMPLETELY HONEST...
WE'RE A GAY COUPLE!
Oha!!

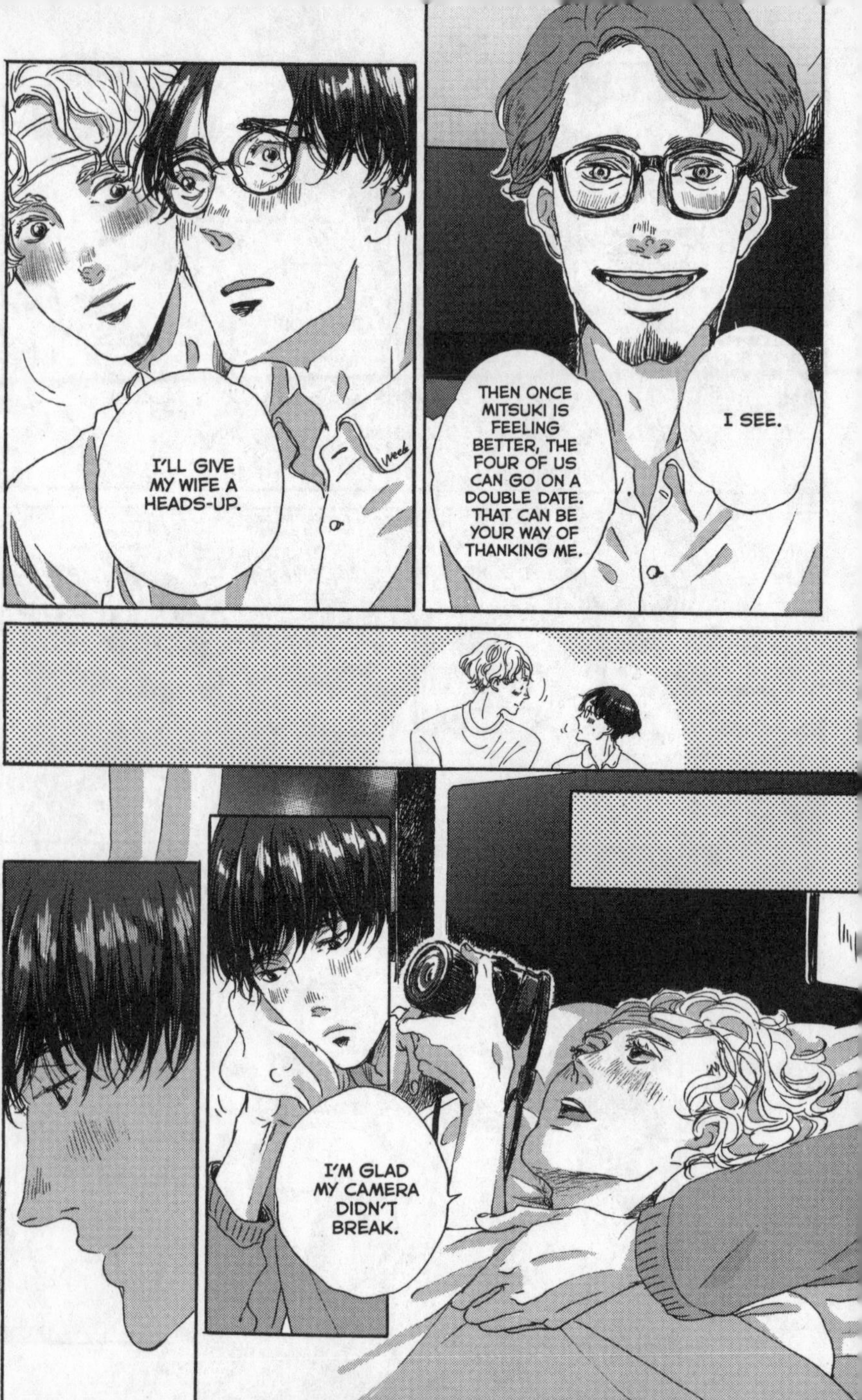
I SEE.
THEN ONCE MITSUKI IS FEELING BETTER, THE FOUR OF US CAN GO ON A DOUBLE DATE. THAT CAN BE YOUR WAY OF THANKING ME.
I'LL GIVE MY WIFE A HEADS-UP.
I'M GLAD MY CAMERA DIDN'T BREAK.

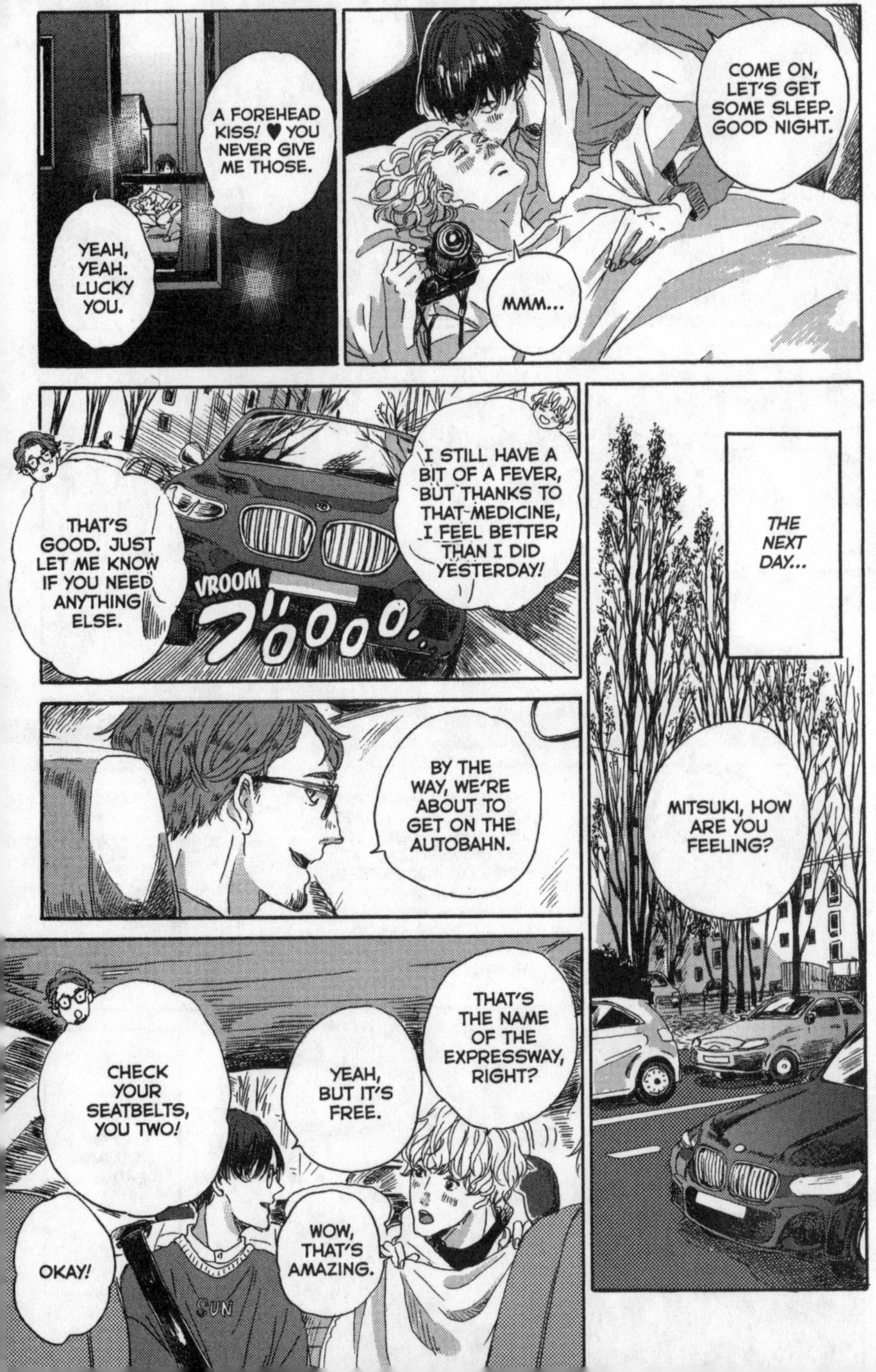
COME ON, LET'S GET SOME SLEEP. GOOD NIGHT.
MMM...
A FOREHEAD KISS! ♥ YOU NEVER GIVE ME THOSE.
YEAH, YEAH. LUCKY YOU.
THE NEXT DAY...
MITSUKI, HOW ARE YOU FEELING?
I STILL HAVE A BIT OF A FEVER, BUT THANKS TO THAT MEDICINE, I FEEL BETTER THAN I DID YESTERDAY!
THAT'S GOOD. JUST LET ME KNOW IF YOU NEED ANYTHING ELSE.
VROOM
BY THE WAY, WE'RE ABOUT TO GET ON THE AUTOBAHN.
THAT'S THE NAME OF THE EXPRESSWAY, RIGHT?
YEAH, BUT IT'S FREE.
CHECK YOUR SEATBELTS, YOU TWO!
WOW, THAT'S AMAZING.
OKAY!

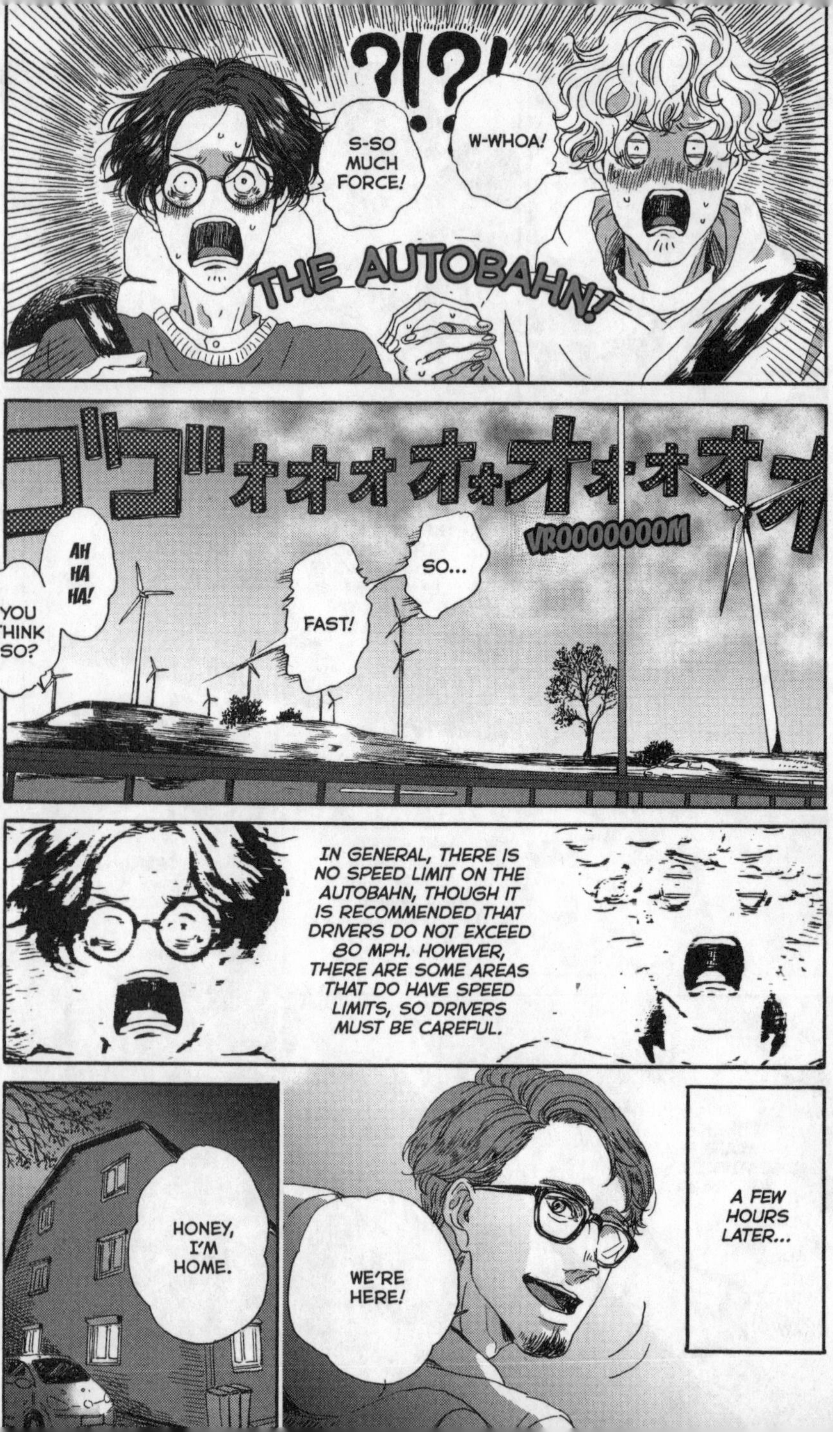
?!?!
W-WHOA!
S-SO MUCH FORCE!
THE AUTOBAHN!
ゴゴオオオオォオォォオ
VROOOOOOOM
SO... FAST!
AH HA HA!
YOU THINK SO?
IN GENERAL, THERE IS NO SPEED LIMIT ON THE AUTOBAHN, THOUGH IT IS RECOMMENDED THAT DRIVERS DO NOT EXCEED 80 MPH. HOWEVER, THERE ARE SOME AREAS THAT DO HAVE SPEED LIMITS, SO DRIVERS MUST BE CAREFUL.
A FEW HOURS LATER...
WE'RE HERE!
HONEY, I'M HOME.

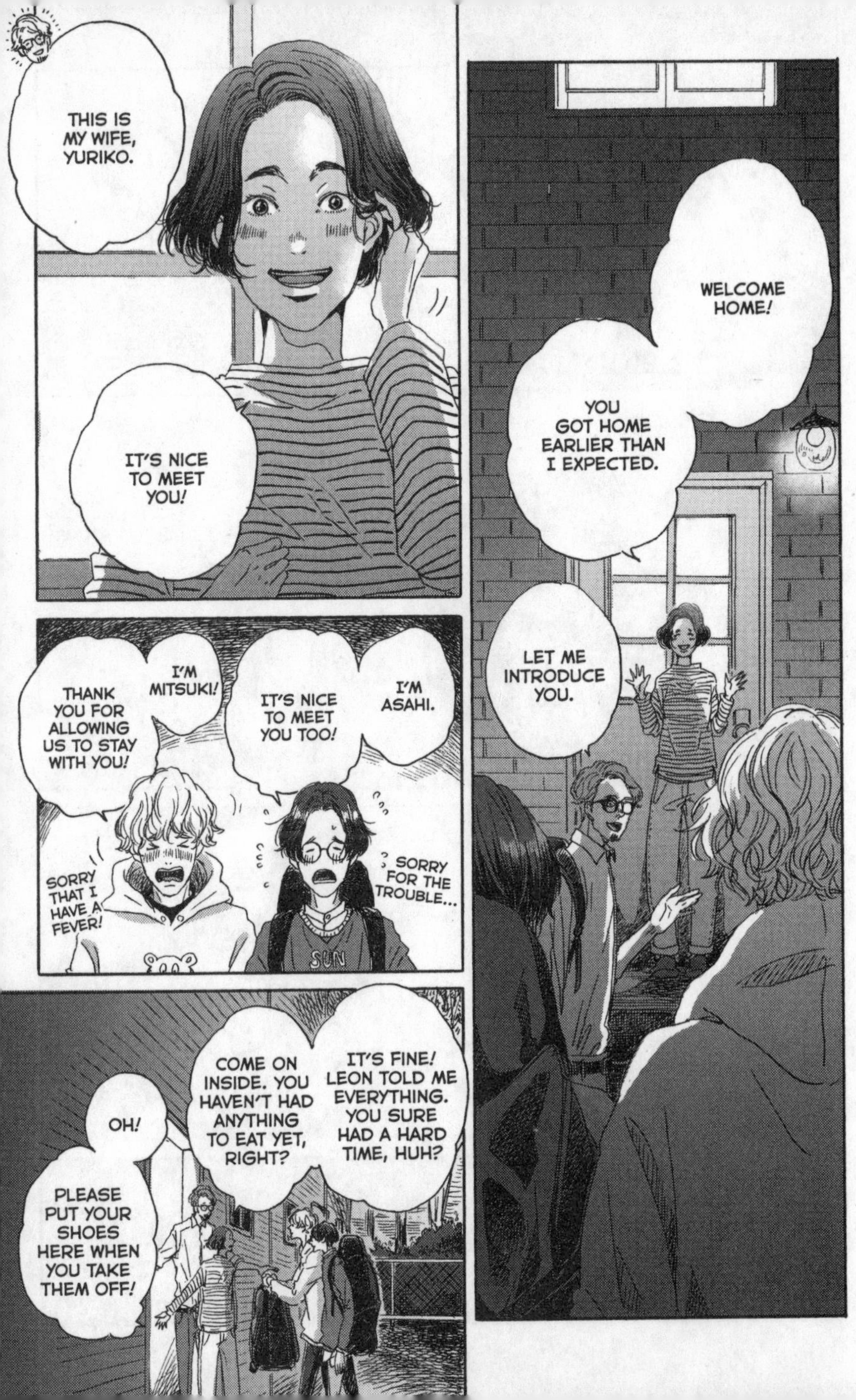
WELCOME HOME!
YOU GOT HOME EARLIER THAN I EXPECTED.
LET ME INTRODUCE YOU.
THIS IS MY WIFE, YURIKO.
IT'S NICE TO MEET YOU!
I'M ASAHI.
IT'S NICE TO MEET YOU TOO!
I'M MITSUKI!
THANK YOU FOR ALLOWING US TO STAY WITH YOU!
SORRY FOR THE TROUBLE...
SORRY THAT I HAVE A FEVER!
SUN
IT'S FINE! LEON TOLD ME EVERYTHING. YOU SURE HAD A HARD TIME, HUH?
COME ON INSIDE. YOU HAVEN'T HAD ANYTHING TO EAT YET, RIGHT?
OH!
PLEASE PUT YOUR SHOES HERE WHEN YOU TAKE THEM OFF!

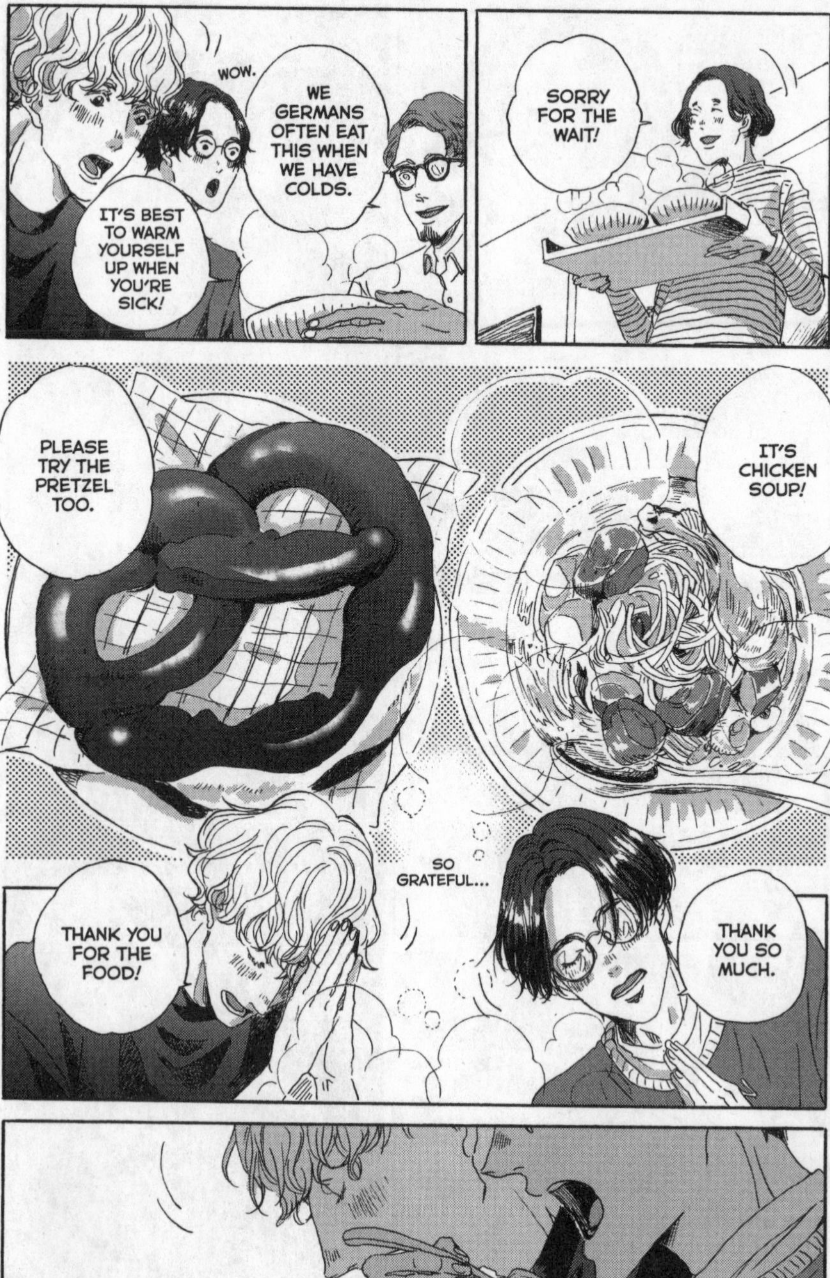
SORRY FOR THE WAIT!
WE GERMANS OFTEN EAT THIS WHEN WE HAVE COLDS.
WOW.
IT'S BEST TO WARM YOURSELF UP WHEN YOU'RE SICK!
IT'S CHICKEN SOUP!
PLEASE TRY THE PRETZEL TOO.
THANK YOU SO MUCH.
SO GRATEFUL...
THANK YOU FOR THE FOOD!

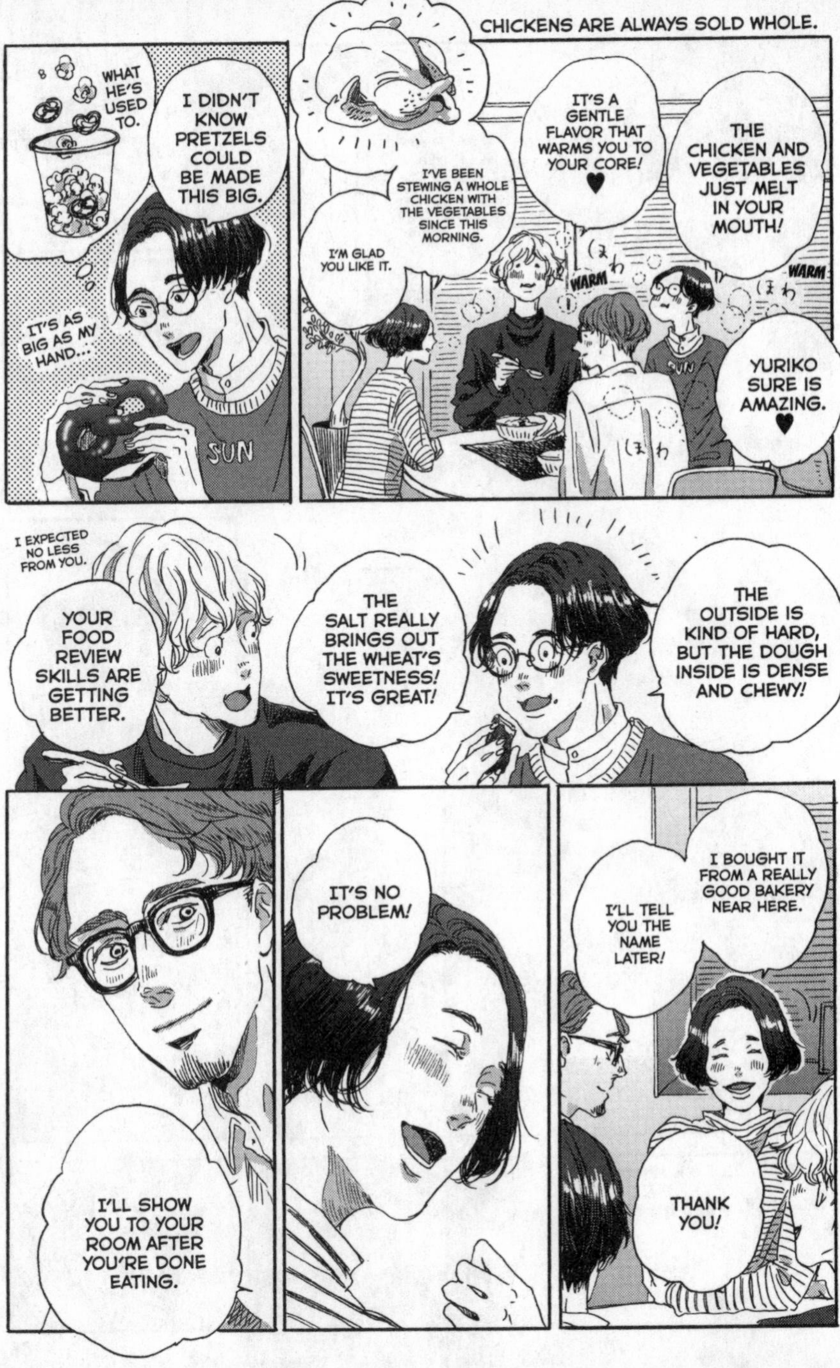
CHICKENS ARE ALWAYS SOLD WHOLE.
THE CHICKEN AND VEGETABLES JUST MELT IN YOUR MOUTH!
WARM
ほわ
IT'S A GENTLE FLAVOR THAT WARMS YOU TO YOUR CORE! ♥
I'VE BEEN STEWING A WHOLE CHICKEN WITH THE VEGETABLES SINCE THIS MORNING.
WARM
ほわ
YURIKO SURE IS AMAZING. ♥
ほわ
I'M GLAD YOU LIKE IT.
I DIDN'T KNOW PRETZELS COULD BE MADE THIS BIG.
WHAT HE'S USED TO.
IT'S AS BIG AS MY HAND...
THE OUTSIDE IS KIND OF HARD, BUT THE DOUGH INSIDE IS DENSE AND CHEWY!
THE SALT REALLY BRINGS OUT THE WHEAT'S SWEETNESS! IT'S GREAT!
I EXPECTED NO LESS FROM YOU.
YOUR FOOD REVIEW SKILLS ARE GETTING BETTER.
I BOUGHT IT FROM A REALLY GOOD BAKERY NEAR HERE.
I'LL TELL YOU THE NAME LATER!
THANK YOU!
IT'S NO PROBLEM!
I'LL SHOW YOU TO YOUR ROOM AFTER YOU'RE DONE EATING.

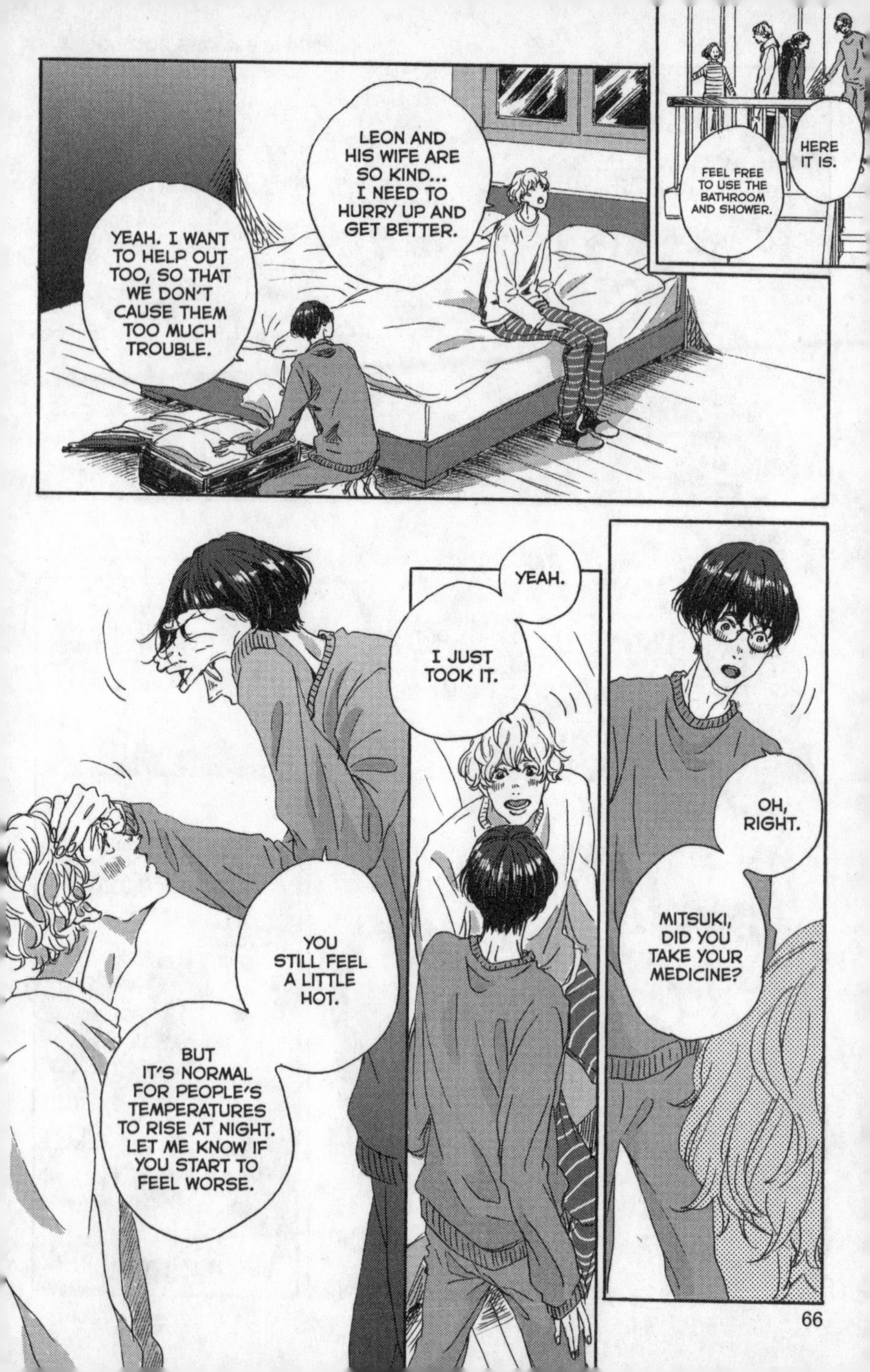
HERE IT IS.
FEEL FREE TO USE THE BATHROOM AND SHOWER.
LEON AND HIS WIFE ARE SO KIND... I NEED TO HURRY UP AND GET BETTER.
YEAH. I WANT TO HELP OUT TOO, SO THAT WE DON'T CAUSE THEM TOO MUCH TROUBLE.
OH, RIGHT.
MITSUKI, DID YOU TAKE YOUR MEDICINE?
YEAH.
I JUST TOOK IT.
YOU STILL FEEL A LITTLE HOT.
BUT IT'S NORMAL FOR PEOPLE'S TEMPERATURES TO RISE AT NIGHT. LET ME KNOW IF YOU START TO FEEL WORSE.

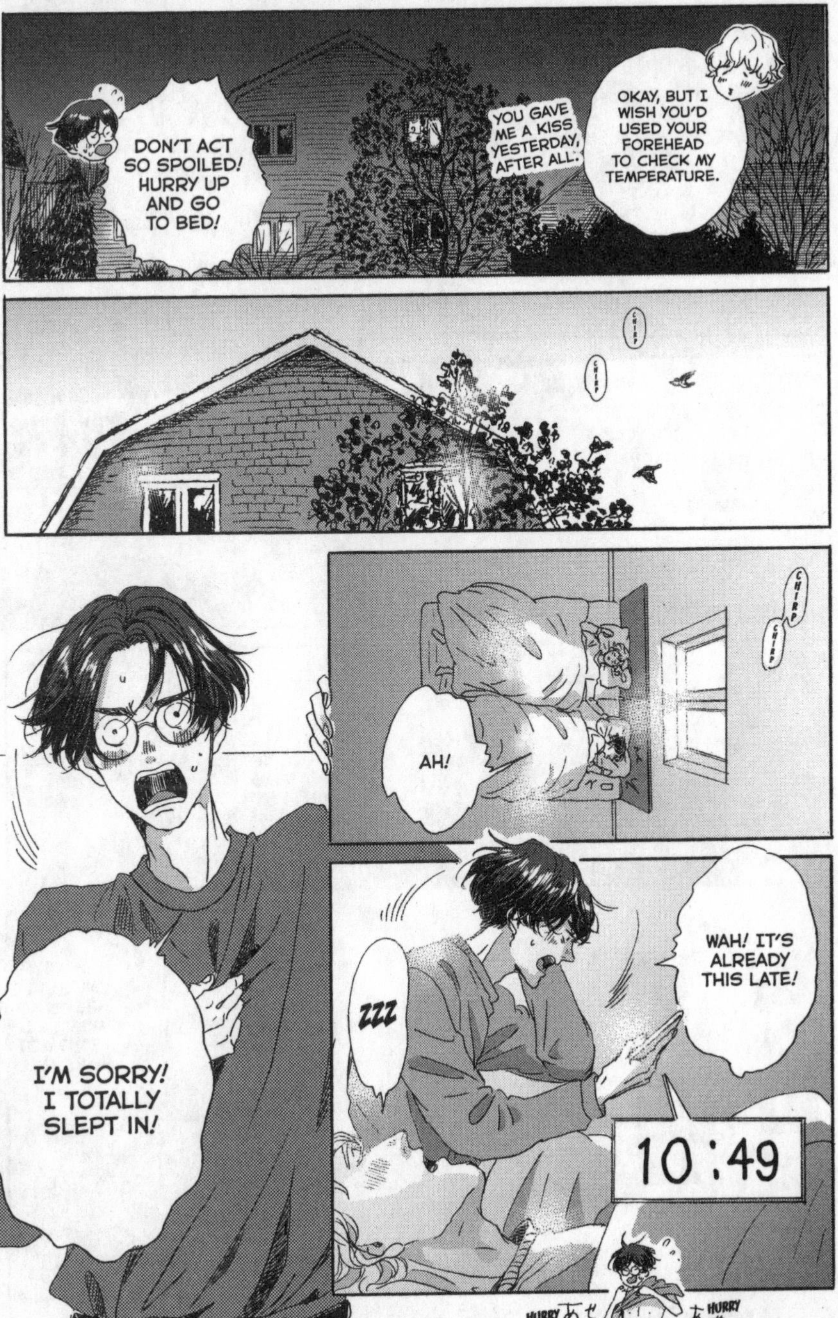
OKAY, BUT I WISH YOU'D USED YOUR FOREHEAD TO CHECK MY TEMPERATURE.
YOU GAVE ME A KISS YESTERDAY, AFTER ALL.
DON'T ACT SO SPOILED! HURRY UP AND GO TO BED!
CHIRP
CHIRP
CHIRP
CHIRP
AH!
WAH! IT'S ALREADY THIS LATE!
ZZZ
10:49
HURRY あせ
あせ HURRY
I'M SORRY! I TOTALLY SLEPT IN!

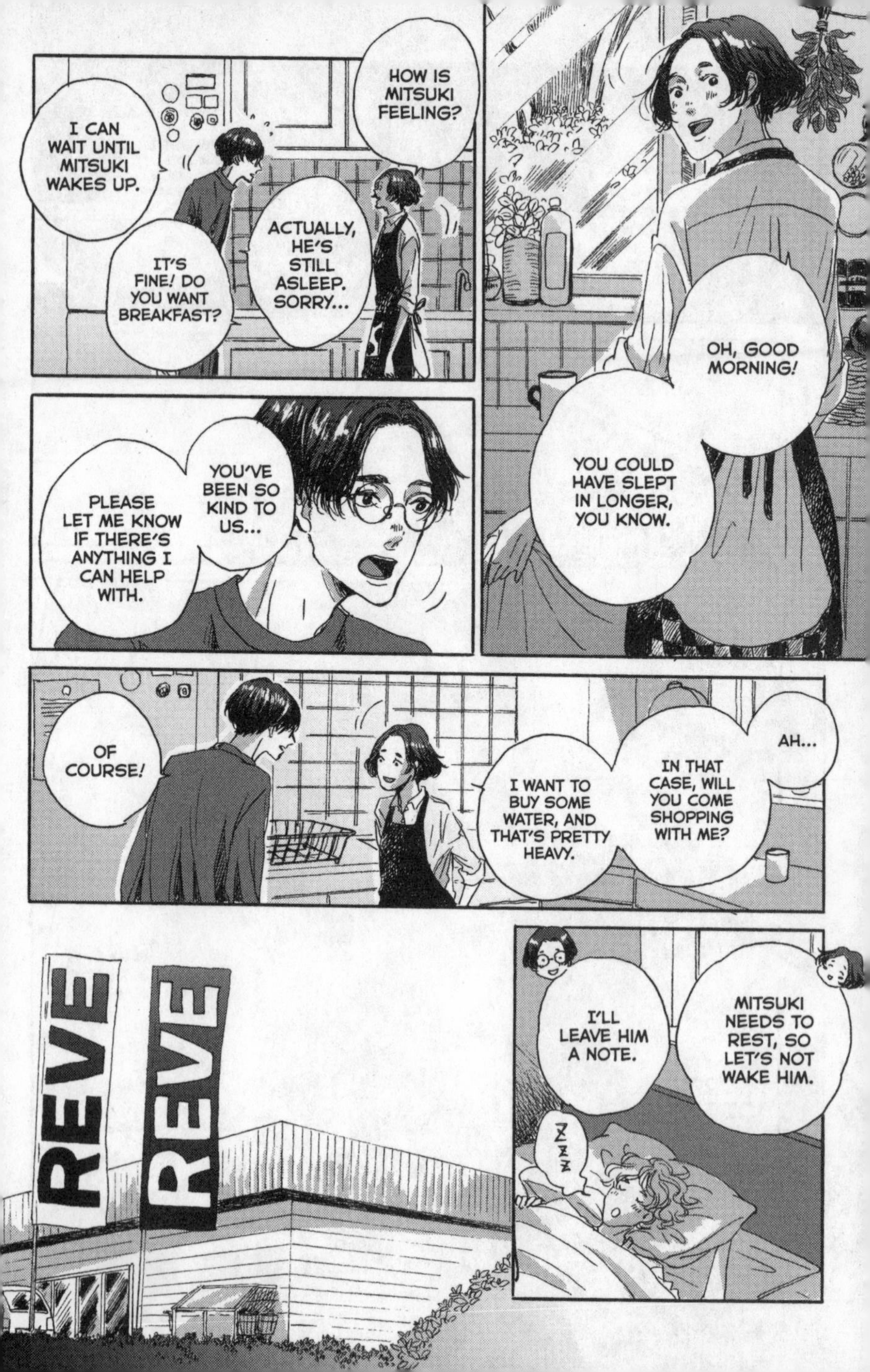
OH, GOOD MORNING!
YOU COULD HAVE SLEPT IN LONGER, YOU KNOW.
HOW IS MITSUKI FEELING?
ACTUALLY, HE'S STILL ASLEEP. SORRY...
IT'S FINE! DO YOU WANT BREAKFAST?
I CAN WAIT UNTIL MITSUKI WAKES UP.
YOU'VE BEEN SO KIND TO US...
PLEASE LET ME KNOW IF THERE'S ANYTHING I CAN HELP WITH.
AH...
IN THAT CASE, WILL YOU COME SHOPPING WITH ME?
I WANT TO BUY SOME WATER, AND THAT'S PRETTY HEAVY.
OF COURSE!
MITSUKI NEEDS TO REST, SO LET'S NOT WAKE HIM.
I'LL LEAVE HIM A NOTE.
ZZZ
REVE
REVE

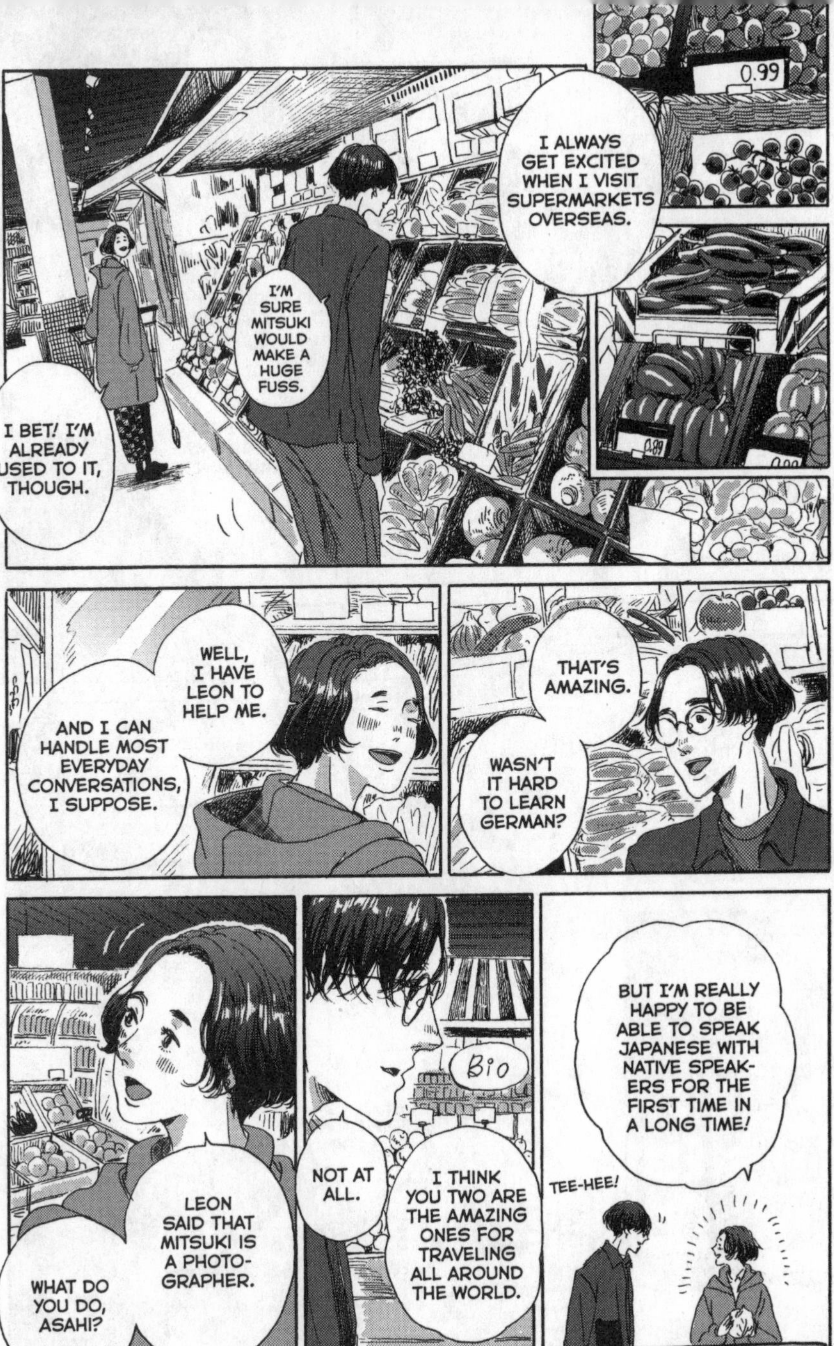
0.99
I ALWAYS GET EXCITED WHEN I VISIT SUPERMARKETS OVERSEAS.
I'M SURE MITSUKI WOULD MAKE A HUGE FUSS.
I BET! I'M ALREADY USED TO IT, THOUGH.
THAT'S AMAZING.
WASN'T IT HARD TO LEARN GERMAN?
WELL, I HAVE LEON TO HELP ME.
AND I CAN HANDLE MOST EVERYDAY CONVERSATIONS, I SUPPOSE.
BUT I'M REALLY HAPPY TO BE ABLE TO SPEAK JAPANESE WITH NATIVE SPEAK-ERS FOR THE FIRST TIME IN A LONG TIME!
TEE-HEE!
Bio
I THINK YOU TWO ARE THE AMAZING ONES FOR TRAVELING ALL AROUND THE WORLD.
NOT AT ALL.
LEON SAID THAT MITSUKI IS A PHOTO-GRAPHER.
WHAT DO YOU DO, ASAHI?

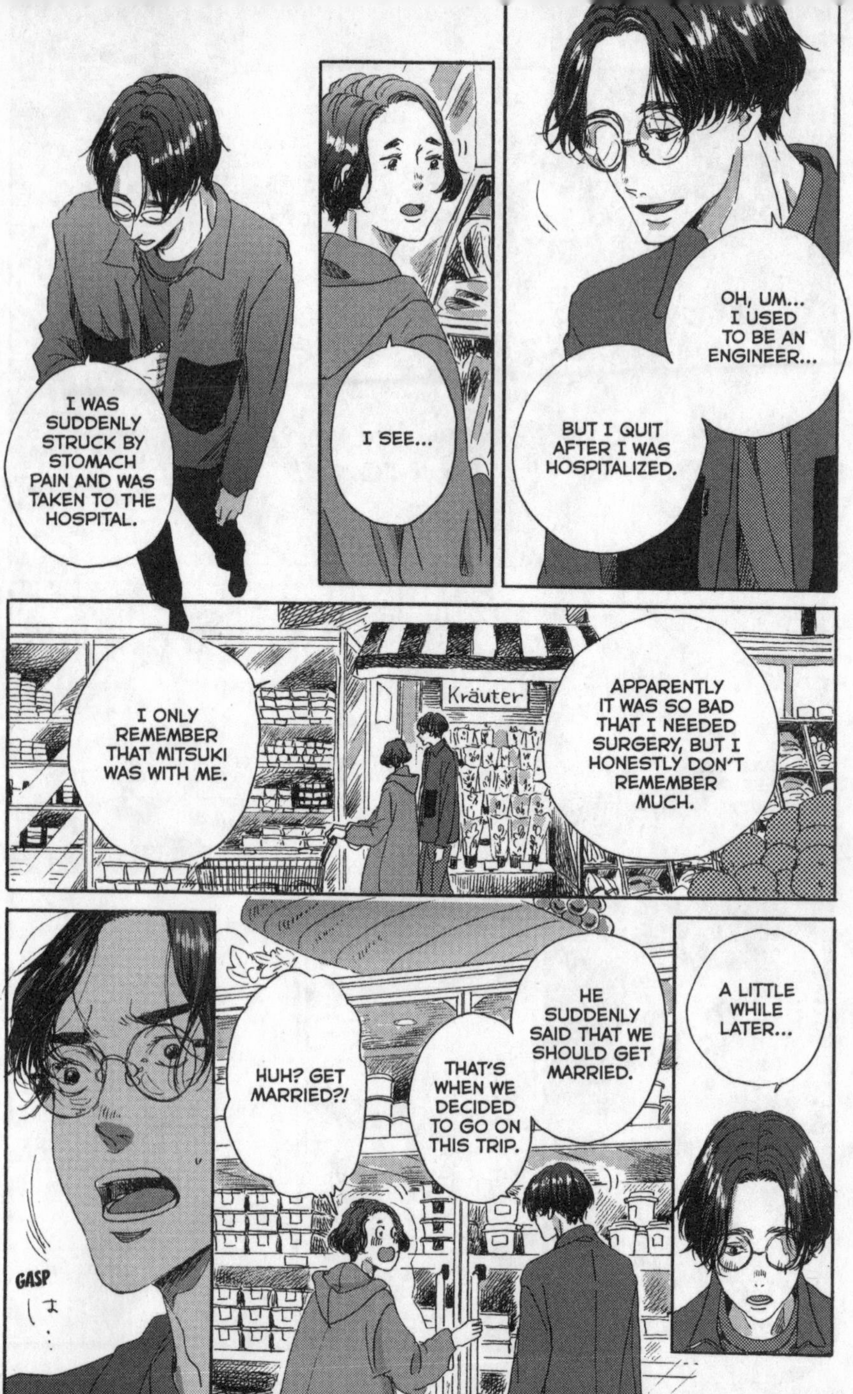
OH, UM... I USED TO BE AN ENGINEER...
BUT I QUIT AFTER I WAS HOSPITALIZED.
I SEE...
I WAS SUDDENLY STRUCK BY STOMACH PAIN AND WAS TAKEN TO THE HOSPITAL.
APPARENTLY IT WAS SO BAD THAT I NEEDED SURGERY, BUT I HONESTLY DON'T REMEMBER MUCH.
Kräuter
I ONLY REMEMBER THAT MITSUKI WAS WITH ME.
A LITTLE WHILE LATER...
HE SUDDENLY SAID THAT WE SHOULD GET MARRIED.
THAT'S WHEN WE DECIDED TO GO ON THIS TRIP.
HUH? GET MARRIED?!
GASP
は…

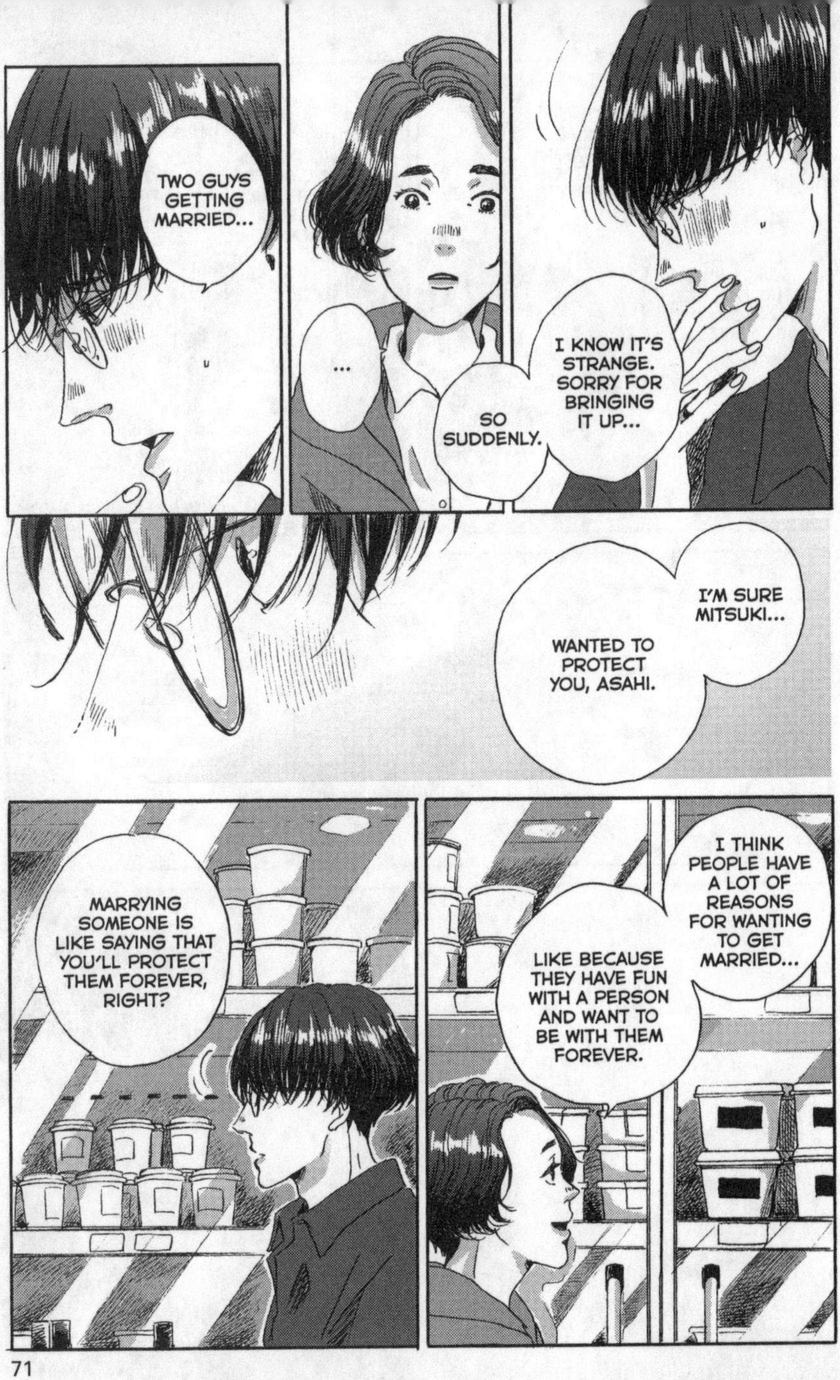
I KNOW IT'S STRANGE. SORRY FOR BRINGING IT UP...
SO SUDDENLY.
...
TWO GUYS GETTING MARRIED...
I'M SURE MITSUKI...
WANTED TO PROTECT YOU, ASAHI.
I THINK PEOPLE HAVE A LOT OF REASONS FOR WANTING TO GET MARRIED...
LIKE BECAUSE THEY HAVE FUN WITH A PERSON AND WANT TO BE WITH THEM FOREVER.
MARRYING SOMEONE IS LIKE SAYING THAT YOU'LL PROTECT THEM FOREVER, RIGHT?

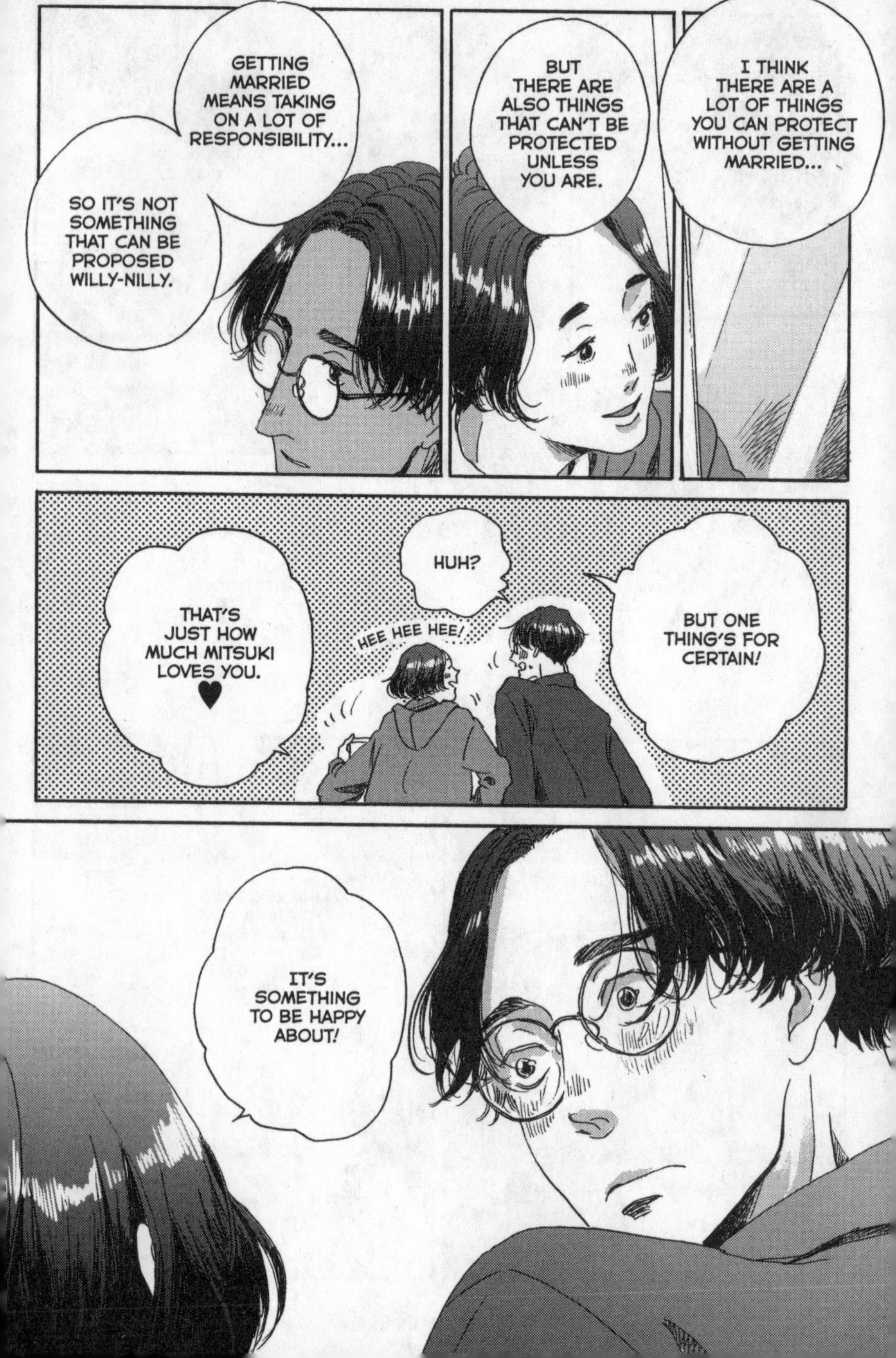
I THINK THERE ARE A LOT OF THINGS YOU CAN PROTECT WITHOUT GETTING MARRIED...
BUT THERE ARE ALSO THINGS THAT CAN'T BE PROTECTED UNLESS YOU ARE.
GETTING MARRIED MEANS TAKING ON A LOT OF RESPONSIBILITY...
SO IT'S NOT SOMETHING THAT CAN BE PROPOSED WILLY-NILLY.
BUT ONE THING'S FOR CERTAIN!
HUH?
HEE HEE HEE!
THAT'S JUST HOW MUCH MITSUKI LOVES YOU. ♥
IT'S SOMETHING TO BE HAPPY ABOUT!

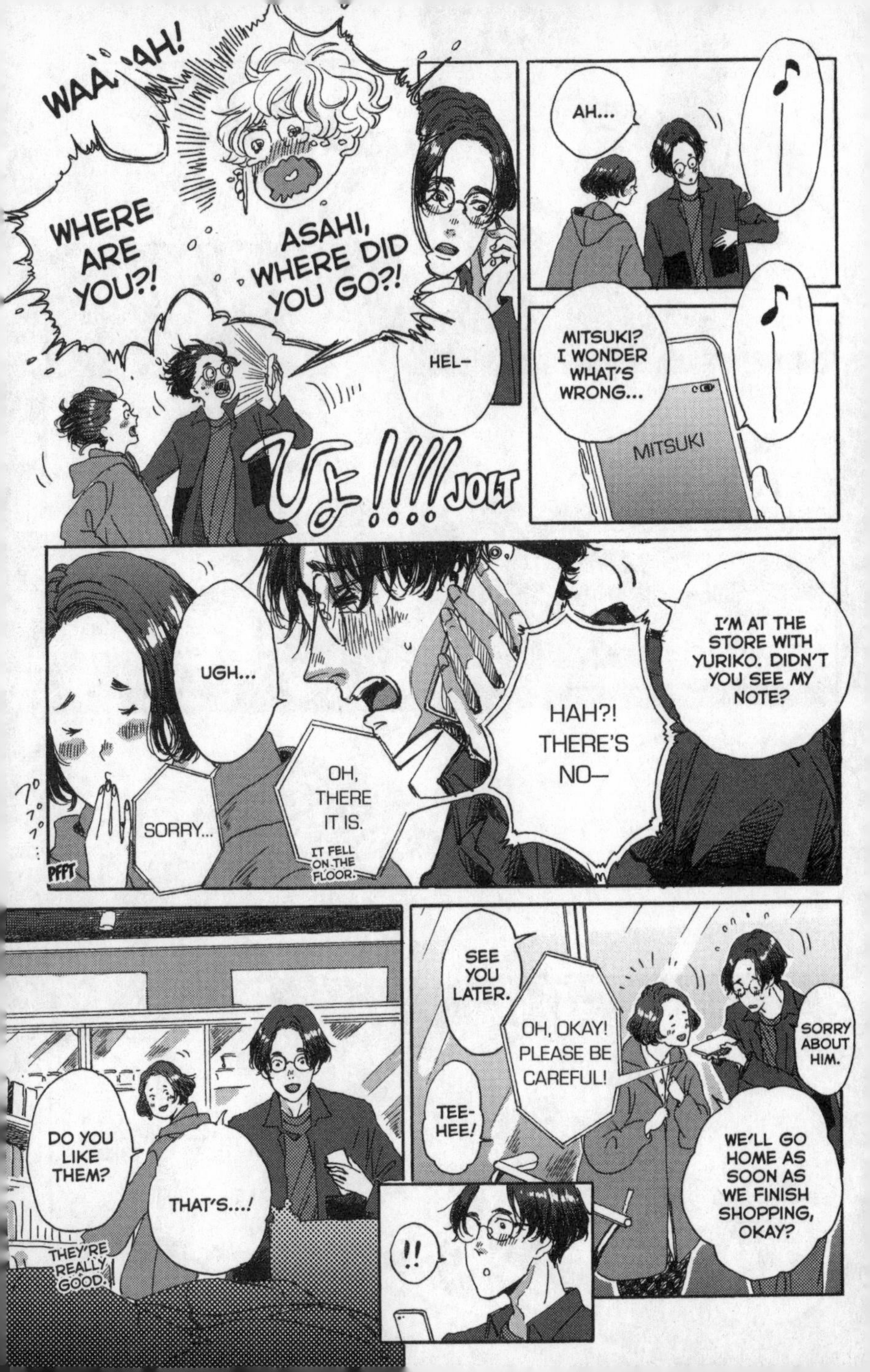
AH...
♪
MITSUKI? I WONDER WHAT'S WRONG...
MITSUKI
♪
HEL—
ASAHI, WHERE DID YOU GO?!
WHERE ARE YOU?!
WAA-AH!
JOLT
I'M AT THE STORE WITH YURIKO. DIDN'T YOU SEE MY NOTE?
HAH?! THERE'S NO—
OH, THERE IT IS.
IT FELL ON THE FLOOR.
UGH...
SORRY...
PFFT
SORRY ABOUT HIM.
WE'LL GO HOME AS SOON AS WE FINISH SHOPPING, OKAY?
OH, OKAY! PLEASE BE CAREFUL!
SEE YOU LATER.
TEE-HEE!
!!
THAT'S...!
DO YOU LIKE THEM?
THEY'RE REALLY GOOD.

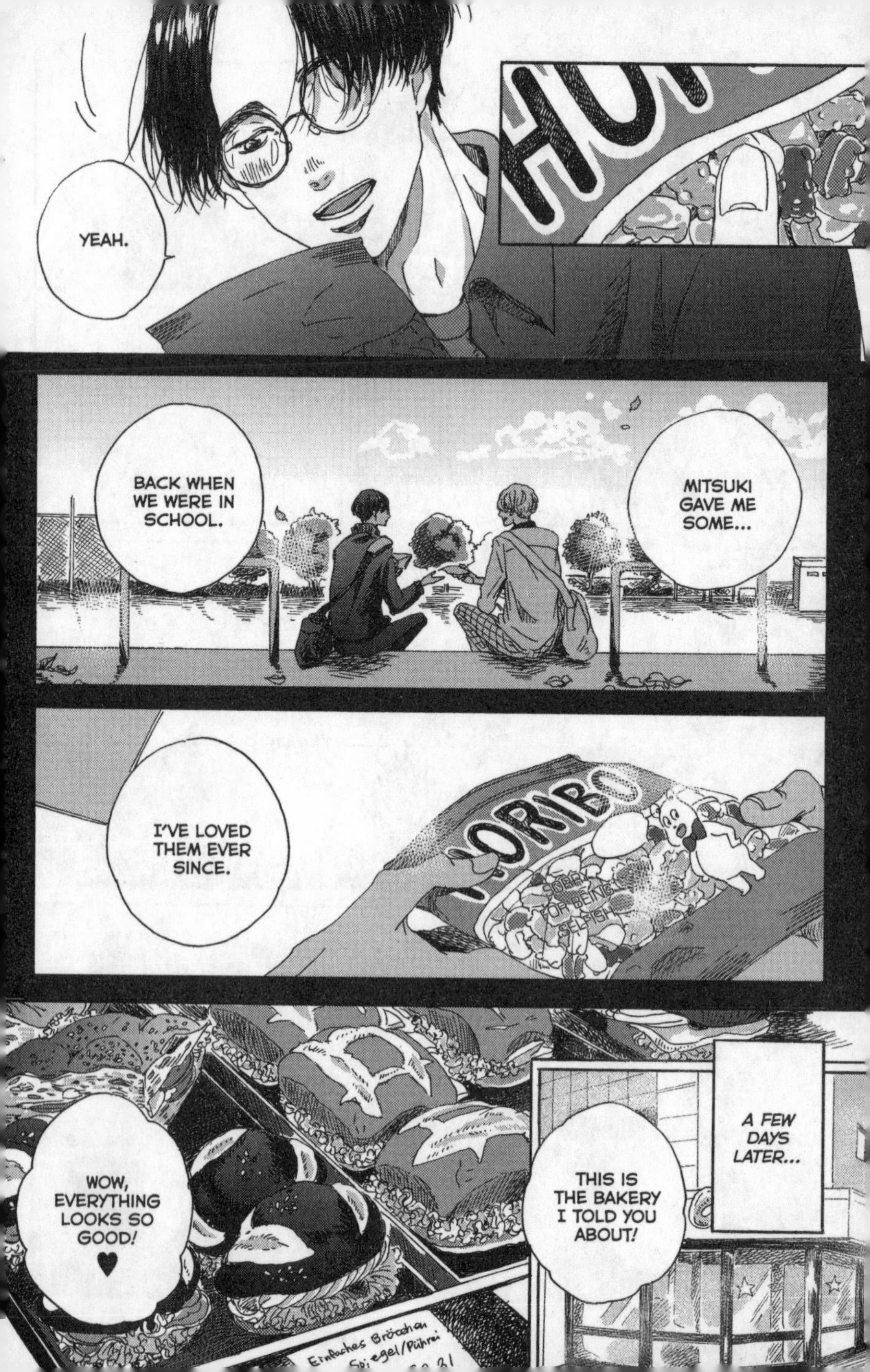
YEAH.
MITSUKI GAVE ME SOME...
BACK WHEN WE WERE IN SCHOOL.
SORRY FOR BEING SELFISH
I'VE LOVED THEM EVER SINCE.
A FEW DAYS LATER...
THIS IS THE BAKERY I TOLD YOU ABOUT!
WOW, EVERYTHING LOOKS SO GOOD! ♥
Einfaches Brötchen
Spiegel/Rührei

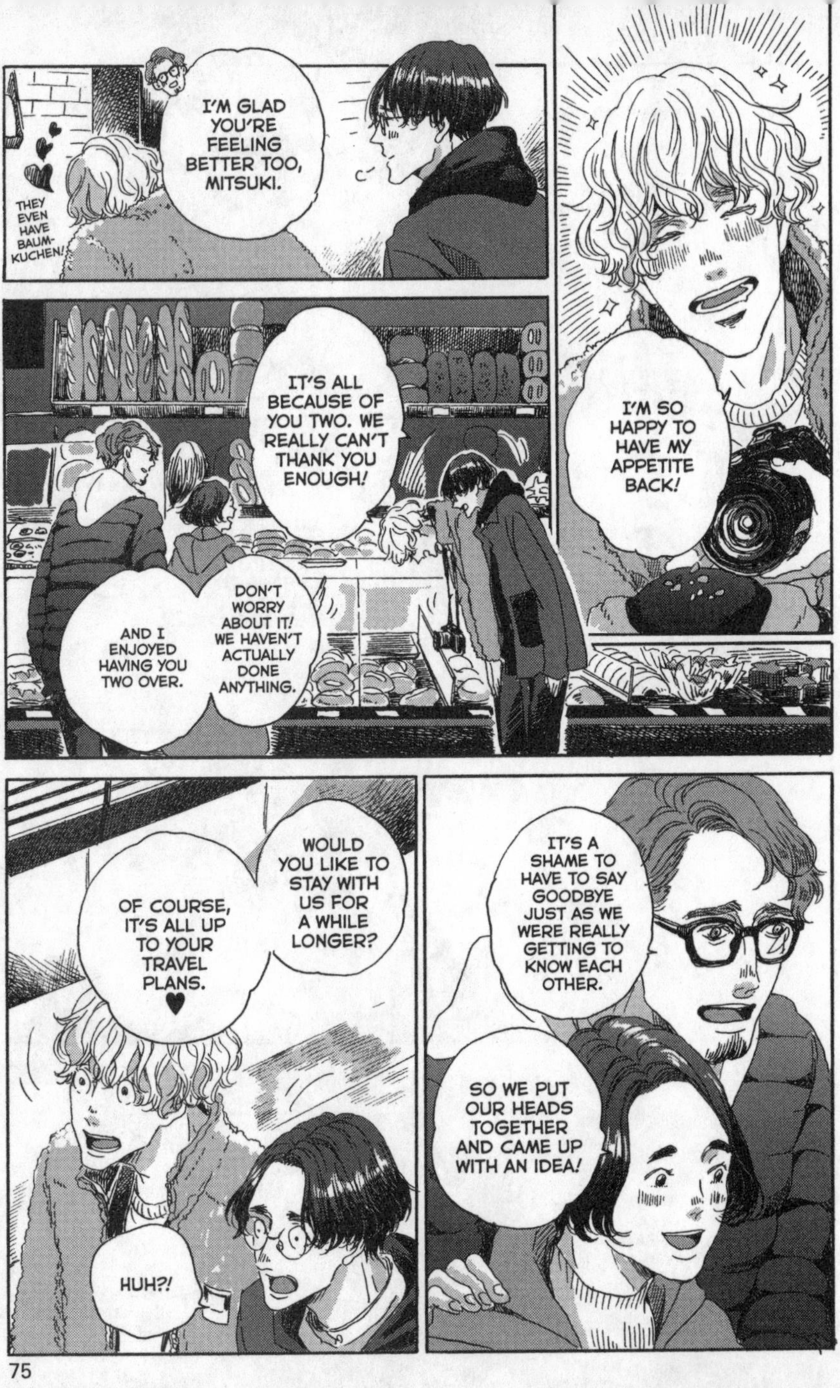
I'M SO HAPPY TO HAVE MY APPETITE BACK!
I'M GLAD YOU'RE FEELING BETTER TOO, MITSUKI.
THEY EVEN HAVE BAUM-KUCHEN!
IT'S ALL BECAUSE OF YOU TWO. WE REALLY CAN'T THANK YOU ENOUGH!
DON'T WORRY ABOUT IT! WE HAVEN'T ACTUALLY DONE ANYTHING.
AND I ENJOYED HAVING YOU TWO OVER.
IT'S A SHAME TO HAVE TO SAY GOODBYE JUST AS WE WERE REALLY GETTING TO KNOW EACH OTHER.
SO WE PUT OUR HEADS TOGETHER AND CAME UP WITH AN IDEA!
WOULD YOU LIKE TO STAY WITH US FOR A WHILE LONGER?
OF COURSE, IT'S ALL UP TO YOUR TRAVEL PLANS. ♥
HUH?!

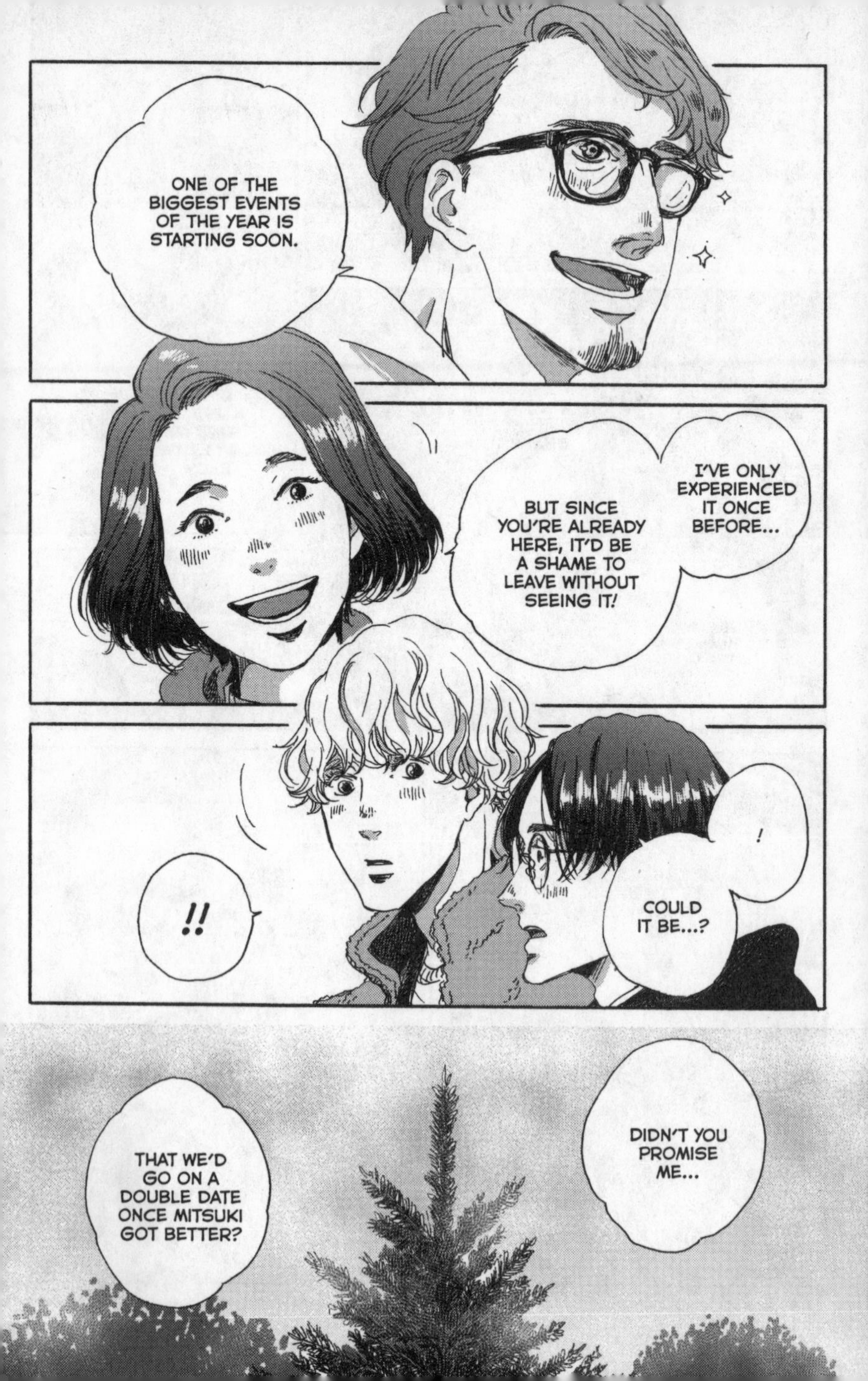
ONE OF THE BIGGEST EVENTS OF THE YEAR IS STARTING SOON.
I'VE ONLY EXPERIENCED IT ONCE BEFORE...
BUT SINCE YOU'RE ALREADY HERE, IT'D BE A SHAME TO LEAVE WITHOUT SEEING IT!
!
COULD IT BE...?
!!
DIDN'T YOU PROMISE ME...
THAT WE'D GO ON A DOUBLE DATE ONCE MITSUKI GOT BETTER?

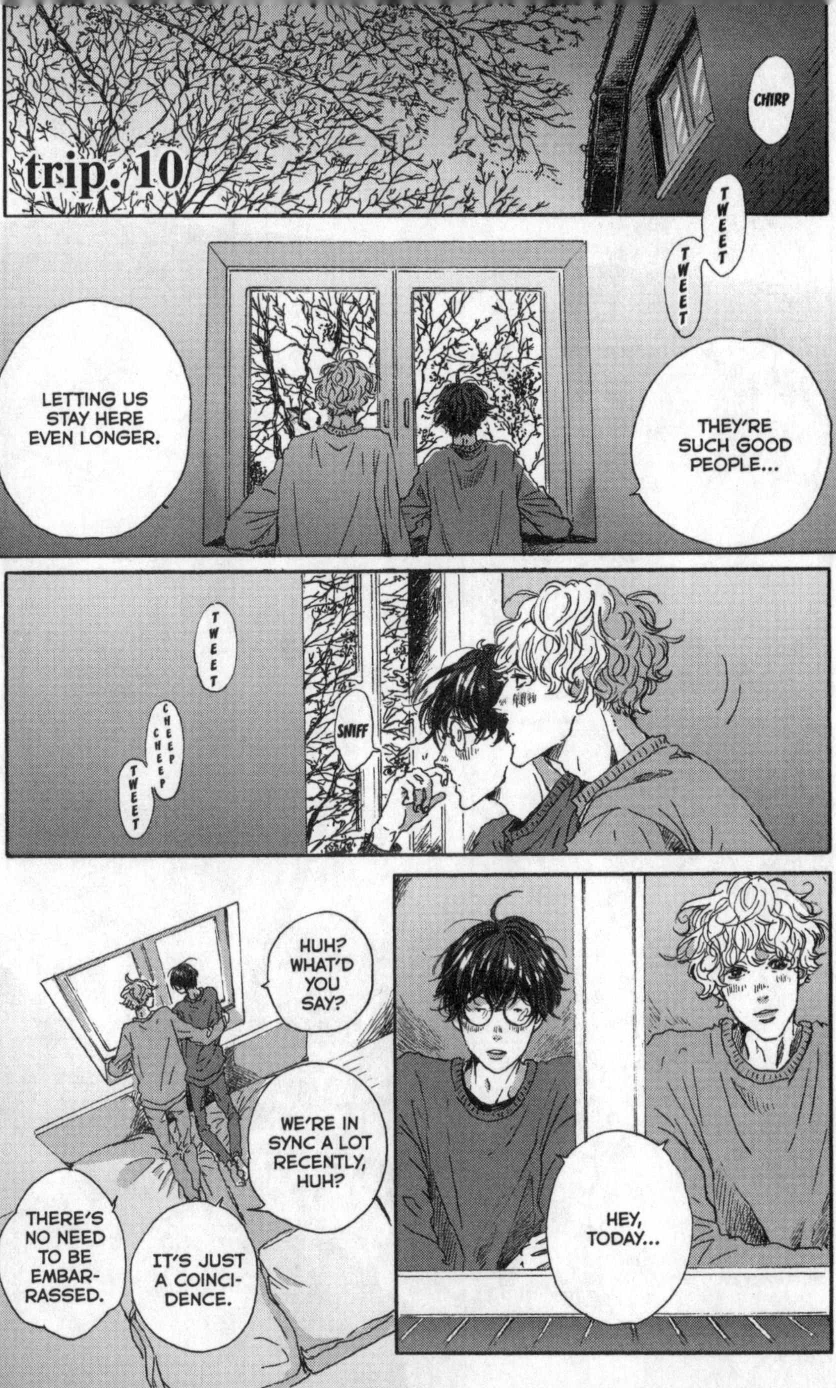
CHIRP
trip. 10
TWEET TWEET
THEY'RE SUCH GOOD PEOPLE...
LETTING US STAY HERE EVEN LONGER.
TWEET
SNIFF
CHEEP CHEEP
TWEET
HEY, TODAY...
HUH? WHAT'D YOU SAY?
WE'RE IN SYNC A LOT RECENTLY, HUH?
IT'S JUST A COINCIDENCE.
THERE'S NO NEED TO BE EMBARRASSED.

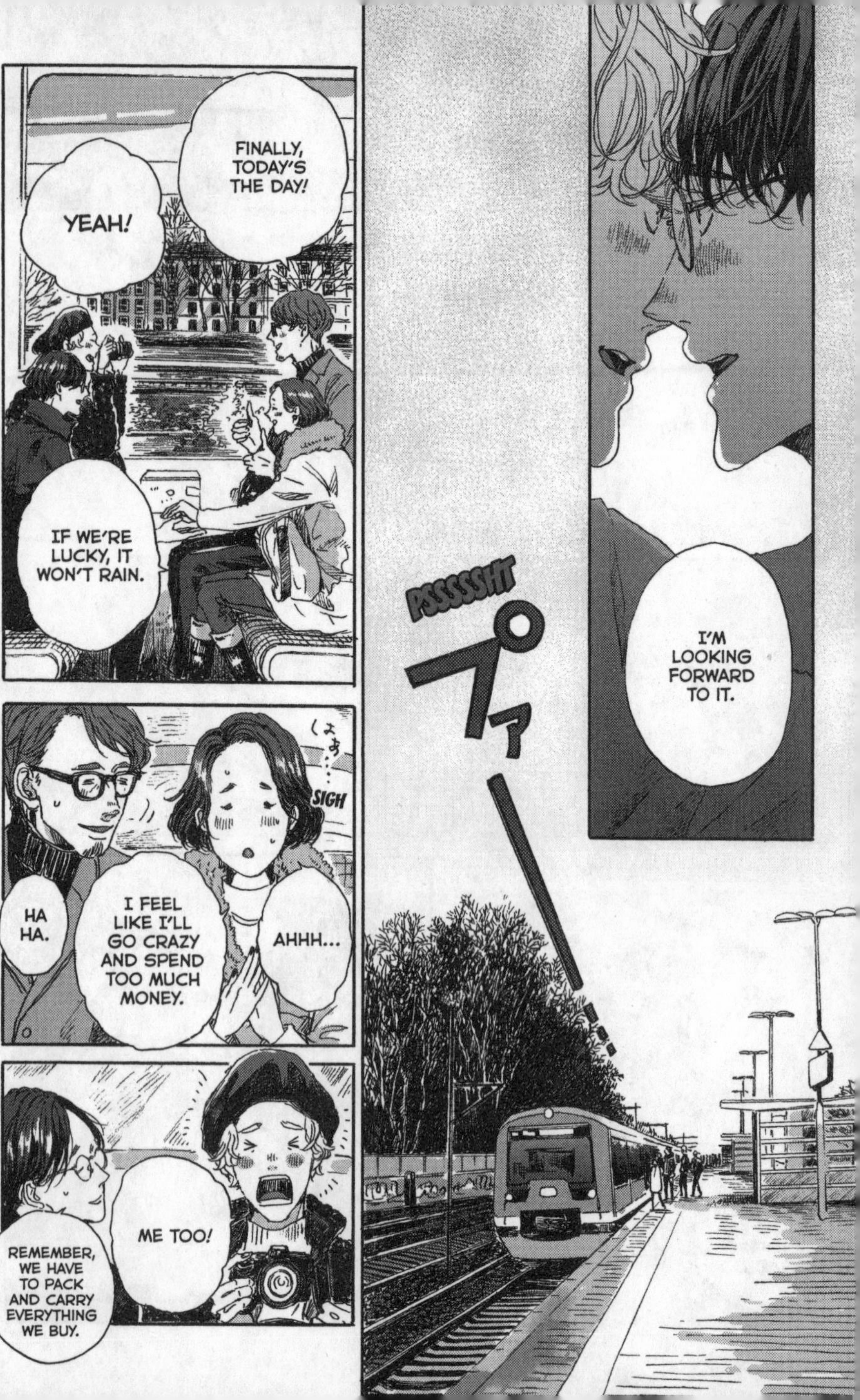
I'M LOOKING FORWARD TO IT.
PSSSSSHT
プァー
FINALLY, TODAY'S THE DAY!
YEAH!
IF WE'RE LUCKY, IT WON'T RAIN.
SIGH
AHHH...
I FEEL LIKE I'LL GO CRAZY AND SPEND TOO MUCH MONEY.
HA HA.
ME TOO!
REMEMBER, WE HAVE TO PACK AND CARRY EVERYTHING WE BUY.

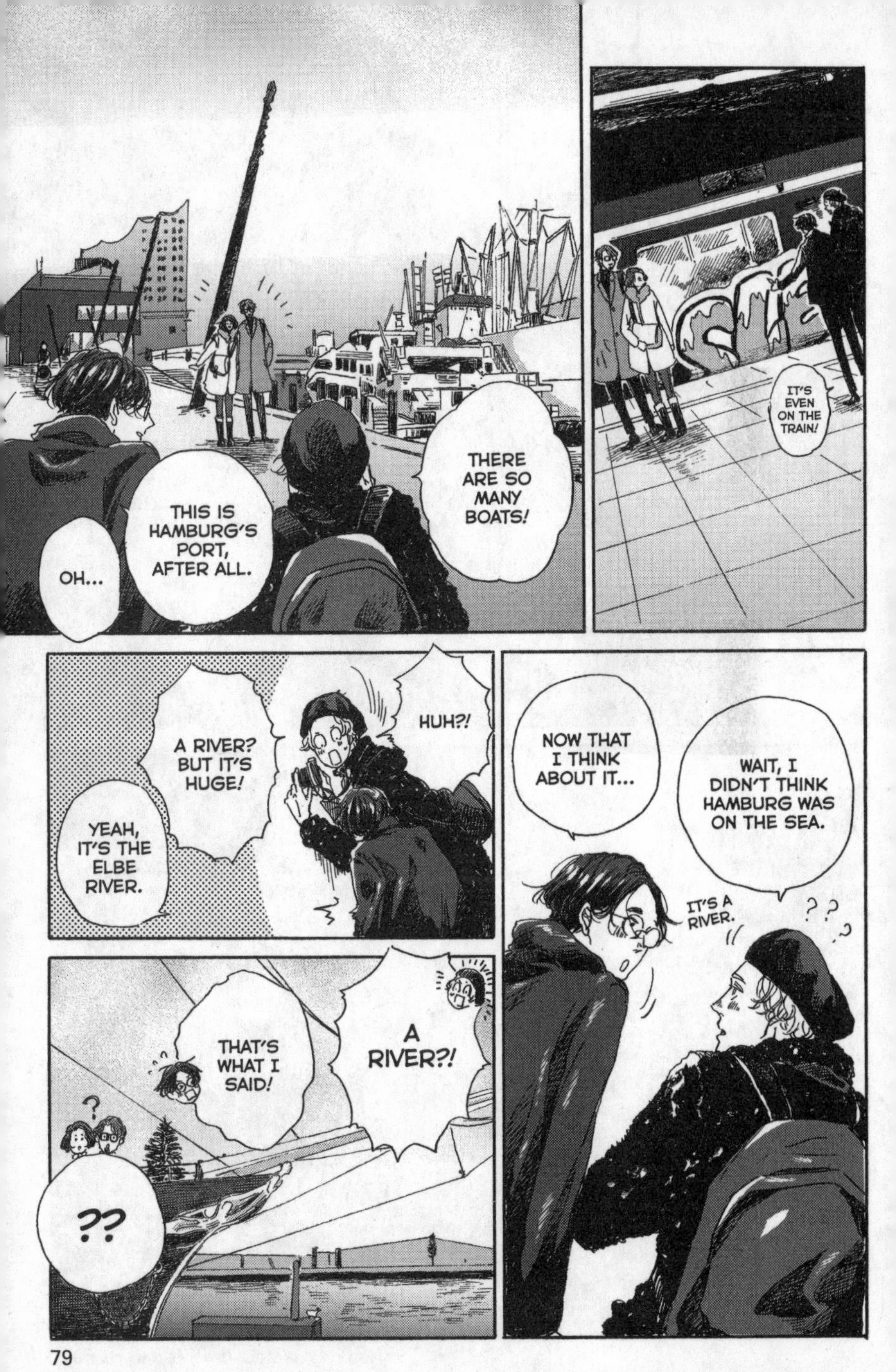

IT'S EVEN ON THE TRAIN!
THERE ARE SO MANY BOATS!
THIS IS HAMBURG'S PORT, AFTER ALL.
OH...
WAIT, I DIDN'T THINK HAMBURG WAS ON THE SEA.
NOW THAT I THINK ABOUT IT...
IT'S A RIVER.
HUH?!
A RIVER? BUT IT'S HUGE!
YEAH, IT'S THE ELBE RIVER.
A RIVER?!
THAT'S WHAT I SAID!
??

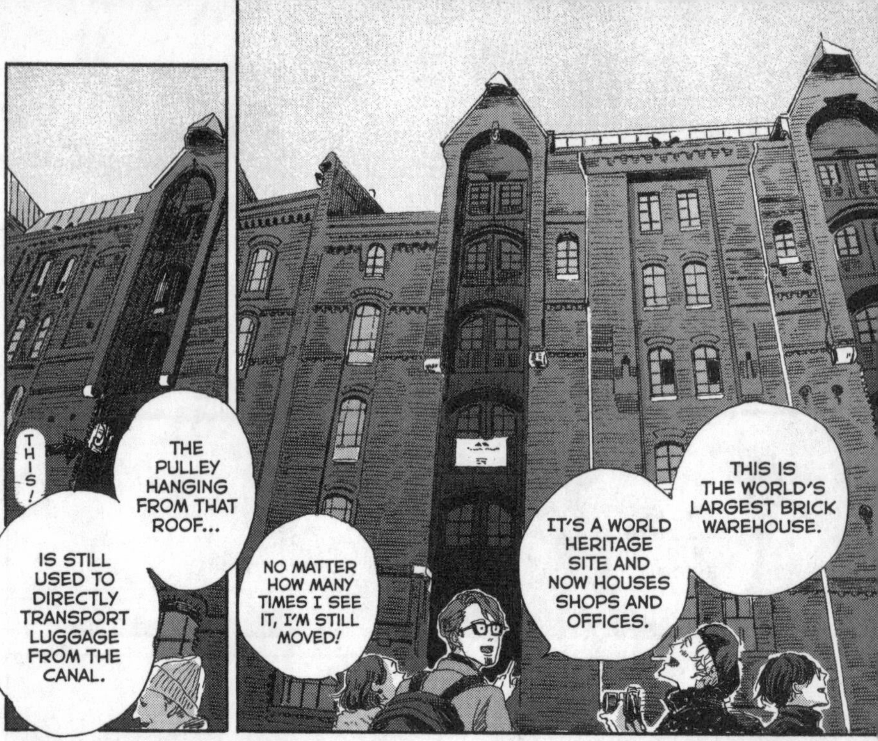
THIS IS THE WORLD'S LARGEST BRICK WAREHOUSE.
IT'S A WORLD HERITAGE SITE AND NOW HOUSES SHOPS AND OFFICES.
NO MATTER HOW MANY TIMES I SEE IT, I'M STILL MOVED!
THE PULLEY HANGING FROM THAT ROOF...
THIS!
IS STILL USED TO DIRECTLY TRANSPORT LUGGAGE FROM THE CANAL.

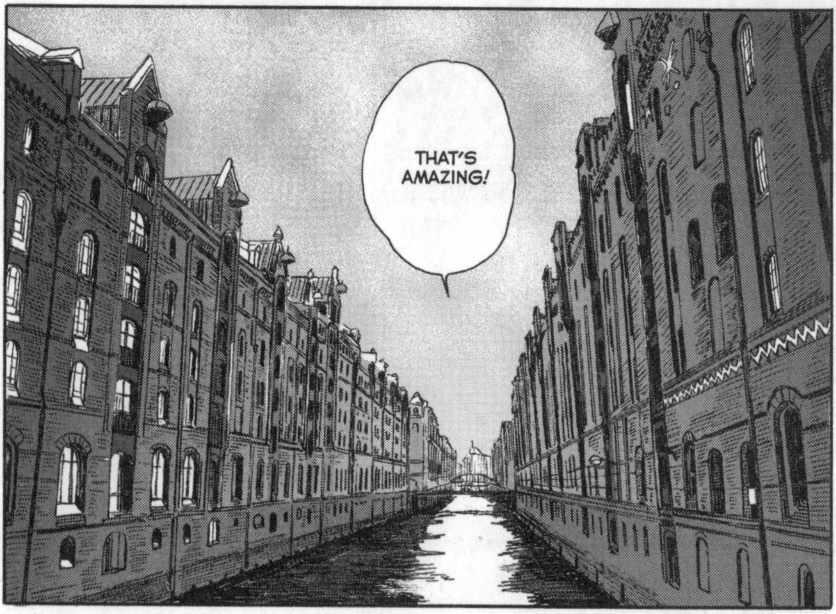
THAT'S AMAZING!

PART OF IT IS STILL USED AS A WAREHOUSE.

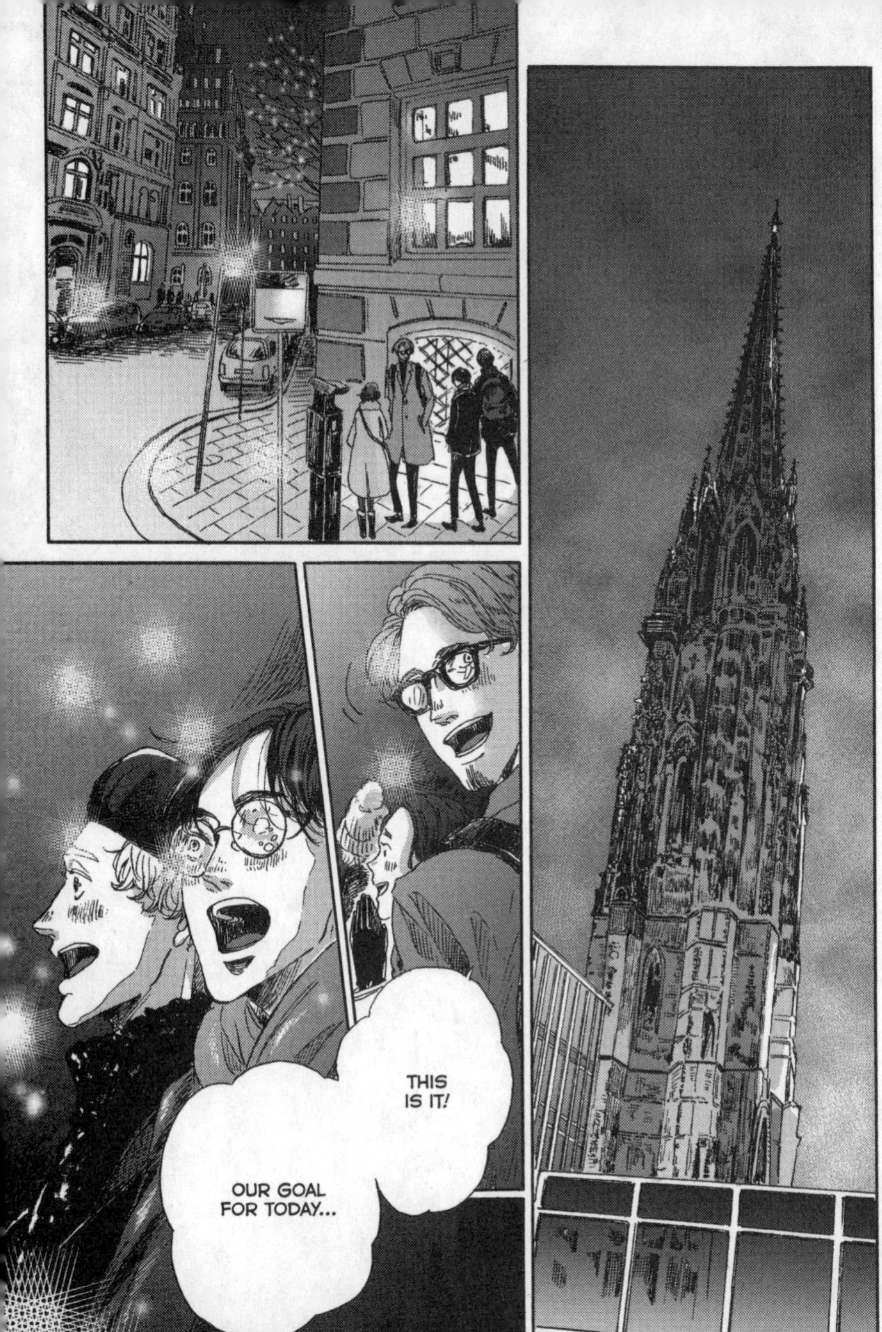
THIS IS IT!
OUR GOAL FOR TODAY...

ST. NIKOLAI WAS BOMBED IN WORLD WAR II AND IS NO LONGER USED AS A PLACE OF WORSHIP, BUT IT IS THE 3RD TALLEST RELIGIOUS BUILDING IN GERMANY AND THE 5TH TALLEST IN THE WORLD. YOU CAN SEE THE MARKS LEFT BY THE BOMBINGS.

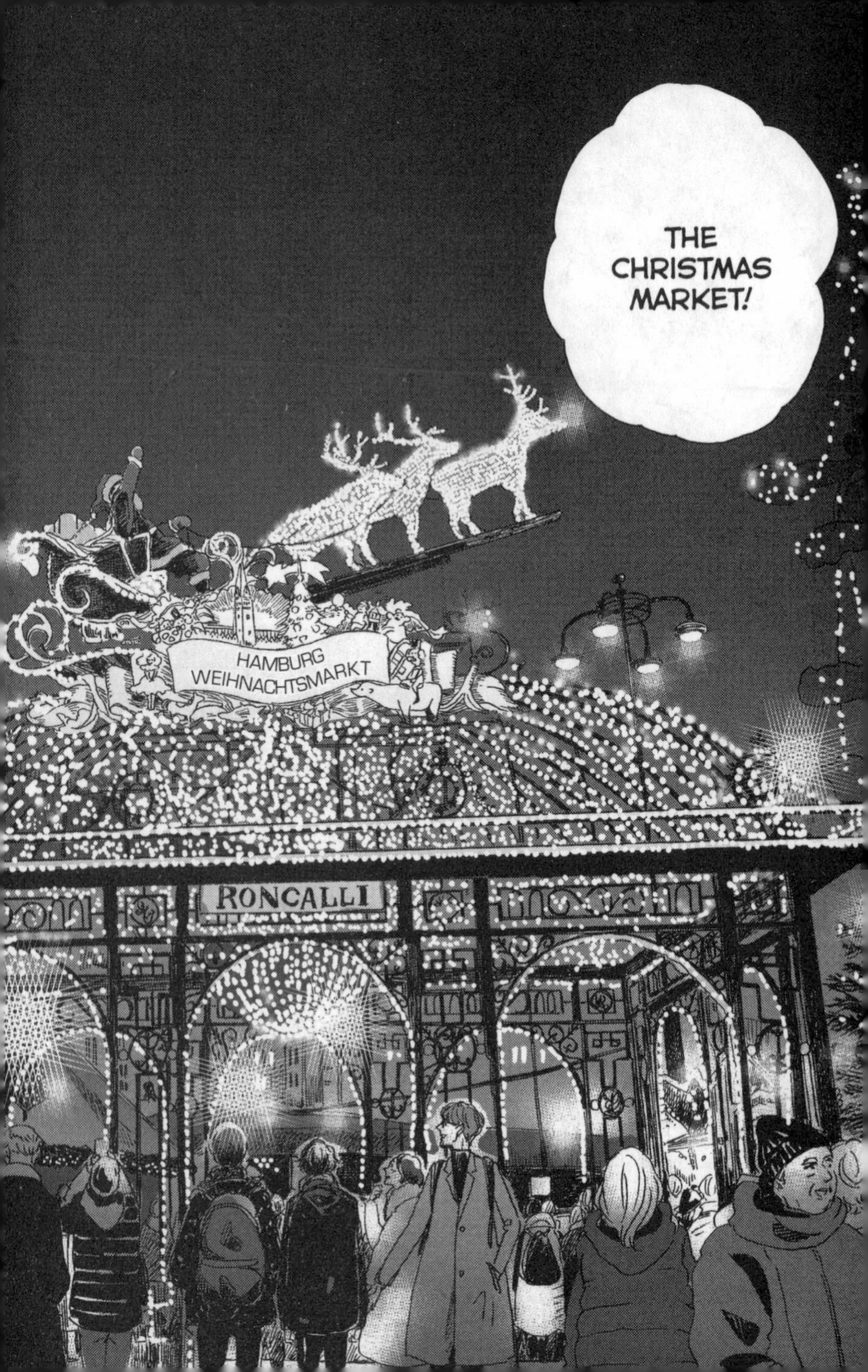
THE CHRISTMAS MARKET!
HAMBURG WEIHNACHTSMARKT
RONCALLI

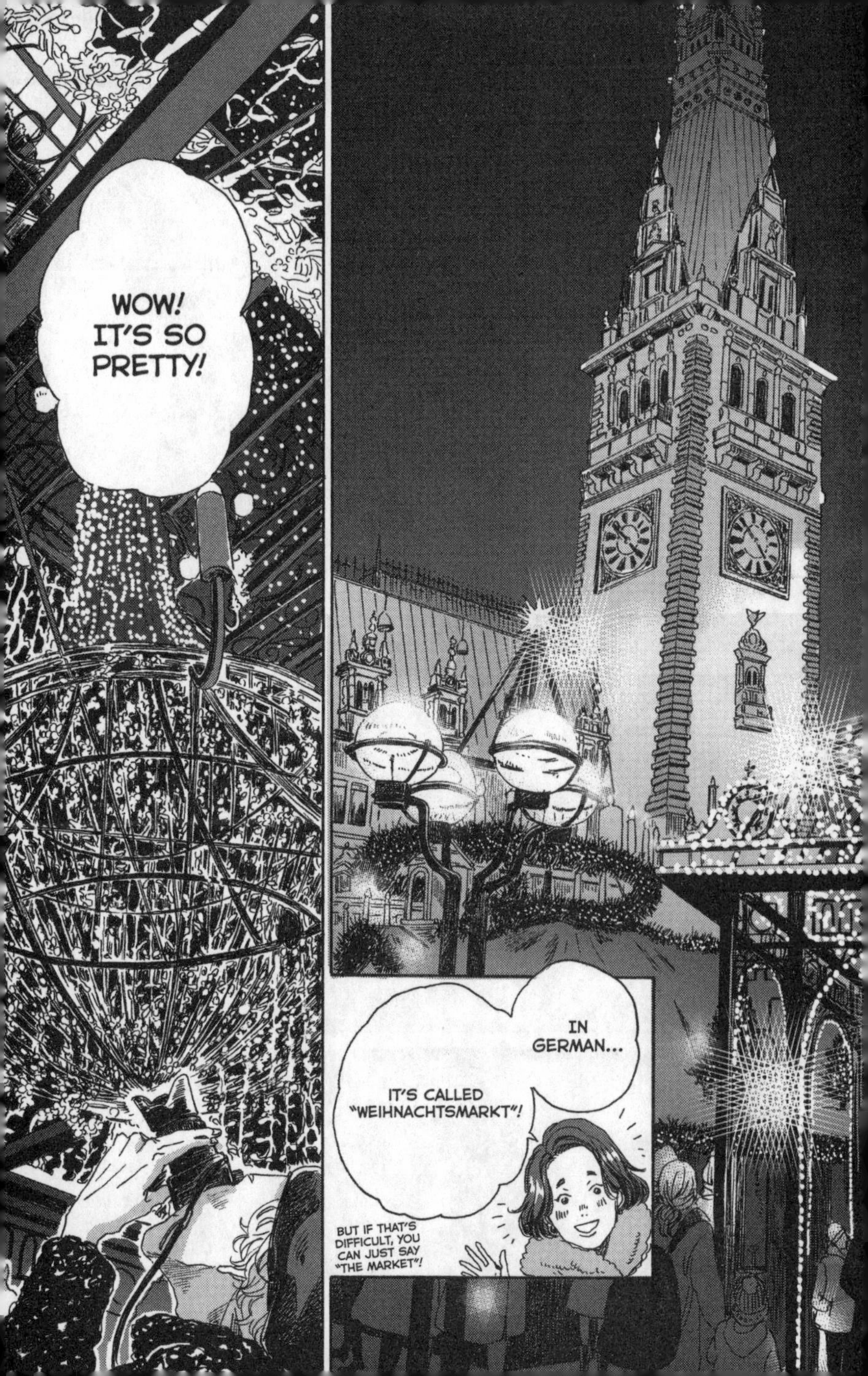
IN GERMAN...
IT'S CALLED "WEIHNACHTSMARKT"!
BUT IF THAT'S DIFFICULT, YOU CAN JUST SAY "THE MARKET"!
WOW! IT'S SO PRETTY!

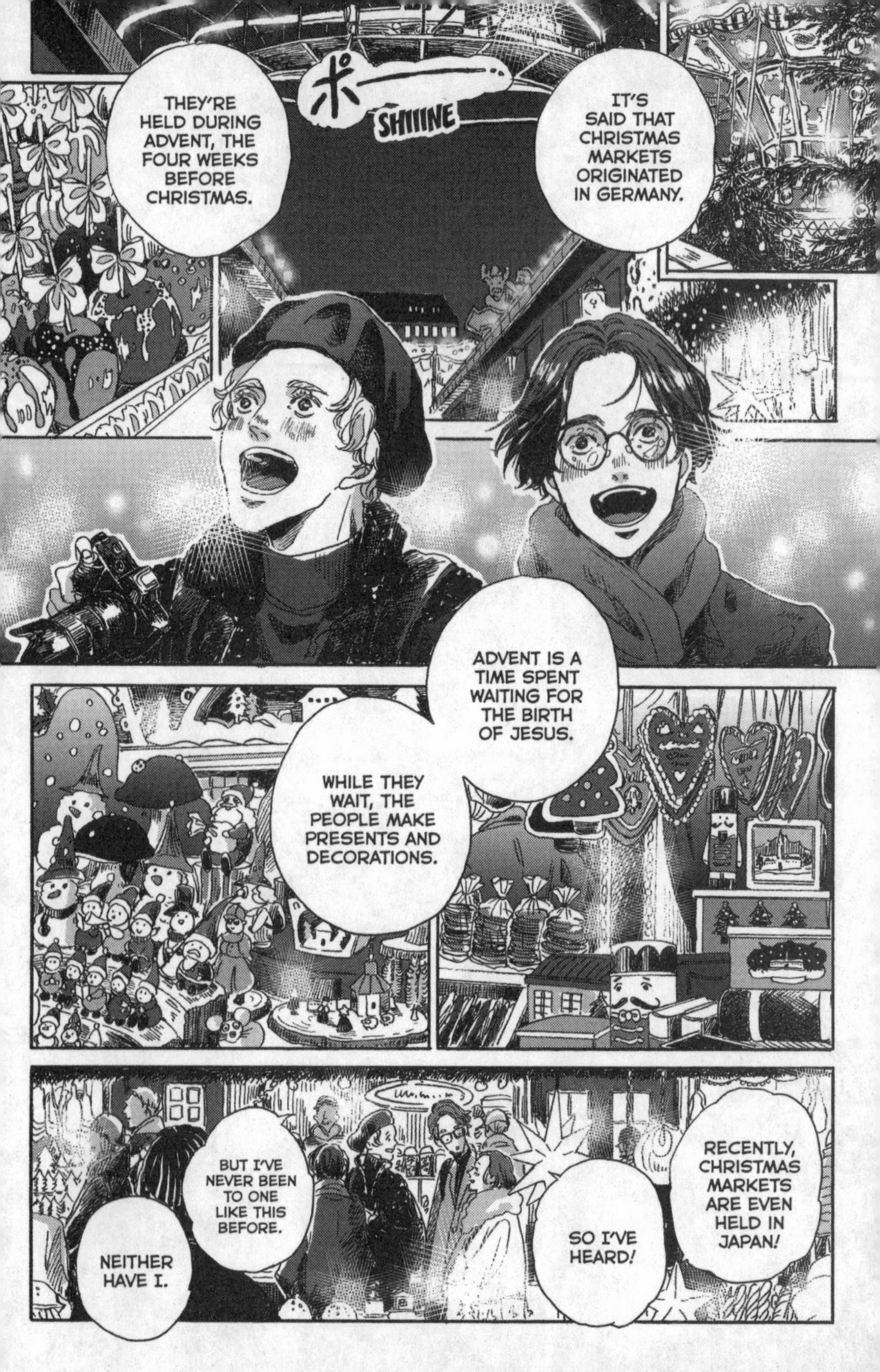
IT'S SAID THAT CHRISTMAS MARKETS ORIGINATED IN GERMANY.
ポー
SHIIINE
THEY'RE HELD DURING ADVENT, THE FOUR WEEKS BEFORE CHRISTMAS.
ADVENT IS A TIME SPENT WAITING FOR THE BIRTH OF JESUS.
WHILE THEY WAIT, THE PEOPLE MAKE PRESENTS AND DECORATIONS.
RECENTLY, CHRISTMAS MARKETS ARE EVEN HELD IN JAPAN!
SO I'VE HEARD!
BUT I'VE NEVER BEEN TO ONE LIKE THIS BEFORE.
NEITHER HAVE I.

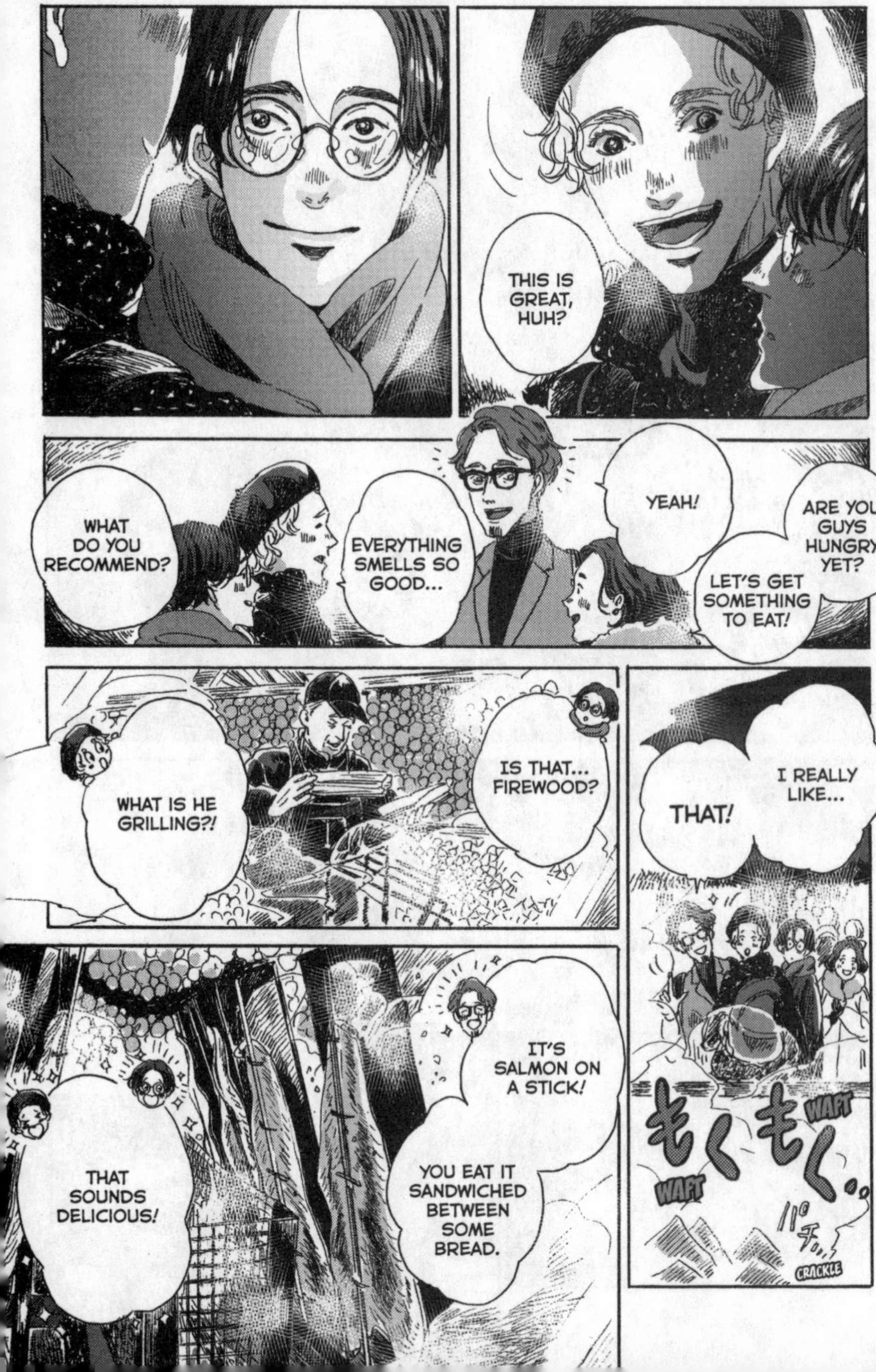
THIS IS GREAT, HUH?
ARE YOU GUYS HUNGRY YET?
LET'S GET SOMETHING TO EAT!
YEAH!
EVERYTHING SMELLS SO GOOD...
WHAT DO YOU RECOMMEND?
I REALLY LIKE...
THAT!
WAFT
もくもく
WAFT
パチ
CRACKLE
IS THAT... FIREWOOD?
WHAT IS HE GRILLING?!
IT'S SALMON ON A STICK!
YOU EAT IT SANDWICHED BETWEEN SOME BREAD.
THAT SOUNDS DELICIOUS!

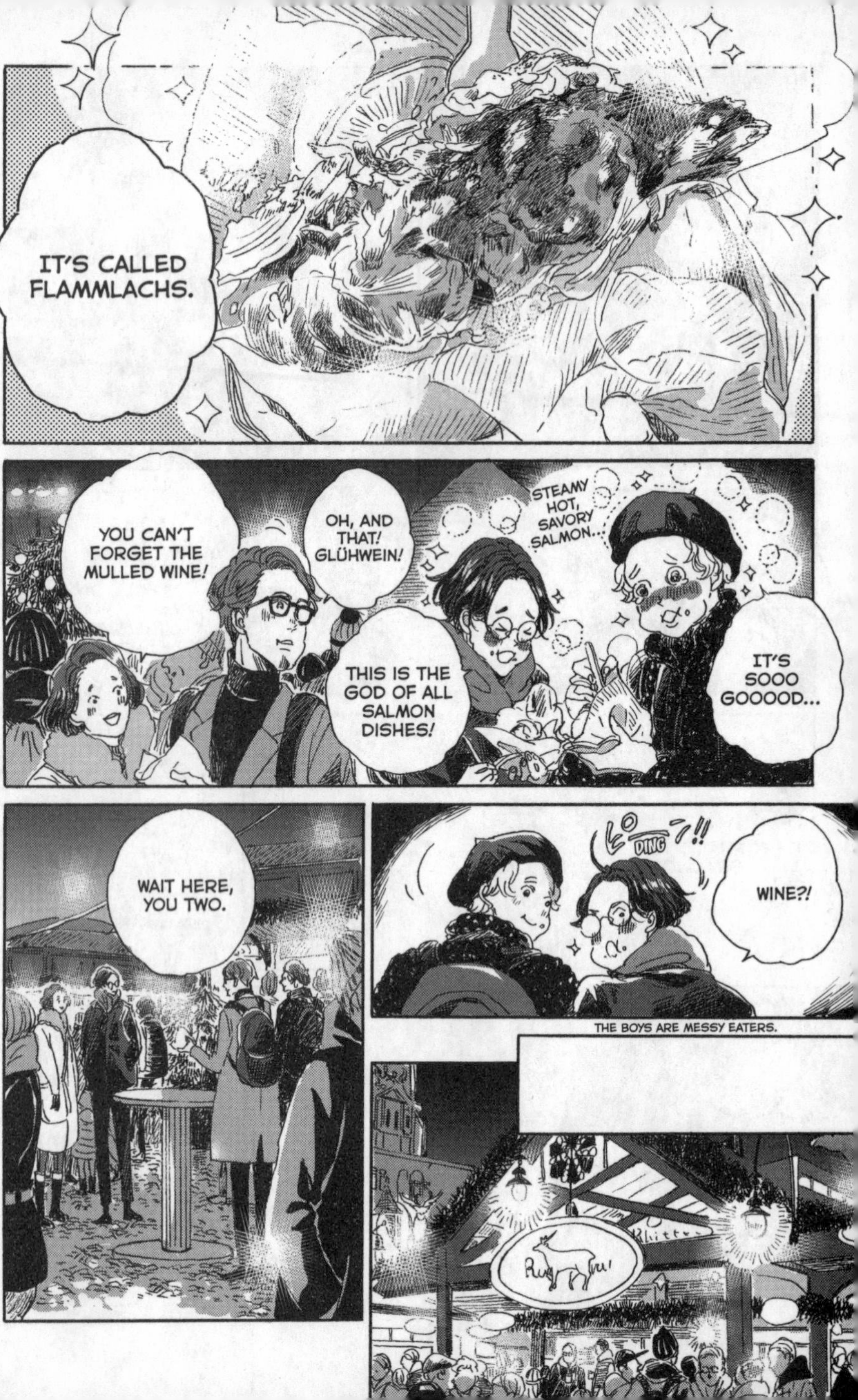
IT'S CALLED FLAMMLACHS.
IT'S SOOO GOOOOD...
STEAMY HOT, SAVORY SALMON...
THIS IS THE GOD OF ALL SALMON DISHES!
OH, AND THAT! GLÜHWEIN!
YOU CAN'T FORGET THE MULLED WINE!
ピーン!!
DING
WINE?!
THE BOYS ARE MESSY EATERS.
WAIT HERE, YOU TWO.

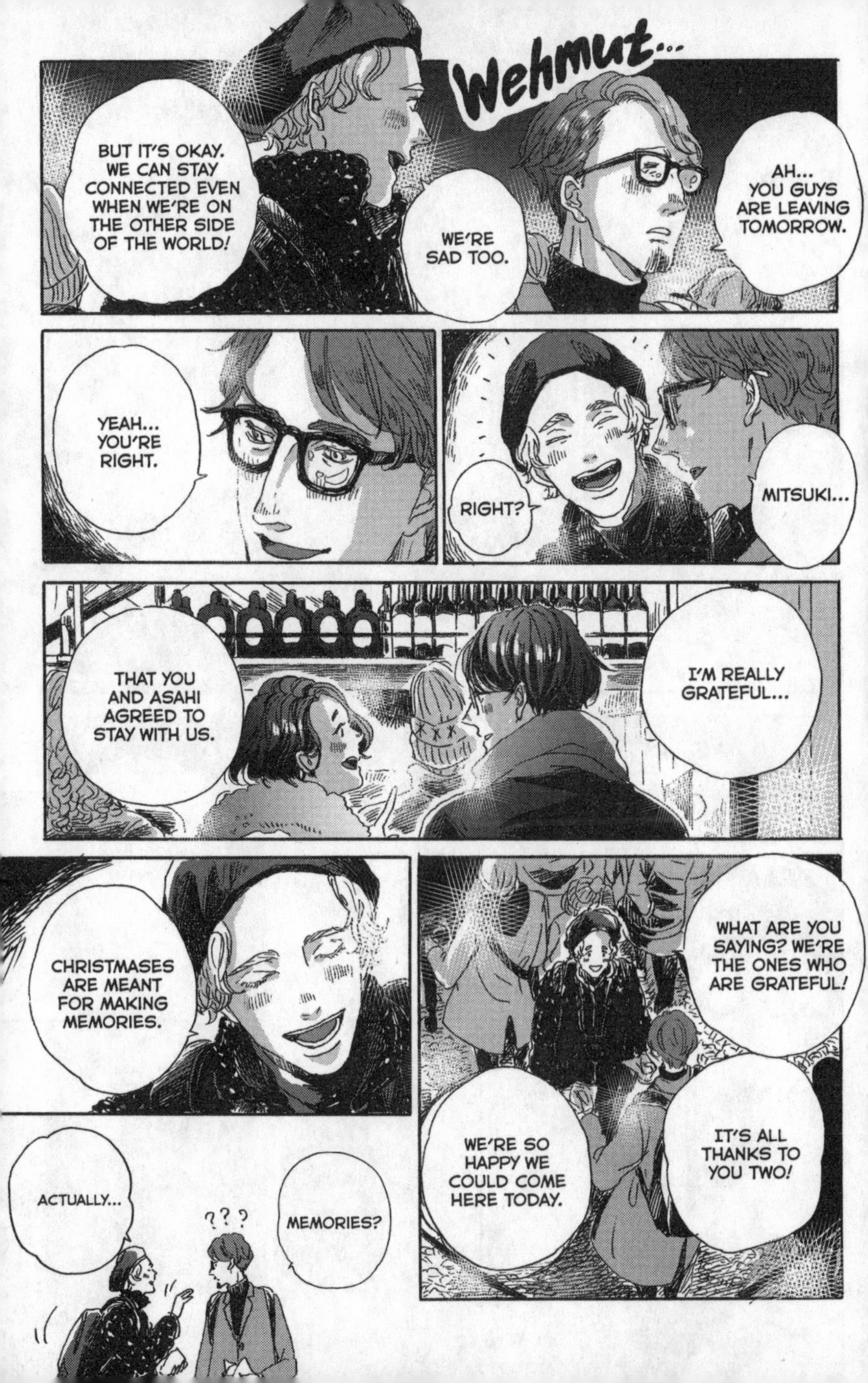
Wehmut...
AH... YOU GUYS ARE LEAVING TOMORROW.
WE'RE SAD TOO.
BUT IT'S OKAY. WE CAN STAY CONNECTED EVEN WHEN WE'RE ON THE OTHER SIDE OF THE WORLD!
MITSUKI...
RIGHT?
YEAH... YOU'RE RIGHT.
I'M REALLY GRATEFUL...
THAT YOU AND ASAHI AGREED TO STAY WITH US.
WHAT ARE YOU SAYING? WE'RE THE ONES WHO ARE GRATEFUL!
IT'S ALL THANKS TO YOU TWO!
WE'RE SO HAPPY WE COULD COME HERE TODAY.
CHRISTMASES ARE MEANT FOR MAKING MEMORIES.
MEMORIES?
???
ACTUALLY...

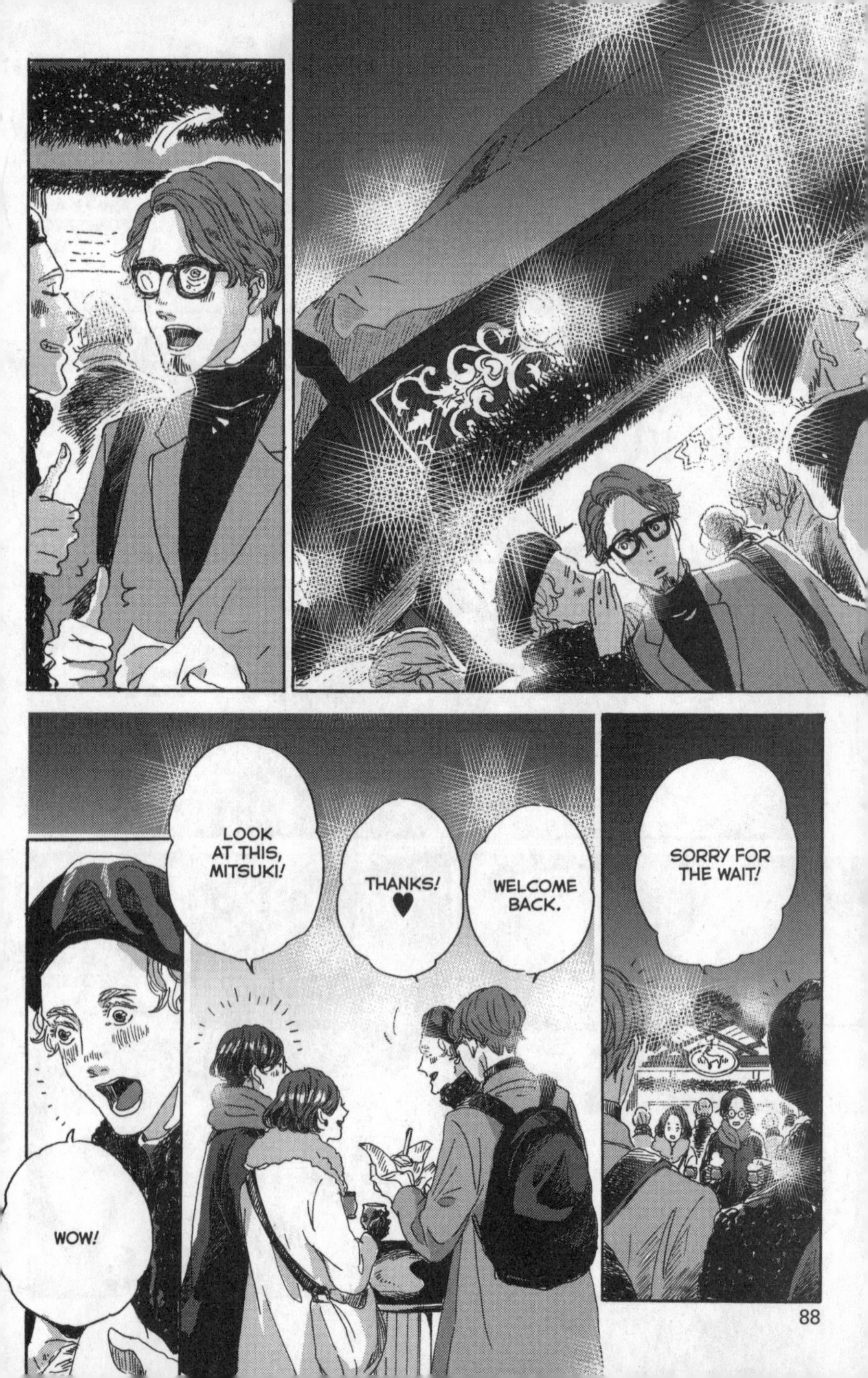
SORRY FOR THE WAIT!
WELCOME BACK.
THANKS! ♥
LOOK AT THIS, MITSUKI!
WOW!

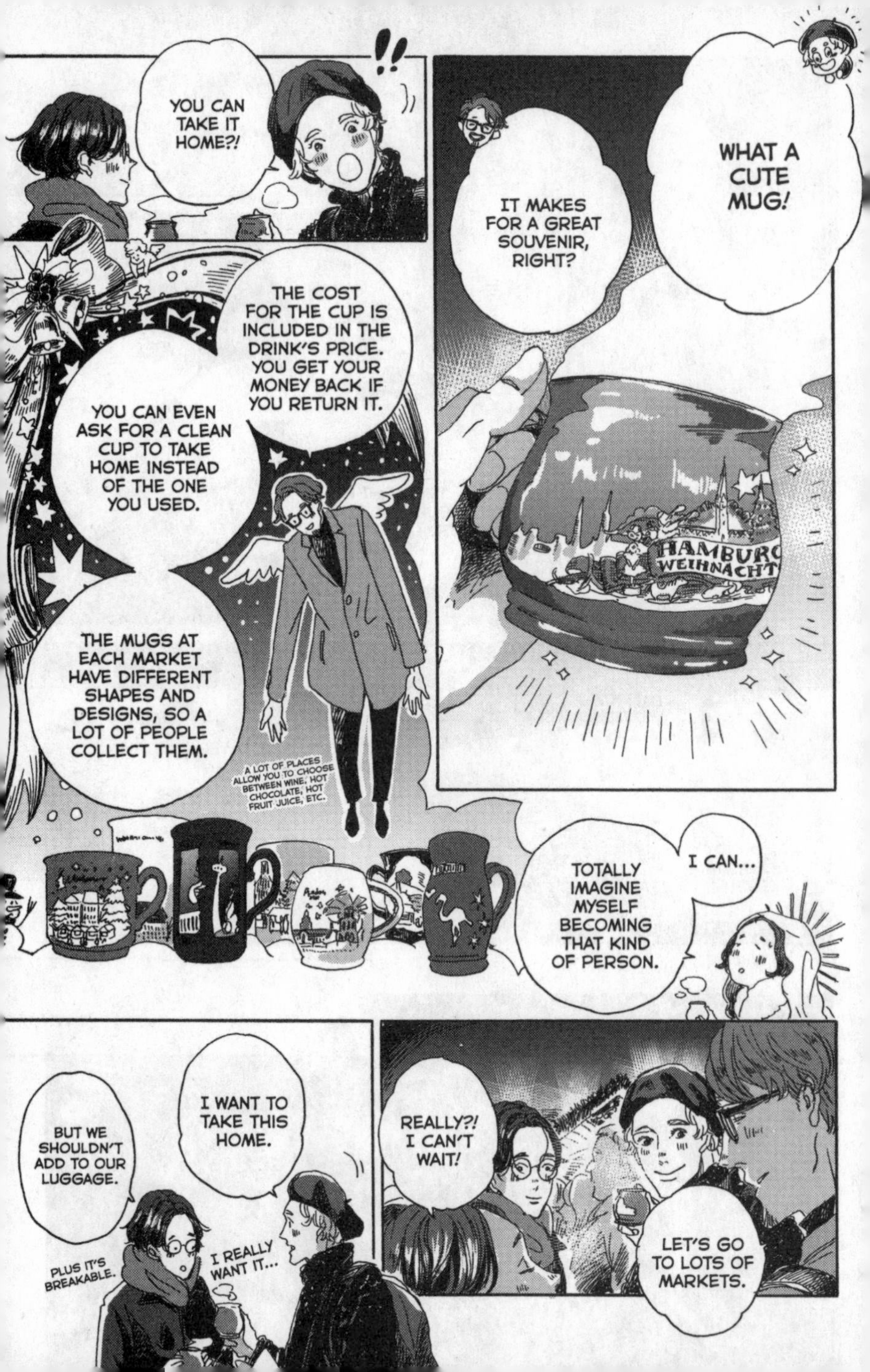
WHAT A CUTE MUG!
IT MAKES FOR A GREAT SOUVENIR, RIGHT?
!!
YOU CAN TAKE IT HOME?!
THE COST FOR THE CUP IS INCLUDED IN THE DRINK'S PRICE. YOU GET YOUR MONEY BACK IF YOU RETURN IT.
YOU CAN EVEN ASK FOR A CLEAN CUP TO TAKE HOME INSTEAD OF THE ONE YOU USED.
THE MUGS AT EACH MARKET HAVE DIFFERENT SHAPES AND DESIGNS, SO A LOT OF PEOPLE COLLECT THEM.
A LOT OF PLACES ALLOW YOU TO CHOOSE BETWEEN WINE, HOT CHOCOLATE, HOT FRUIT JUICE, ETC.
I CAN...
TOTALLY IMAGINE MYSELF BECOMING THAT KIND OF PERSON.
LET'S GO TO LOTS OF MARKETS.
REALLY?! I CAN'T WAIT!
I WANT TO TAKE THIS HOME.
I REALLY WANT IT...
BUT WE SHOULDN'T ADD TO OUR LUGGAGE.
PLUS IT'S BREAKABLE.

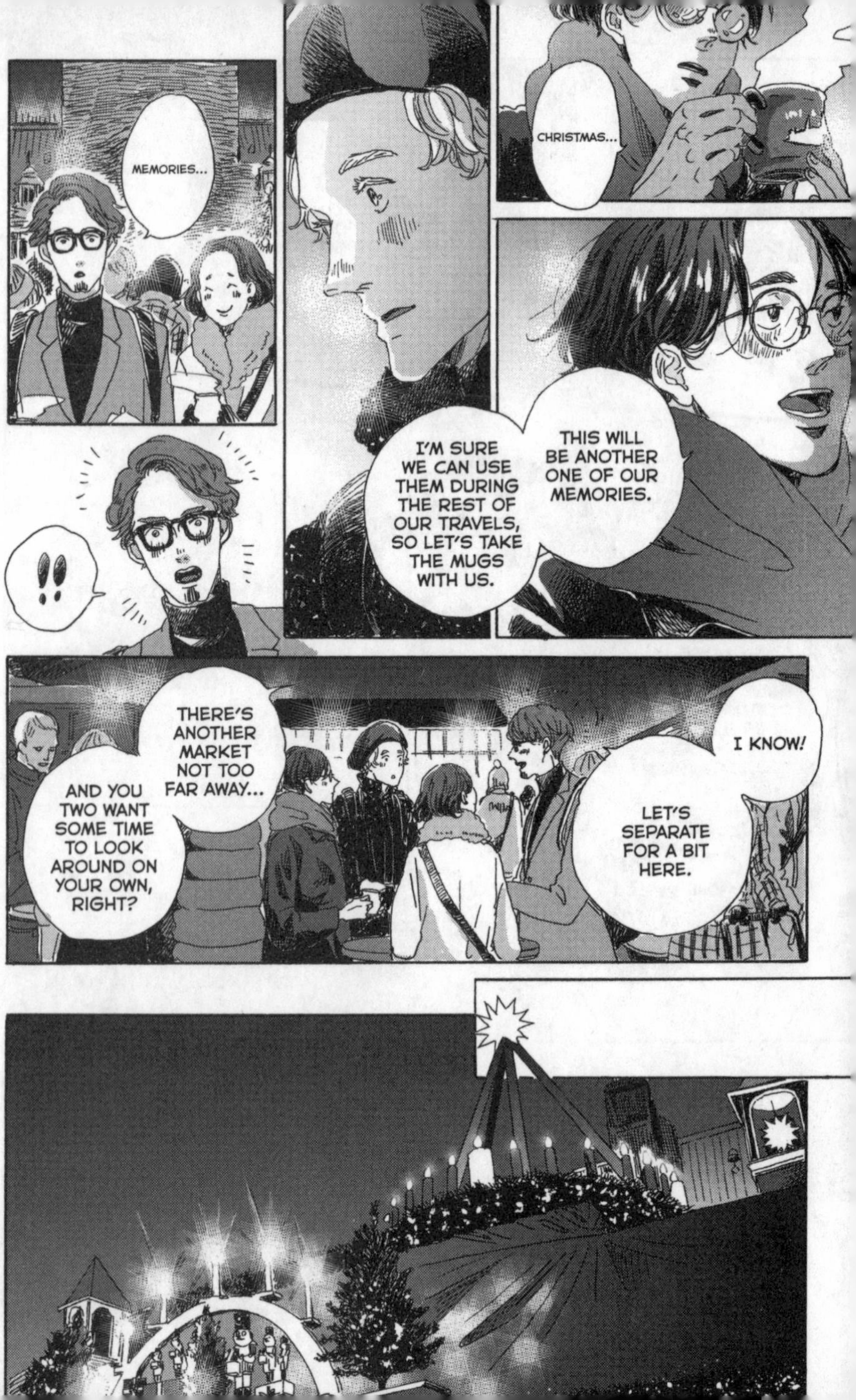
CHRISTMAS...
THIS WILL BE ANOTHER ONE OF OUR MEMORIES.
I'M SURE WE CAN USE THEM DURING THE REST OF OUR TRAVELS, SO LET'S TAKE THE MUGS WITH US.
MEMORIES...
!!
I KNOW!
LET'S SEPARATE FOR A BIT HERE.
THERE'S ANOTHER MARKET NOT TOO FAR AWAY...
AND YOU TWO WANT SOME TIME TO LOOK AROUND ON YOUR OWN, RIGHT?

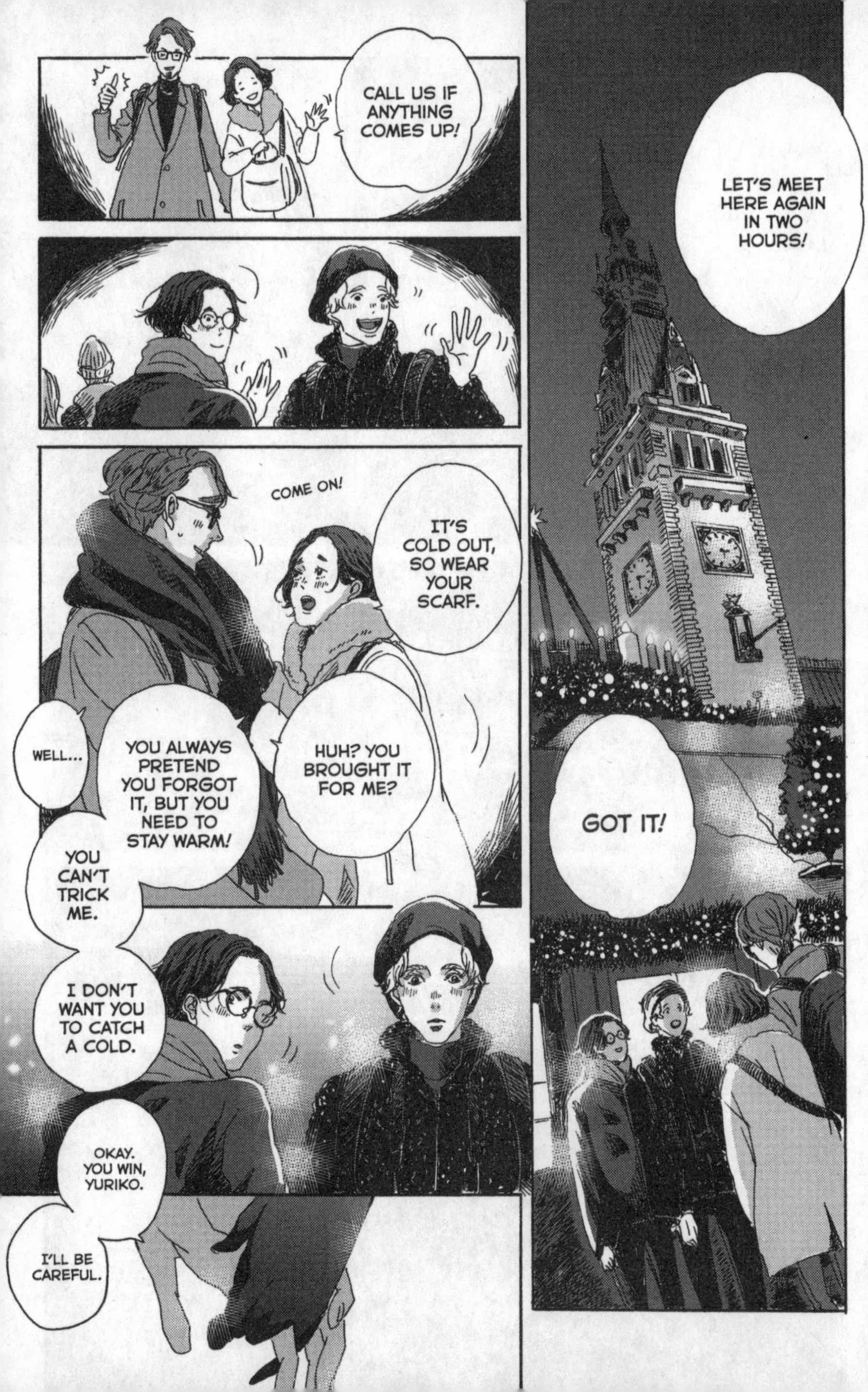
LET'S MEET HERE AGAIN IN TWO HOURS!
GOT IT!
CALL US IF ANYTHING COMES UP!
COME ON!
IT'S COLD OUT, SO WEAR YOUR SCARF.
HUH? YOU BROUGHT IT FOR ME?
YOU ALWAYS PRETEND YOU FORGOT IT, BUT YOU NEED TO STAY WARM!
WELL...
YOU CAN'T TRICK ME.
I DON'T WANT YOU TO CATCH A COLD.
OKAY. YOU WIN, YURIKO.
I'LL BE CAREFUL.

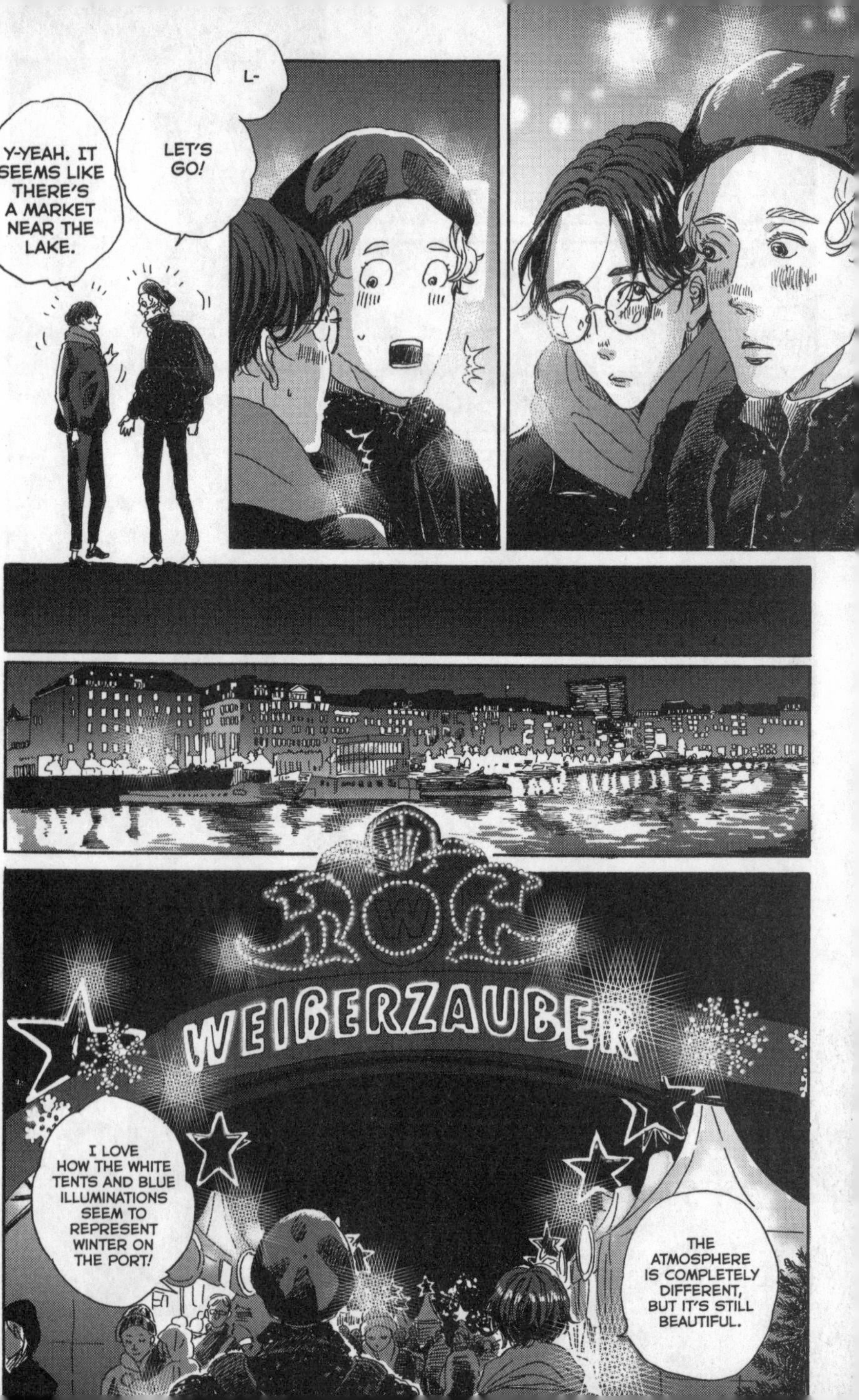
L-
LET'S GO!
Y-YEAH. IT SEEMS LIKE THERE'S A MARKET NEAR THE LAKE.
WEIßERZAUBER
THE ATMOSPHERE IS COMPLETELY DIFFERENT, BUT IT'S STILL BEAUTIFUL.
I LOVE HOW THE WHITE TENTS AND BLUE ILLUMINATIONS SEEM TO REPRESENT WINTER ON THE PORT!

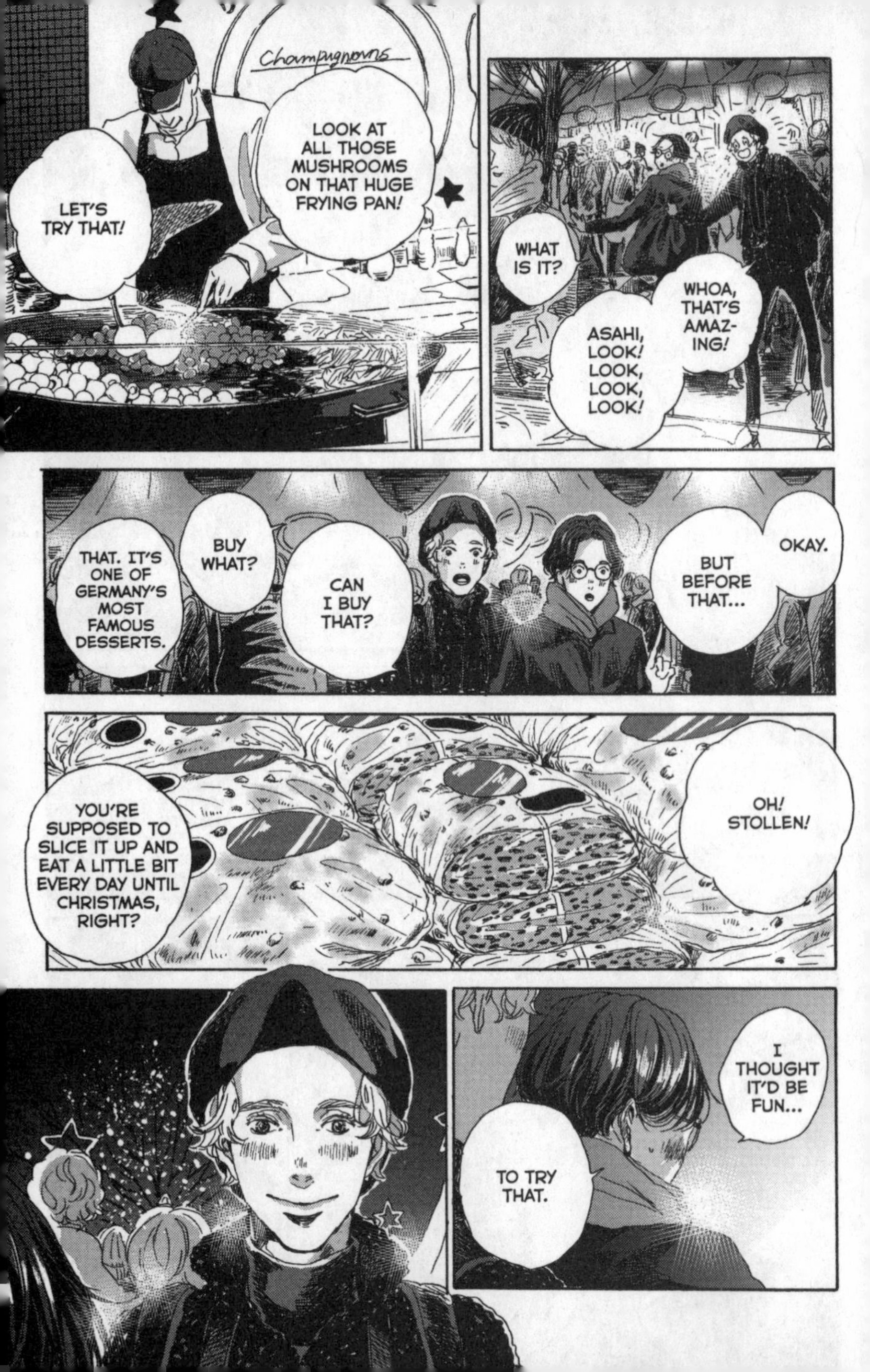
WHOA, THAT'S AMAZ-ING!
ASAHI, LOOK! LOOK, LOOK, LOOK!
WHAT IS IT?
Champignons
LOOK AT ALL THOSE MUSHROOMS ON THAT HUGE FRYING PAN!
LET'S TRY THAT!
OKAY.
BUT BEFORE THAT...
CAN I BUY THAT?
BUY WHAT?
THAT. IT'S ONE OF GERMANY'S MOST FAMOUS DESSERTS.
OH! STOLLEN!
YOU'RE SUPPOSED TO SLICE IT UP AND EAT A LITTLE BIT EVERY DAY UNTIL CHRISTMAS, RIGHT?
I THOUGHT IT'D BE FUN...
TO TRY THAT.

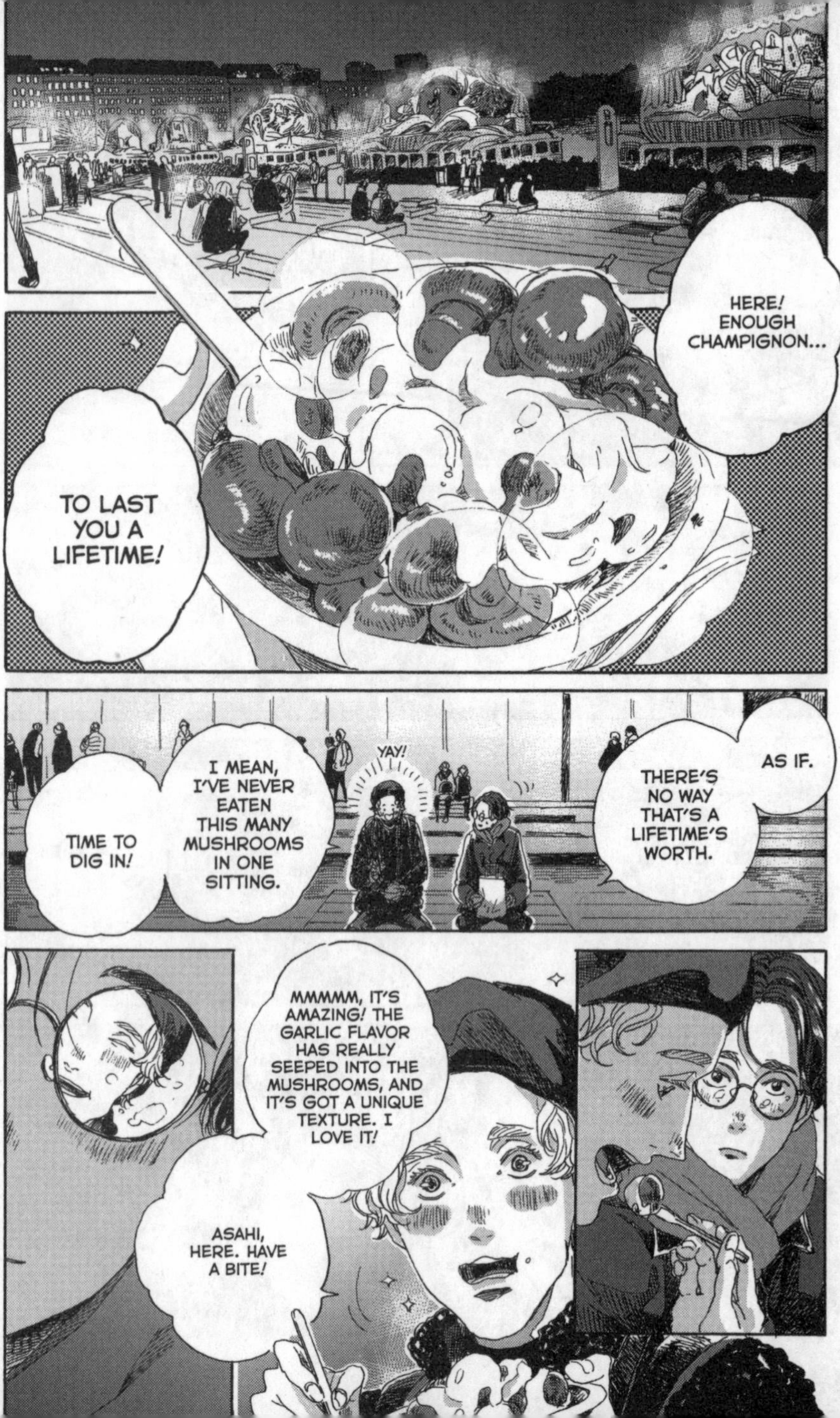
HERE! ENOUGH CHAMPIGNON...
TO LAST YOU A LIFETIME!
AS IF.
THERE'S NO WAY THAT'S A LIFETIME'S WORTH.
YAY!
I MEAN, I'VE NEVER EATEN THIS MANY MUSHROOMS IN ONE SITTING.
TIME TO DIG IN!
MMMMM, IT'S AMAZING! THE GARLIC FLAVOR HAS REALLY SEEPED INTO THE MUSHROOMS, AND IT'S GOT A UNIQUE TEXTURE. I LOVE IT!
ASAHI, HERE. HAVE A BITE!

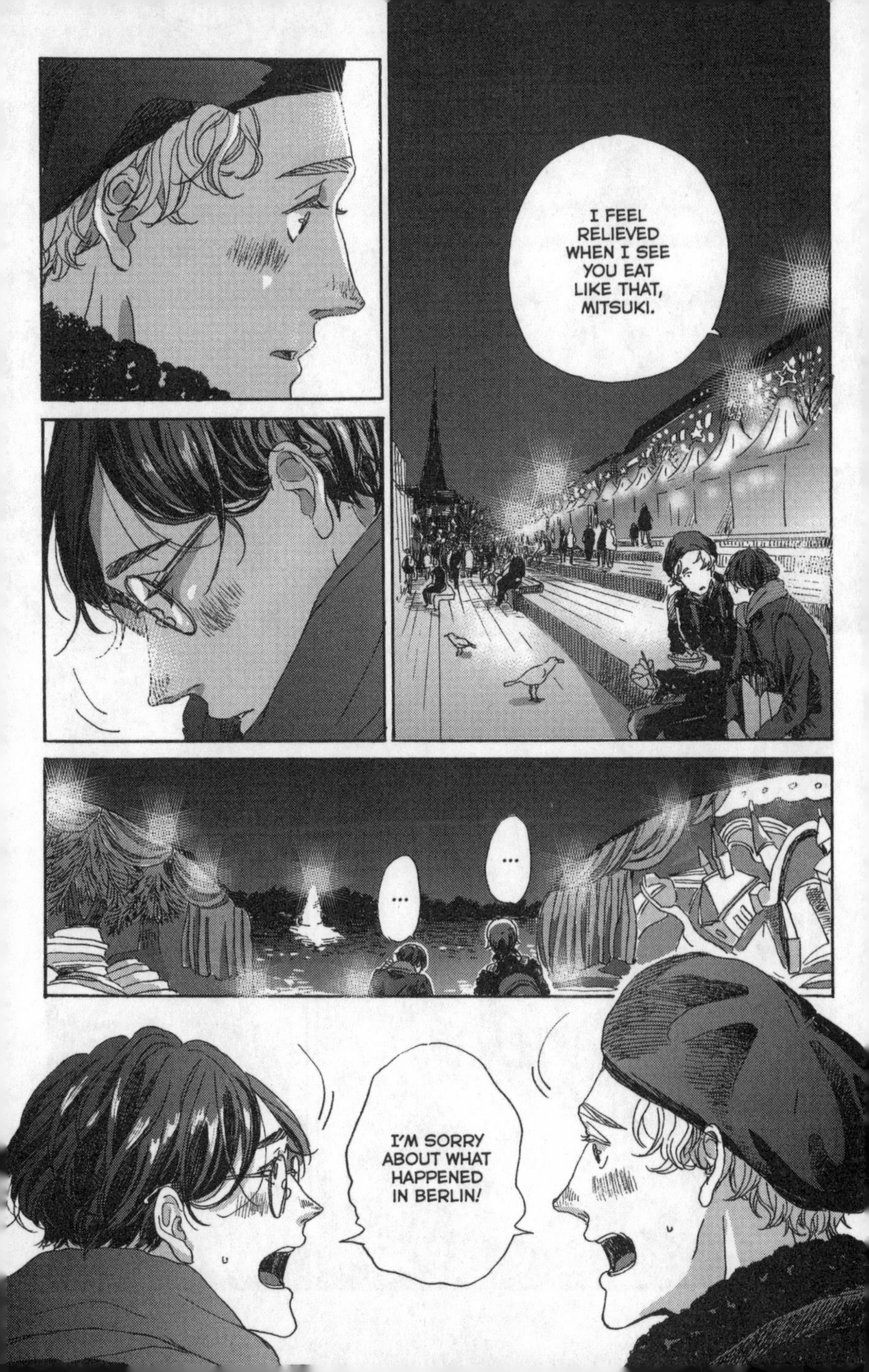
I FEEL RELIEVED WHEN I SEE YOU EAT LIKE THAT, MITSUKI.
...
...
I'M SORRY ABOUT WHAT HAPPENED IN BERLIN!

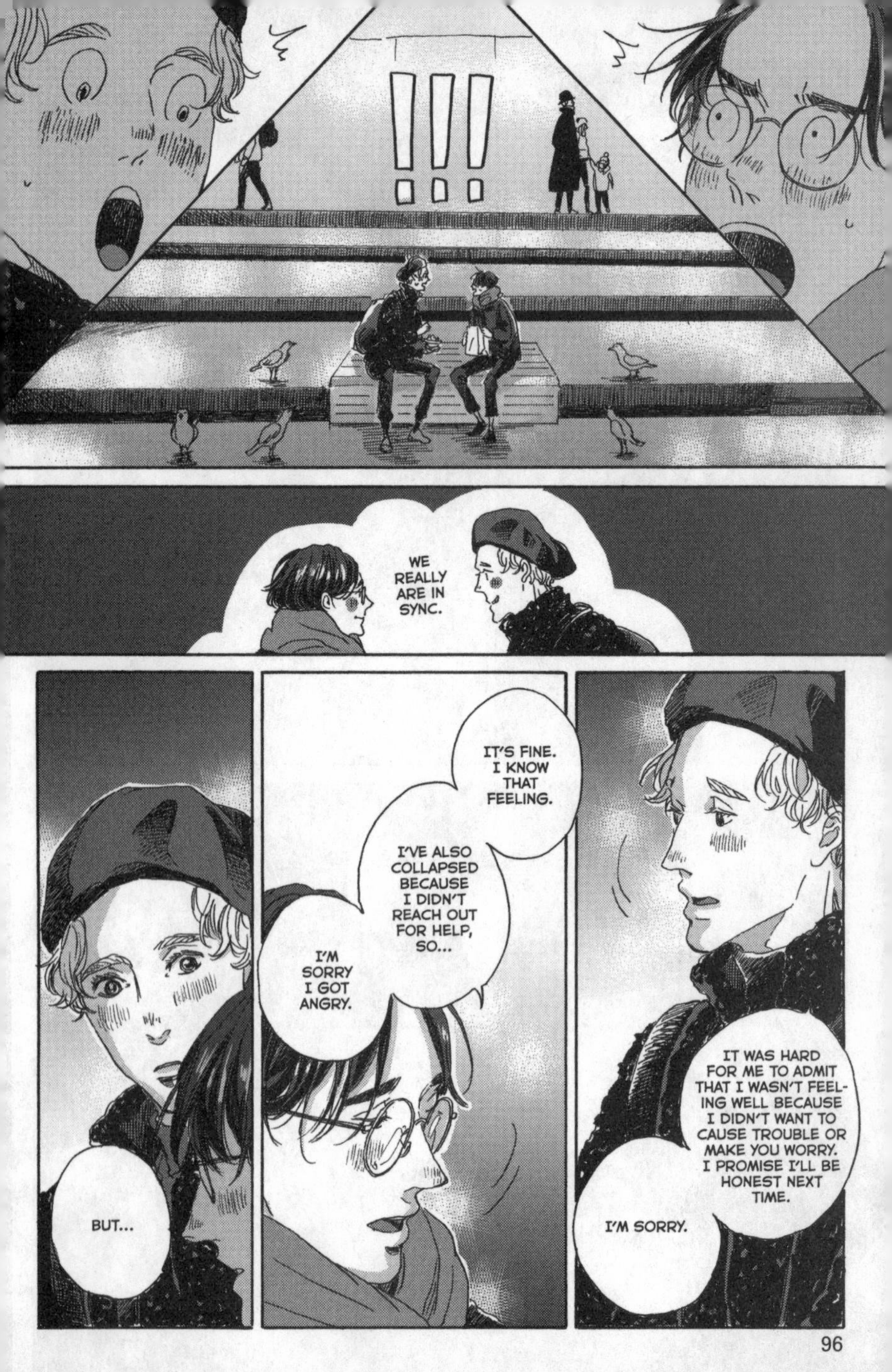
!!!
WE REALLY ARE IN SYNC.
IT WAS HARD FOR ME TO ADMIT THAT I WASN'T FEELING WELL BECAUSE I DIDN'T WANT TO CAUSE TROUBLE OR MAKE YOU WORRY. I PROMISE I'LL BE HONEST NEXT TIME.
I'M SORRY.
IT'S FINE. I KNOW THAT FEELING.
I'VE ALSO COLLAPSED BECAUSE I DIDN'T REACH OUT FOR HELP, SO...
I'M SORRY I GOT ANGRY.
BUT...

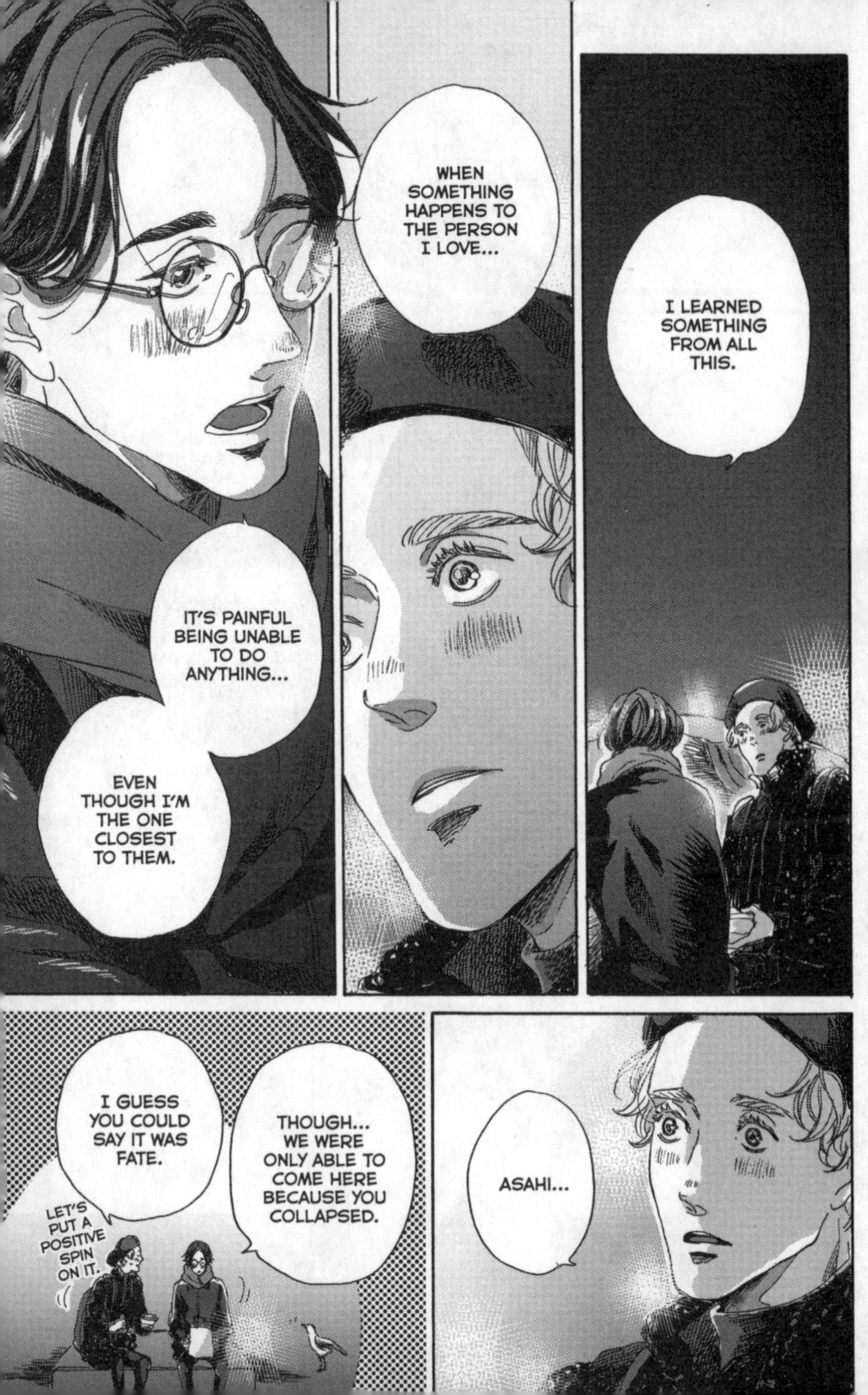
I LEARNED SOMETHING FROM ALL THIS.
WHEN SOMETHING HAPPENS TO THE PERSON I LOVE...
IT'S PAINFUL BEING UNABLE TO DO ANYTHING...
EVEN THOUGH I'M THE ONE CLOSEST TO THEM.
ASAHI...
THOUGH... WE WERE ONLY ABLE TO COME HERE BECAUSE YOU COLLAPSED.
I GUESS YOU COULD SAY IT WAS FATE.
LET'S PUT A POSITIVE SPIN ON IT.

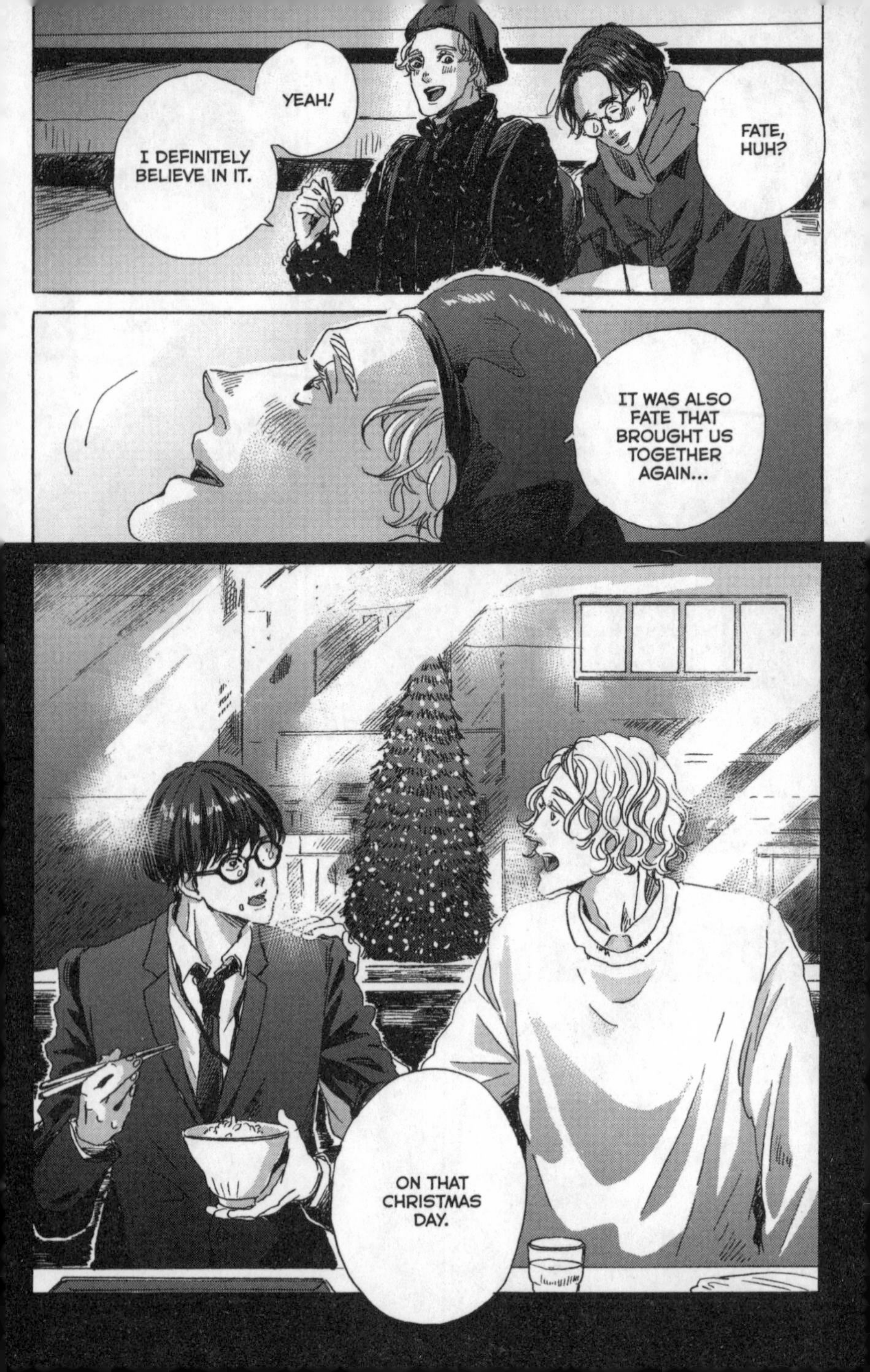
FATE, HUH?
YEAH!
I DEFINITELY BELIEVE IN IT.
IT WAS ALSO FATE THAT BROUGHT US TOGETHER AGAIN...
ON THAT CHRISTMAS DAY.

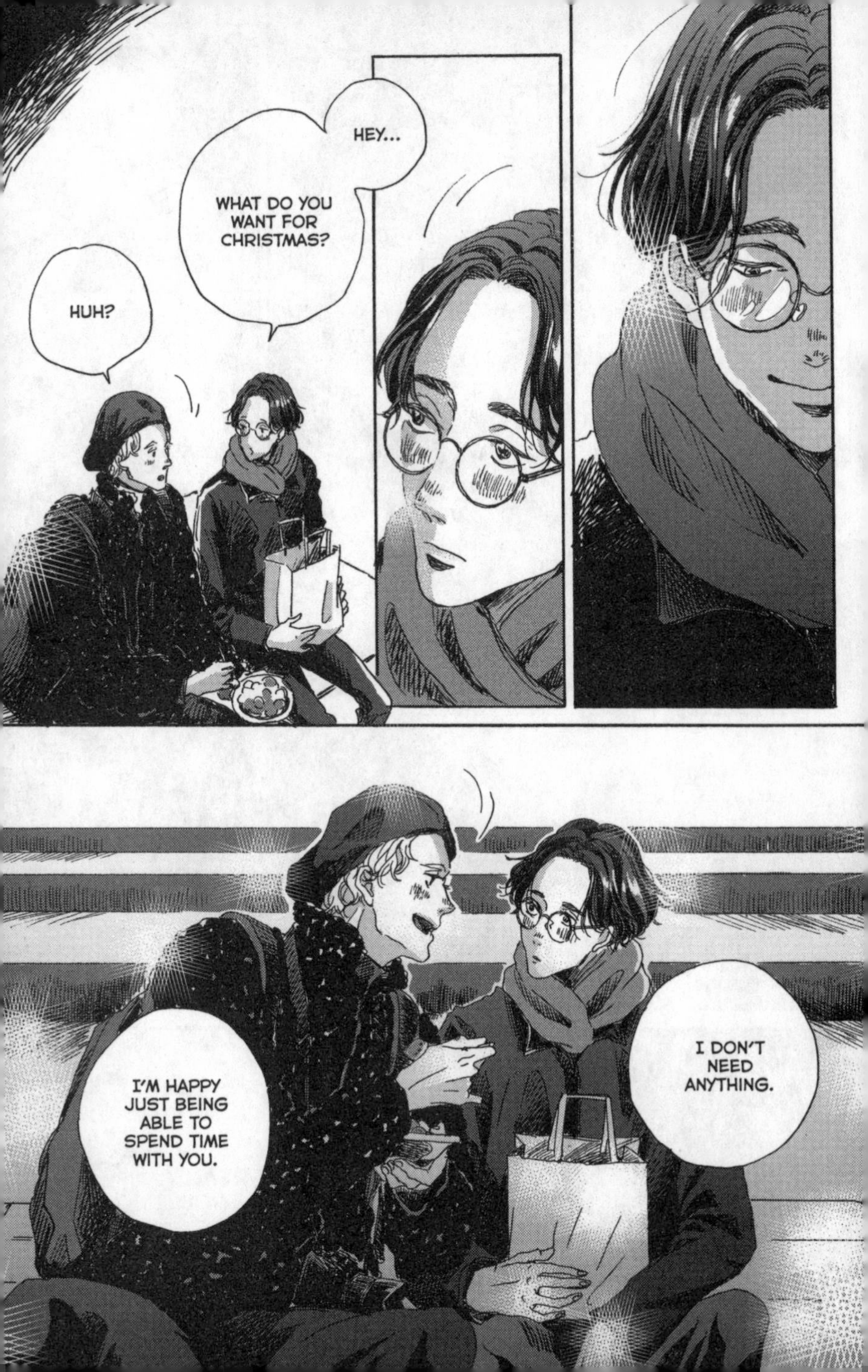
HEY...
WHAT DO YOU WANT FOR CHRISTMAS?
HUH?
I DON'T NEED ANYTHING.
I'M HAPPY JUST BEING ABLE TO SPEND TIME WITH YOU.

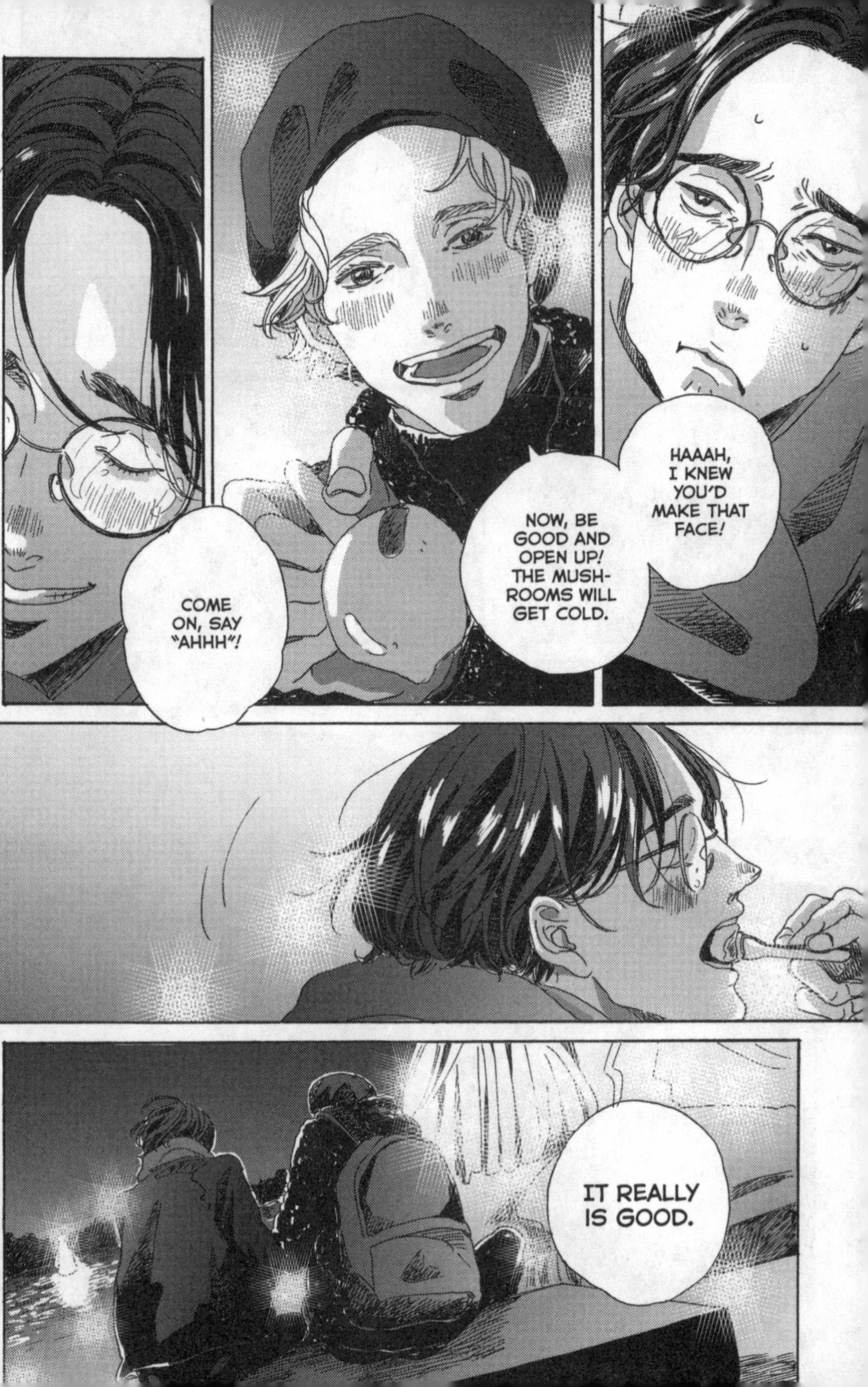
HAAAH, I KNEW YOU'D MAKE THAT FACE!
NOW, BE GOOD AND OPEN UP! THE MUSH-ROOMS WILL GET COLD.
COME ON, SAY "AHHH"!
IT REALLY IS GOOD.

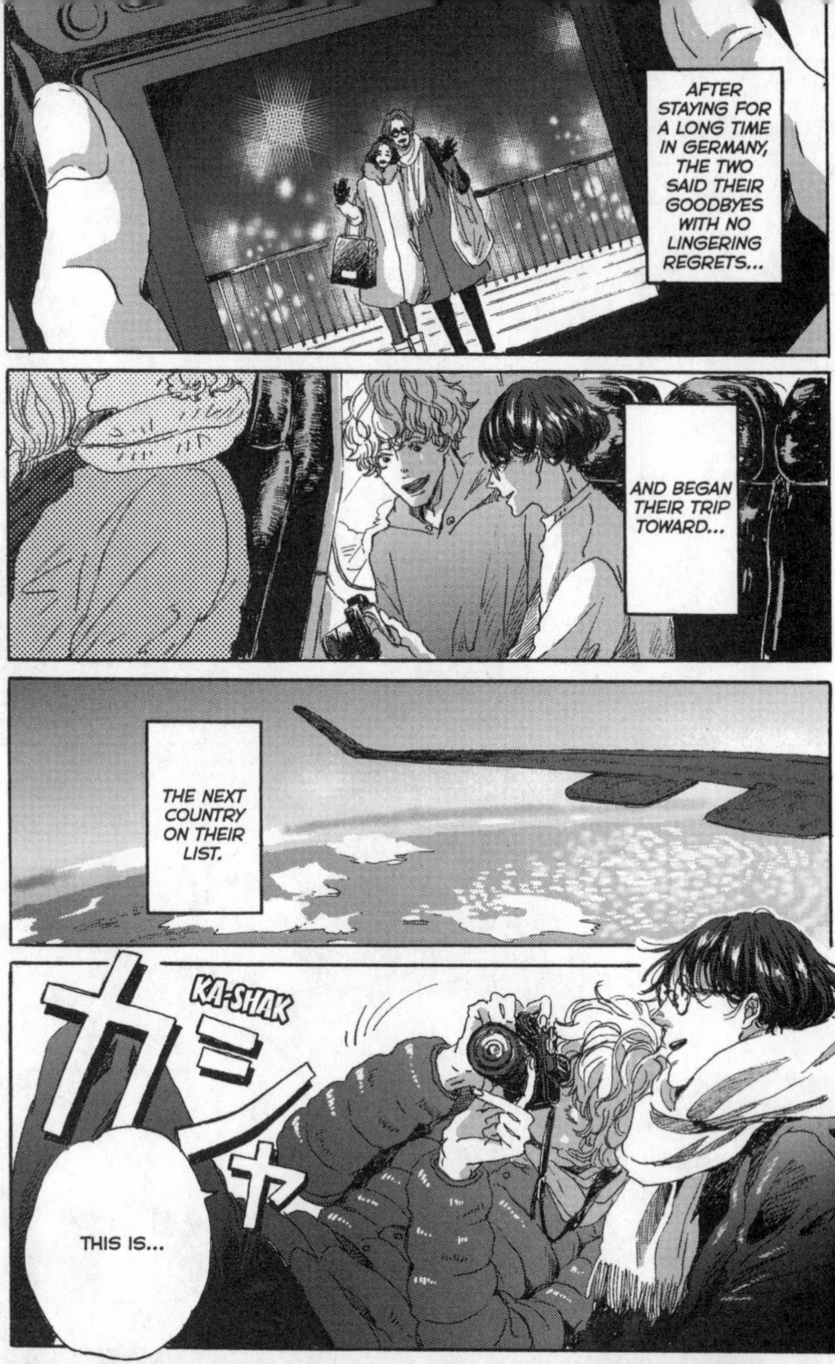
AFTER STAYING FOR A LONG TIME IN GERMANY, THE TWO SAID THEIR GOODBYES WITH NO LINGERING REGRETS...
AND BEGAN THEIR TRIP TOWARD...
THE NEXT COUNTRY ON THEIR LIST.
KA-SHAK
カシャ
THIS IS...

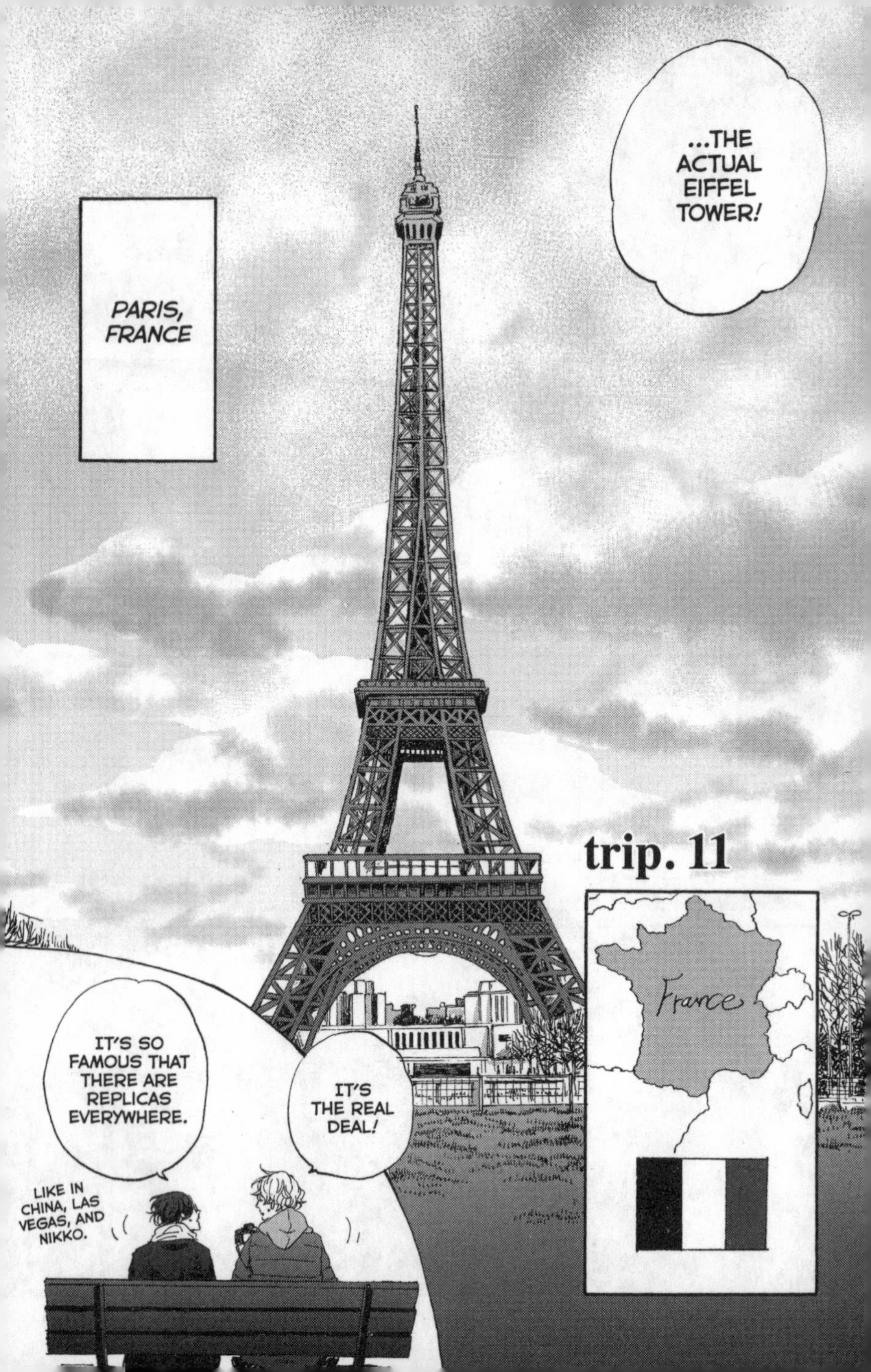
...THE ACTUAL EIFFEL TOWER!
PARIS, FRANCE
trip. 11
France
IT'S THE REAL DEAL!
IT'S SO FAMOUS THAT THERE ARE REPLICAS EVERYWHERE.
LIKE IN CHINA, LAS VEGAS, AND NIKKO.

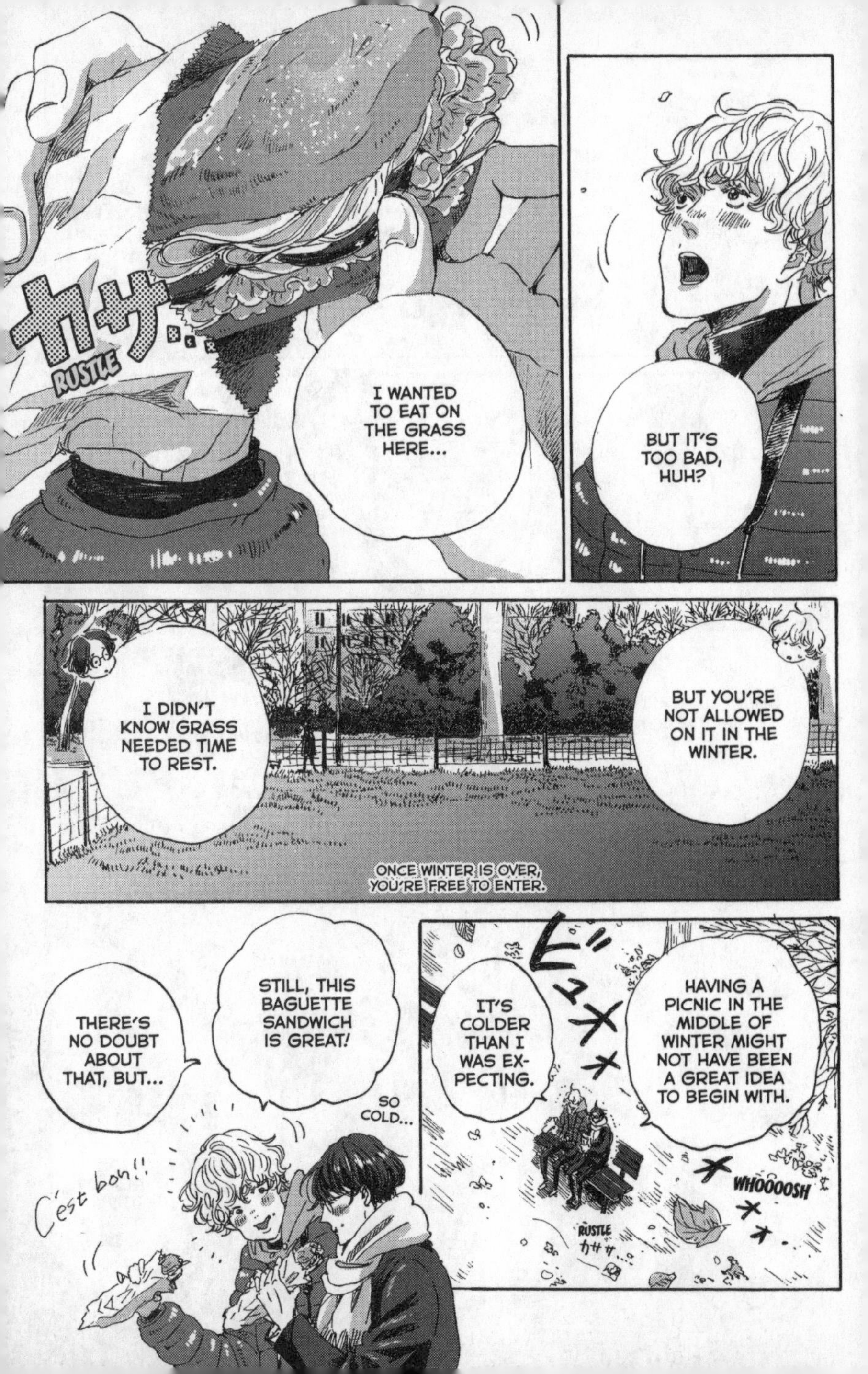

BUT IT'S TOO BAD, HUH?
カサ...
RUSTLE
I WANTED TO EAT ON THE GRASS HERE...
BUT YOU'RE NOT ALLOWED ON IT IN THE WINTER.
I DIDN'T KNOW GRASS NEEDED TIME TO REST.
ONCE WINTER IS OVER, YOU'RE FREE TO ENTER.
HAVING A PICNIC IN THE MIDDLE OF WINTER MIGHT NOT HAVE BEEN A GREAT IDEA TO BEGIN WITH.
WHOOOOSH
IT'S COLDER THAN I WAS EX-PECTING.
RUSTLE
カサ...
SO COLD...
STILL, THIS BAGUETTE SANDWICH IS GREAT!
THERE'S NO DOUBT ABOUT THAT, BUT...
C'est bon!!

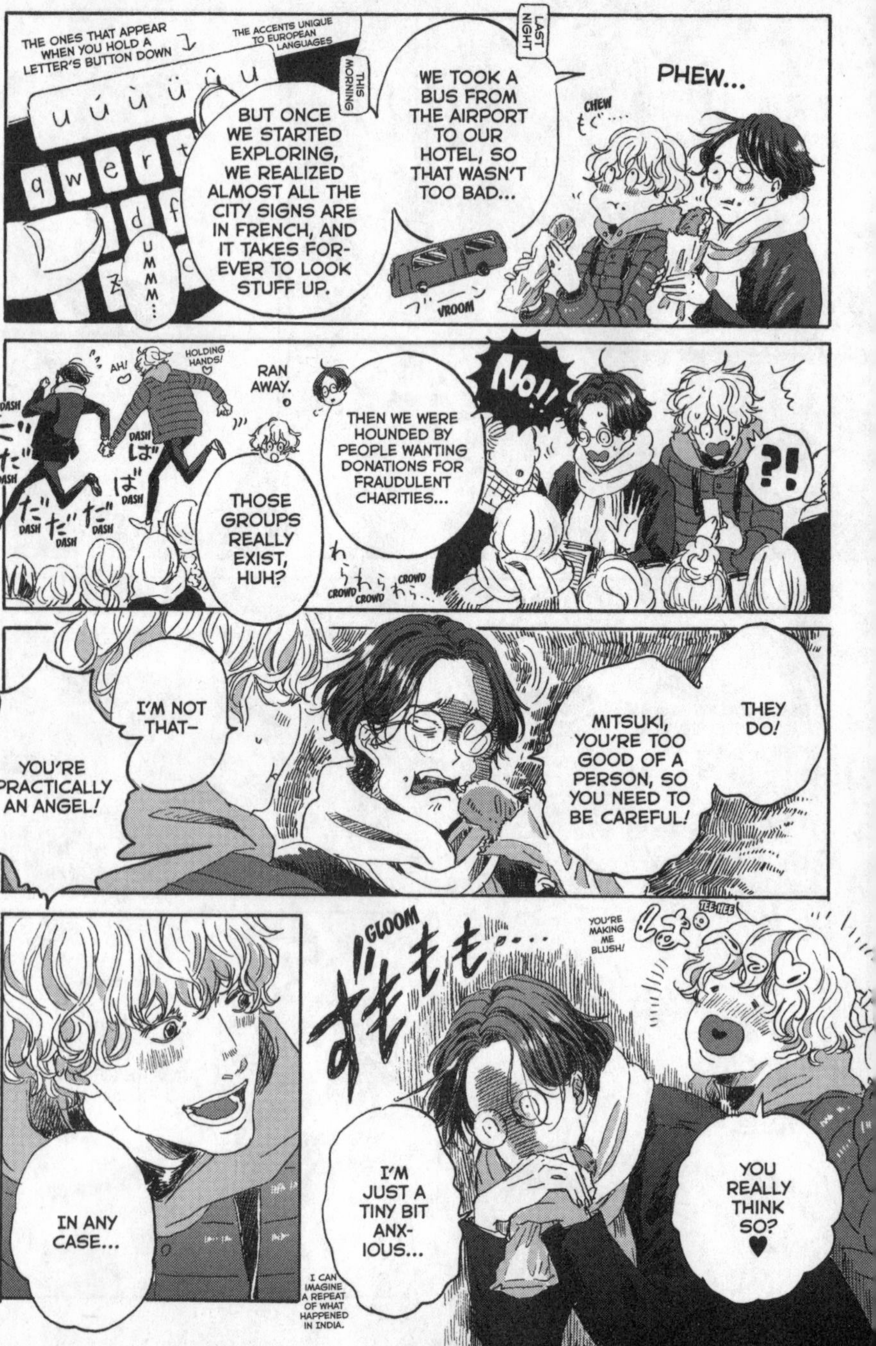
PHEW...
CHEW
LAST NIGHT
WE TOOK A BUS FROM THE AIRPORT TO OUR HOTEL, SO THAT WASN'T TOO BAD...
VROOM
THIS MORNING
BUT ONCE WE STARTED EXPLORING, WE REALIZED ALMOST ALL THE CITY SIGNS ARE IN FRENCH, AND IT TAKES FOREVER TO LOOK STUFF UP.
UMMM...
THE ACCENTS UNIQUE TO EUROPEAN LANGUAGES
THE ONES THAT APPEAR WHEN YOU HOLD A LETTER'S BUTTON DOWN
?!
No!!
THEN WE WERE HOUNDED BY PEOPLE WANTING DONATIONS FOR FRAUDULENT CHARITIES...
CROWD CROWD CROWD
THOSE GROUPS REALLY EXIST, HUH?
RAN AWAY.
HOLDING HANDS!
AH!
DASH DASH DASH DASH DASH DASH DASH
THEY DO!
MITSUKI, YOU'RE TOO GOOD OF A PERSON, SO YOU NEED TO BE CAREFUL!
I'M NOT THAT–
YOU'RE PRACTICALLY AN ANGEL!
TEE-HEE
YOU'RE MAKING ME BLUSH!
GLOOM
YOU REALLY THINK SO? ♥
I'M JUST A TINY BIT ANXIOUS...
I CAN IMAGINE A REPEAT OF WHAT HAPPENED IN INDIA.
IN ANY CASE...

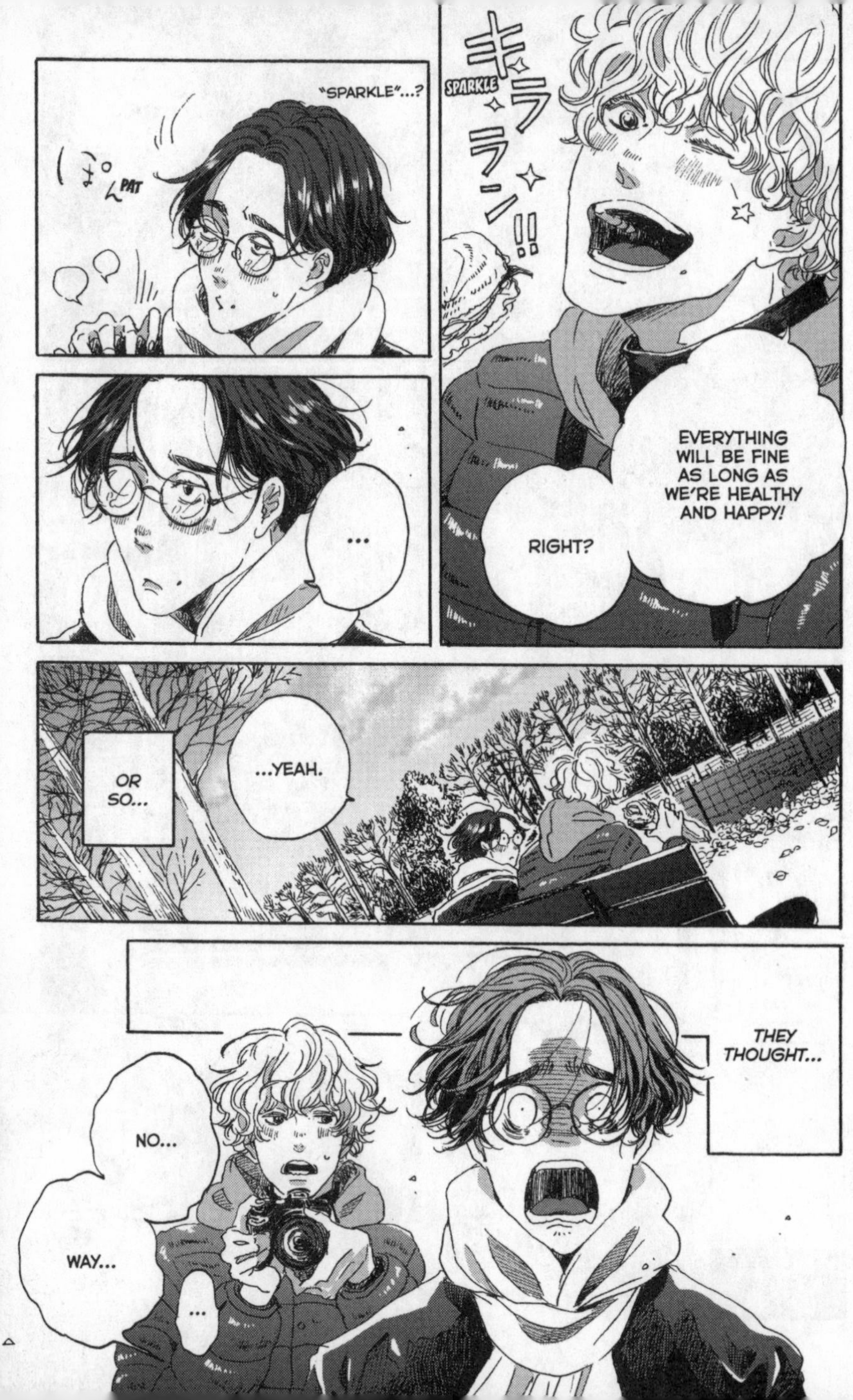
キラ
SPARKLE
ラーン!!
EVERYTHING WILL BE FINE AS LONG AS WE'RE HEALTHY AND HAPPY!
RIGHT?
"SPARKLE"...?
ぽん
PAT
...
...YEAH.
OR SO...
THEY THOUGHT...
NO...
WAY...
...

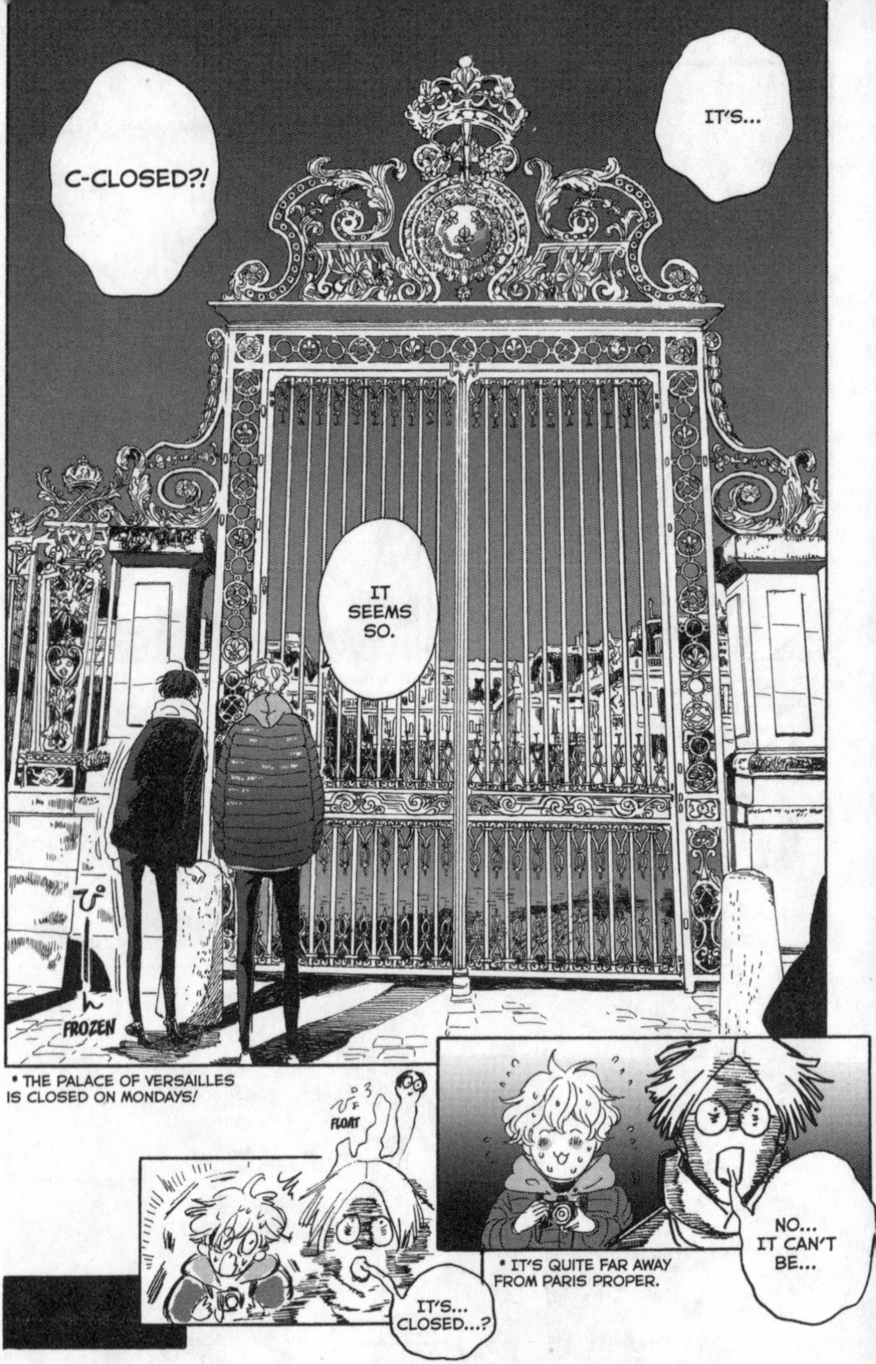
IT'S...
C-CLOSED?!
IT SEEMS SO.
ぴーん
FROZEN
* THE PALACE OF VERSAILLES IS CLOSED ON MONDAYS!
NO... IT CAN'T BE...
* IT'S QUITE FAR AWAY FROM PARIS PROPER.
FLOAT
IT'S... CLOSED...?

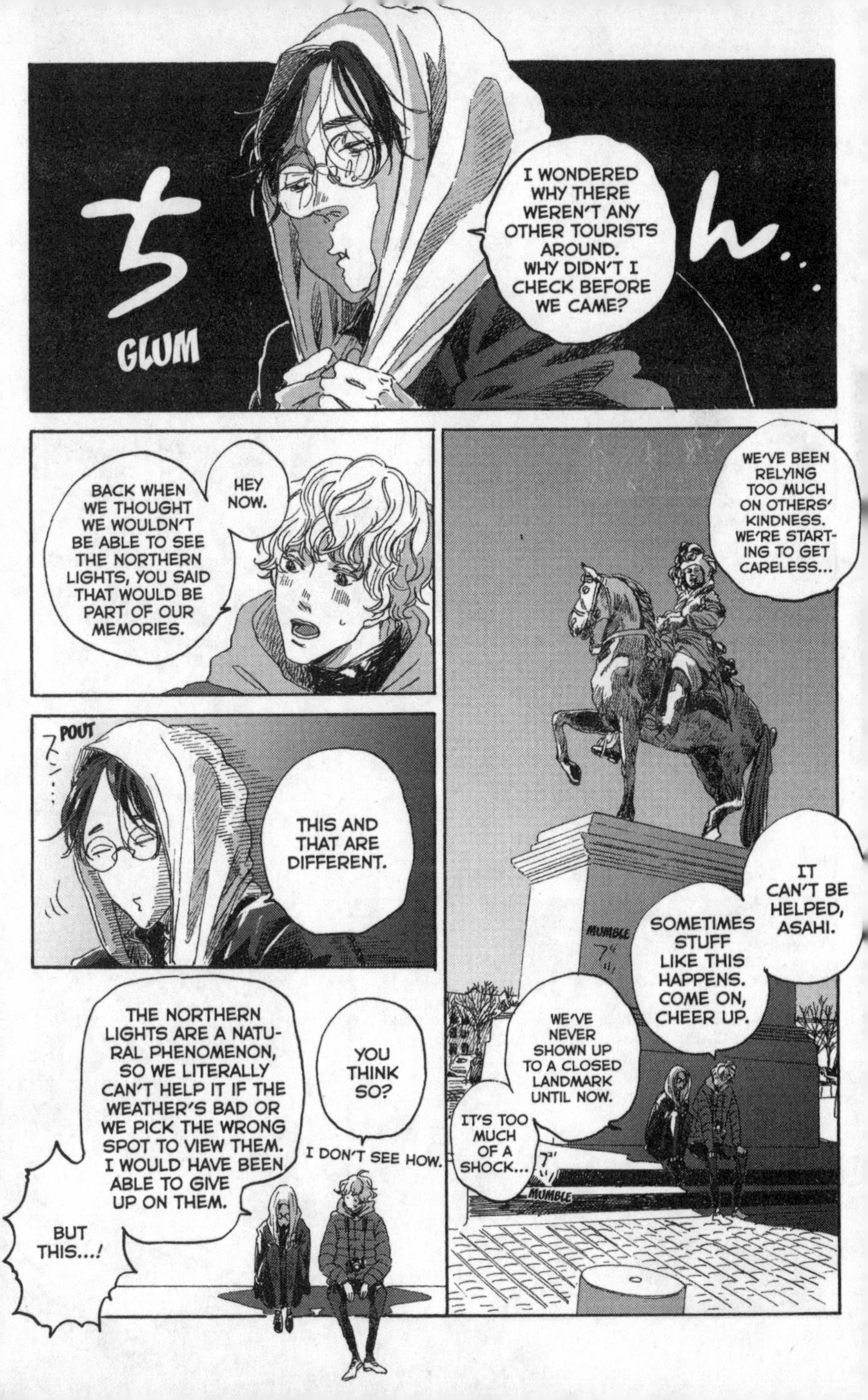
ちん…
GLUM
I WONDERED WHY THERE WEREN'T ANY OTHER TOURISTS AROUND. WHY DIDN'T I CHECK BEFORE WE CAME?
WE'VE BEEN RELYING TOO MUCH ON OTHERS' KINDNESS. WE'RE STARTING TO GET CARELESS...
IT CAN'T BE HELPED, ASAHI.
SOMETIMES STUFF LIKE THIS HAPPENS. COME ON, CHEER UP.
MUMBLE
WE'VE NEVER SHOWN UP TO A CLOSED LANDMARK UNTIL NOW.
IT'S TOO MUCH OF A SHOCK...
MUMBLE
HEY NOW.
BACK WHEN WE THOUGHT WE WOULDN'T BE ABLE TO SEE THE NORTHERN LIGHTS, YOU SAID THAT WOULD BE PART OF OUR MEMORIES.
POUT
THIS AND THAT ARE DIFFERENT.
YOU THINK SO?
I DON'T SEE HOW.
THE NORTHERN LIGHTS ARE A NATURAL PHENOMENON, SO WE LITERALLY CAN'T HELP IT IF THE WEATHER'S BAD OR WE PICK THE WRONG SPOT TO VIEW THEM. I WOULD HAVE BEEN ABLE TO GIVE UP ON THEM.
BUT THIS...!

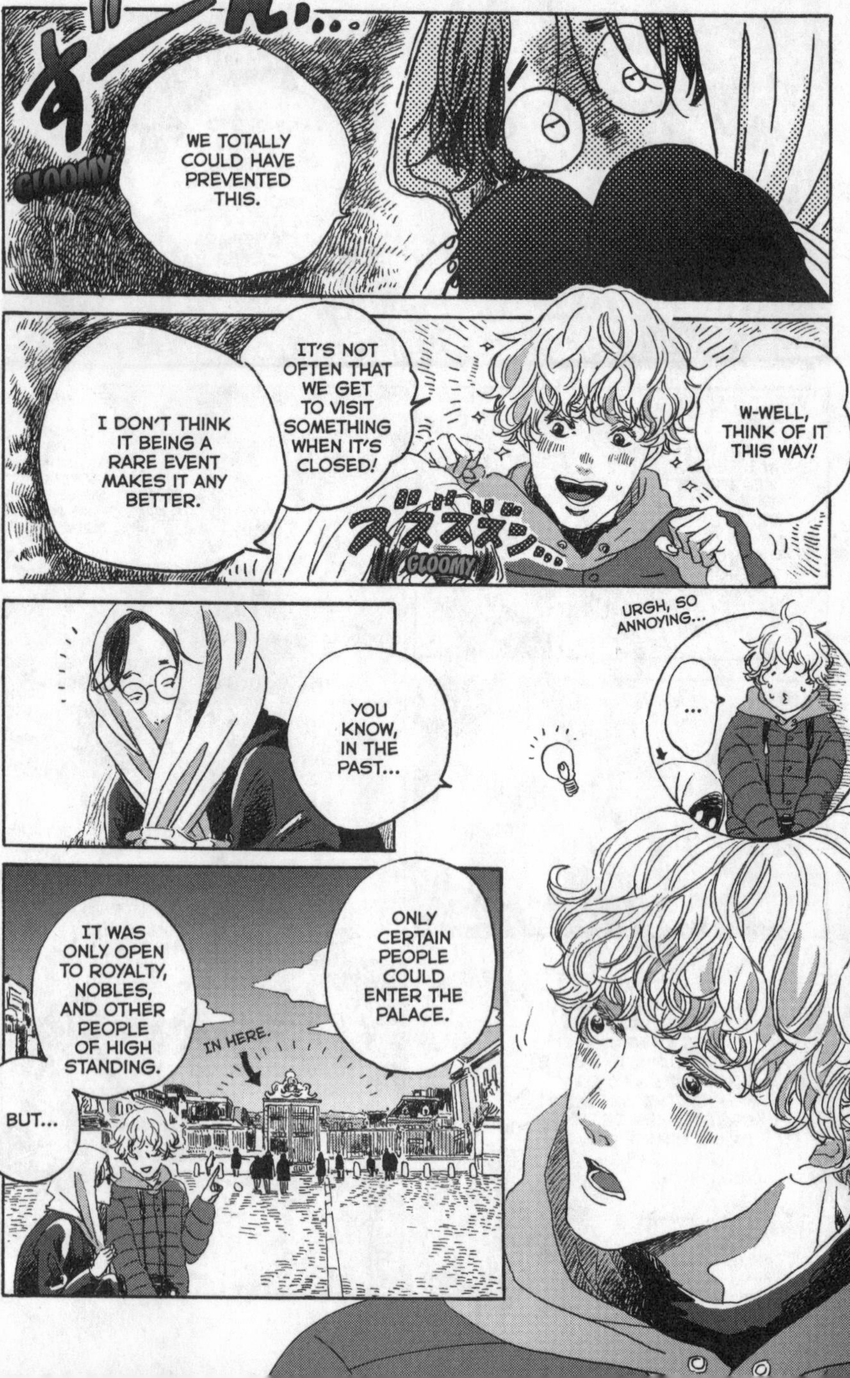
ずーん…
GLOOMY
WE TOTALLY COULD HAVE PREVENTED THIS.
W-WELL, THINK OF IT THIS WAY!
IT'S NOT OFTEN THAT WE GET TO VISIT SOMETHING WHEN IT'S CLOSED!
ズズズズン…
GLOOMY
I DON'T THINK IT BEING A RARE EVENT MAKES IT ANY BETTER.
URGH, SO ANNOYING...
...
YOU KNOW, IN THE PAST...
ONLY CERTAIN PEOPLE COULD ENTER THE PALACE.
IT WAS ONLY OPEN TO ROYALTY, NOBLES, AND OTHER PEOPLE OF HIGH STANDING.
IN HERE.
BUT...

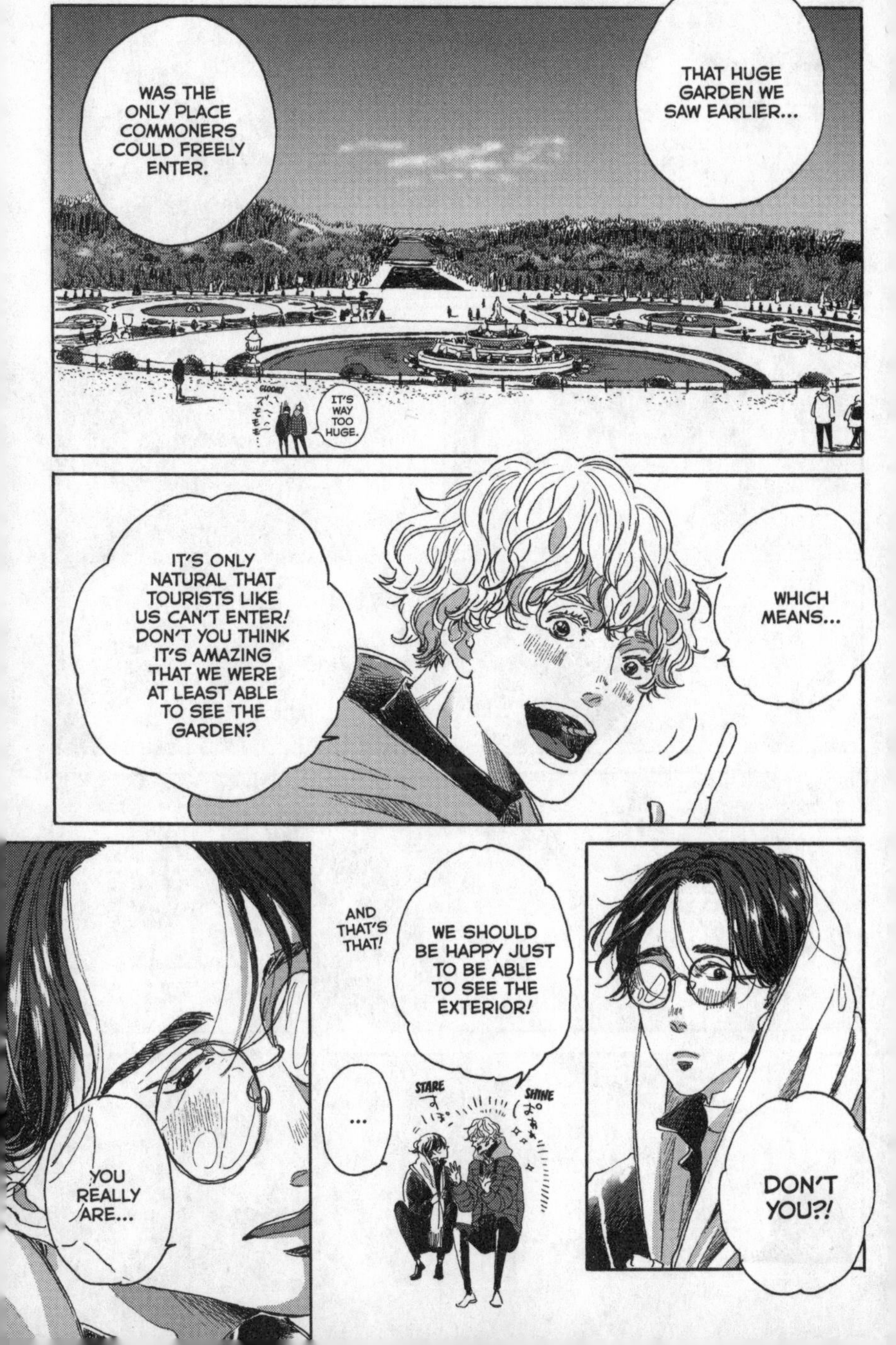

THAT HUGE GARDEN WE SAW EARLIER...
WAS THE ONLY PLACE COMMONERS COULD FREELY ENTER.
GLOOMY
IT'S WAY TOO HUGE.
WHICH MEANS...
IT'S ONLY NATURAL THAT TOURISTS LIKE US CAN'T ENTER! DON'T YOU THINK IT'S AMAZING THAT WE WERE AT LEAST ABLE TO SEE THE GARDEN?
DON'T YOU?!
WE SHOULD BE HAPPY JUST TO BE ABLE TO SEE THE EXTERIOR!
AND THAT'S THAT!
SHINE
STARE
...
YOU REALLY ARE...

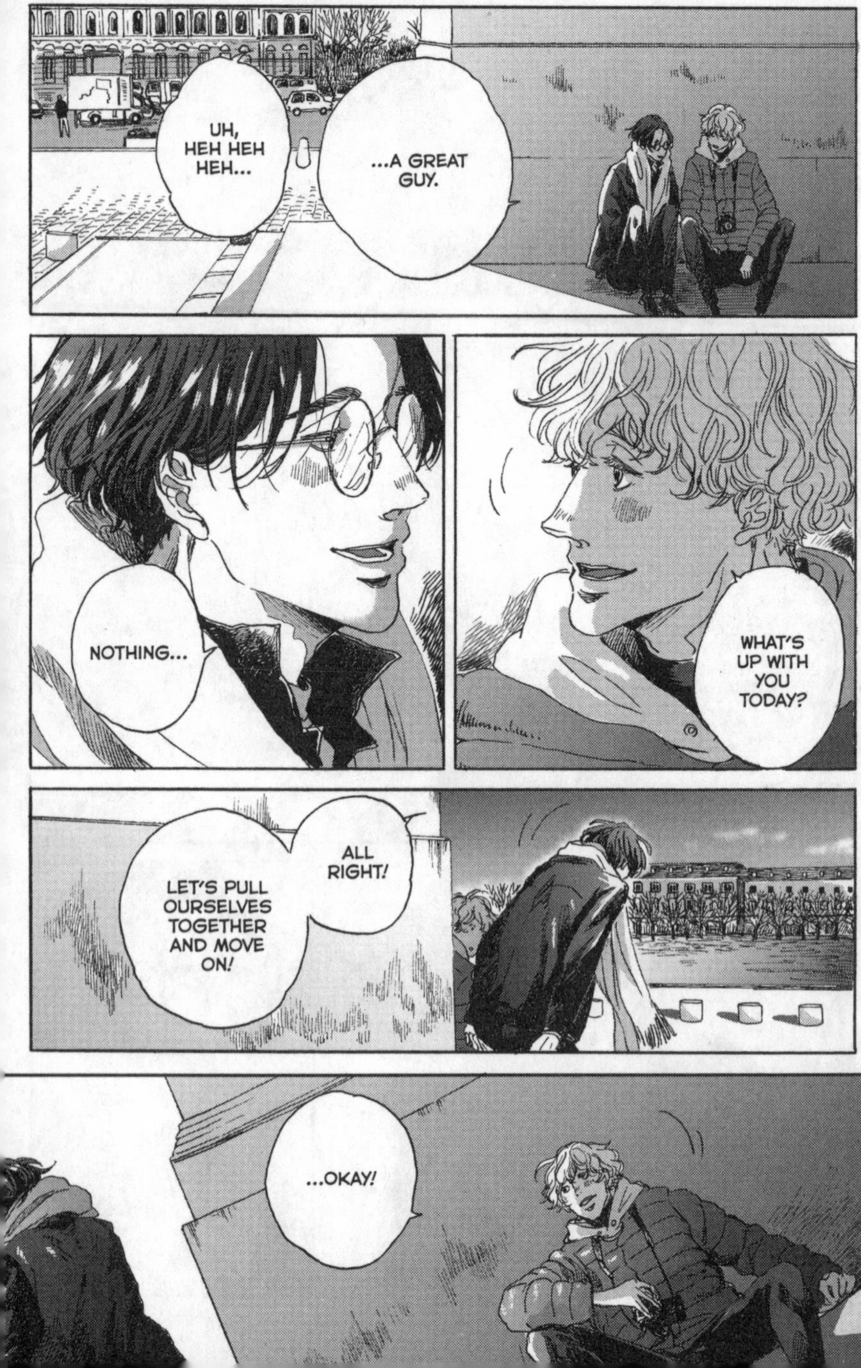
...A GREAT GUY.
UH, HEH HEH HEH...
WHAT'S UP WITH YOU TODAY?
NOTHING...
ALL RIGHT!
LET'S PULL OURSELVES TOGETHER AND MOVE ON!
...OKAY!

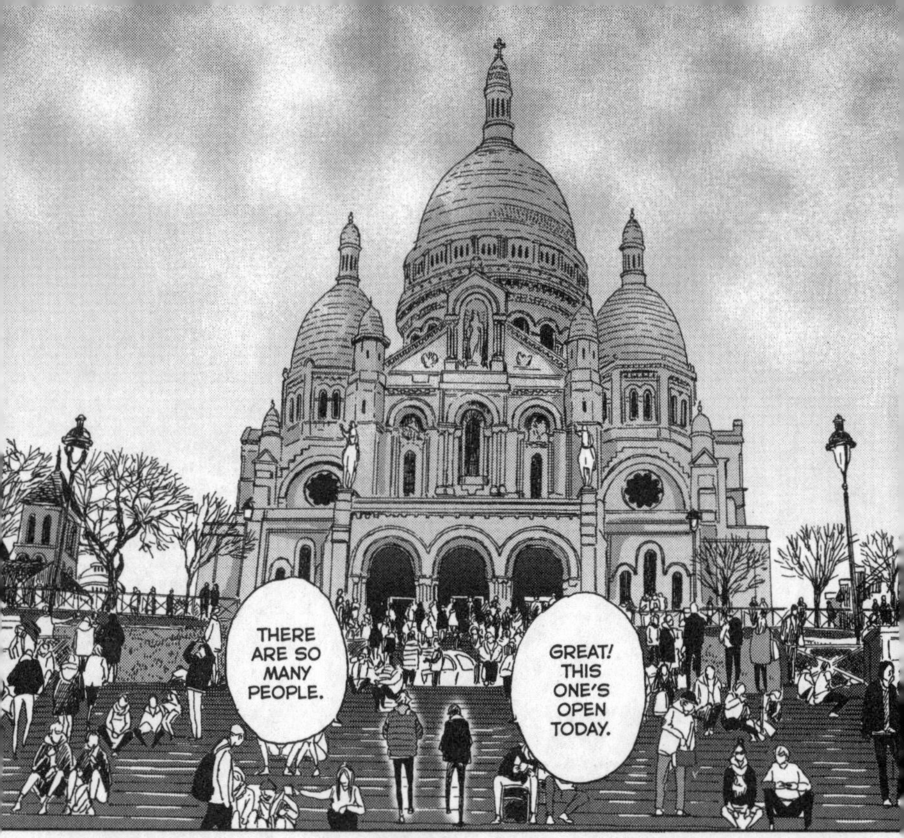
GREAT! THIS ONE'S OPEN TODAY.
THERE ARE SO MANY PEOPLE.

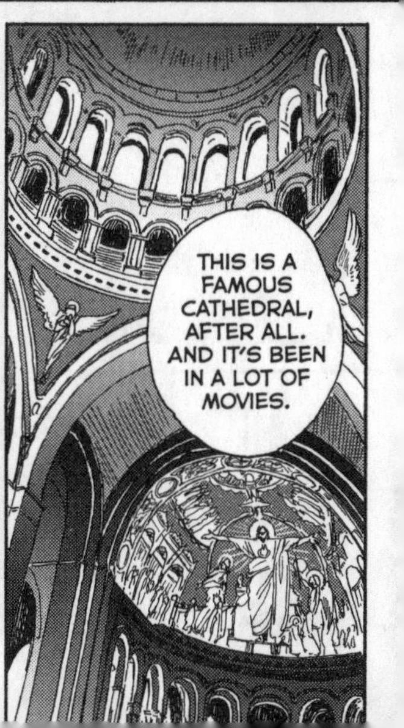
THIS IS A FAMOUS CATHEDRAL, AFTER ALL. AND IT'S BEEN IN A LOT OF MOVIES.

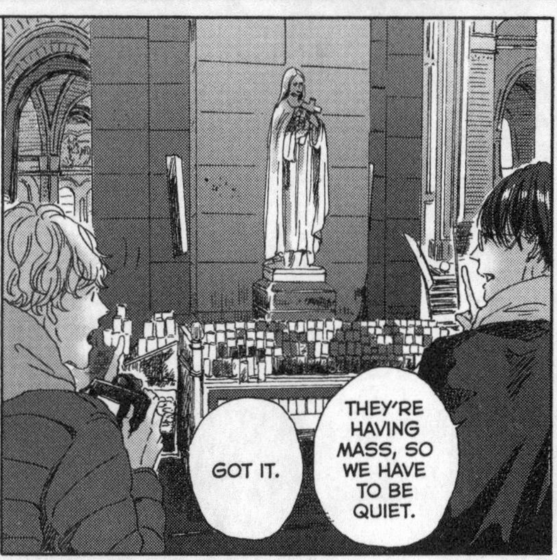
THEY'RE HAVING MASS, SO WE HAVE TO BE QUIET.
GOT IT.

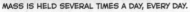

MASS IS HELD SEVERAL TIMES A DAY, EVERY DAY.

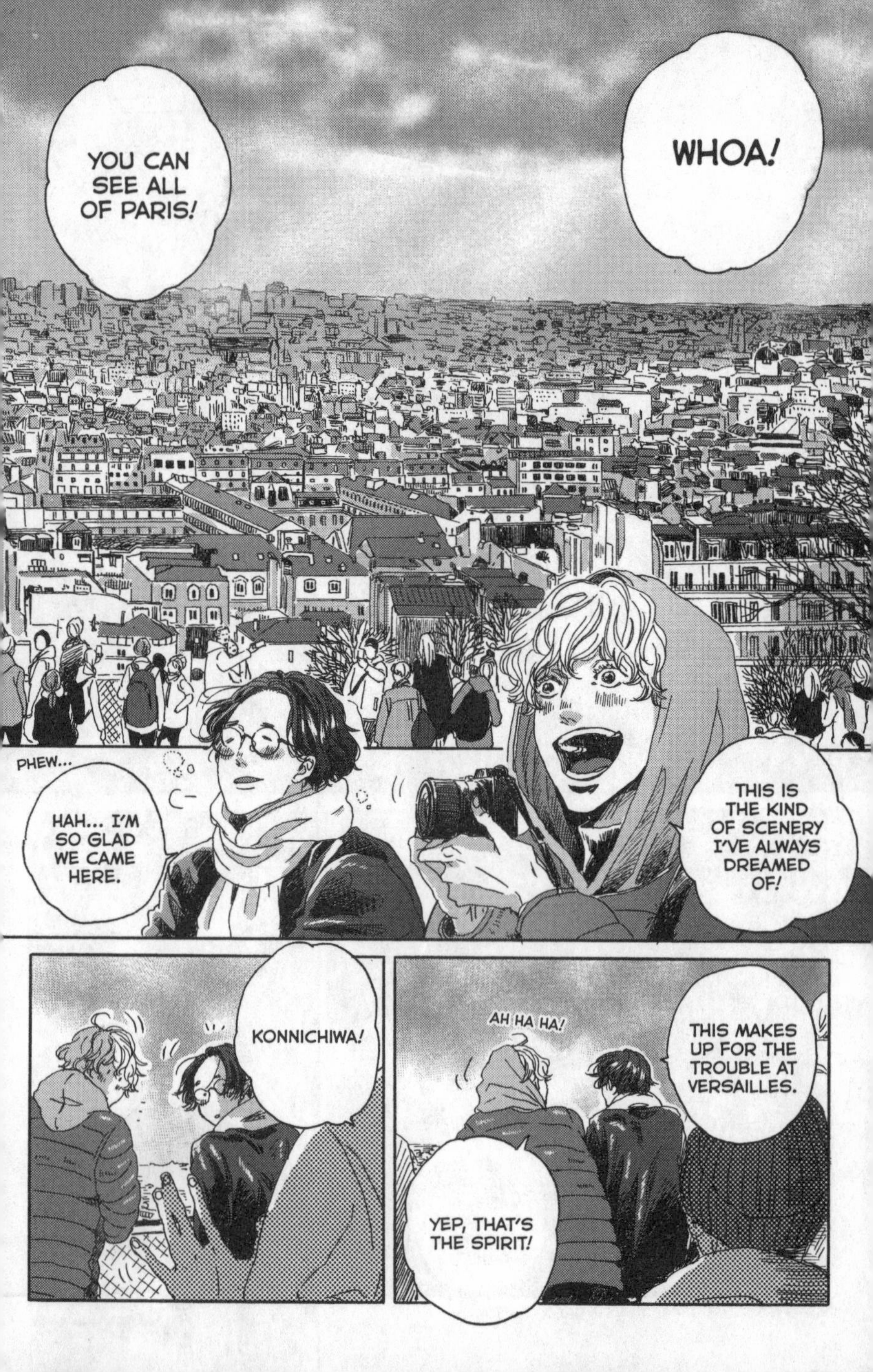
WHOA!
YOU CAN SEE ALL OF PARIS!
THIS IS THE KIND OF SCENERY I'VE ALWAYS DREAMED OF!
PHEW...
HAH... I'M SO GLAD WE CAME HERE.
THIS MAKES UP FOR THE TROUBLE AT VERSAILLES.
AH HA HA!
YEP, THAT'S THE SPIRIT!
KONNICHIWA!

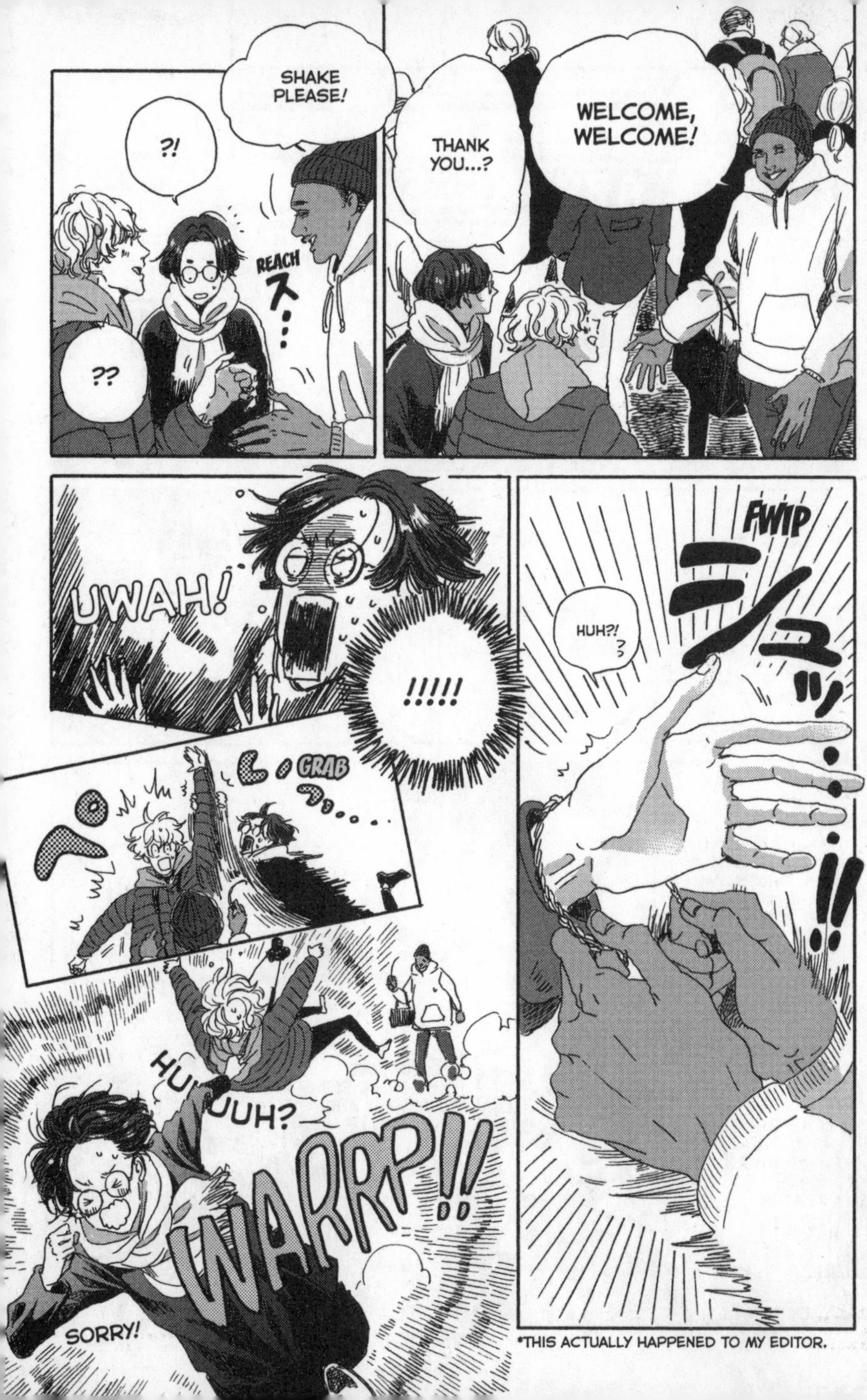
WELCOME, WELCOME!
THANK YOU...?
SHAKE PLEASE!
?!
REACH
??
FWIP
HUH?!
!!
UWAH!
!!!!!
GRAB
HUUUUH?
WARRP!!
SORRY!

*THIS ACTUALLY HAPPENED TO MY EDITOR.

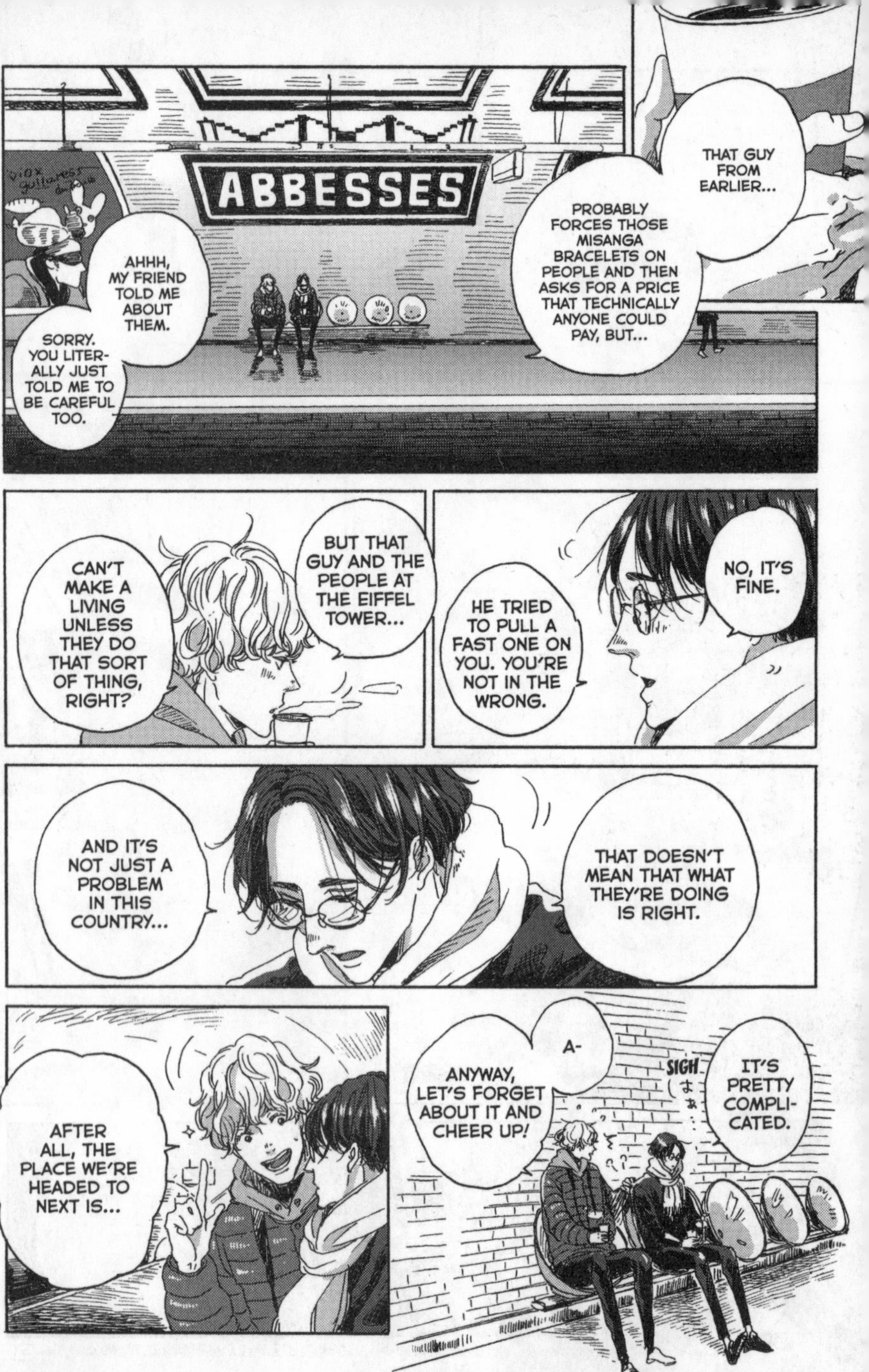
THAT GUY FROM EARLIER...
PROBABLY FORCES THOSE MISANGA BRACELETS ON PEOPLE AND THEN ASKS FOR A PRICE THAT TECHNICALLY ANYONE COULD PAY, BUT...
ABBESSES
AHHH, MY FRIEND TOLD ME ABOUT THEM.
SORRY. YOU LITER-ALLY JUST TOLD ME TO BE CAREFUL TOO.
NO, IT'S FINE.
HE TRIED TO PULL A FAST ONE ON YOU. YOU'RE NOT IN THE WRONG.
BUT THAT GUY AND THE PEOPLE AT THE EIFFEL TOWER...
CAN'T MAKE A LIVING UNLESS THEY DO THAT SORT OF THING, RIGHT?
THAT DOESN'T MEAN THAT WHAT THEY'RE DOING IS RIGHT.
AND IT'S NOT JUST A PROBLEM IN THIS COUNTRY...
IT'S PRETTY COMPLI-CATED.
SIGH はぁ…
A-
ANYWAY, LET'S FORGET ABOUT IT AND CHEER UP!
AFTER ALL, THE PLACE WE'RE HEADED TO NEXT IS...

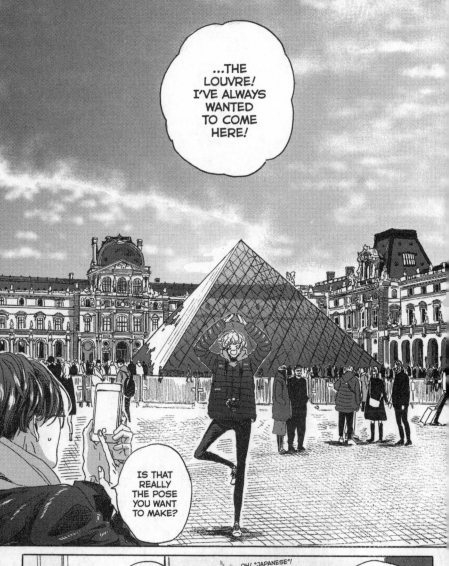

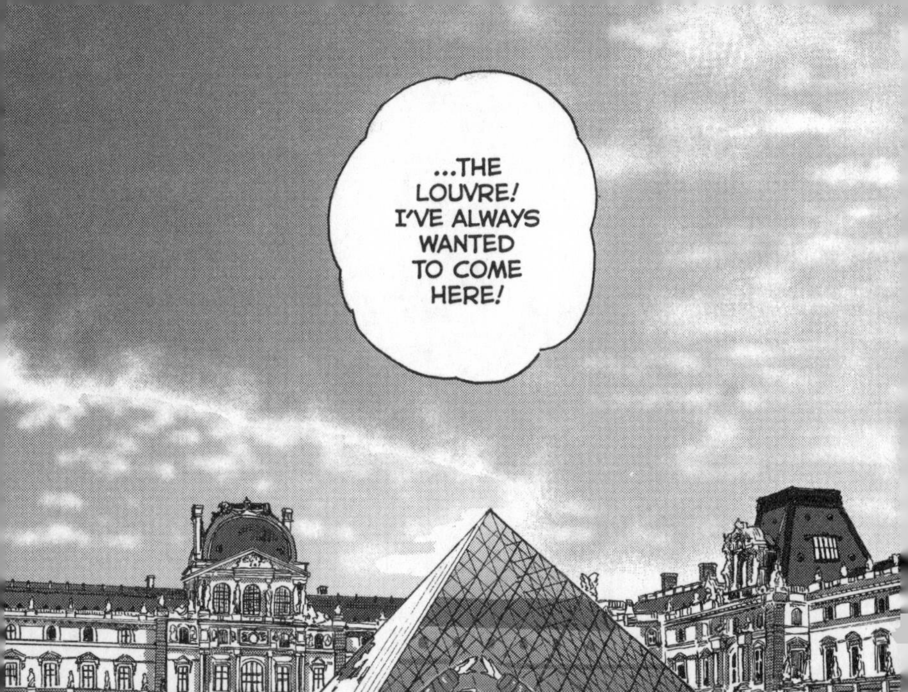
...THE LOUVRE! I'VE ALWAYS WANTED TO COME HERE!
IS THAT REALLY THE POSE YOU WANT TO MAKE?

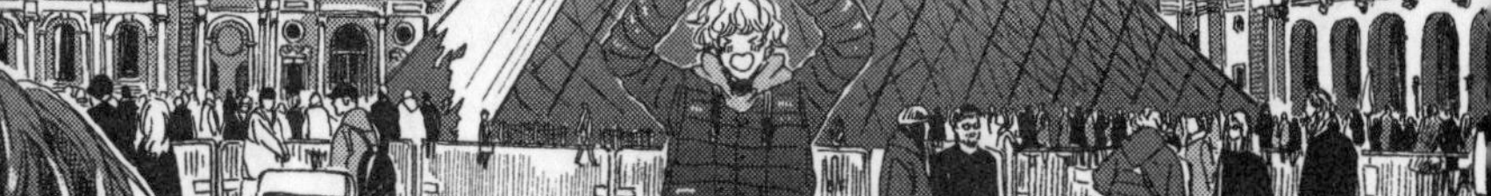
I THOUGHT THERE'D BE A LINE TO GET IN, BUT THERE'S NOT.
OH! "JAPANESE"!
THE SECURITY CHECK JUST TOOK A LITTLE TIME.
THERE PROBABLY AREN'T MANY PEOPLE SINCE WINTER IS THE OFF-SEASON FOR TOUR-ISTS.

THERE ARE OTHER VENDING MACHINES NEAR THE TICKET MACHINES. YOU CAN EVEN SET THE LANGUAGE TO JAPANESE!

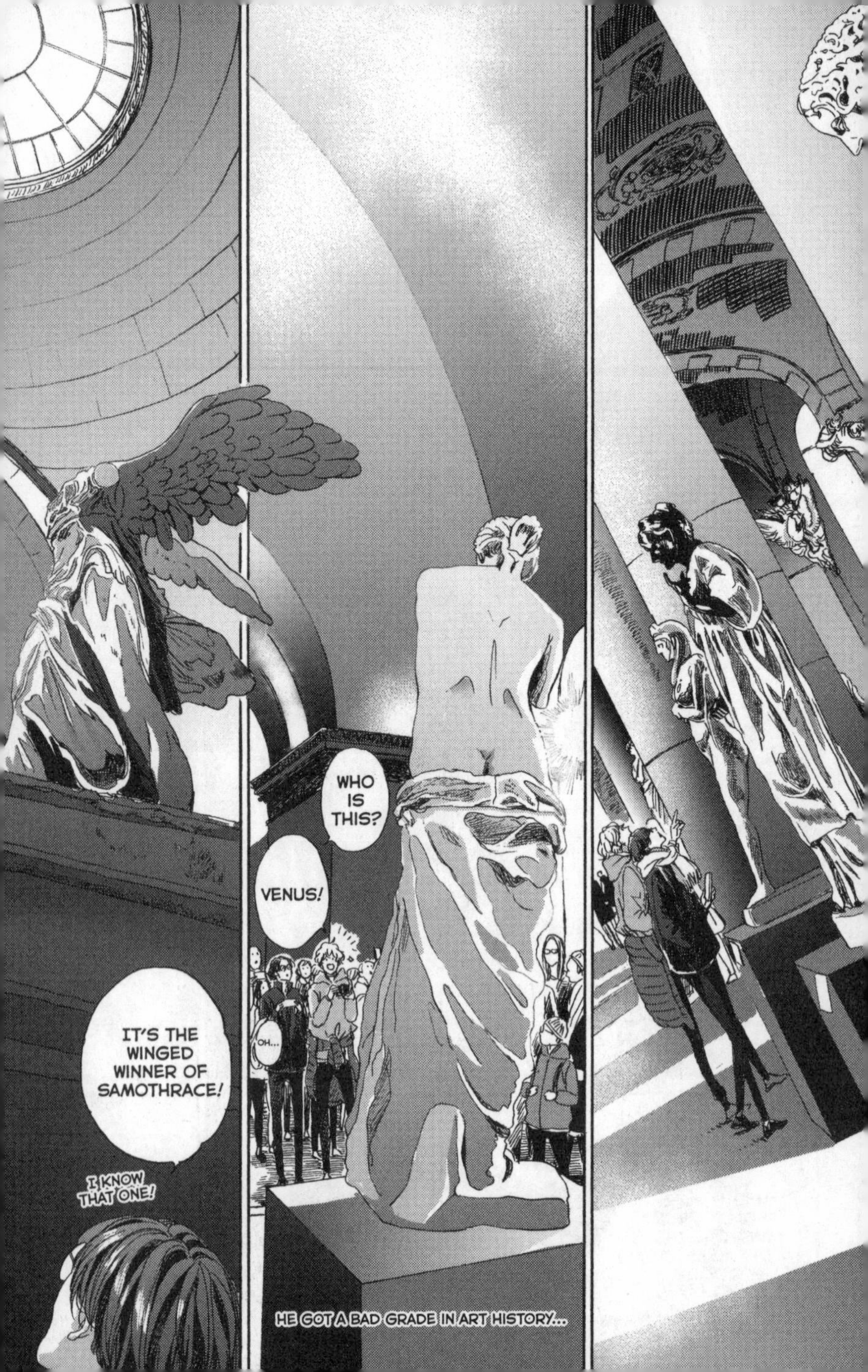
WHO IS THIS?
VENUS!
OH...
HE GOT A BAD GRADE IN ART HISTORY...
IT'S THE WINGED WINNER OF SAMOTHRACE!
I KNOW THAT ONE!

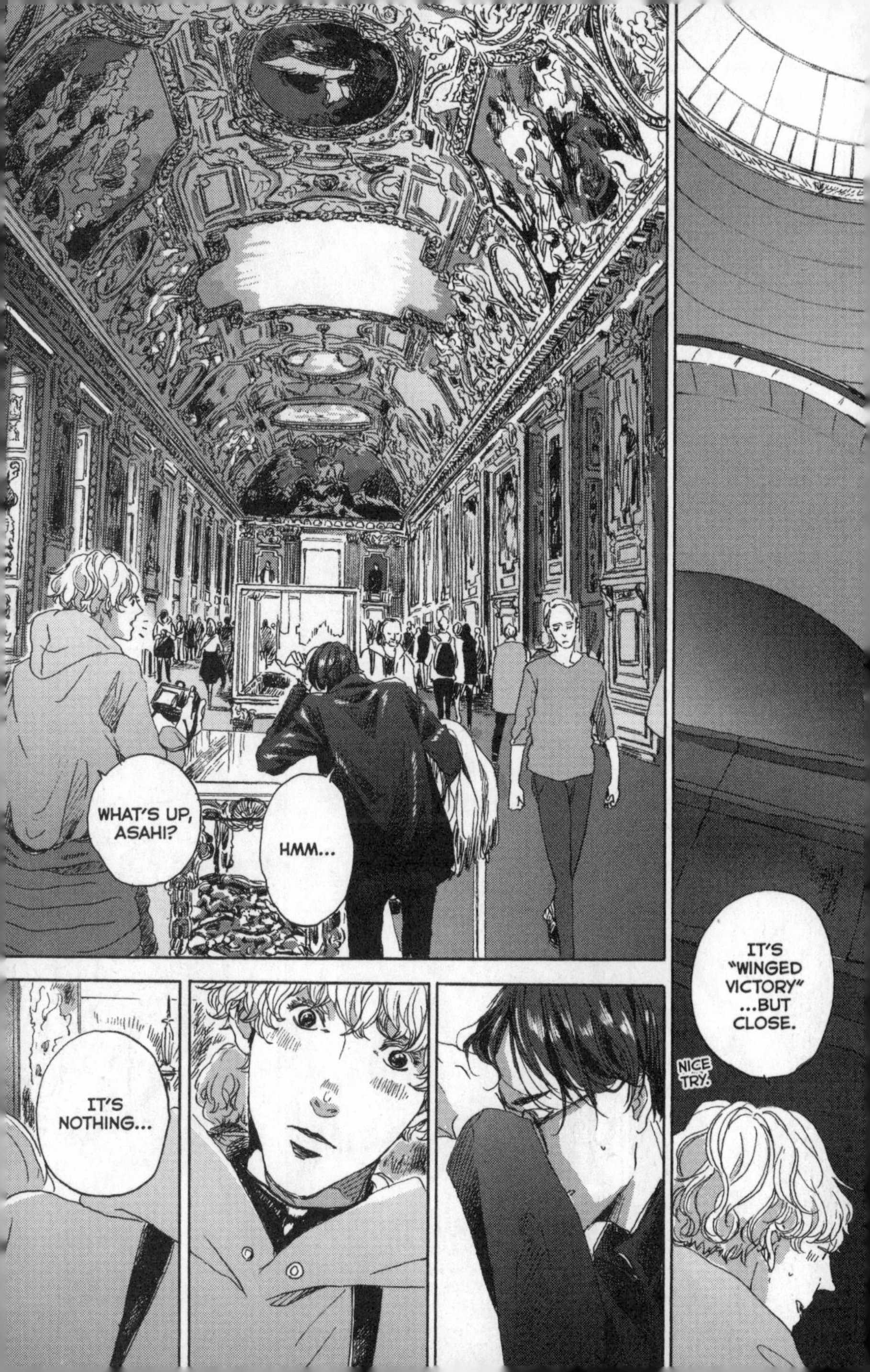
IT'S "WINGED VICTORY" ...BUT CLOSE.
NICE TRY.
HMM...
WHAT'S UP, ASAHI?
IT'S NOTHING...

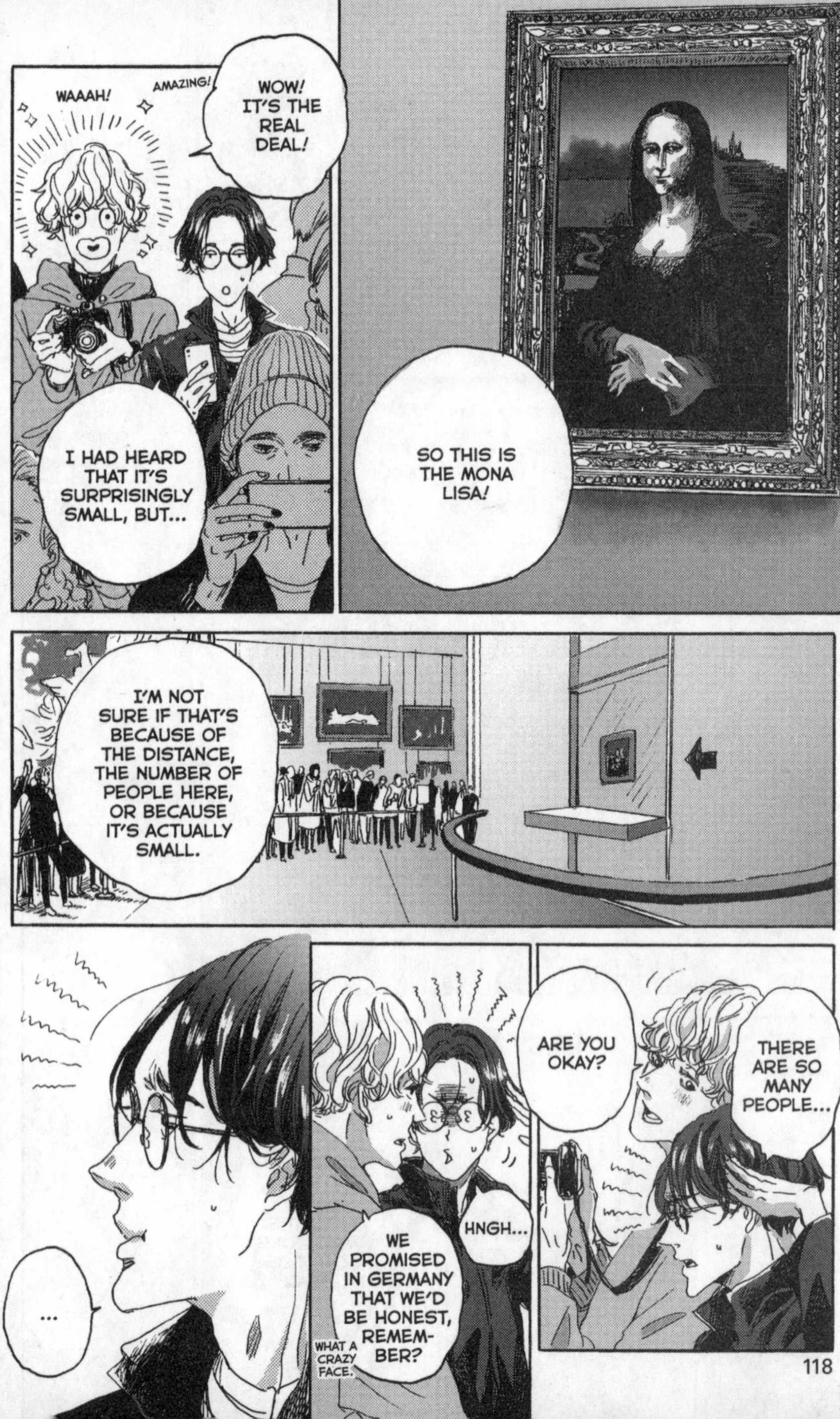
SO THIS IS THE MONA LISA!
WOW! IT'S THE REAL DEAL!
AMAZING!
WAAAH!
I HAD HEARD THAT IT'S SURPRISINGLY SMALL, BUT...
I'M NOT SURE IF THAT'S BECAUSE OF THE DISTANCE, THE NUMBER OF PEOPLE HERE, OR BECAUSE IT'S ACTUALLY SMALL.
THERE ARE SO MANY PEOPLE...
ARE YOU OKAY?
HNGH...
WE PROMISED IN GERMANY THAT WE'D BE HONEST, REMEMBER?
WHAT A CRAZY FACE.
...

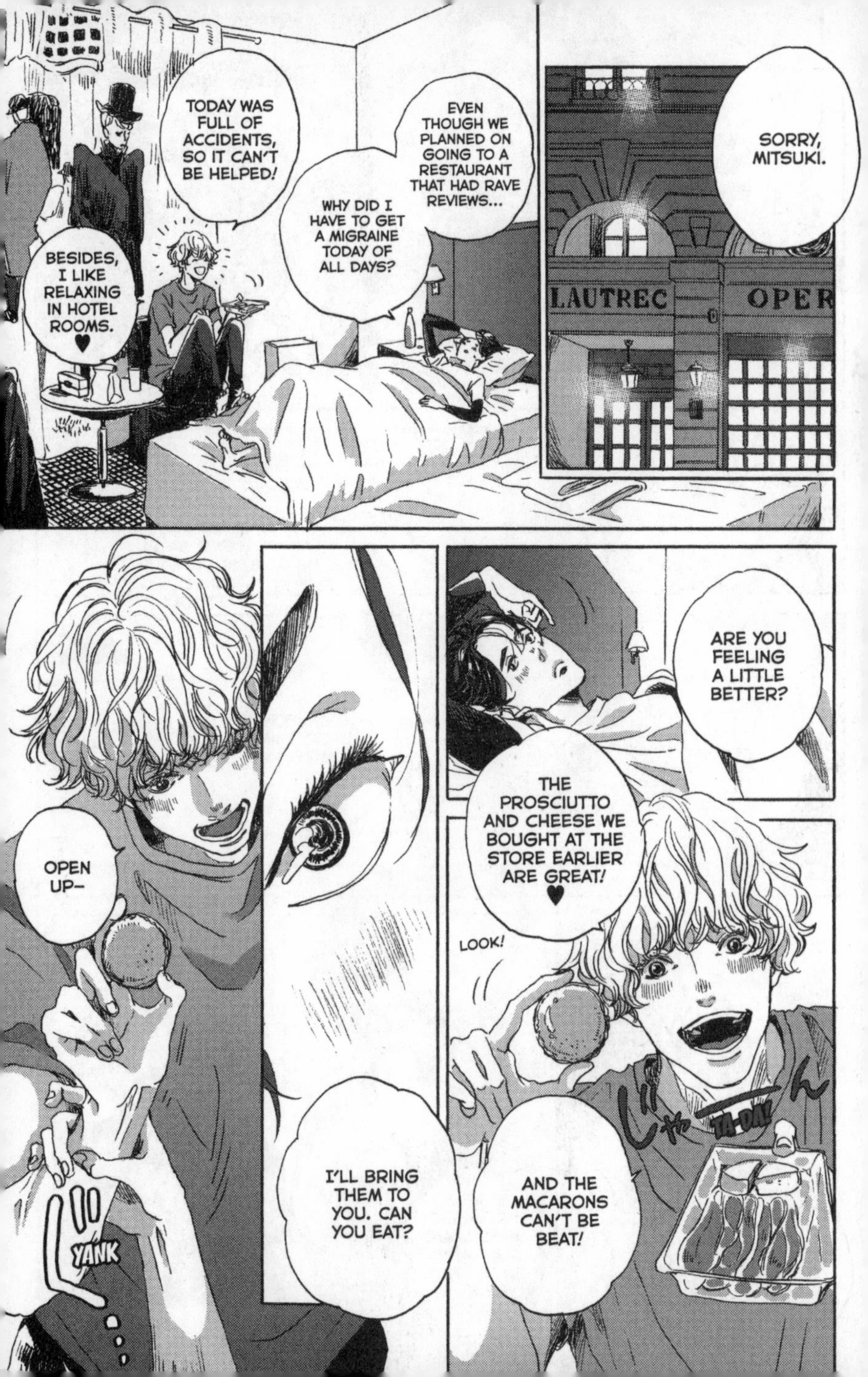
LAUTREC
OPER
SORRY, MITSUKI.
EVEN THOUGH WE PLANNED ON GOING TO A RESTAURANT THAT HAD RAVE REVIEWS...
WHY DID I HAVE TO GET A MIGRAINE TODAY OF ALL DAYS?
TODAY WAS FULL OF ACCIDENTS, SO IT CAN'T BE HELPED!
BESIDES, I LIKE RELAXING IN HOTEL ROOMS. ♥
ARE YOU FEELING A LITTLE BETTER?
THE PROSCIUTTO AND CHEESE WE BOUGHT AT THE STORE EARLIER ARE GREAT! ♥
LOOK!
TA-DA!
AND THE MACARONS CAN'T BE BEAT!
I'LL BRING THEM TO YOU. CAN YOU EAT?
OPEN UP–
YANK

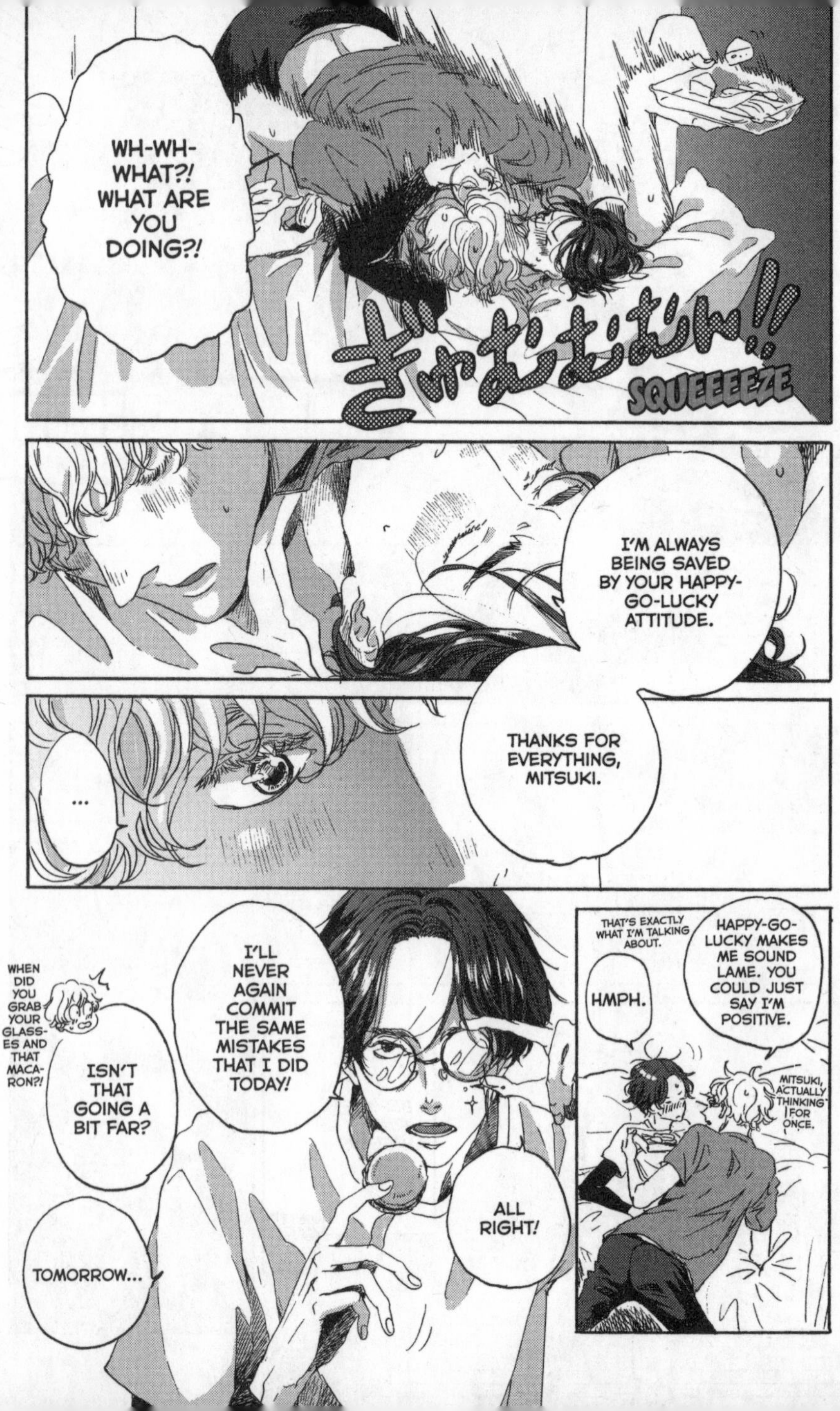
WH-WH-WHAT?! WHAT ARE YOU DOING?!
SQUEEEEEZE
I'M ALWAYS BEING SAVED BY YOUR HAPPY-GO-LUCKY ATTITUDE.
THANKS FOR EVERYTHING, MITSUKI.
...
HAPPY-GO-LUCKY MAKES ME SOUND LAME. YOU COULD JUST SAY I'M POSITIVE.
THAT'S EXACTLY WHAT I'M TALKING ABOUT.
HMPH.
MITSUKI, ACTUALLY THINKING FOR ONCE.
I'LL NEVER AGAIN COMMIT THE SAME MISTAKES THAT I DID TODAY!
ISN'T THAT GOING A BIT FAR?
WHEN DID YOU GRAB YOUR GLASSES AND THAT MACARON?!
ALL RIGHT!
TOMORROW...

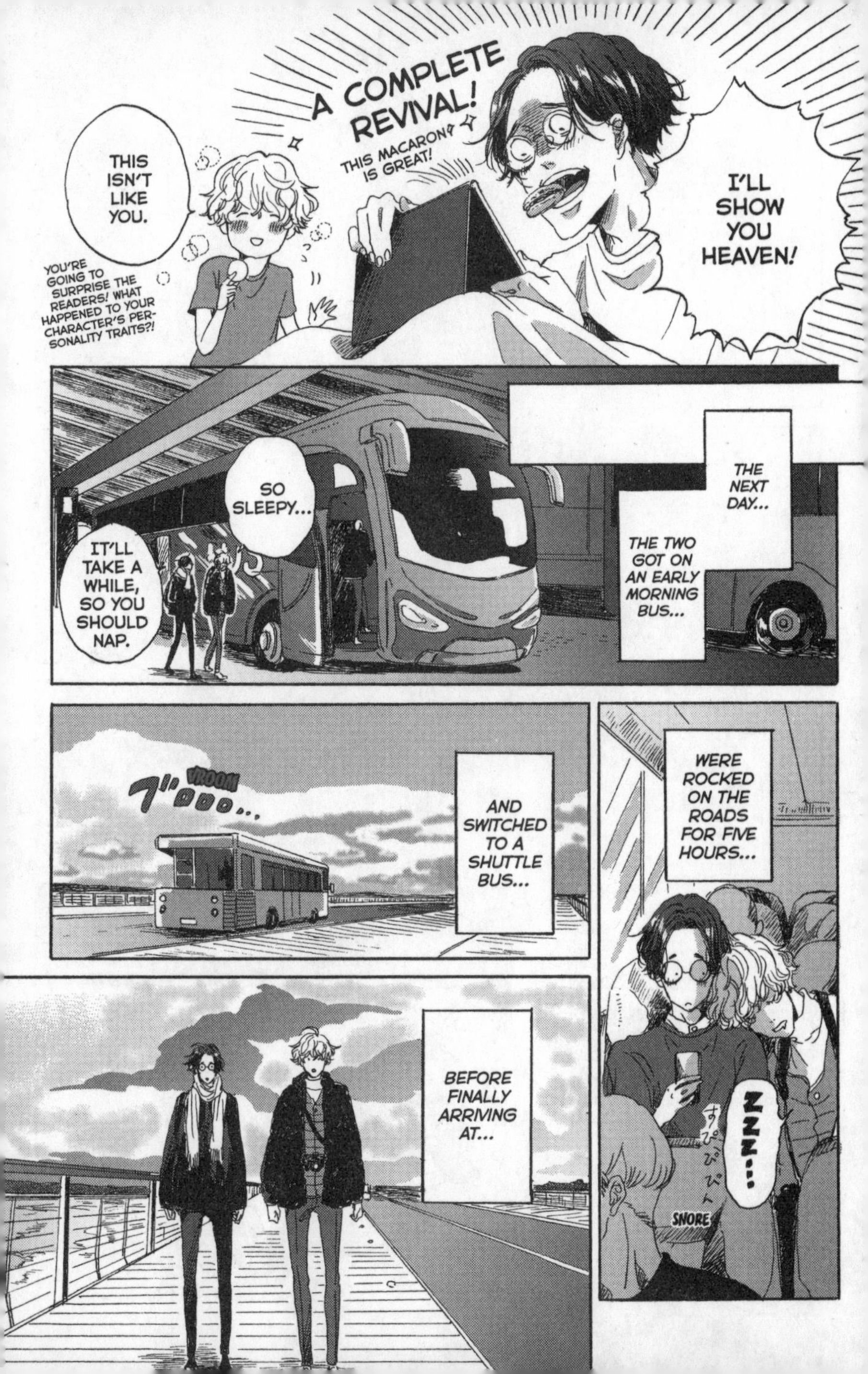
I'LL SHOW YOU HEAVEN!
A COMPLETE REVIVAL!
THIS MACARON♡ IS GREAT!
THIS ISN'T LIKE YOU.
YOU'RE GOING TO SURPRISE THE READERS! WHAT HAPPENED TO YOUR CHARACTER'S PER-SONALITY TRAITS?!
THE NEXT DAY...
THE TWO GOT ON AN EARLY MORNING BUS...
SO SLEEPY...
IT'LL TAKE A WHILE, SO YOU SHOULD NAP.
WERE ROCKED ON THE ROADS FOR FIVE HOURS...
ZZZ...
すぴぴぴん
SNORE
AND SWITCHED TO A SHUTTLE BUS...
ブロロロ...
VROOM
BEFORE FINALLY ARRIVING AT...

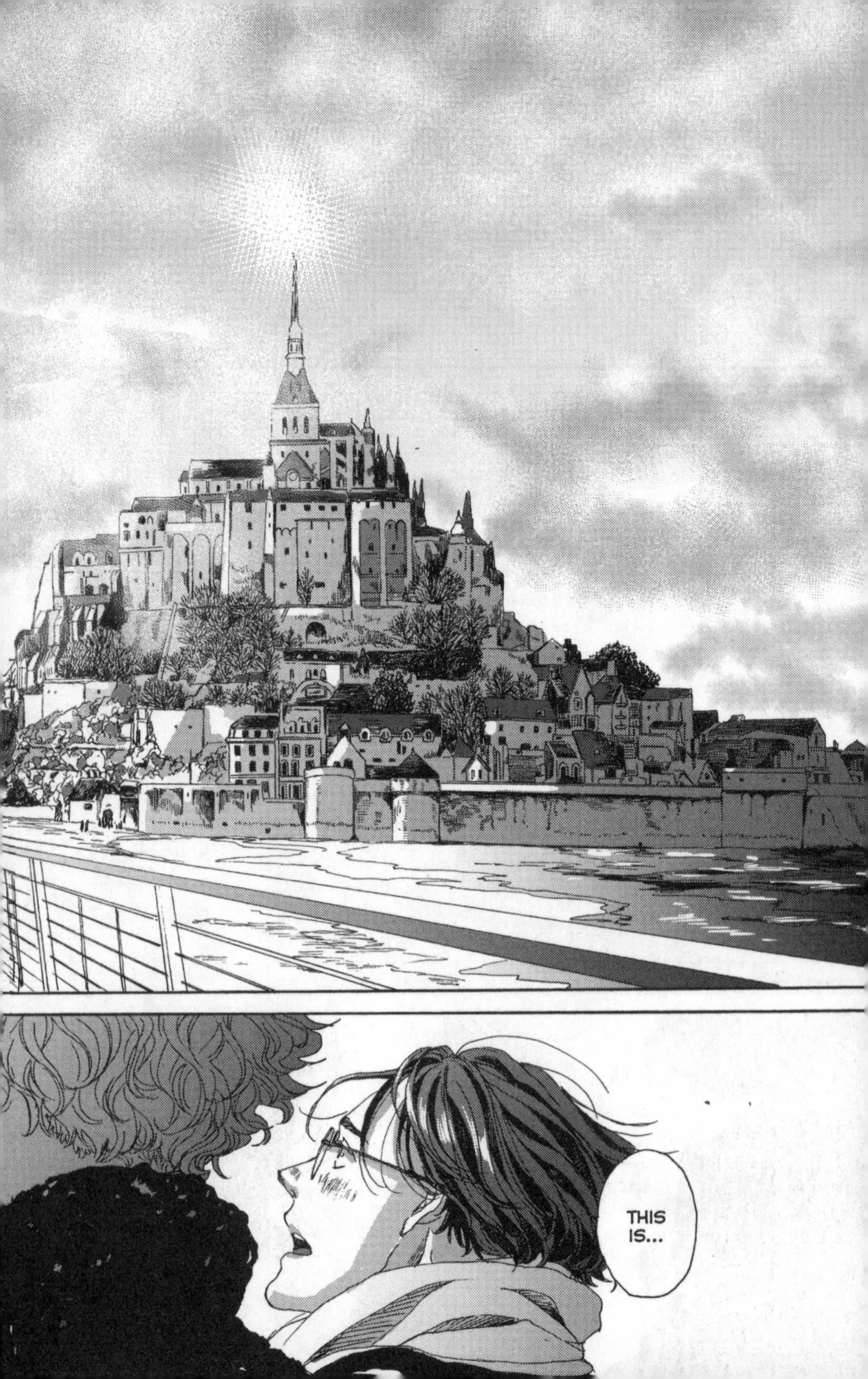
THIS IS...

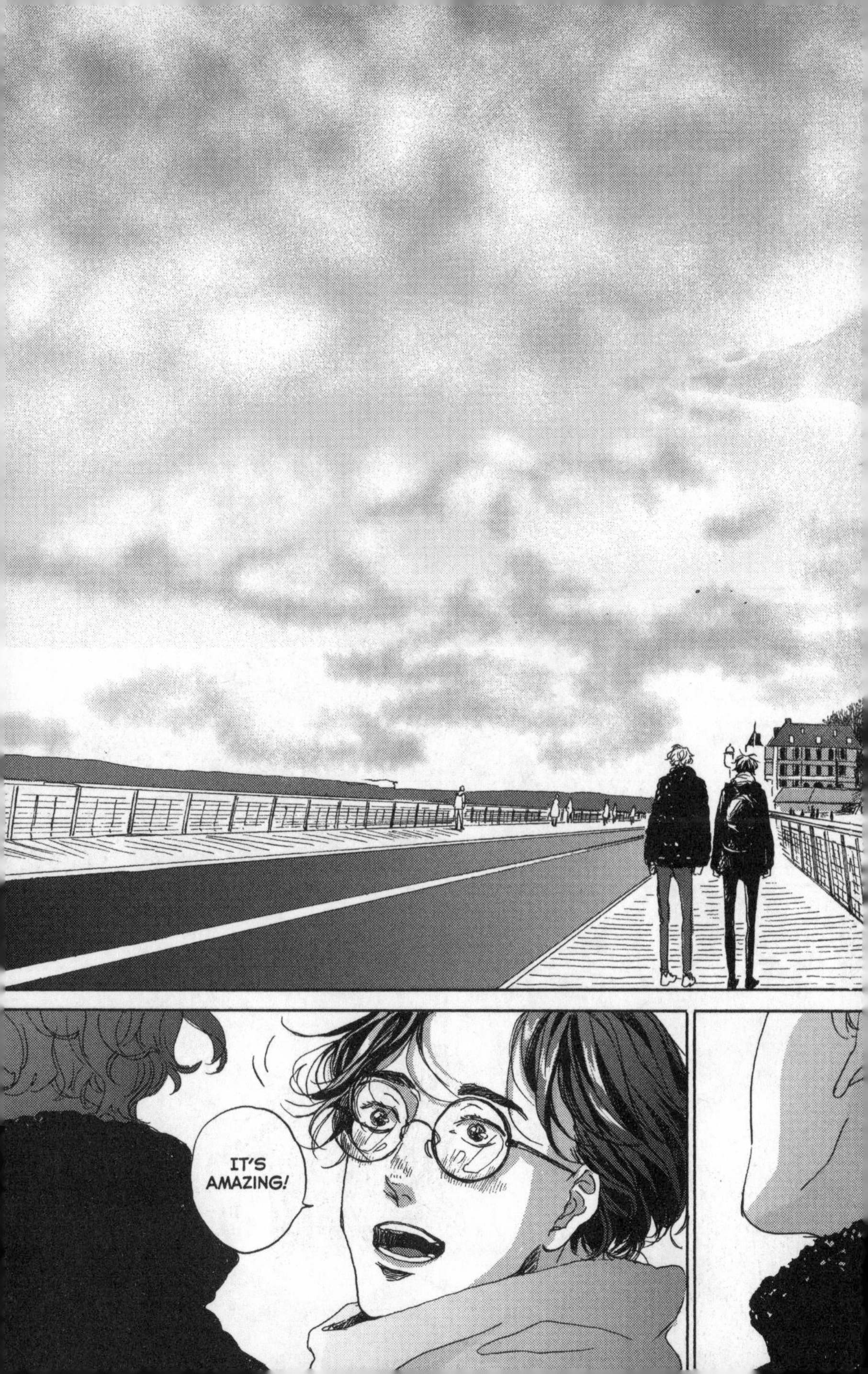
IT'S AMAZING!

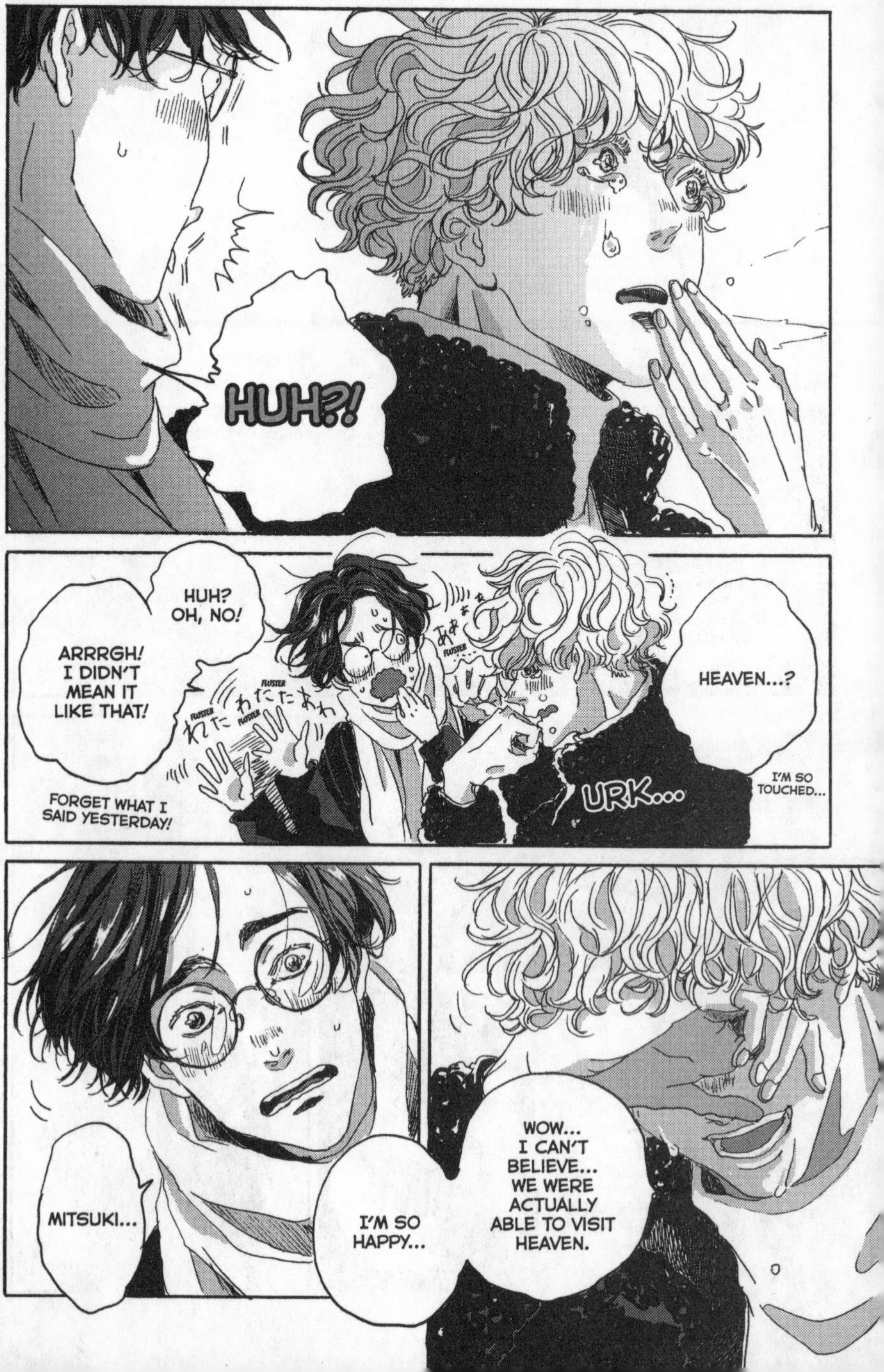
HUH?!
HEAVEN...?
I'M SO TOUCHED...
URK...
FLUSTER
HUH? OH, NO!
ARRRGH! I DIDN'T MEAN IT LIKE THAT!
FLUSTER FLUSTER FLUSTER
FORGET WHAT I SAID YESTERDAY!
WOW... I CAN'T BELIEVE... WE WERE ACTUALLY ABLE TO VISIT HEAVEN.
I'M SO HAPPY...
MITSUKI...

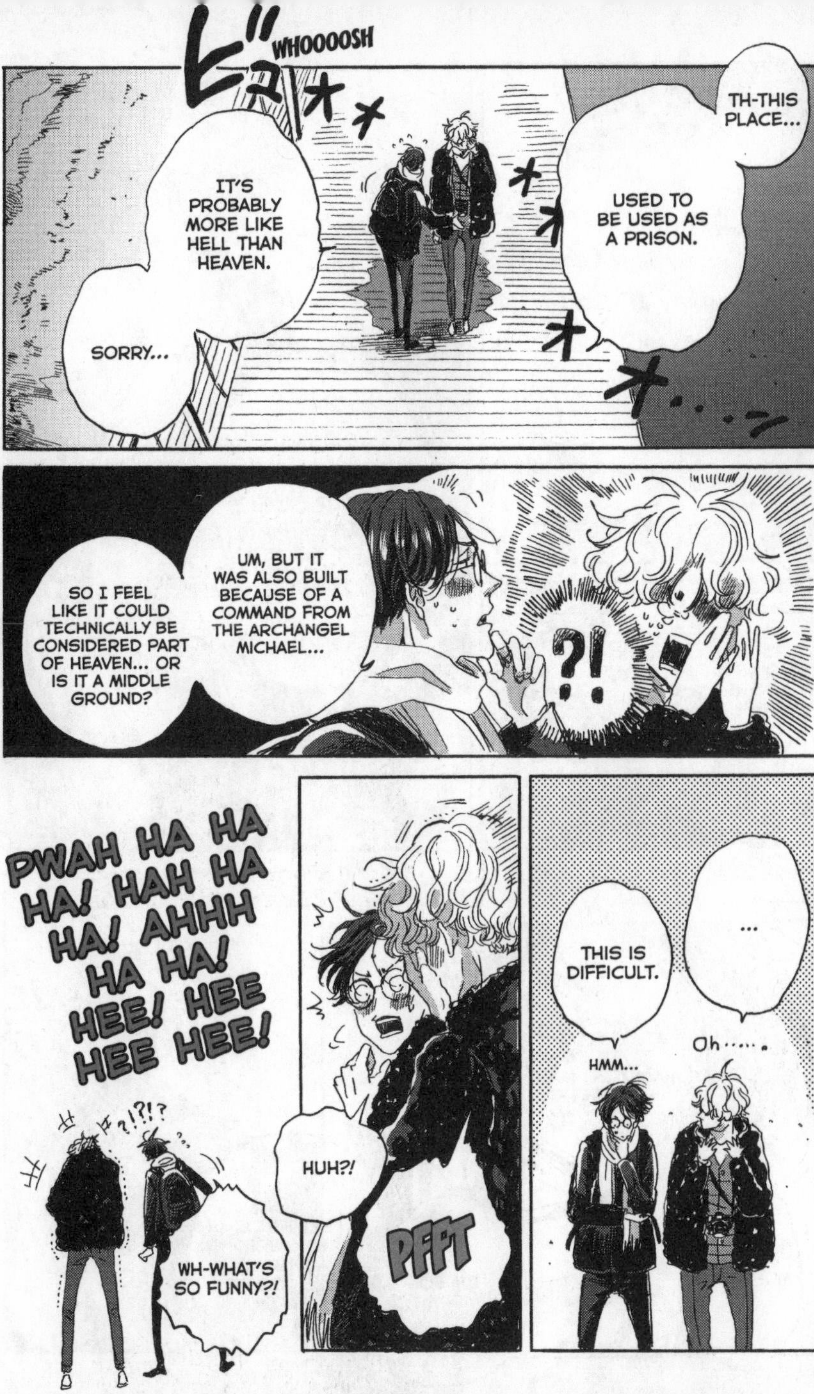
WHOOOOSH
TH-THIS PLACE...
USED TO BE USED AS A PRISON.
IT'S PROBABLY MORE LIKE HELL THAN HEAVEN.
SORRY...
UM, BUT IT WAS ALSO BUILT BECAUSE OF A COMMAND FROM THE ARCHANGEL MICHAEL...
SO I FEEL LIKE IT COULD TECHNICALLY BE CONSIDERED PART OF HEAVEN... OR IS IT A MIDDLE GROUND?
?!
...
THIS IS DIFFICULT.
Oh.....
HMM...
HUH?!
PFFT
PWAH HA HA HA! HAH HA HA! AHHH HA HA! HEE! HEE HEE HEE!
WH-WHAT'S SO FUNNY?!

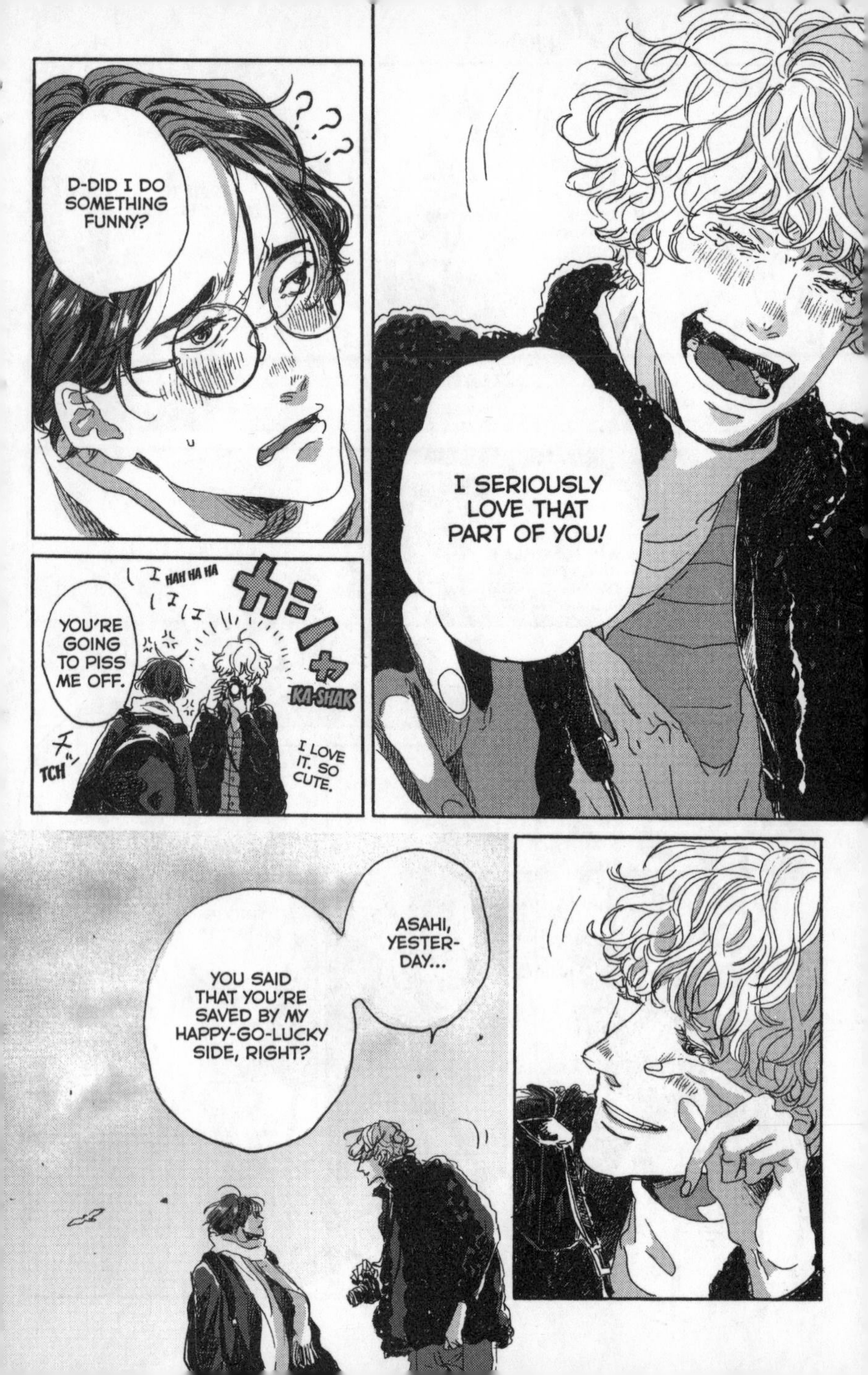
I SERIOUSLY LOVE THAT PART OF YOU!
D-DID I DO SOMETHING FUNNY?
KA-SHAK
HAH HA HA
YOU'RE GOING TO PISS ME OFF.
I LOVE IT. SO CUTE.
TCH
ASAHI, YESTER-DAY...
YOU SAID THAT YOU'RE SAVED BY MY HAPPY-GO-LUCKY SIDE, RIGHT?

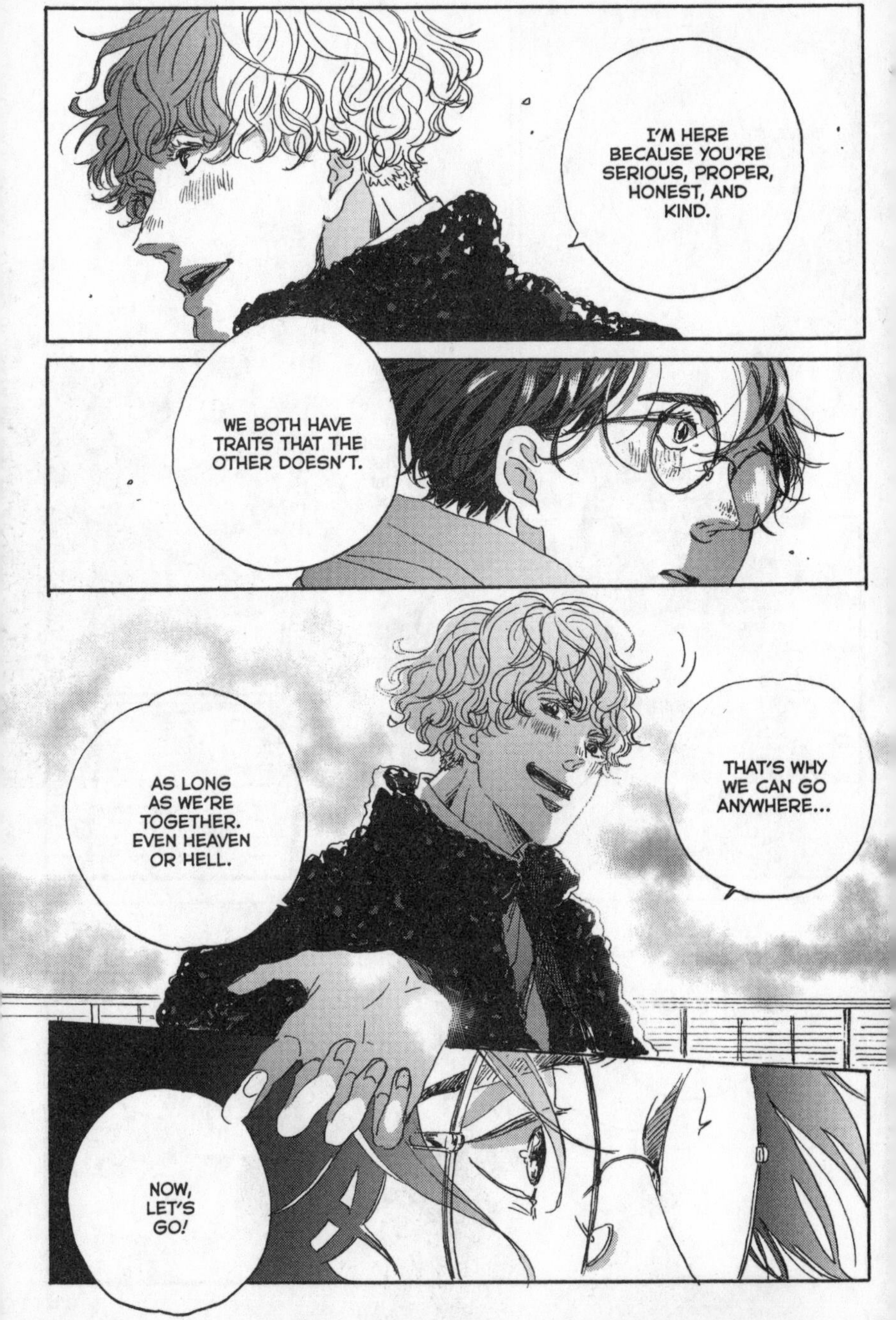
I'M HERE BECAUSE YOU'RE SERIOUS, PROPER, HONEST, AND KIND.
WE BOTH HAVE TRAITS THAT THE OTHER DOESN'T.
THAT'S WHY WE CAN GO ANYWHERE...
AS LONG AS WE'RE TOGETHER. EVEN HEAVEN OR HELL.
NOW, LET'S GO!

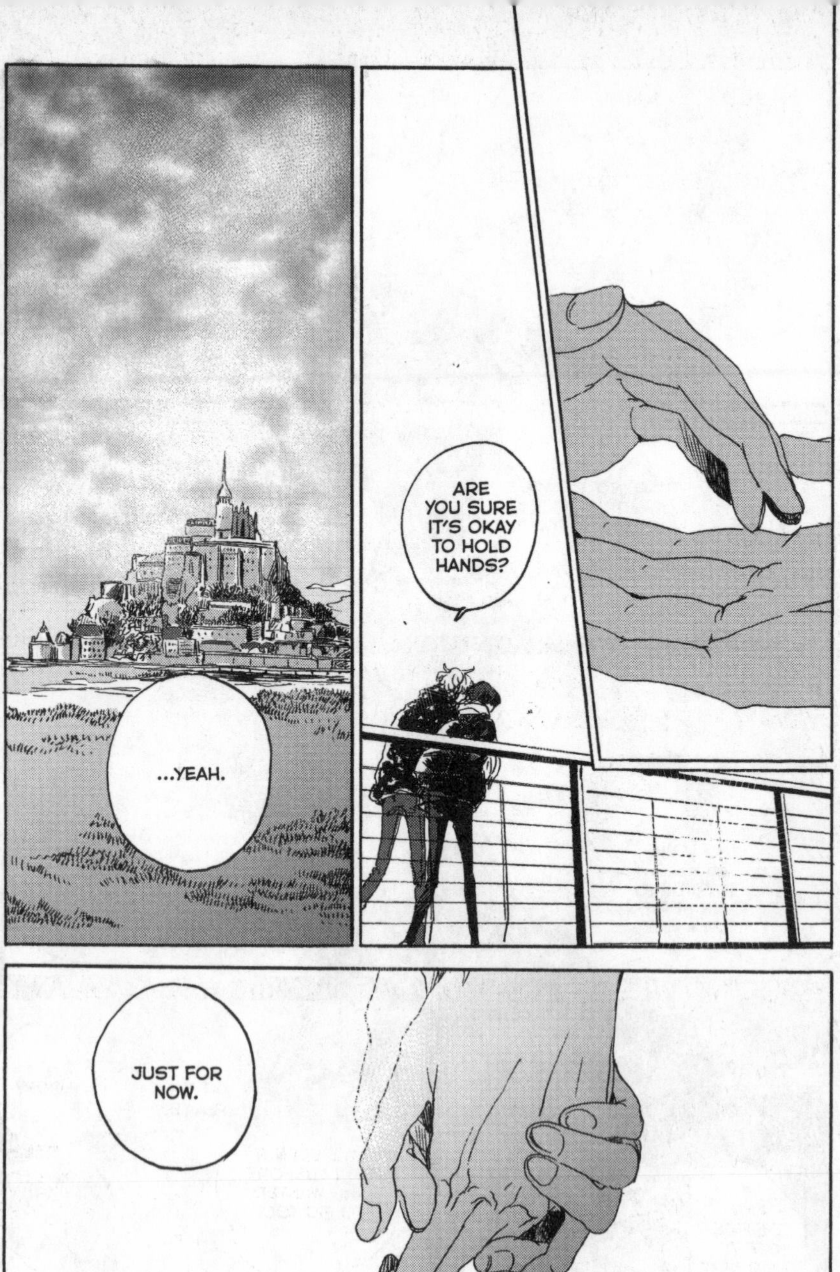
ARE YOU SURE IT'S OKAY TO HOLD HANDS?
...YEAH.
JUST FOR NOW.

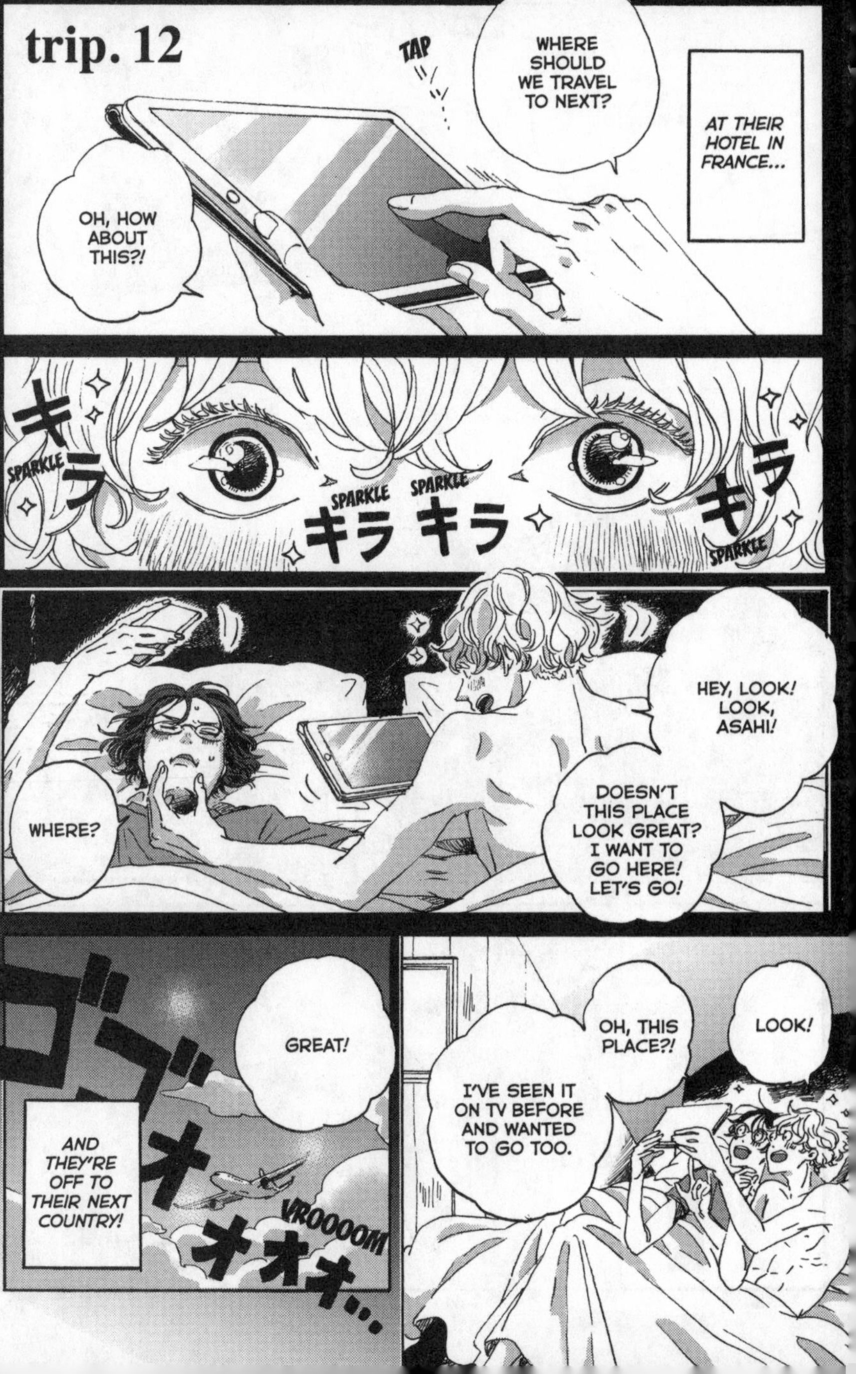
trip. 12
AT THEIR HOTEL IN FRANCE...
WHERE SHOULD WE TRAVEL TO NEXT?
TAP
OH, HOW ABOUT THIS?!
キラ
SPARKLE
キラ
SPARKLE
キラ
SPARKLE
キラ
SPARKLE
HEY, LOOK! LOOK, ASAHI!
DOESN'T THIS PLACE LOOK GREAT? I WANT TO GO HERE! LET'S GO!
WHERE?
LOOK!
OH, THIS PLACE?!
I'VE SEEN IT ON TV BEFORE AND WANTED TO GO TOO.
GREAT!
AND THEY'RE OFF TO THEIR NEXT COUNTRY!
VROOOOOM

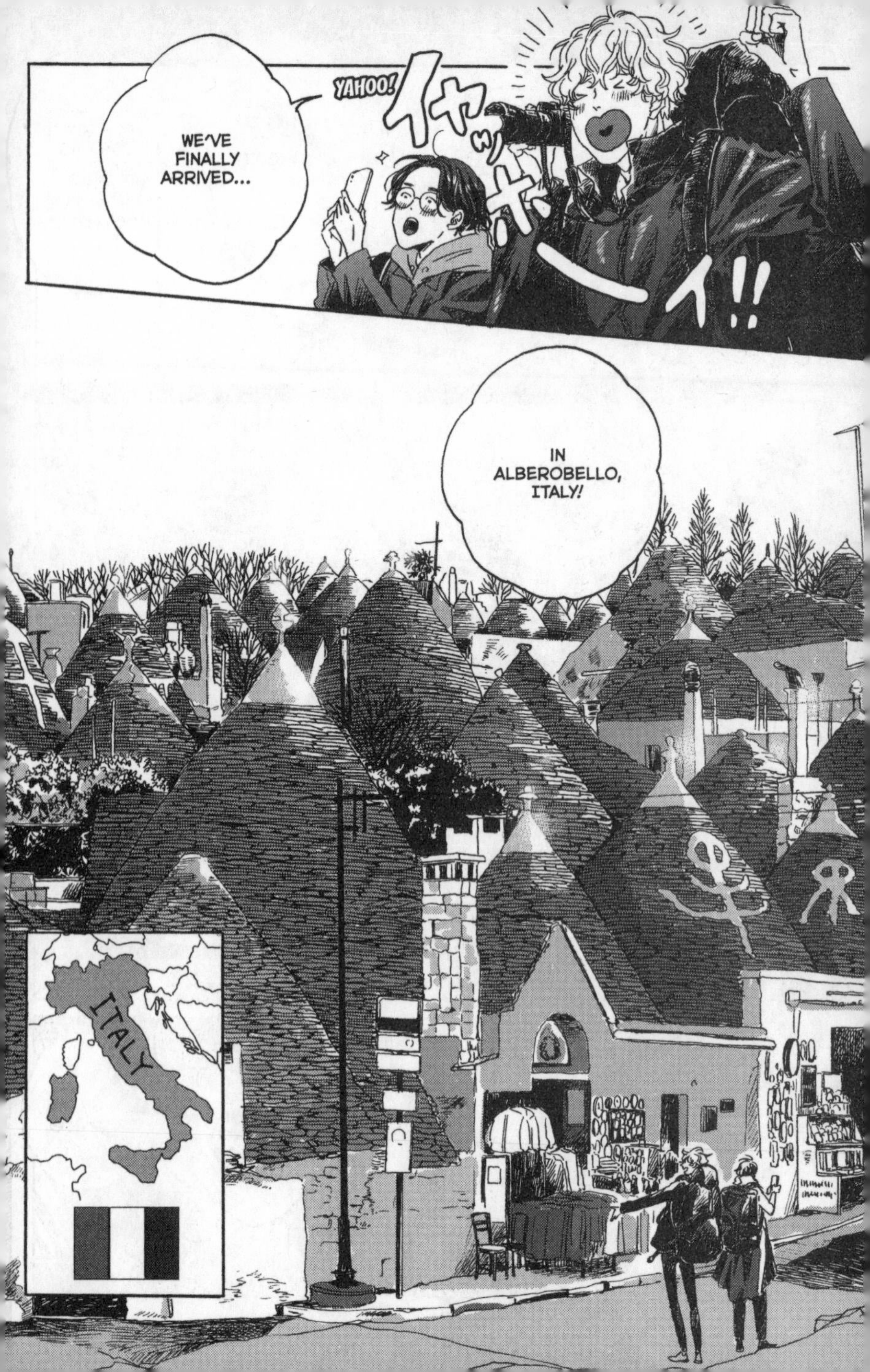
YAHOO!
イヤッホーイ!!
WE'VE FINALLY ARRIVED...
IN ALBEROBELLO, ITALY!
ITALY

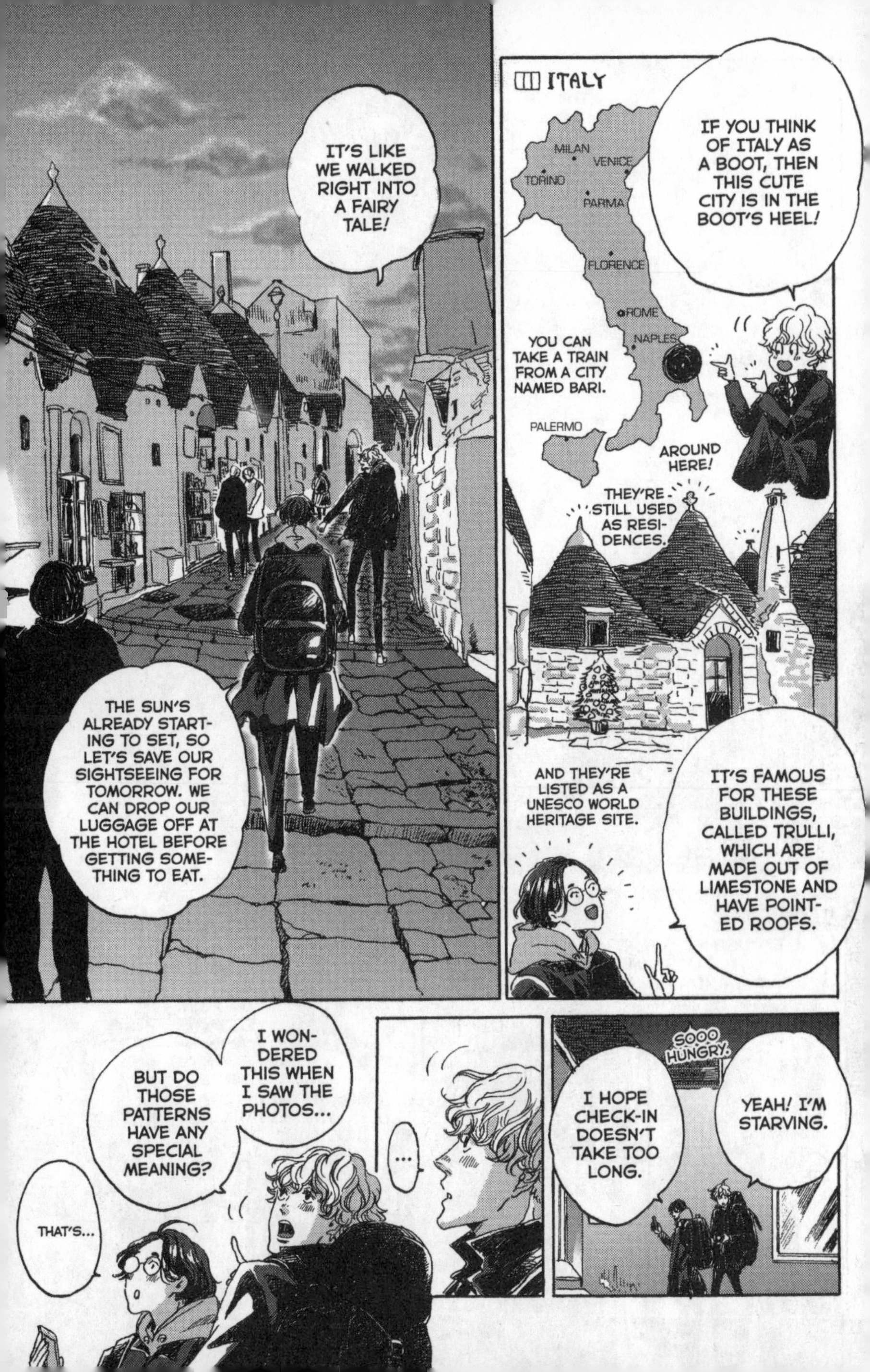
IF YOU THINK OF ITALY AS A BOOT, THEN THIS CUTE CITY IS IN THE BOOT'S HEEL!
ITALY
MILAN
VENICE
TORINO
PARMA
FLORENCE
ROME
NAPLES
PALERMO
YOU CAN TAKE A TRAIN FROM A CITY NAMED BARI.
AROUND HERE!
THEY'RE STILL USED AS RESIDENCES.
IT'S FAMOUS FOR THESE BUILDINGS, CALLED TRULLI, WHICH ARE MADE OUT OF LIMESTONE AND HAVE POINTED ROOFS.
AND THEY'RE LISTED AS A UNESCO WORLD HERITAGE SITE.
IT'S LIKE WE WALKED RIGHT INTO A FAIRY TALE!
THE SUN'S ALREADY STARTING TO SET, SO LET'S SAVE OUR SIGHTSEEING FOR TOMORROW. WE CAN DROP OUR LUGGAGE OFF AT THE HOTEL BEFORE GETTING SOMETHING TO EAT.
SOOO HUNGRY.
YEAH! I'M STARVING.
I HOPE CHECK-IN DOESN'T TAKE TOO LONG.
...
I WONDERED THIS WHEN I SAW THE PHOTOS...
BUT DO THOSE PATTERNS HAVE ANY SPECIAL MEANING?
THAT'S...

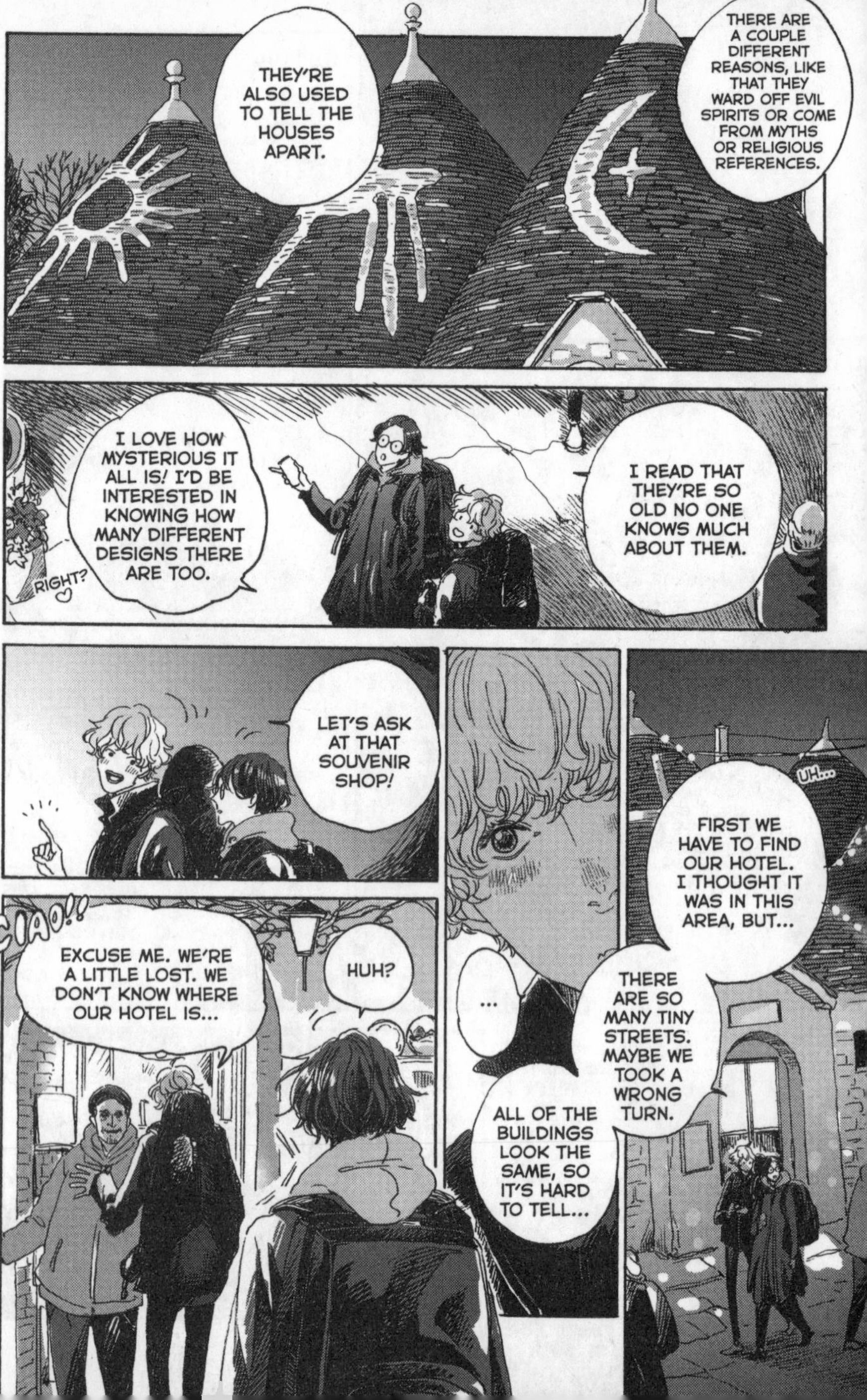
THERE ARE A COUPLE DIFFERENT REASONS, LIKE THAT THEY WARD OFF EVIL SPIRITS OR COME FROM MYTHS OR RELIGIOUS REFERENCES.
THEY'RE ALSO USED TO TELL THE HOUSES APART.
I READ THAT THEY'RE SO OLD NO ONE KNOWS MUCH ABOUT THEM.
I LOVE HOW MYSTERIOUS IT ALL IS! I'D BE INTERESTED IN KNOWING HOW MANY DIFFERENT DESIGNS THERE ARE TOO.
RIGHT? ♡
UH...
FIRST WE HAVE TO FIND OUR HOTEL. I THOUGHT IT WAS IN THIS AREA, BUT...
THERE ARE SO MANY TINY STREETS. MAYBE WE TOOK A WRONG TURN.
...
ALL OF THE BUILDINGS LOOK THE SAME, SO IT'S HARD TO TELL...
LET'S ASK AT THAT SOUVENIR SHOP!
CIAO!!
EXCUSE ME. WE'RE A LITTLE LOST. WE DON'T KNOW WHERE OUR HOTEL IS...
HUH?

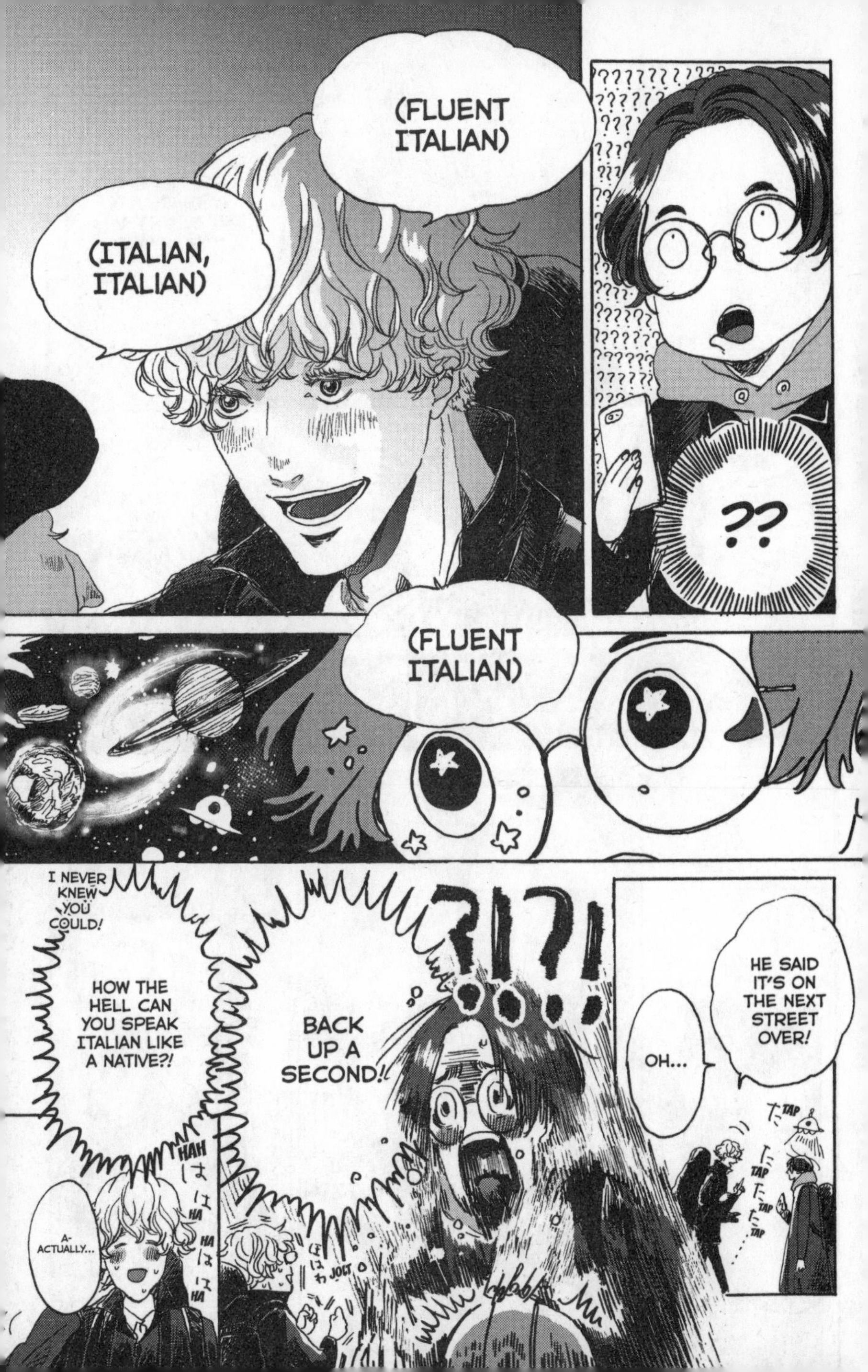
??
(FLUENT ITALIAN)
(ITALIAN, ITALIAN)
(FLUENT ITALIAN)
HE SAID IT'S ON THE NEXT STREET OVER!
OH...
TAP TAP TAP TAP
?!?!
BACK UP A SECOND!
HOW THE HELL CAN YOU SPEAK ITALIAN LIKE A NATIVE?!
I NEVER KNEW YOU COULD!
JOLT
HAH HA HA HA
A- ACTUALLY...

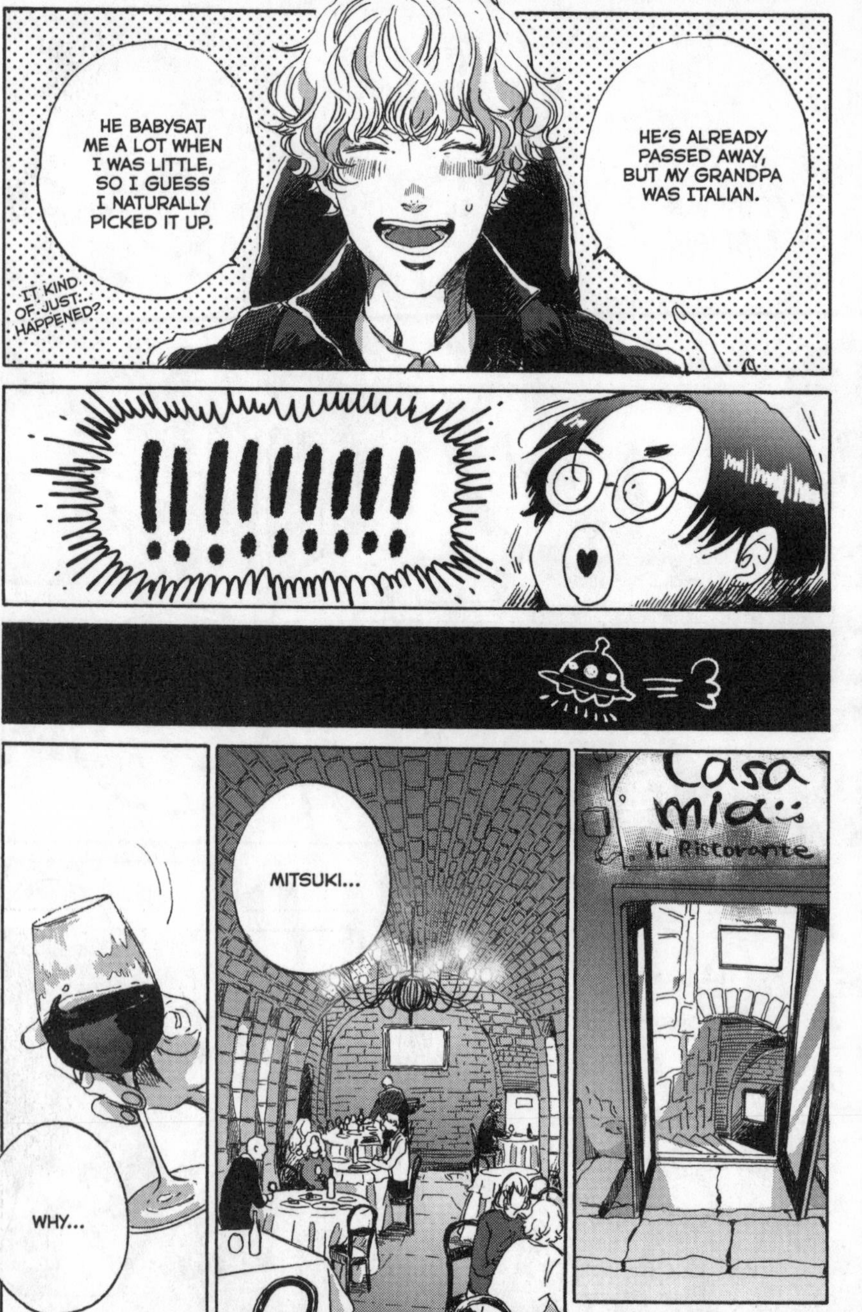
HE'S ALREADY PASSED AWAY, BUT MY GRANDPA WAS ITALIAN.
HE BABYSAT ME A LOT WHEN I WAS LITTLE, SO I GUESS I NATURALLY PICKED IT UP.
IT KIND OF JUST... HAPPENED?
!!!!!!!!
Casa mia
Il Ristorante
MITSUKI...
WHY...

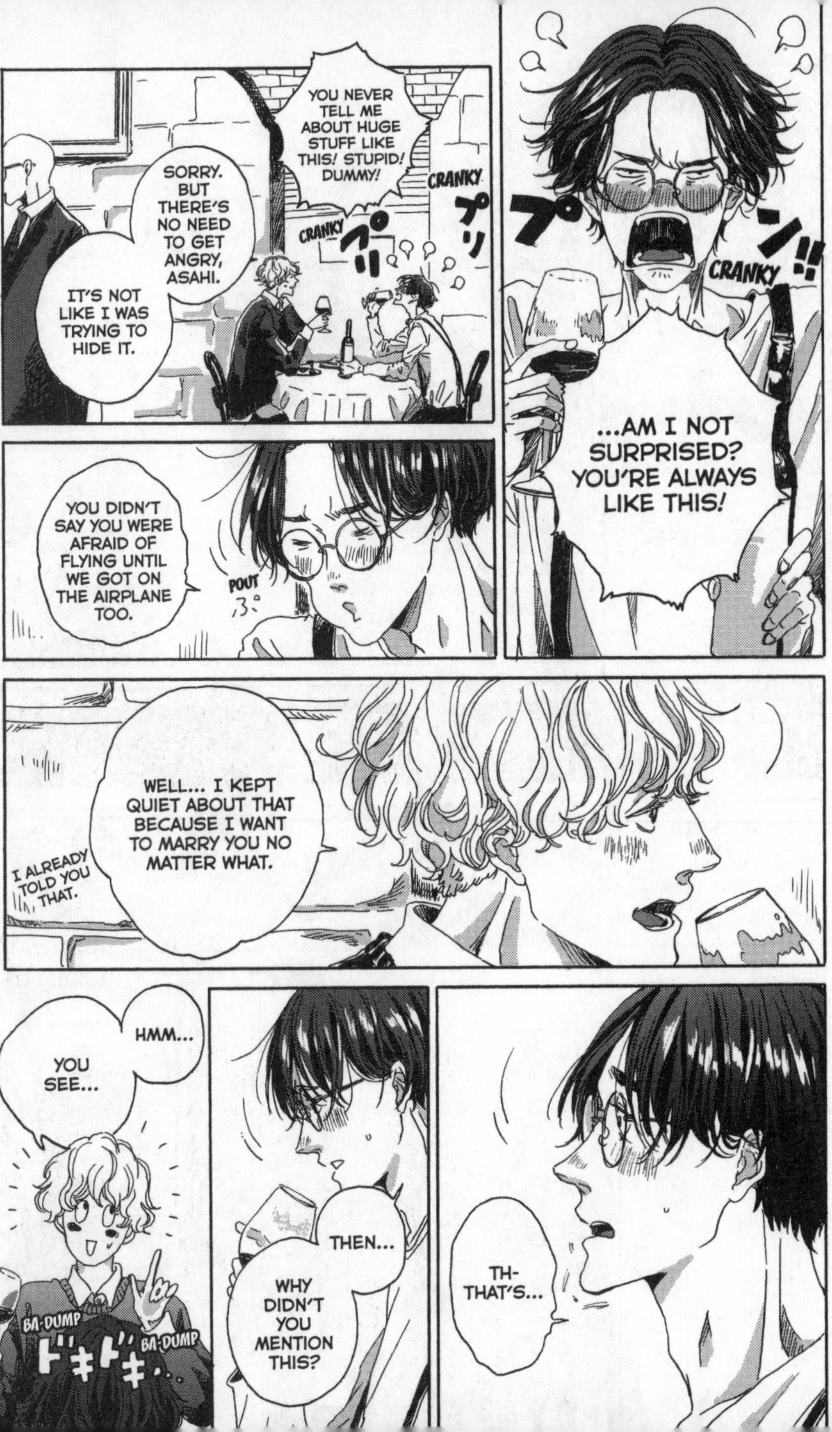
CRANKY
プンッ!!
CRANKY
...AM I NOT SURPRISED? YOU'RE ALWAYS LIKE THIS!
YOU NEVER TELL ME ABOUT HUGE STUFF LIKE THIS! STUPID! DUMMY!
CRANKY
プリ
CRANKY
プリ
SORRY. BUT THERE'S NO NEED TO GET ANGRY, ASAHI.
IT'S NOT LIKE I WAS TRYING TO HIDE IT.
POUT
ぷ
YOU DIDN'T SAY YOU WERE AFRAID OF FLYING UNTIL WE GOT ON THE AIRPLANE TOO.
WELL... I KEPT QUIET ABOUT THAT BECAUSE I WANT TO MARRY YOU NO MATTER WHAT.
I ALREADY TOLD YOU THAT.
TH- THAT'S...
THEN...
WHY DIDN'T YOU MENTION THIS?
HMM...
YOU SEE...
BA-DUMP
ドキドキ...
BA-DUMP

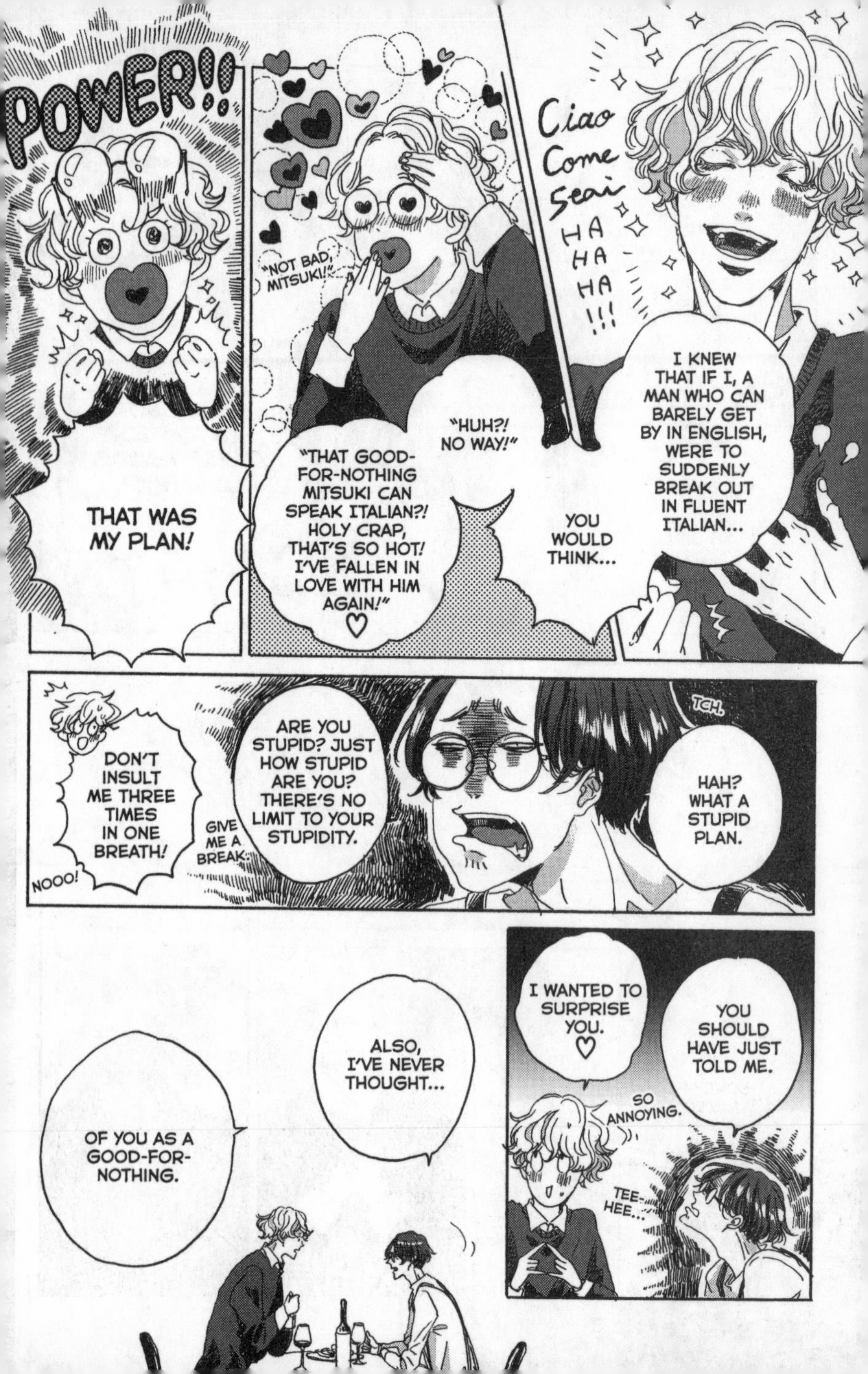
Ciao Come Seai
HA HA HA!!!
I KNEW THAT IF I, A MAN WHO CAN BARELY GET BY IN ENGLISH, WERE TO SUDDENLY BREAK OUT IN FLUENT ITALIAN...
YOU WOULD THINK...
"HUH?! NO WAY!"
"THAT GOOD-FOR-NOTHING MITSUKI CAN SPEAK ITALIAN?! HOLY CRAP, THAT'S SO HOT! I'VE FALLEN IN LOVE WITH HIM AGAIN!" ♡
"NOT BAD, MITSUKI!"
POWER!!
THAT WAS MY PLAN!
TCH.
HAH? WHAT A STUPID PLAN.
ARE YOU STUPID? JUST HOW STUPID ARE YOU? THERE'S NO LIMIT TO YOUR STUPIDITY.
GIVE ME A BREAK.
DON'T INSULT ME THREE TIMES IN ONE BREATH!
NOOO!
YOU SHOULD HAVE JUST TOLD ME.
SO ANNOYING.
I WANTED TO SURPRISE YOU. ♡
TEE-HEE...
ALSO, I'VE NEVER THOUGHT...
OF YOU AS A GOOD-FOR-NOTHING.

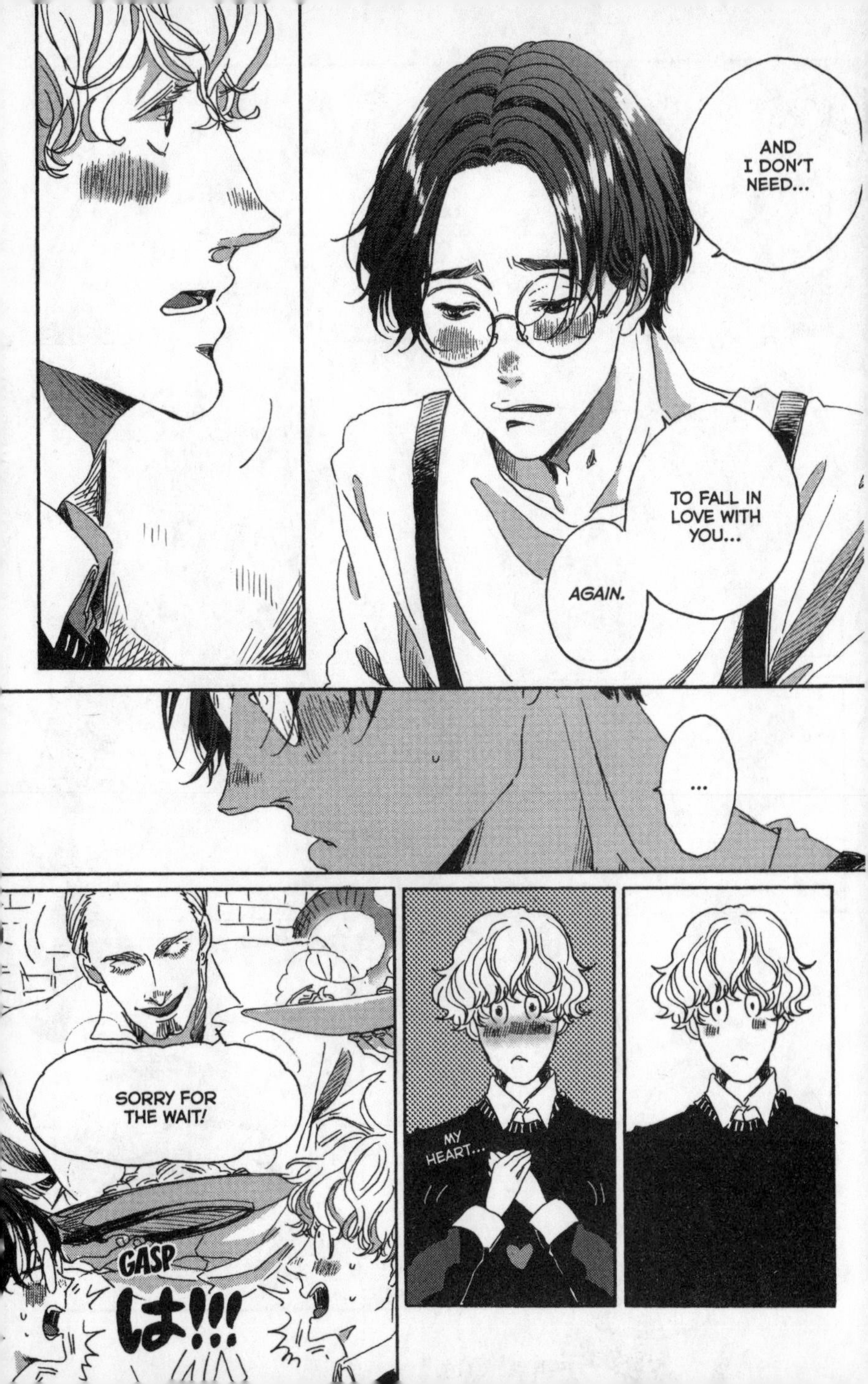
AND I DON'T NEED...
TO FALL IN LOVE WITH YOU...
AGAIN.
...
MY HEART...
SORRY FOR THE WAIT!
GASP
は!!!

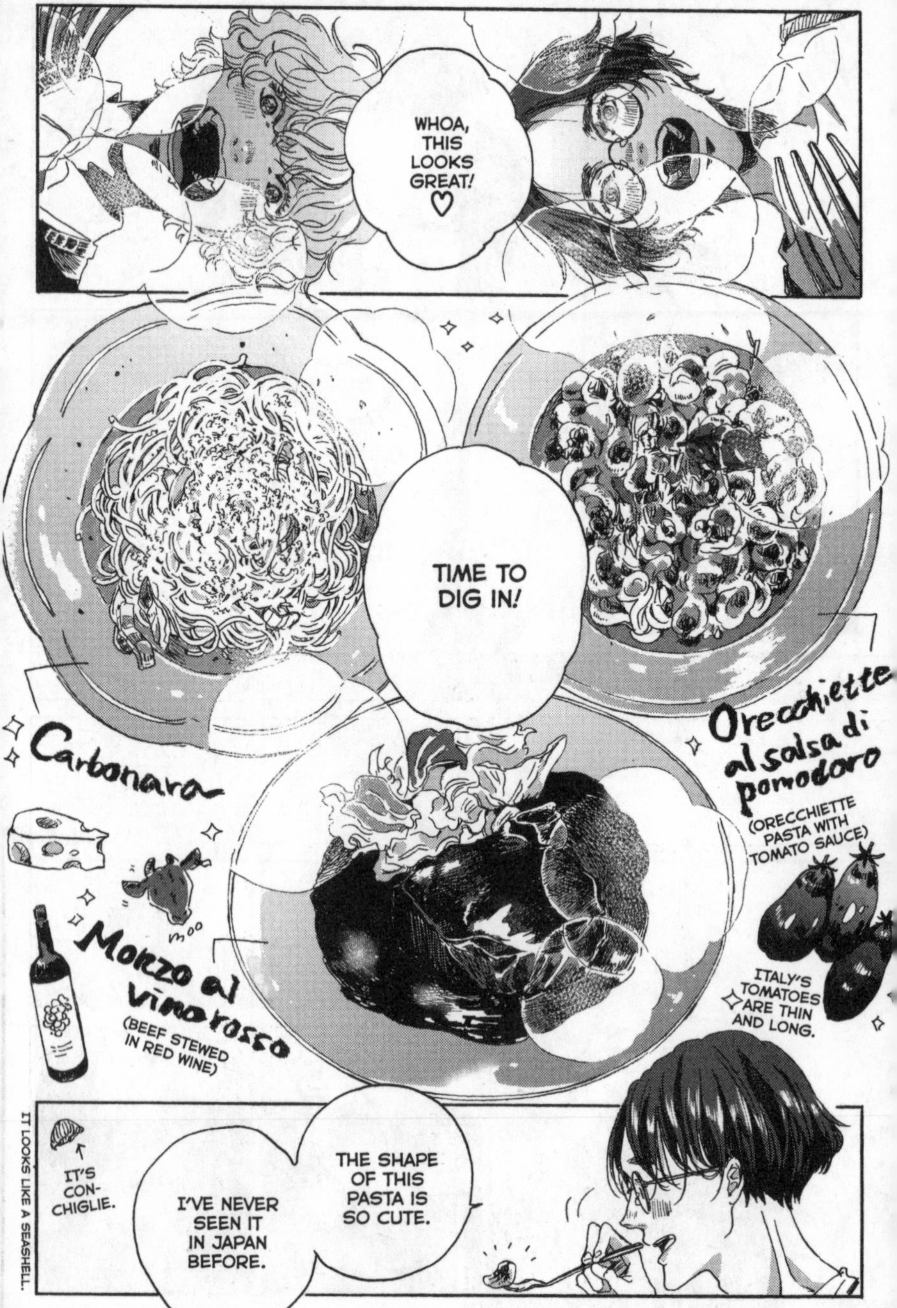
WHOA, THIS LOOKS GREAT! ♡
Orecchiette al salsa di pomodoro
(ORECCHIETTE PASTA WITH TOMATO SAUCE)
TIME TO DIG IN!
ITALY'S TOMATOES ARE THIN AND LONG.
Carbonara
MOO
Manzo al vino rosso
(BEEF STEWED IN RED WINE)
THE SHAPE OF THIS PASTA IS SO CUTE.
I'VE NEVER SEEN IT IN JAPAN BEFORE.
IT'S CONCHIGLIE.
IT LOOKS LIKE A SEASHELL.

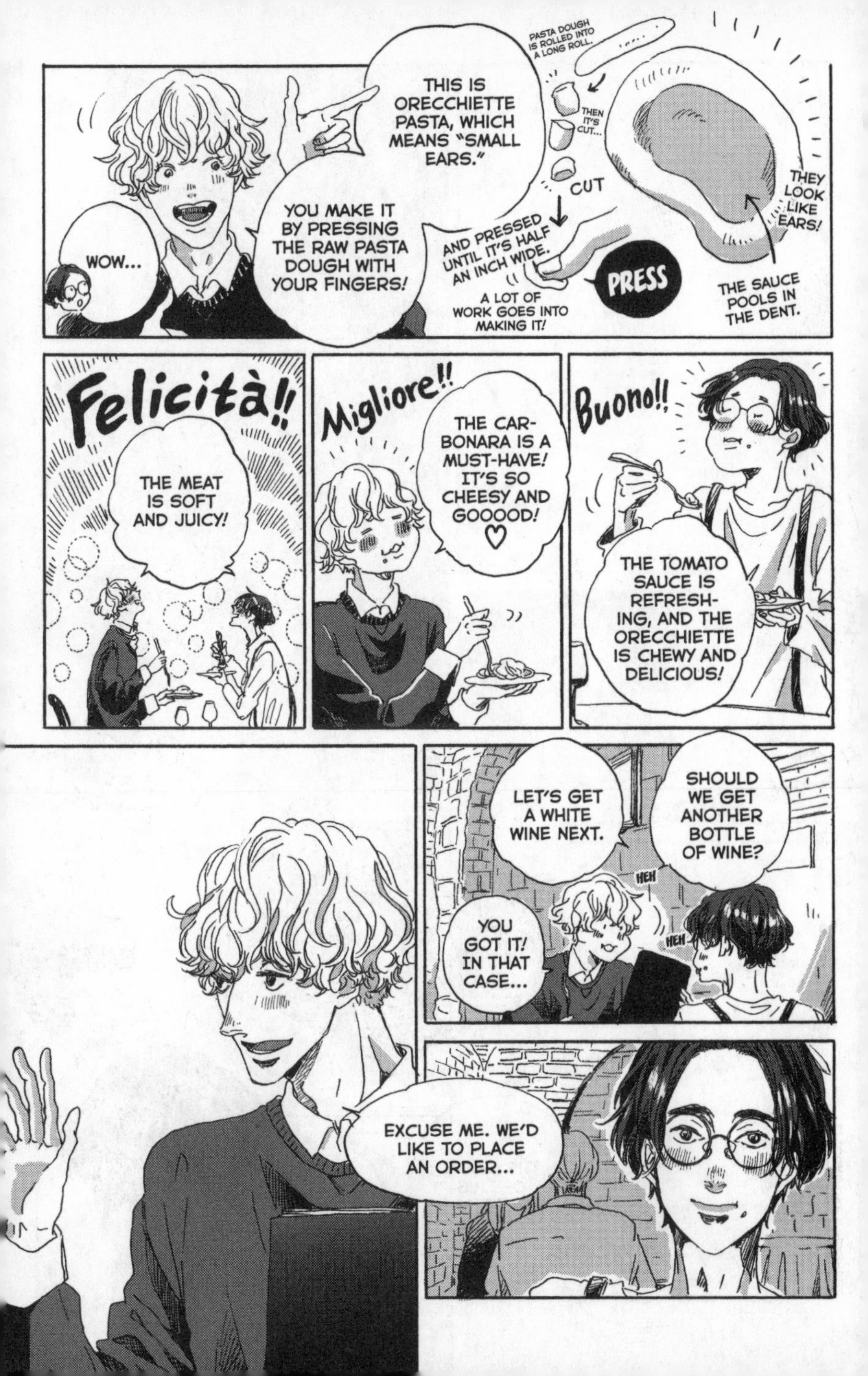
THIS IS ORECCHIETTE PASTA, WHICH MEANS "SMALL EARS."
PASTA DOUGH IS ROLLED INTO A LONG ROLL.
THEN IT'S CUT...
THEY LOOK LIKE EARS!
CUT
YOU MAKE IT BY PRESSING THE RAW PASTA DOUGH WITH YOUR FINGERS!
AND PRESSED UNTIL IT'S HALF AN INCH WIDE.
PRESS
THE SAUCE POOLS IN THE DENT.
A LOT OF WORK GOES INTO MAKING IT!
WOW...
Buono!!
THE TOMATO SAUCE IS REFRESHING, AND THE ORECCHIETTE IS CHEWY AND DELICIOUS!
Migliore!!
THE CARBONARA IS A MUST-HAVE! IT'S SO CHEESY AND GOOOOD! ♡
Felicità!!
THE MEAT IS SOFT AND JUICY!
SHOULD WE GET ANOTHER BOTTLE OF WINE?
LET'S GET A WHITE WINE NEXT.
HEH
HEH
YOU GOT IT! IN THAT CASE...
EXCUSE ME. WE'D LIKE TO PLACE AN ORDER...

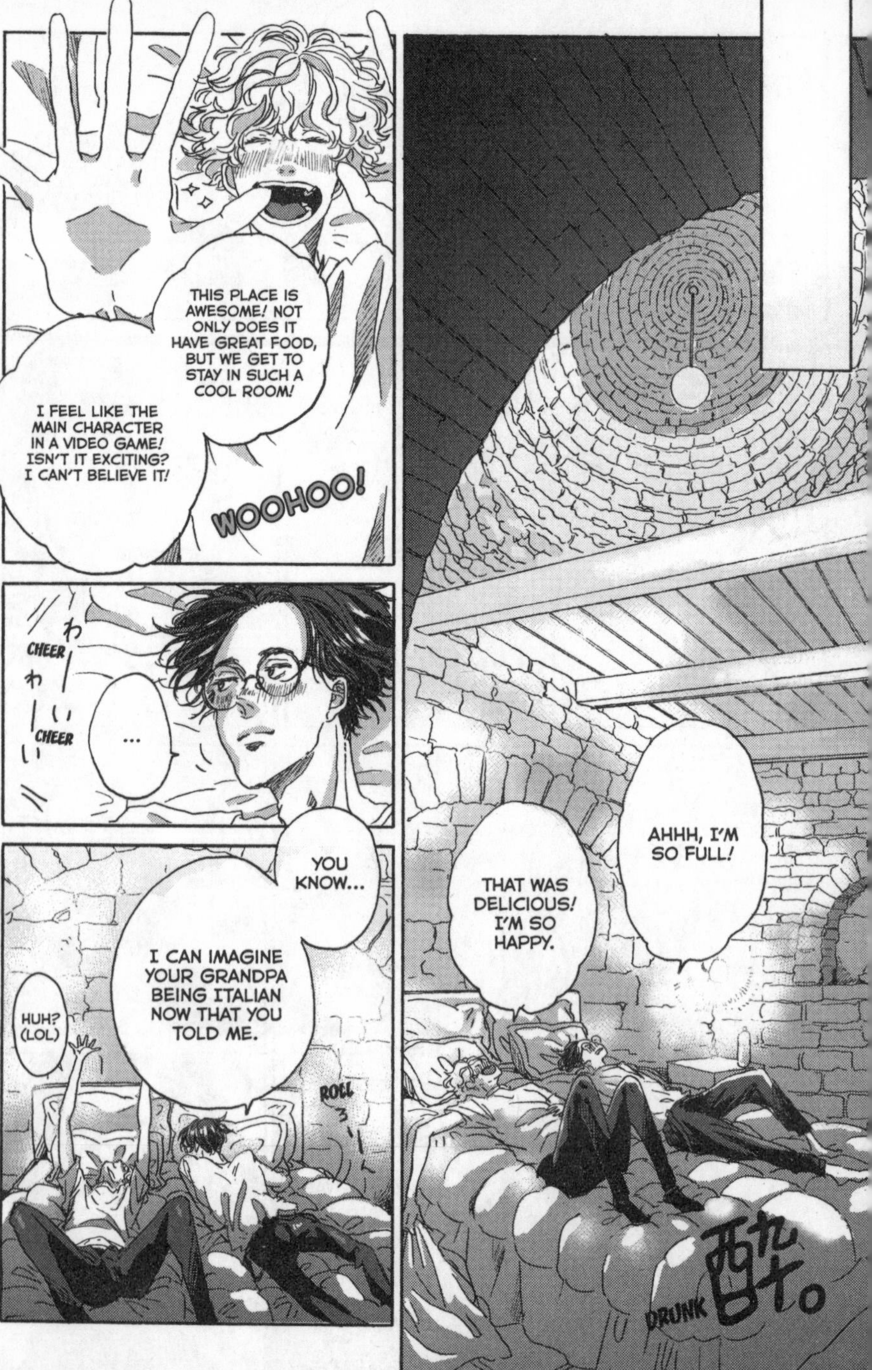
AHHH, I'M SO FULL!
THAT WAS DELICIOUS! I'M SO HAPPY.
DRUNK
酔。
THIS PLACE IS AWESOME! NOT ONLY DOES IT HAVE GREAT FOOD, BUT WE GET TO STAY IN SUCH A COOL ROOM!
I FEEL LIKE THE MAIN CHARACTER IN A VIDEO GAME! ISN'T IT EXCITING? I CAN'T BELIEVE IT!
WOOHOO!
わーい
CHEER
わーい
CHEER
...
YOU KNOW...
I CAN IMAGINE YOUR GRANDPA BEING ITALIAN NOW THAT YOU TOLD ME.
HUH? (LOL)
ROLL

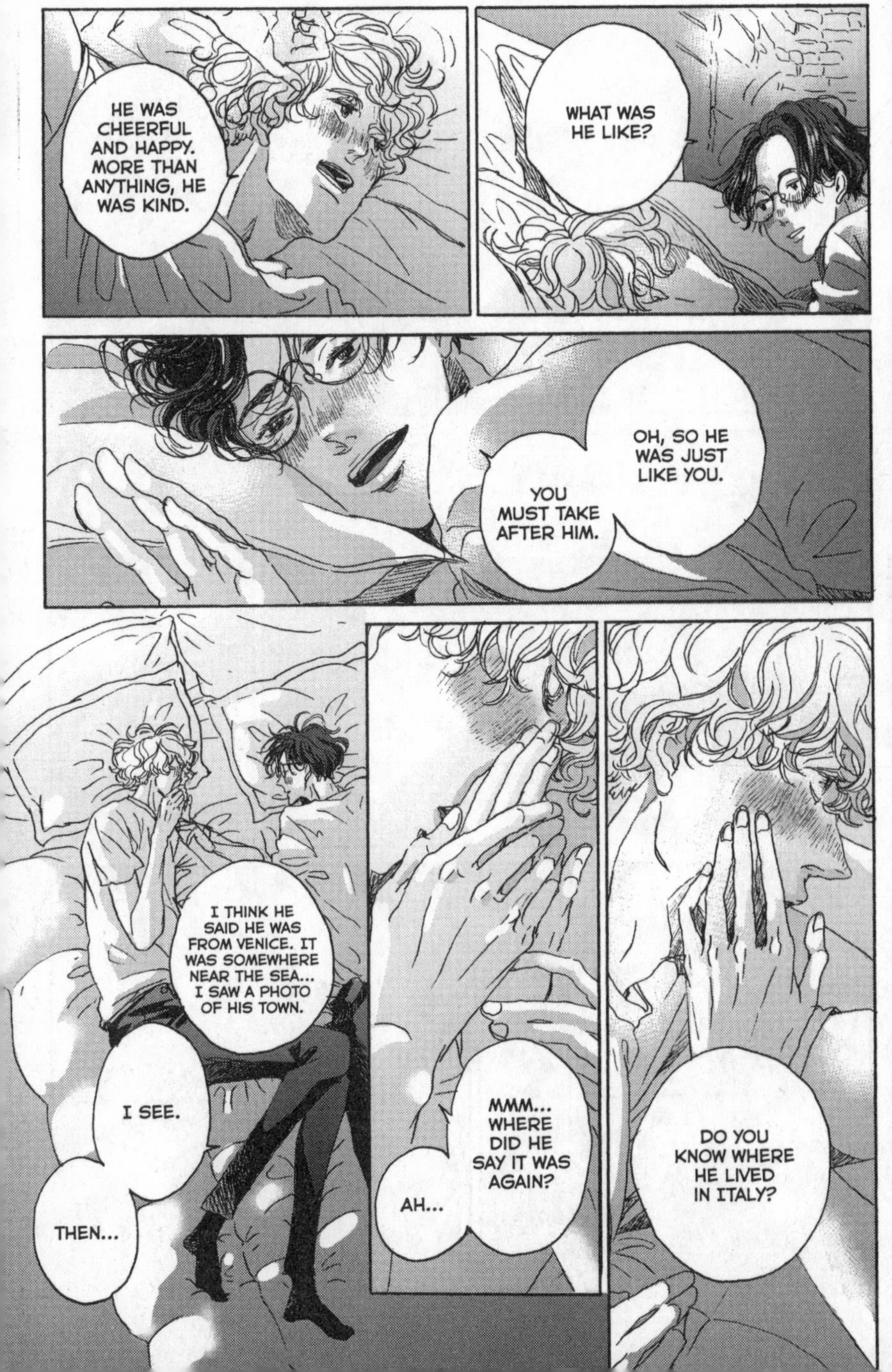
WHAT WAS HE LIKE?
HE WAS CHEERFUL AND HAPPY. MORE THAN ANYTHING, HE WAS KIND.
OH, SO HE WAS JUST LIKE YOU.
YOU MUST TAKE AFTER HIM.
DO YOU KNOW WHERE HE LIVED IN ITALY?
MMM... WHERE DID HE SAY IT WAS AGAIN?
AH...
I THINK HE SAID HE WAS FROM VENICE. IT WAS SOMEWHERE NEAR THE SEA... I SAW A PHOTO OF HIS TOWN.
I SEE.
THEN...

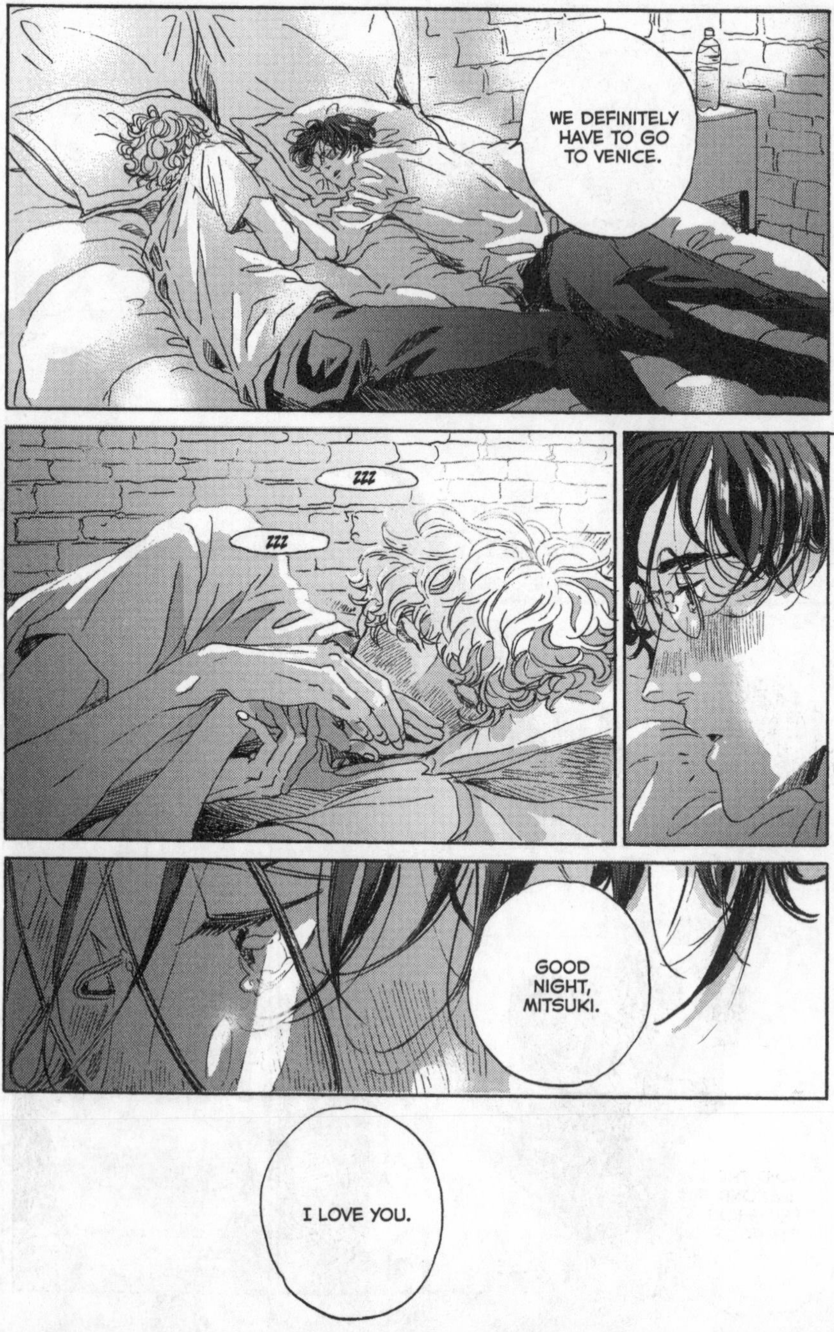
WE DEFINITELY HAVE TO GO TO VENICE.
ZZZ
ZZZ
GOOD NIGHT, MITSUKI.
I LOVE YOU.

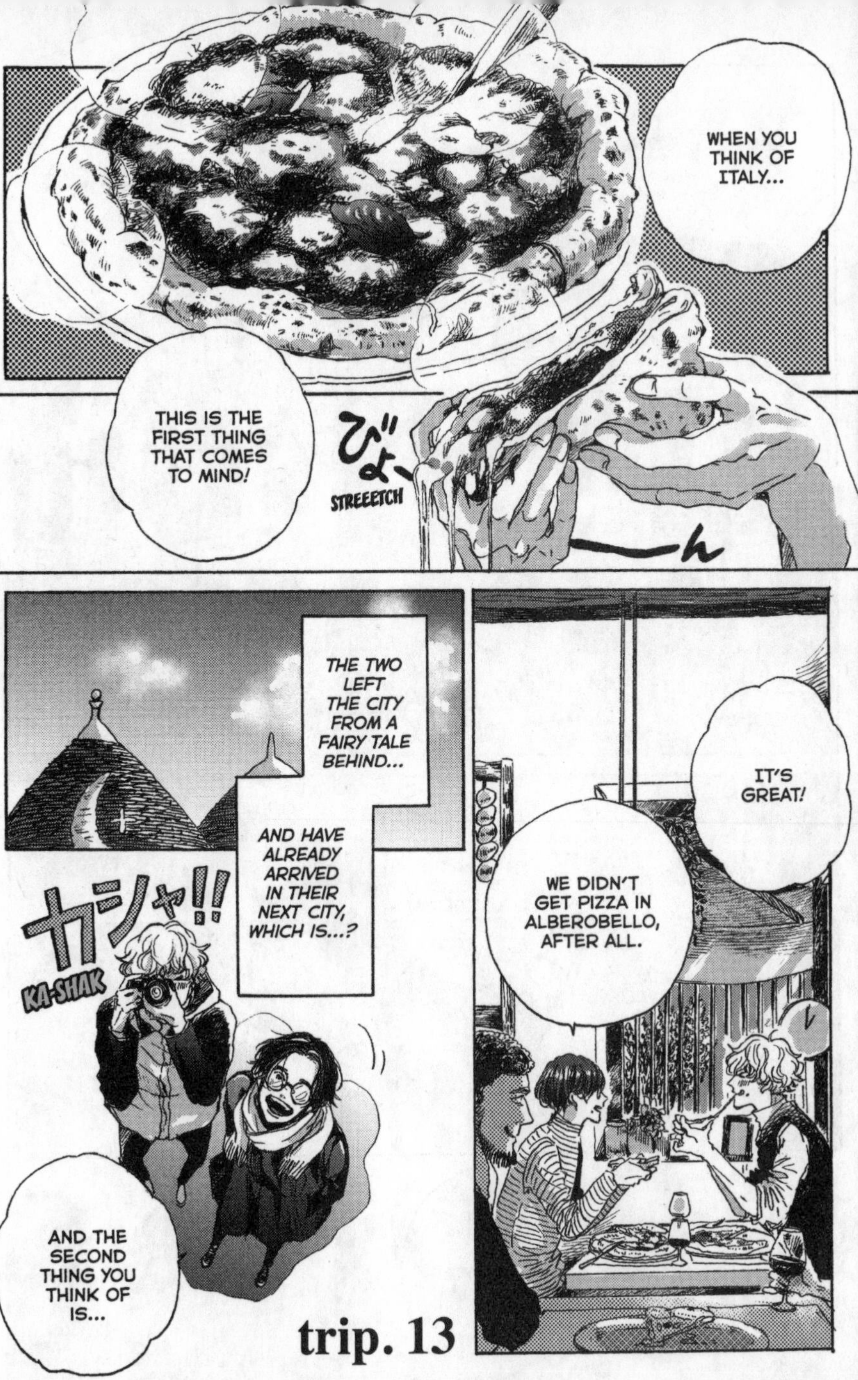
WHEN YOU THINK OF ITALY...
THIS IS THE FIRST THING THAT COMES TO MIND!
びよーん
STREEETCH
IT'S GREAT!
WE DIDN'T GET PIZZA IN ALBEROBELLO, AFTER ALL.
THE TWO LEFT THE CITY FROM A FAIRY TALE BEHIND...
AND HAVE ALREADY ARRIVED IN THEIR NEXT CITY, WHICH IS...?
カシャ!!
KA-SHAK
AND THE SECOND THING YOU THINK OF IS...

trip. 13

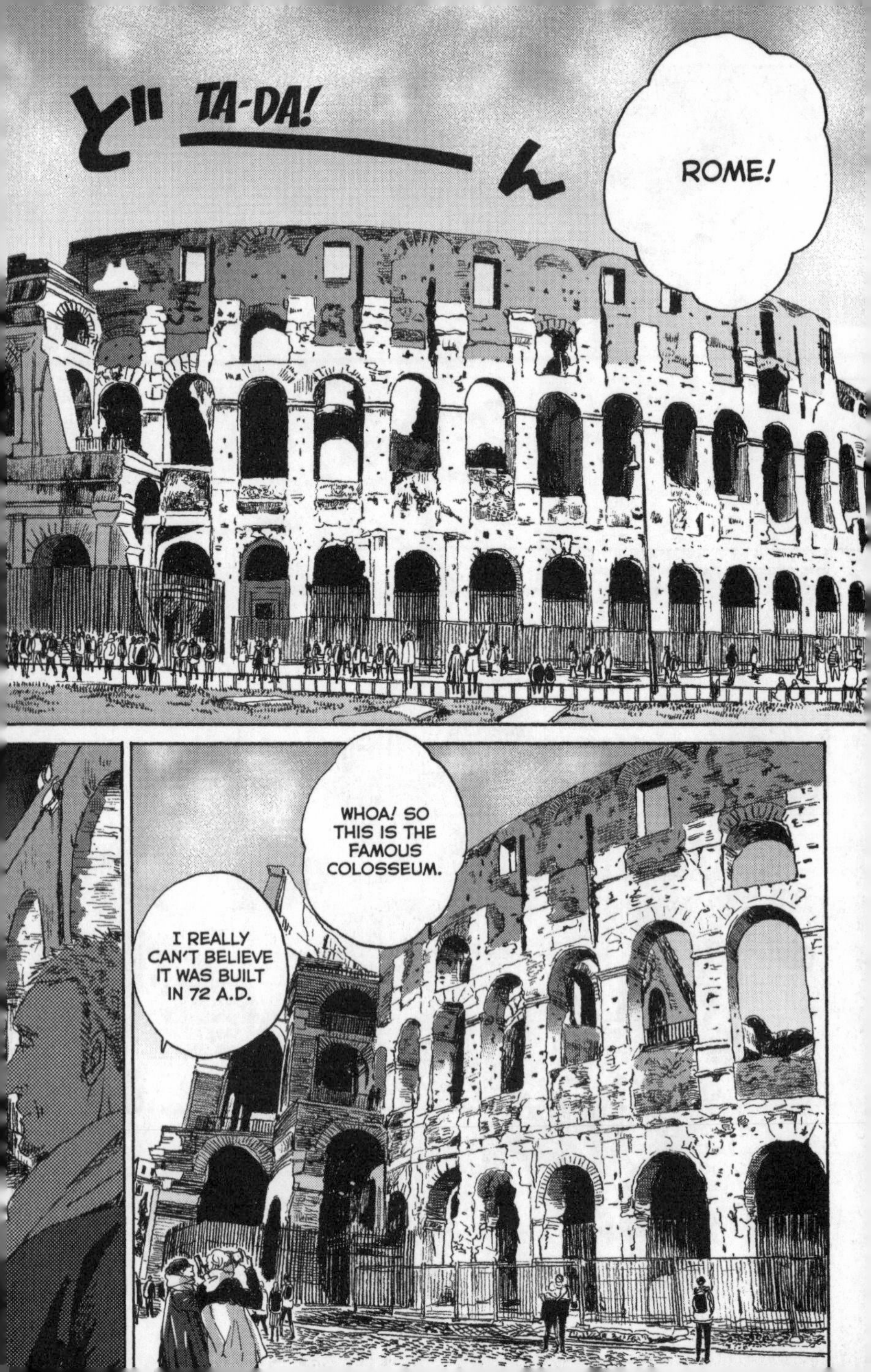
ROME!
どーん
TA-DA!
WHOA! SO THIS IS THE FAMOUS COLOSSEUM.
I REALLY CAN'T BELIEVE IT WAS BUILT IN 72 A.D.

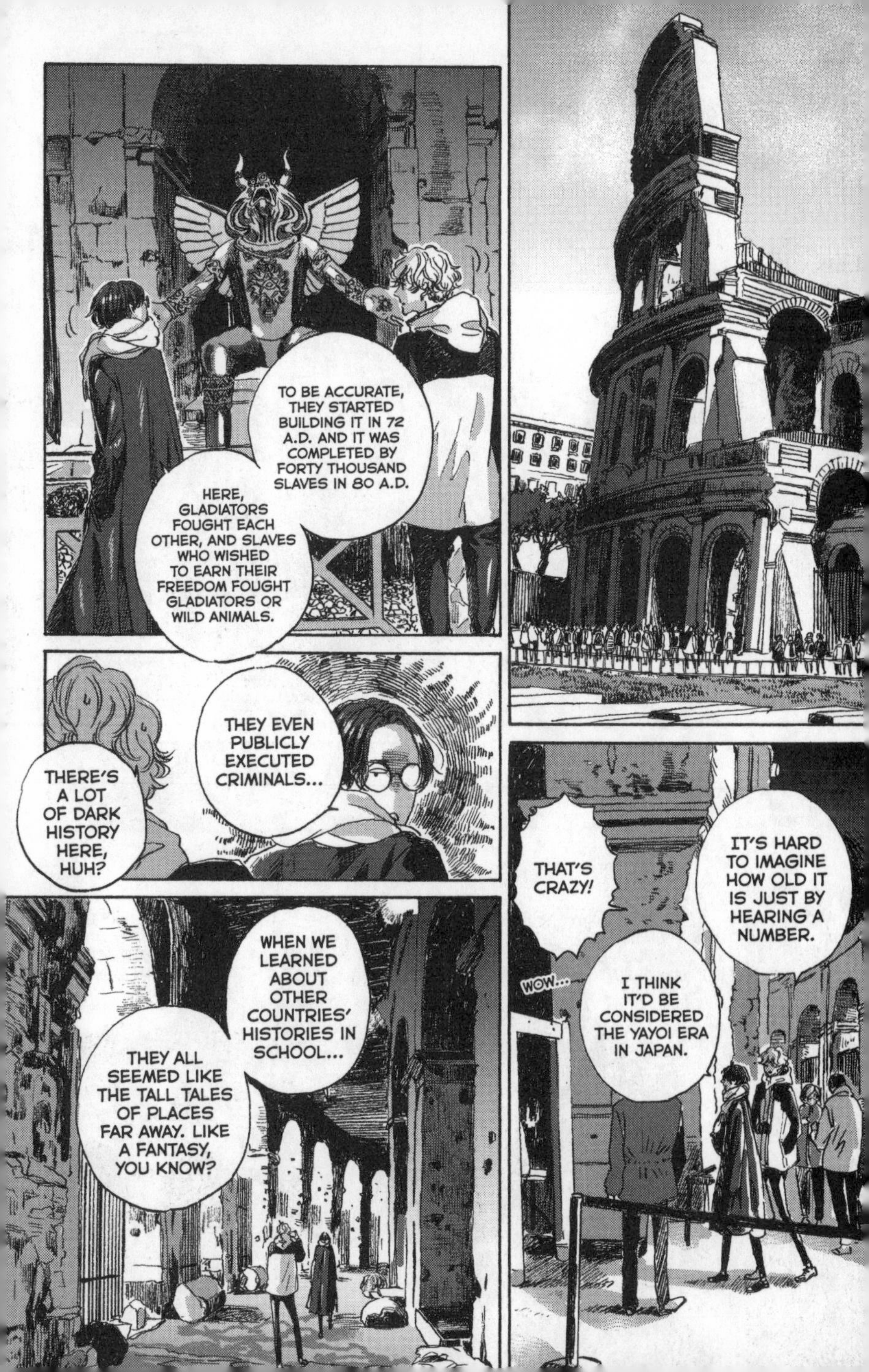
IT'S HARD TO IMAGINE HOW OLD IT IS JUST BY HEARING A NUMBER.
THAT'S CRAZY!
I THINK IT'D BE CONSIDERED THE YAYOI ERA IN JAPAN.
WOW...
TO BE ACCURATE, THEY STARTED BUILDING IT IN 72 A.D. AND IT WAS COMPLETED BY FORTY THOUSAND SLAVES IN 80 A.D.
HERE, GLADIATORS FOUGHT EACH OTHER, AND SLAVES WHO WISHED TO EARN THEIR FREEDOM FOUGHT GLADIATORS OR WILD ANIMALS.
THEY EVEN PUBLICLY EXECUTED CRIMINALS...
THERE'S A LOT OF DARK HISTORY HERE, HUH?
WHEN WE LEARNED ABOUT OTHER COUNTRIES' HISTORIES IN SCHOOL...
THEY ALL SEEMED LIKE THE TALL TALES OF PLACES FAR AWAY. LIKE A FANTASY, YOU KNOW?

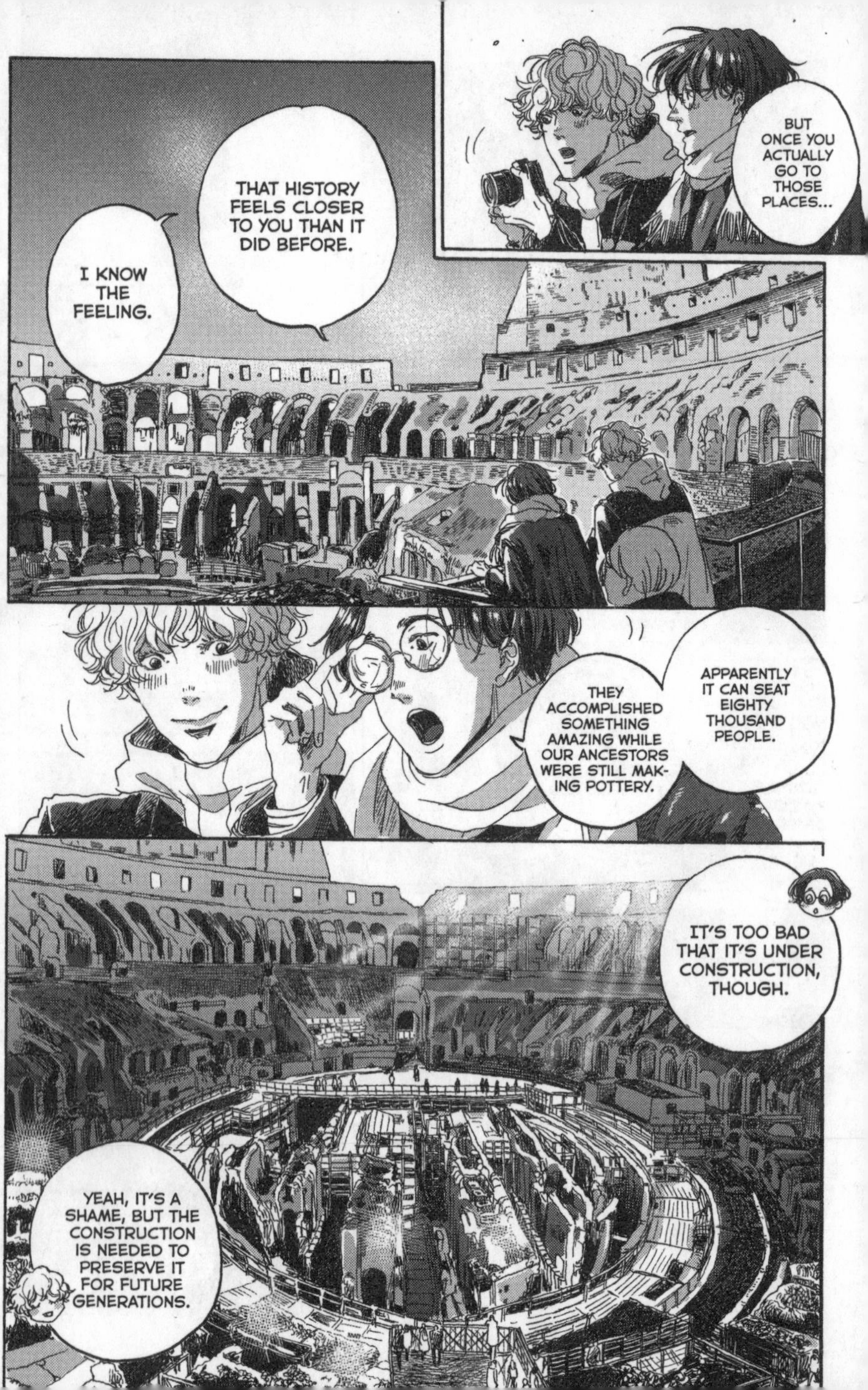
BUT ONCE YOU ACTUALLY GO TO THOSE PLACES...
THAT HISTORY FEELS CLOSER TO YOU THAN IT DID BEFORE.
I KNOW THE FEELING.
APPARENTLY IT CAN SEAT EIGHTY THOUSAND PEOPLE.
THEY ACCOMPLISHED SOMETHING AMAZING WHILE OUR ANCESTORS WERE STILL MAKING POTTERY.
IT'S TOO BAD THAT IT'S UNDER CONSTRUCTION, THOUGH.
YEAH, IT'S A SHAME, BUT THE CONSTRUCTION IS NEEDED TO PRESERVE IT FOR FUTURE GENERATIONS.

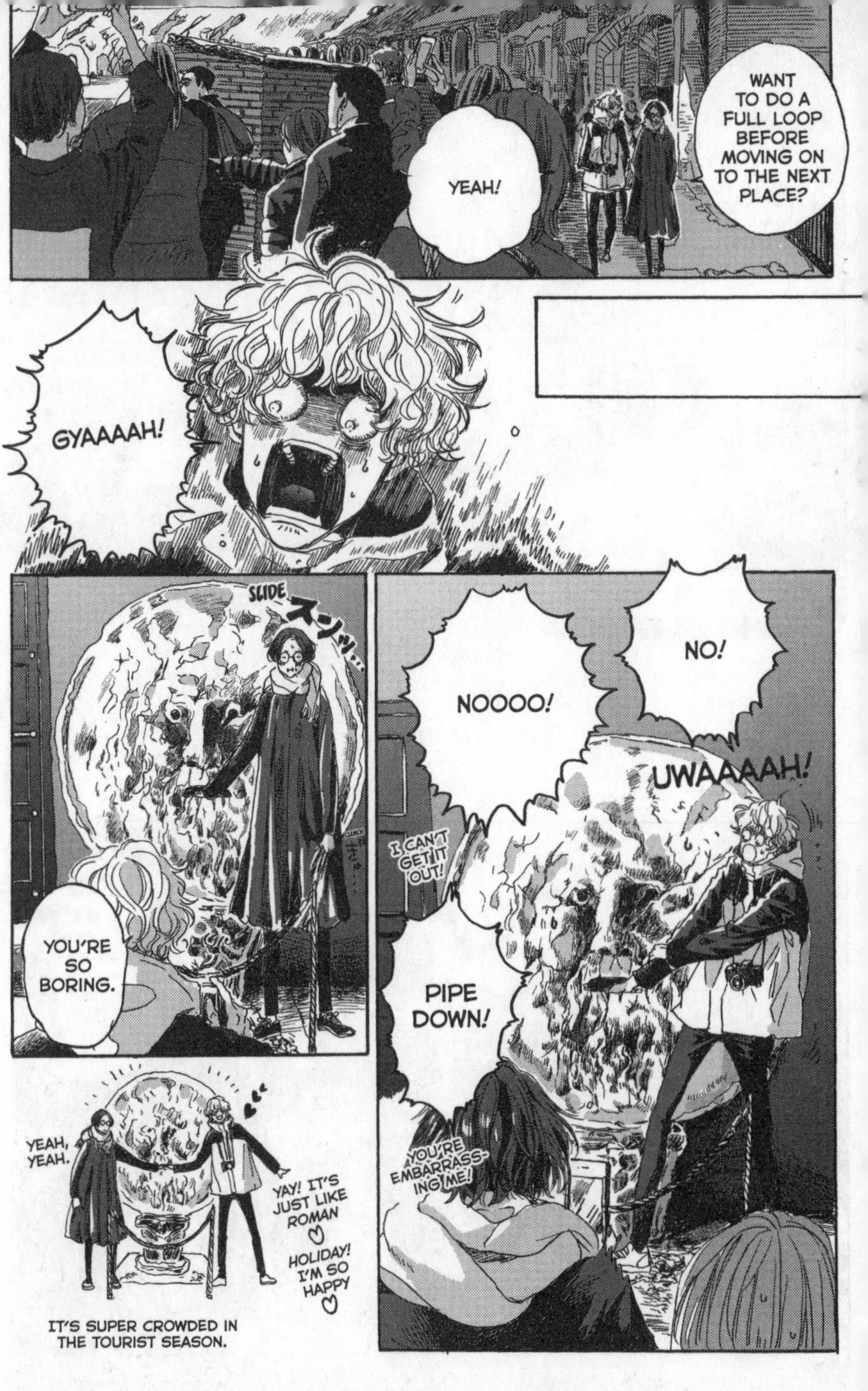
WANT TO DO A FULL LOOP BEFORE MOVING ON TO THE NEXT PLACE?
YEAH!
GYAAAAH!
NO!
NOOOO!
UWAAAAH!
I CAN'T GET IT OUT!
PIPE DOWN!
YOU'RE EMBARRASSING ME!
SLIDE
YOU'RE SO BORING.
YAY! IT'S JUST LIKE ROMAN HOLIDAY! I'M SO HAPPY
YEAH, YEAH.
IT'S SUPER CROWDED IN THE TOURIST SEASON.

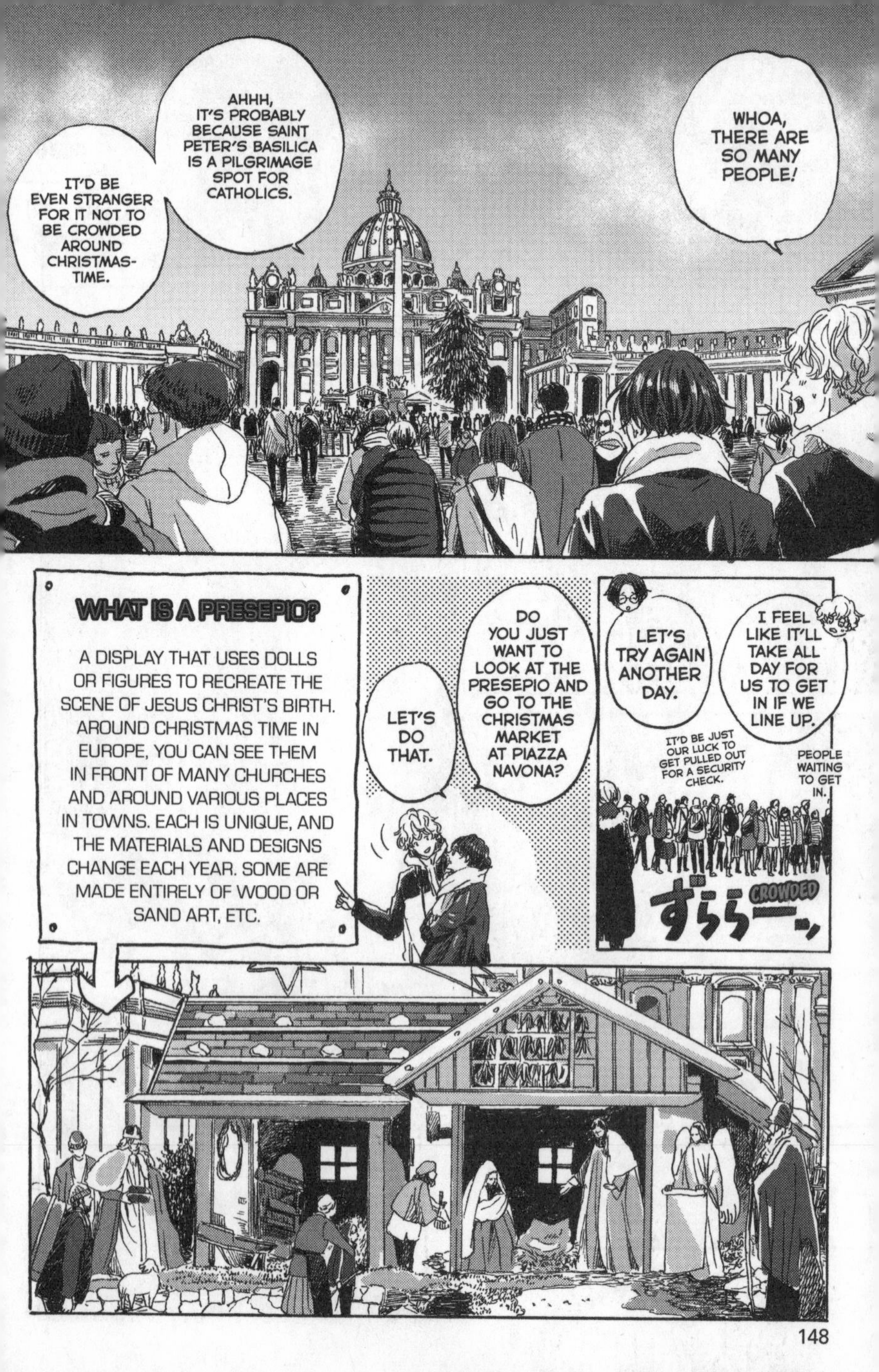
WHOA, THERE ARE SO MANY PEOPLE!
AHHH, IT'S PROBABLY BECAUSE SAINT PETER'S BASILICA IS A PILGRIMAGE SPOT FOR CATHOLICS.
IT'D BE EVEN STRANGER FOR IT NOT TO BE CROWDED AROUND CHRISTMAS-TIME.
I FEEL LIKE IT'LL TAKE ALL DAY FOR US TO GET IN IF WE LINE UP.
LET'S TRY AGAIN ANOTHER DAY.
PEOPLE WAITING TO GET IN.
IT'D BE JUST OUR LUCK TO GET PULLED OUT FOR A SECURITY CHECK.
ずらら—っ
CROWDED
DO YOU JUST WANT TO LOOK AT THE PRESEPIO AND GO TO THE CHRISTMAS MARKET AT PIAZZA NAVONA?
LET'S DO THAT.
WHAT IS A PRESEPIO?
A DISPLAY THAT USES DOLLS OR FIGURES TO RECREATE THE SCENE OF JESUS CHRIST'S BIRTH. AROUND CHRISTMAS TIME IN EUROPE, YOU CAN SEE THEM IN FRONT OF MANY CHURCHES AND AROUND VARIOUS PLACES IN TOWNS. EACH IS UNIQUE, AND THE MATERIALS AND DESIGNS CHANGE EACH YEAR. SOME ARE MADE ENTIRELY OF WOOD OR SAND ART, ETC.

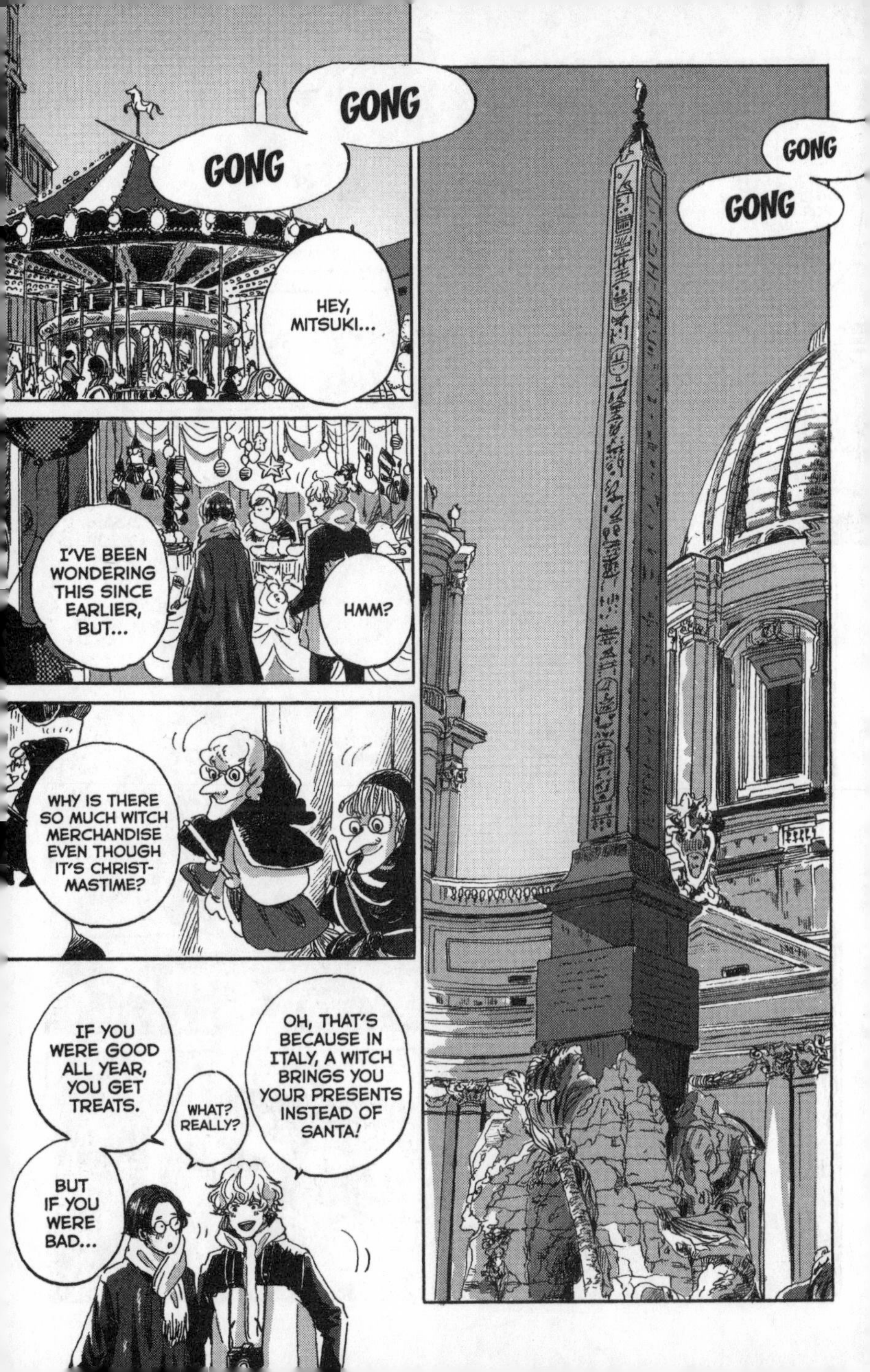
GONG
GONG
GONG
GONG
HEY, MITSUKI...
HMM?
I'VE BEEN WONDERING THIS SINCE EARLIER, BUT...
WHY IS THERE SO MUCH WITCH MERCHANDISE EVEN THOUGH IT'S CHRIST-MASTIME?
OH, THAT'S BECAUSE IN ITALY, A WITCH BRINGS YOU YOUR PRESENTS INSTEAD OF SANTA!
WHAT? REALLY?
IF YOU WERE GOOD ALL YEAR, YOU GET TREATS.
BUT IF YOU WERE BAD...

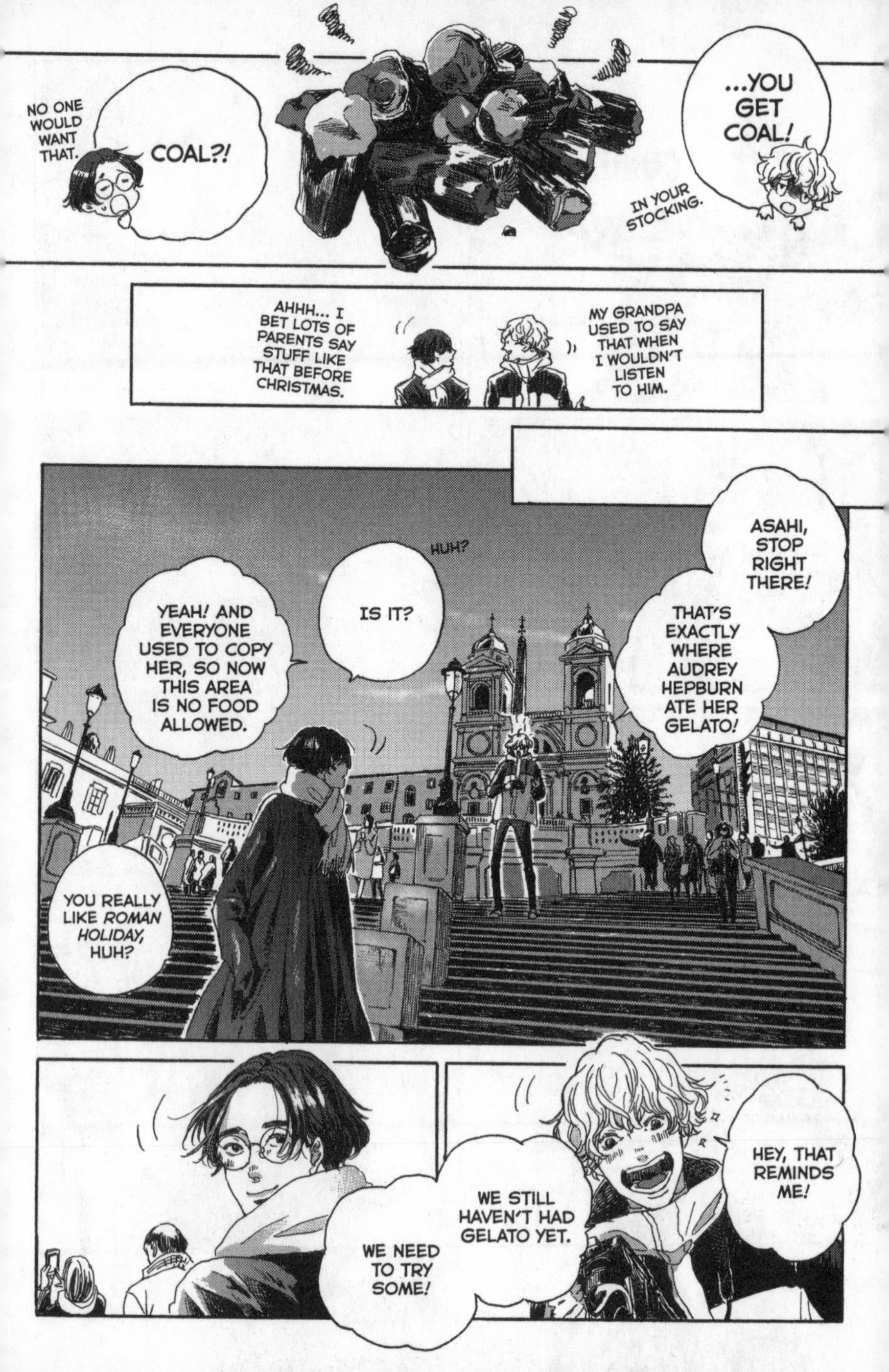
...YOU GET COAL!
IN YOUR STOCKING.
COAL?!
NO ONE WOULD WANT THAT.
MY GRANDPA USED TO SAY THAT WHEN I WOULDN'T LISTEN TO HIM.
AHHH... I BET LOTS OF PARENTS SAY STUFF LIKE THAT BEFORE CHRISTMAS.
ASAHI, STOP RIGHT THERE!
THAT'S EXACTLY WHERE AUDREY HEPBURN ATE HER GELATO!
HUH?
IS IT?
YEAH! AND EVERYONE USED TO COPY HER, SO NOW THIS AREA IS NO FOOD ALLOWED.
YOU REALLY LIKE *ROMAN HOLIDAY*, HUH?
HEY, THAT REMINDS ME!
WE STILL HAVEN'T HAD GELATO YET.
WE NEED TO TRY SOME!

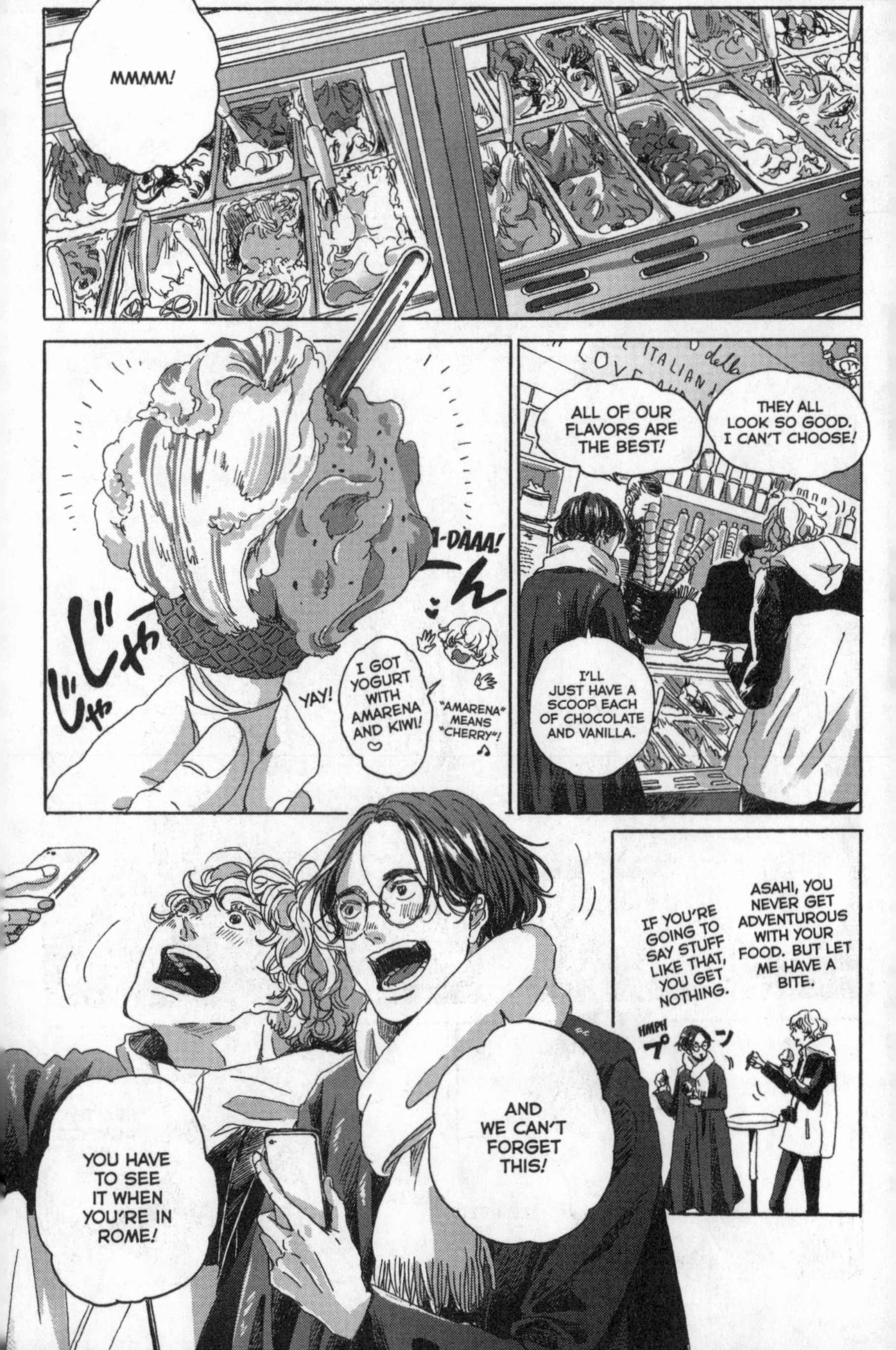
MMMM!
THEY ALL LOOK SO GOOD. I CAN'T CHOOSE!
ALL OF OUR FLAVORS ARE THE BEST!
I'LL JUST HAVE A SCOOP EACH OF CHOCOLATE AND VANILLA.
-DAAA!
じゃじゃーん
"AMARENA" MEANS "CHERRY"!
I GOT YOGURT WITH AMARENA AND KIWI!
YAY!
ASAHI, YOU NEVER GET ADVENTUROUS WITH YOUR FOOD. BUT LET ME HAVE A BITE.
IF YOU'RE GOING TO SAY STUFF LIKE THAT, YOU GET NOTHING.
HMPH
プン
AND WE CAN'T FORGET THIS!
YOU HAVE TO SEE IT WHEN YOU'RE IN ROME!

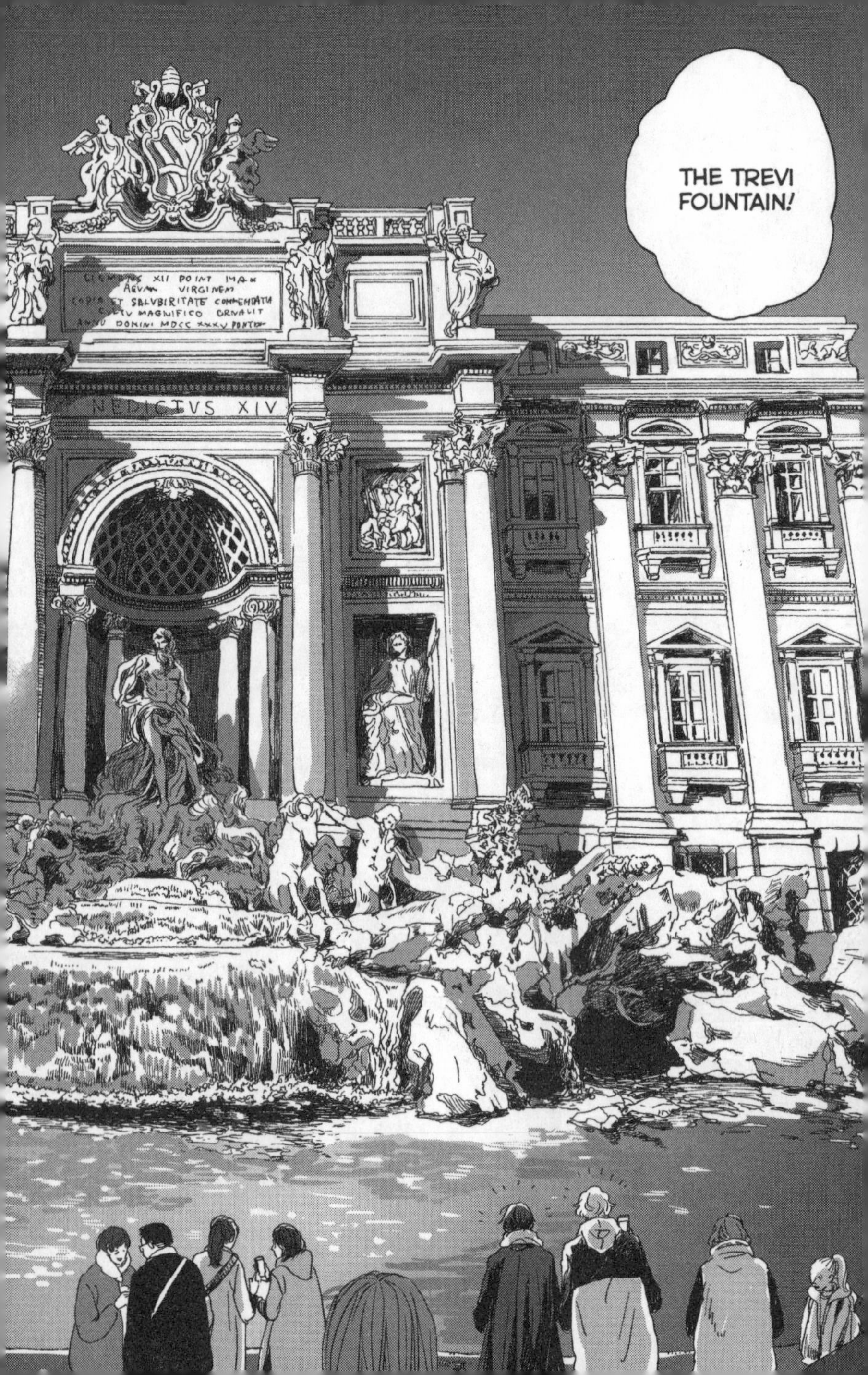
THE TREVI FOUNTAIN!

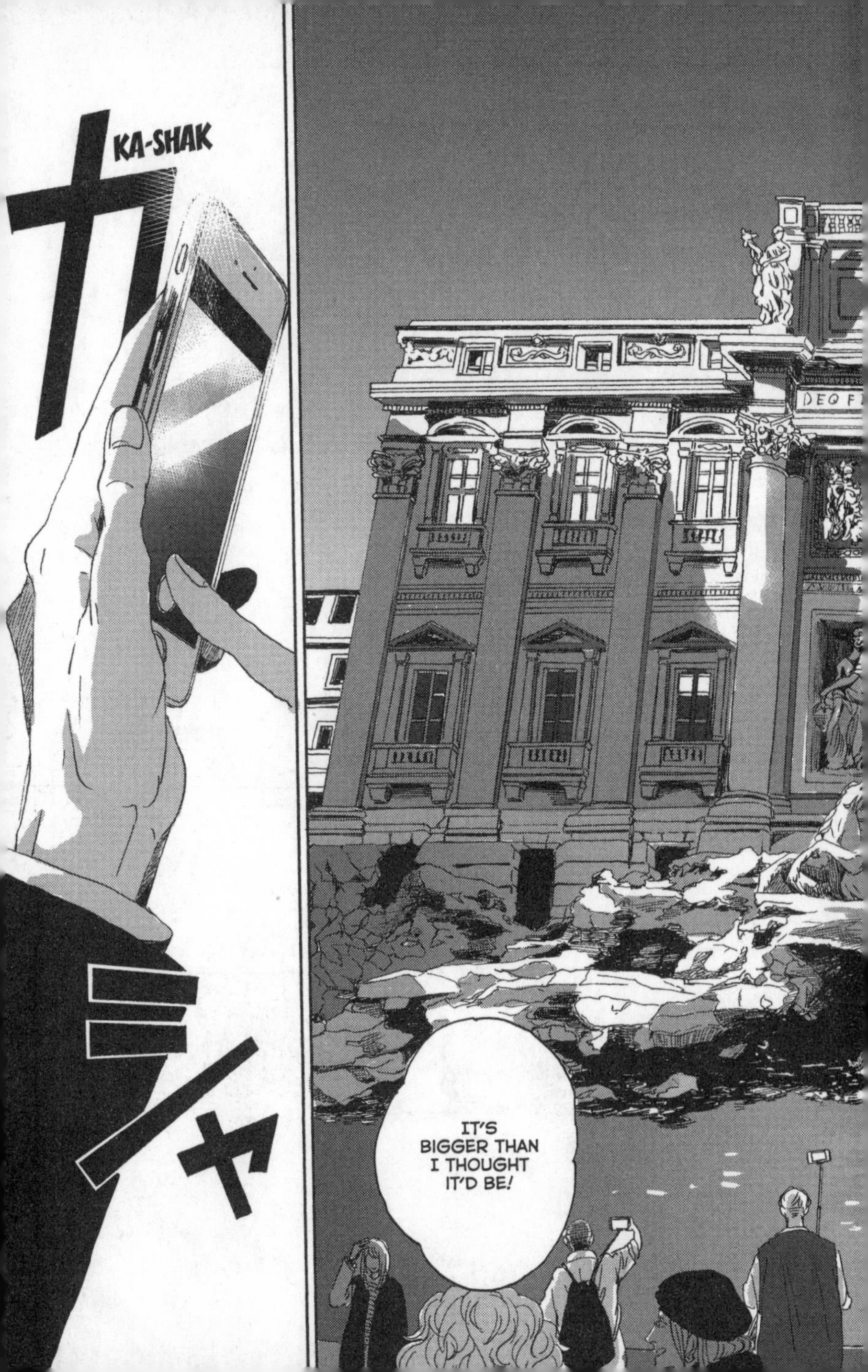
IT'S BIGGER THAN I THOUGHT IT'D BE!
KA-SHAK

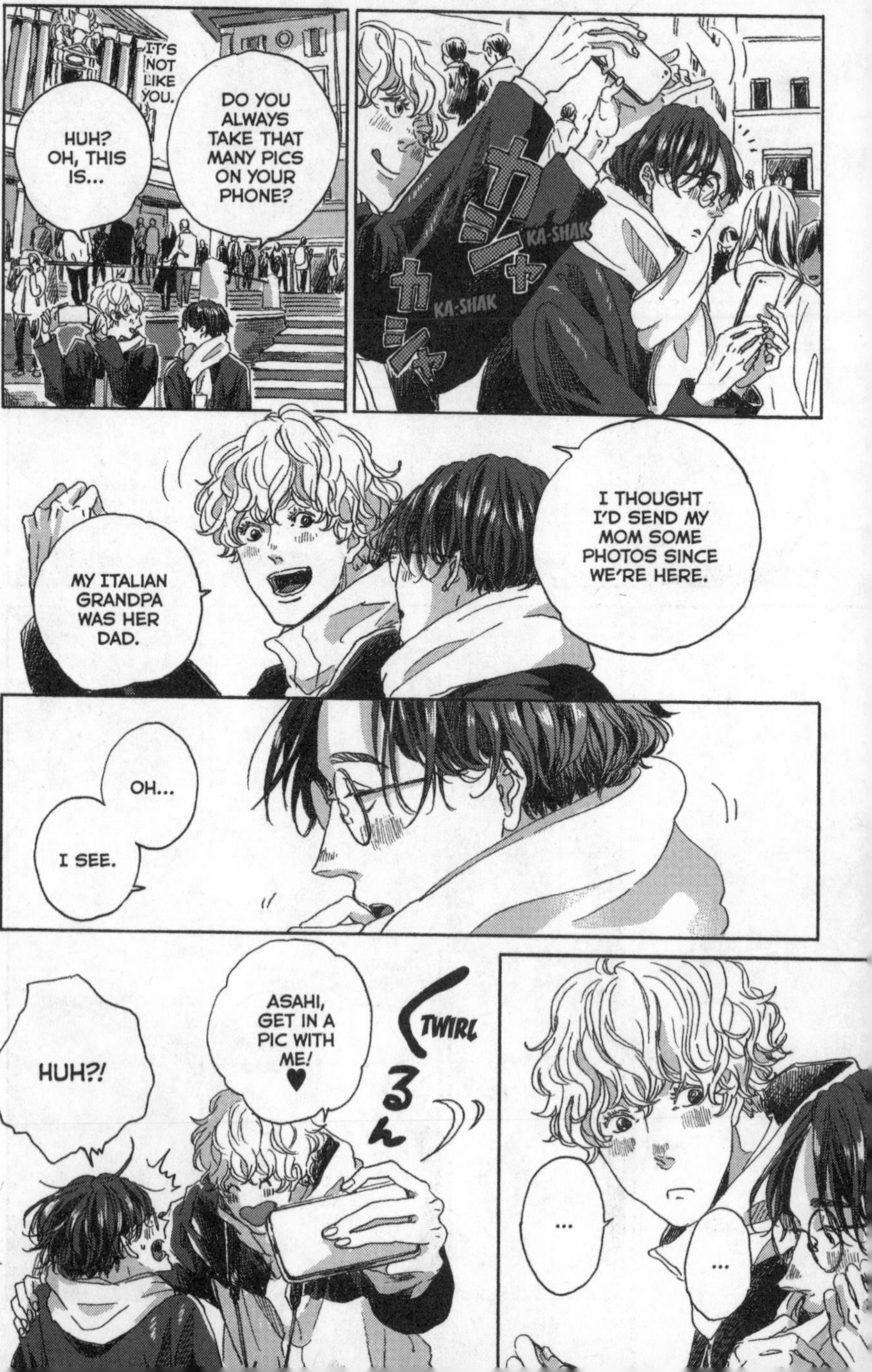
カシャ
KA-SHAK
カシャ
KA-SHAK
DO YOU ALWAYS TAKE THAT MANY PICS ON YOUR PHONE?
IT'S NOT LIKE YOU.
HUH? OH, THIS IS...
I THOUGHT I'D SEND MY MOM SOME PHOTOS SINCE WE'RE HERE.
MY ITALIAN GRANDPA WAS HER DAD.
OH...
I SEE.
...
...
ASAHI, GET IN A PIC WITH ME! ♥
TWIRL
るん
HUH?!

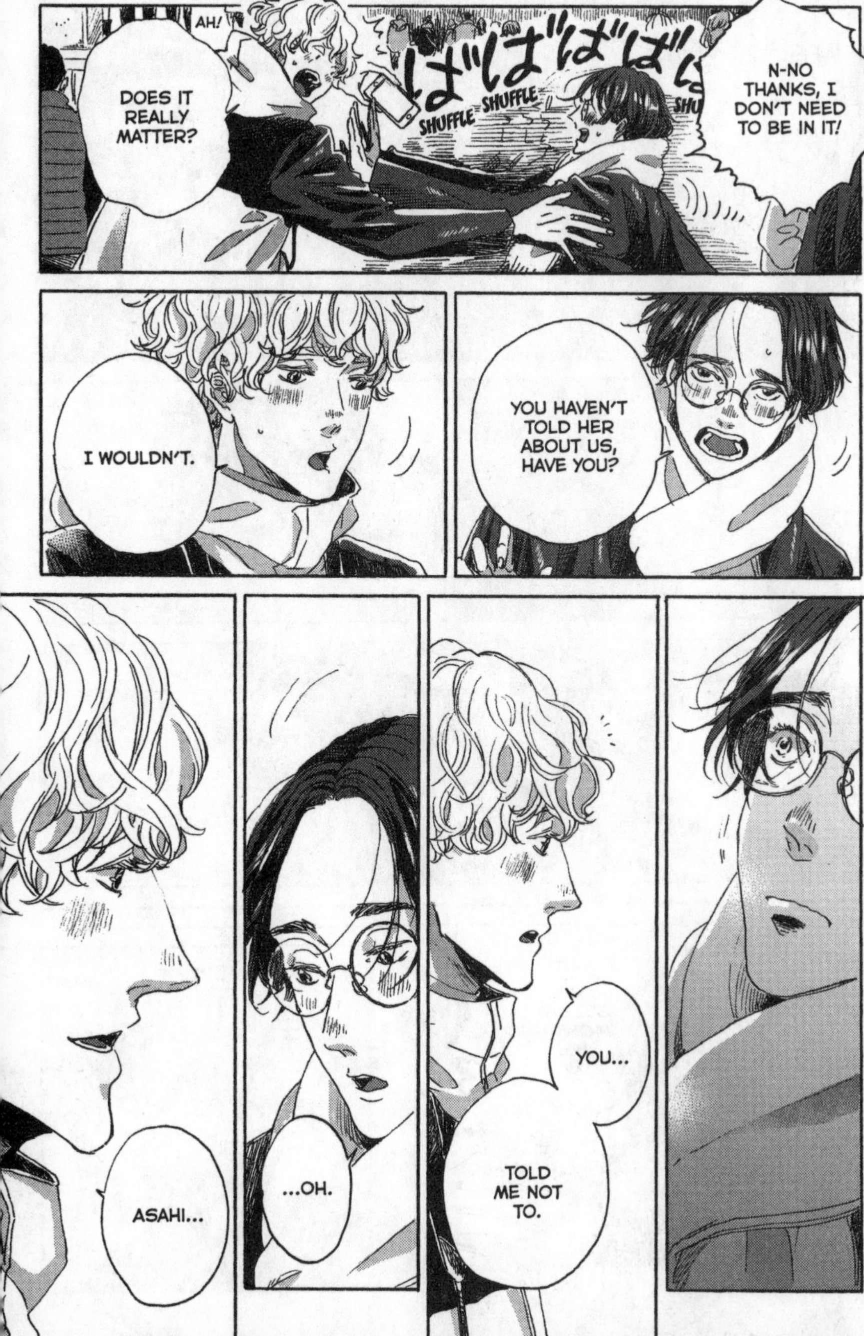
N-NO THANKS, I DON'T NEED TO BE IN IT!
ばばばば
SHUFFLE SHUFFLE
AH!
DOES IT REALLY MATTER?
YOU HAVEN'T TOLD HER ABOUT US, HAVE YOU?
I WOULDN'T.
YOU...
TOLD ME NOT TO.
...OH.
ASAHI...

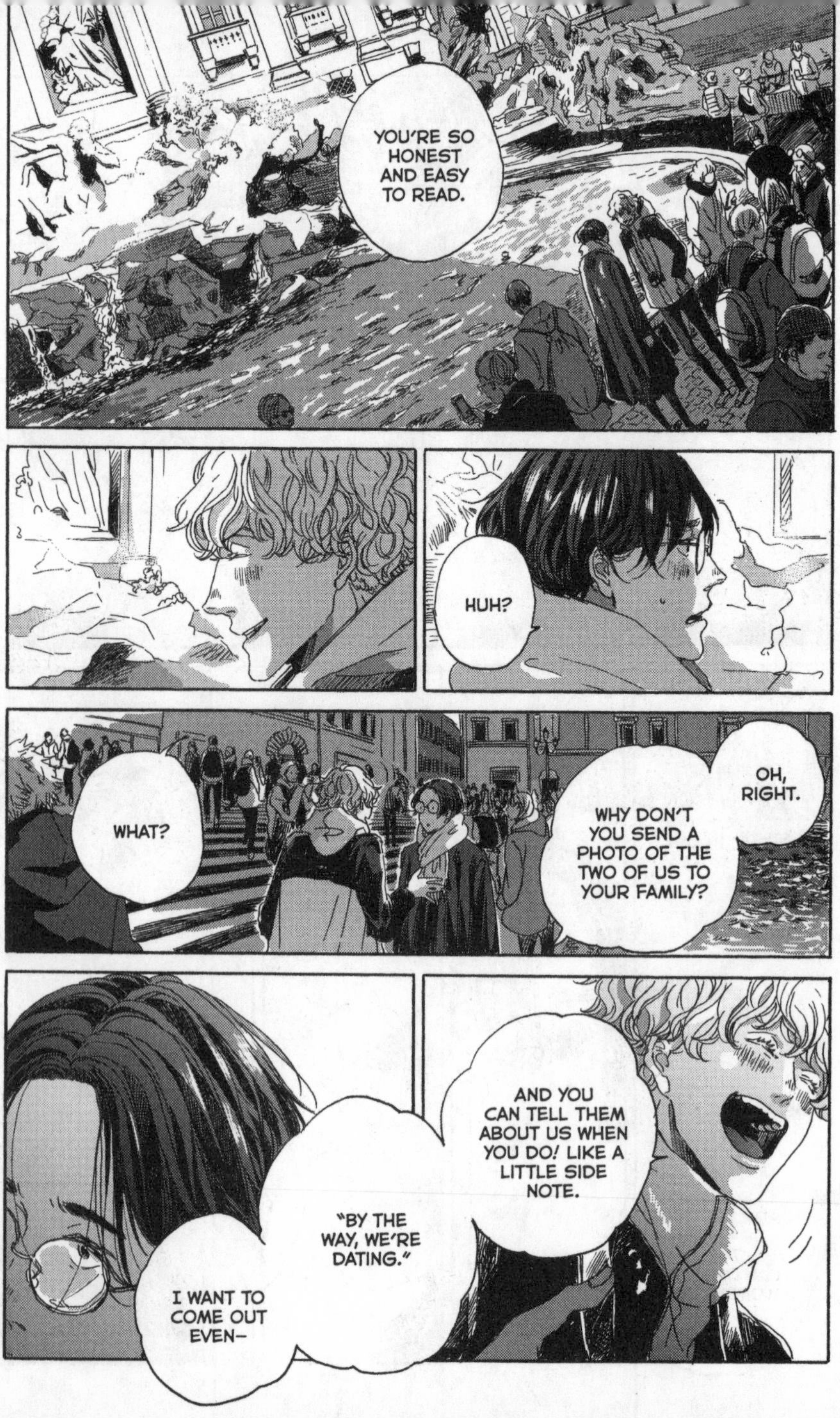
YOU'RE SO HONEST AND EASY TO READ.
HUH?
OH, RIGHT.
WHY DON'T YOU SEND A PHOTO OF THE TWO OF US TO YOUR FAMILY?
WHAT?
AND YOU CAN TELL THEM ABOUT US WHEN YOU DO! LIKE A LITTLE SIDE NOTE.
"BY THE WAY, WE'RE DATING."
I WANT TO COME OUT EVEN–

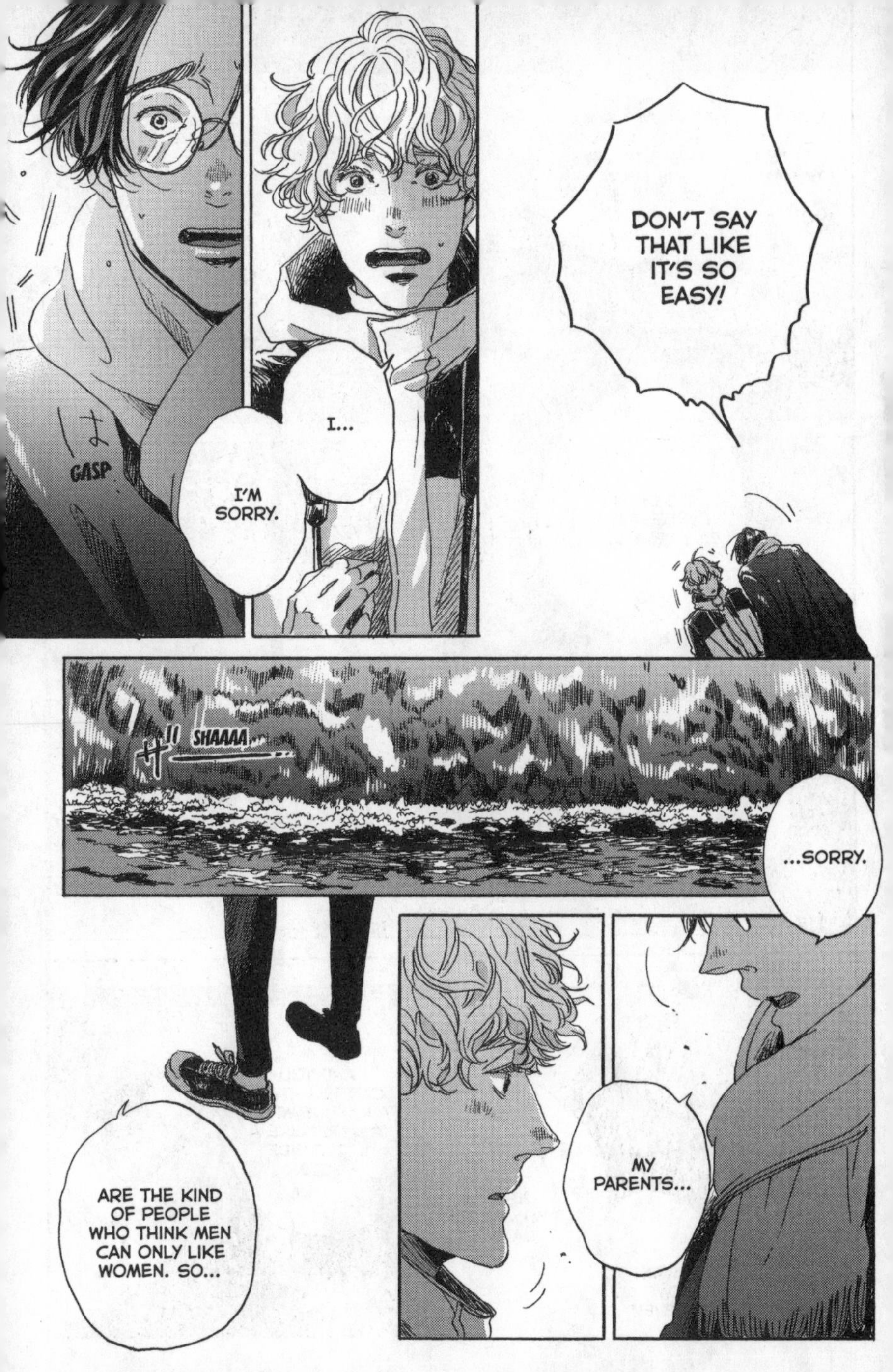
DON'T SAY THAT LIKE IT'S SO EASY!
I...
は
GASP
I'M SORRY.
SHAAAA
...SORRY.
MY PARENTS...
ARE THE KIND OF PEOPLE WHO THINK MEN CAN ONLY LIKE WOMEN. SO...

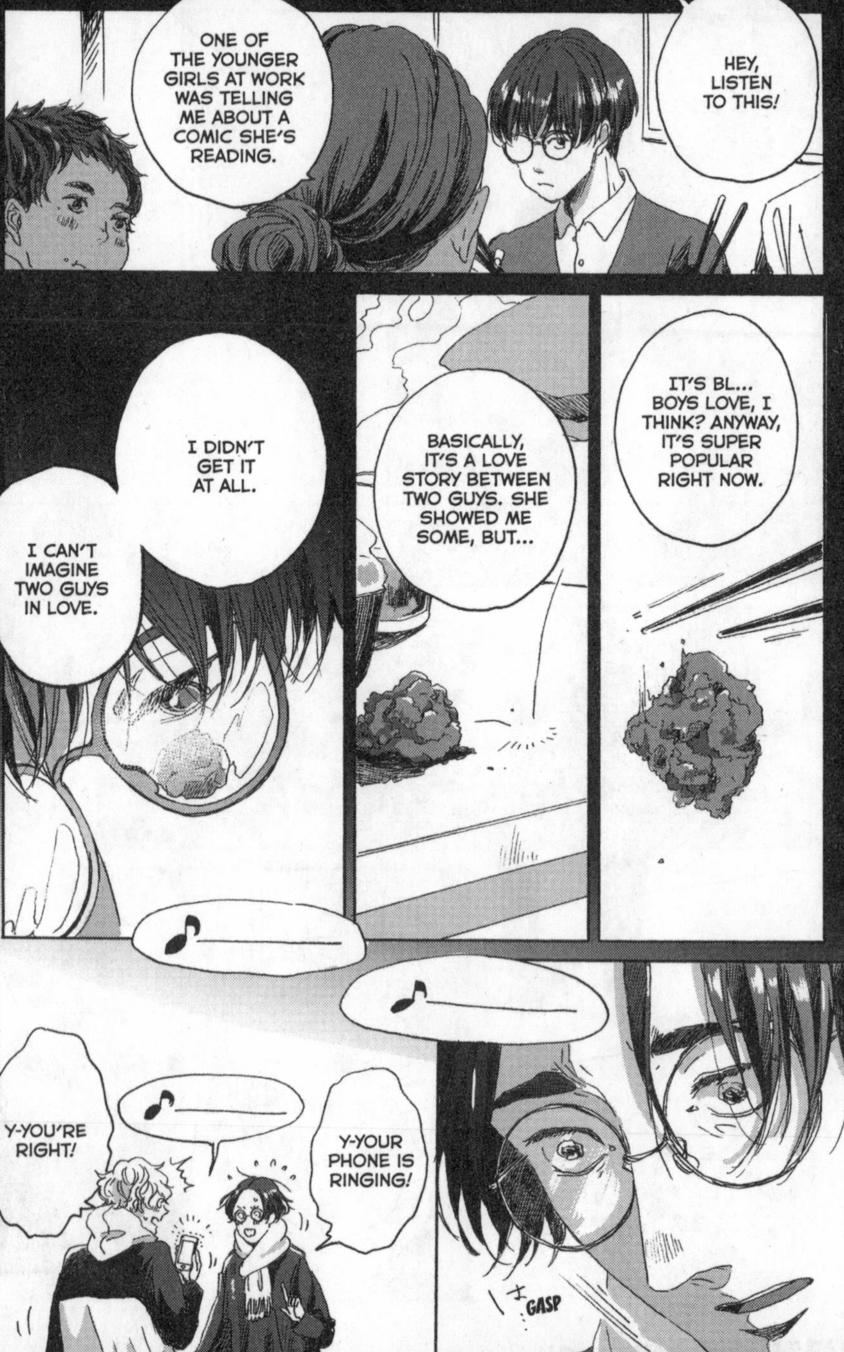
HEY, LISTEN TO THIS!
ONE OF THE YOUNGER GIRLS AT WORK WAS TELLING ME ABOUT A COMIC SHE'S READING.
IT'S BL... BOYS LOVE, I THINK? ANYWAY, IT'S SUPER POPULAR RIGHT NOW.
BASICALLY, IT'S A LOVE STORY BETWEEN TWO GUYS. SHE SHOWED ME SOME, BUT...
I DIDN'T GET IT AT ALL.
I CAN'T IMAGINE TWO GUYS IN LOVE.
♪——
♪——
GASP
♪——
Y-YOUR PHONE IS RINGING!
Y-YOU'RE RIGHT!

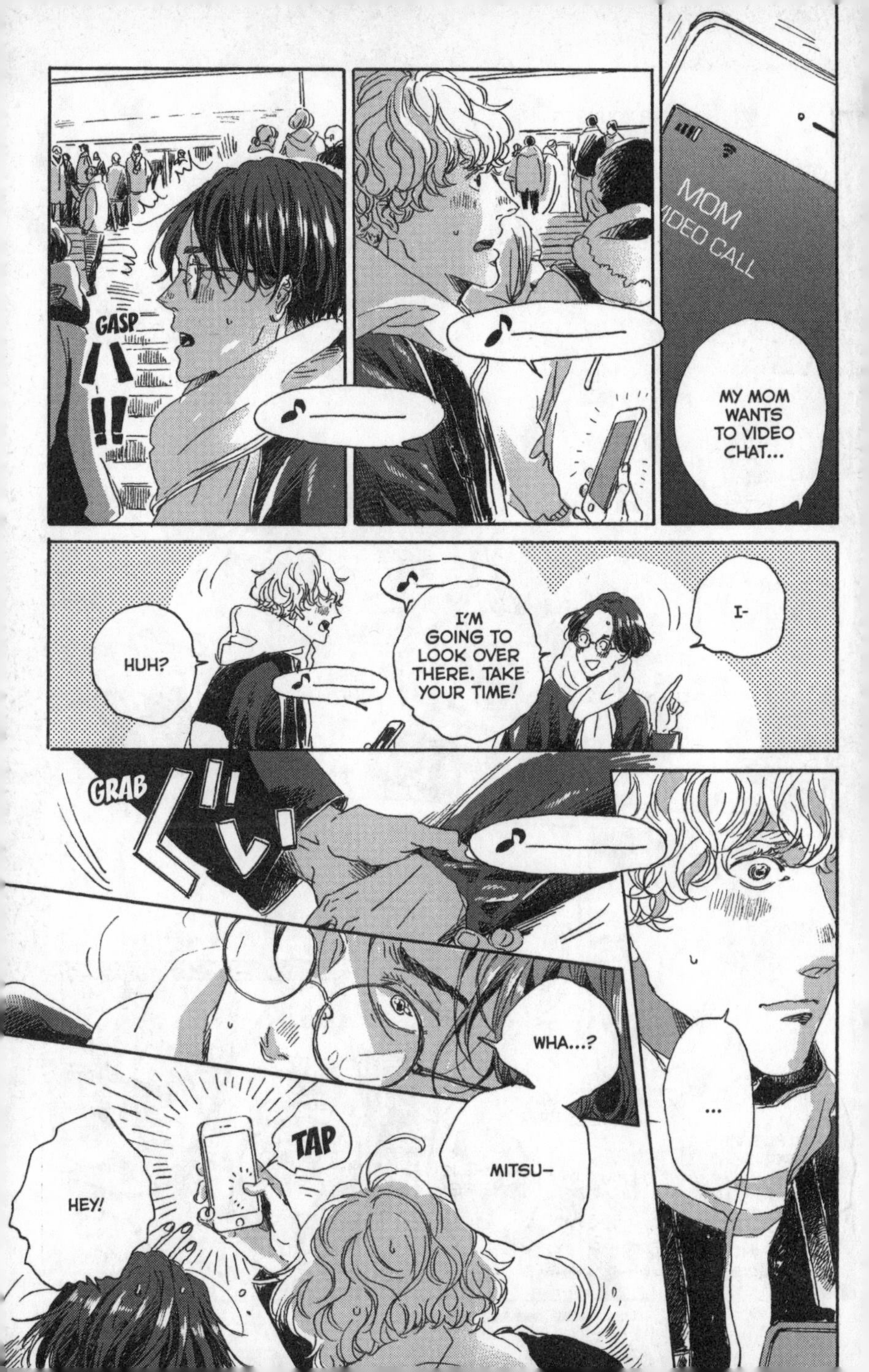
MOM
VIDEO CALL
MY MOM WANTS TO VIDEO CHAT...
♪—
GASP
!!
♪—
I-
I'M GOING TO LOOK OVER THERE. TAKE YOUR TIME!
♪—
HUH?
♪—
...
♪—
GRAB
WHA...?
MITSU-
TAP
HEY!

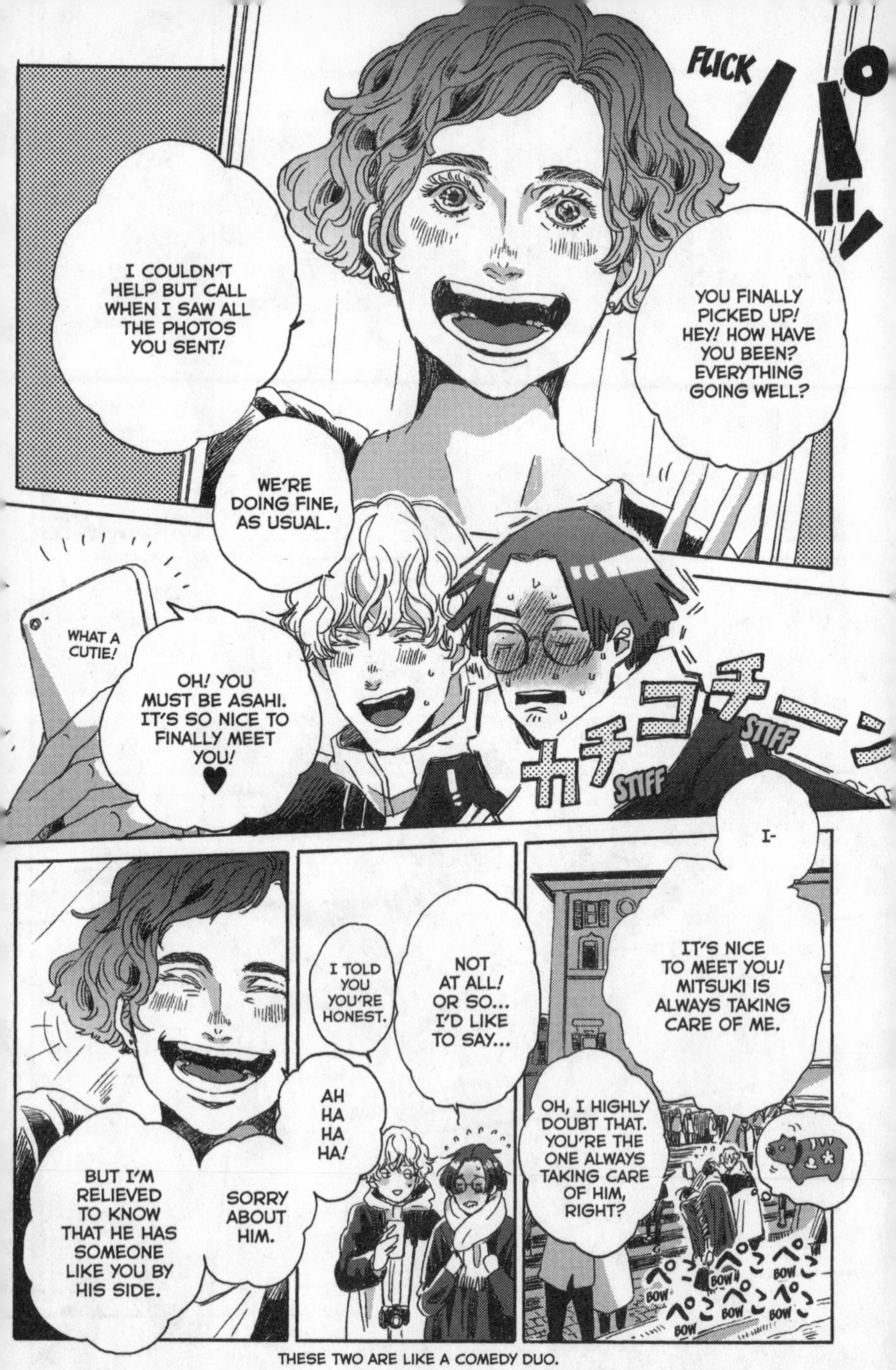

FLICK
YOU FINALLY PICKED UP! HEY! HOW HAVE YOU BEEN? EVERYTHING GOING WELL?
I COULDN'T HELP BUT CALL WHEN I SAW ALL THE PHOTOS YOU SENT!
WE'RE DOING FINE, AS USUAL.
STIFF
STIFF
OH! YOU MUST BE ASAHI. IT'S SO NICE TO FINALLY MEET YOU! ♥
WHAT A CUTIE!
I-
IT'S NICE TO MEET YOU! MITSUKI IS ALWAYS TAKING CARE OF ME.
OH, I HIGHLY DOUBT THAT. YOU'RE THE ONE ALWAYS TAKING CARE OF HIM, RIGHT?
BOW BOW BOW BOW BOW BOW
NOT AT ALL! OR SO... I'D LIKE TO SAY...
I TOLD YOU YOU'RE HONEST.
AH HA HA HA!
SORRY ABOUT HIM.
BUT I'M RELIEVED TO KNOW THAT HE HAS SOMEONE LIKE YOU BY HIS SIDE.

THESE TWO ARE LIKE A COMEDY DUO.

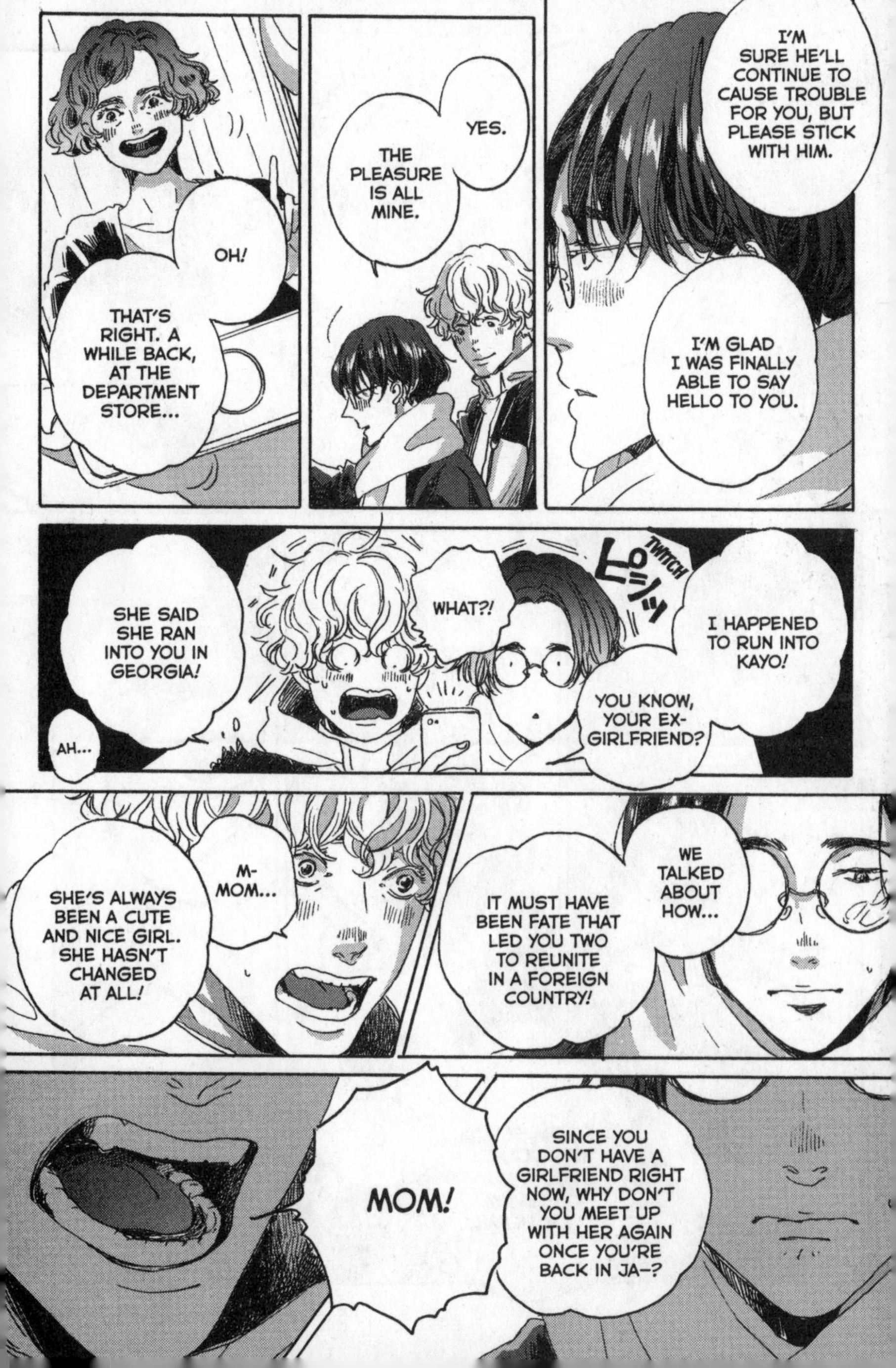
I'M SURE HE'LL CONTINUE TO CAUSE TROUBLE FOR YOU, BUT PLEASE STICK WITH HIM.
I'M GLAD I WAS FINALLY ABLE TO SAY HELLO TO YOU.
YES.
THE PLEASURE IS ALL MINE.
OH!
THAT'S RIGHT. A WHILE BACK, AT THE DEPARTMENT STORE...
I HAPPENED TO RUN INTO KAYO!
YOU KNOW, YOUR EX-GIRLFRIEND?
TWITCH
WHAT?!
SHE SAID SHE RAN INTO YOU IN GEORGIA!
AH...
WE TALKED ABOUT HOW...
IT MUST HAVE BEEN FATE THAT LED YOU TWO TO REUNITE IN A FOREIGN COUNTRY!
M-MOM...
SHE'S ALWAYS BEEN A CUTE AND NICE GIRL. SHE HASN'T CHANGED AT ALL!
SINCE YOU DON'T HAVE A GIRLFRIEND RIGHT NOW, WHY DON'T YOU MEET UP WITH HER AGAIN ONCE YOU'RE BACK IN JA-?
MOM!

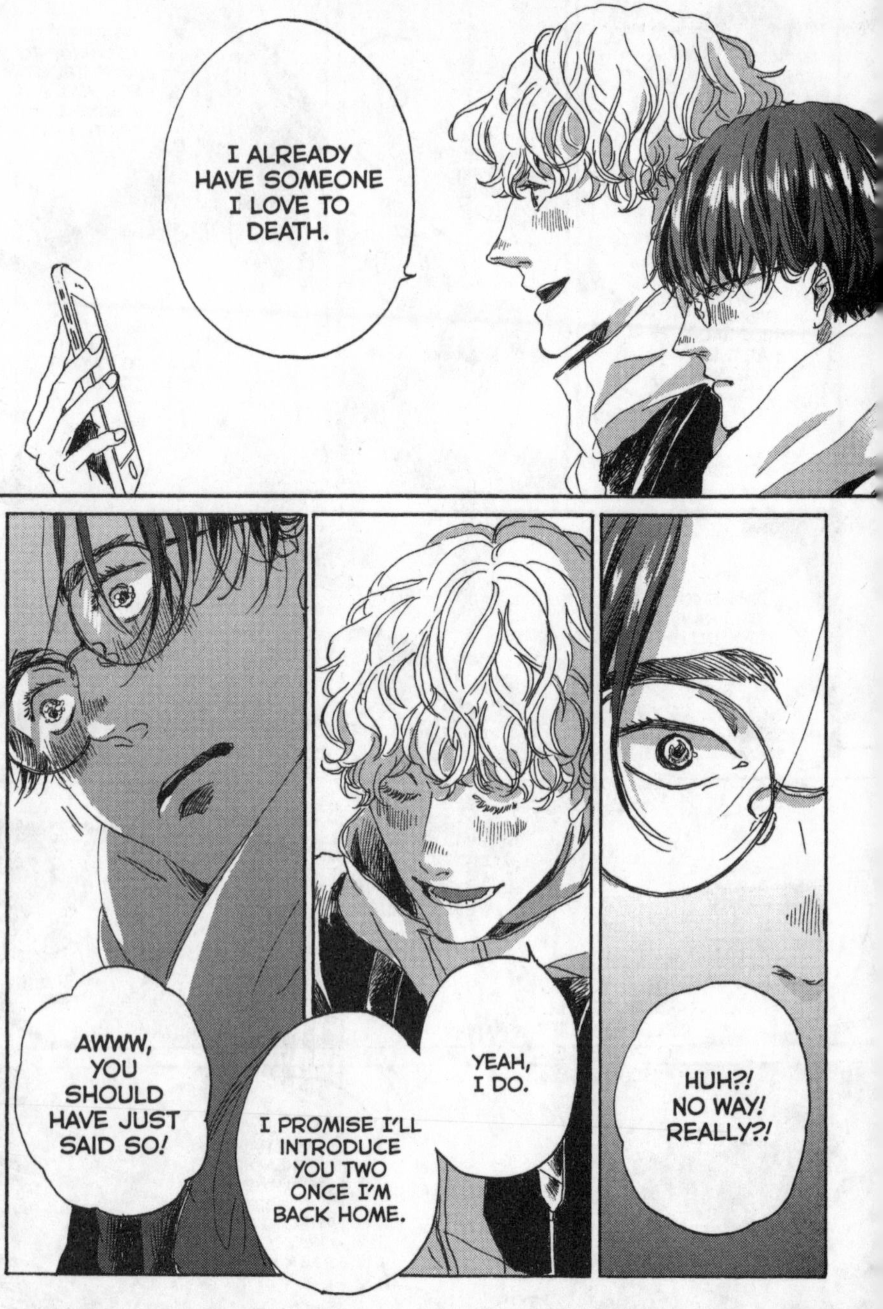
I ALREADY HAVE SOMEONE I LOVE TO DEATH.
HUH?! NO WAY! REALLY?!
YEAH, I DO.
AWWW, YOU SHOULD HAVE JUST SAID SO!
I PROMISE I'LL INTRODUCE YOU TWO ONCE I'M BACK HOME.

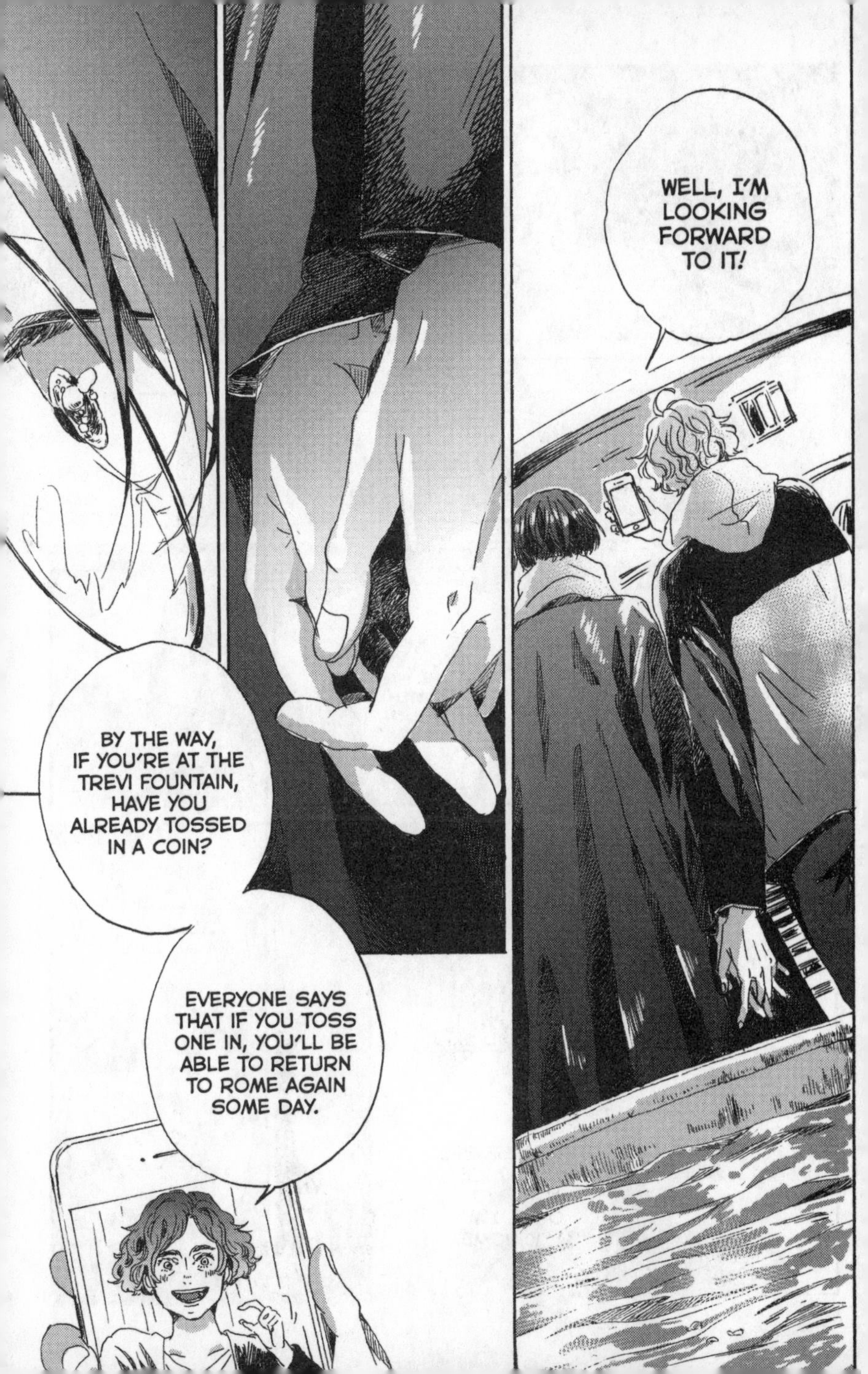
WELL, I'M LOOKING FORWARD TO IT!
BY THE WAY, IF YOU'RE AT THE TREVI FOUNTAIN, HAVE YOU ALREADY TOSSED IN A COIN?
EVERYONE SAYS THAT IF YOU TOSS ONE IN, YOU'LL BE ABLE TO RETURN TO ROME AGAIN SOME DAY.

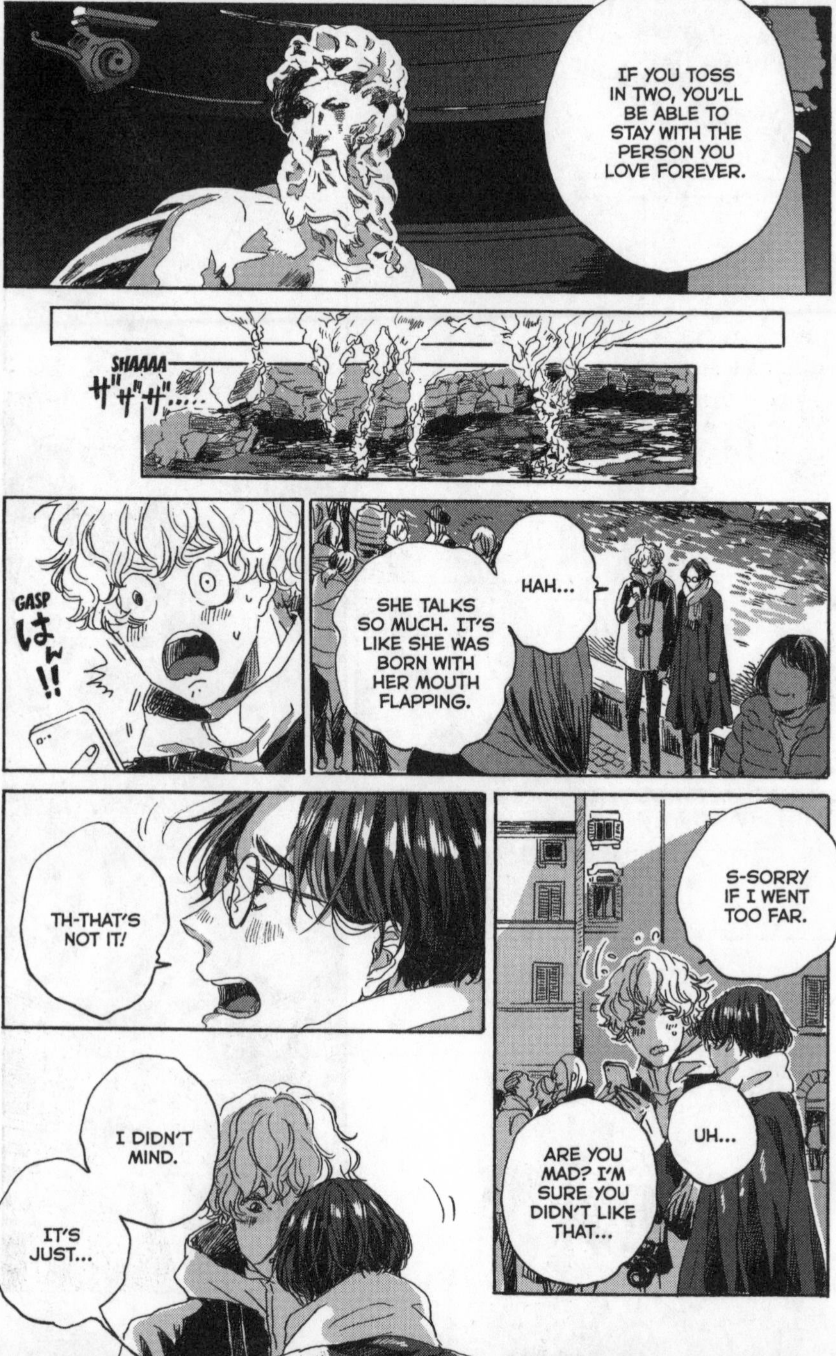
IF YOU TOSS IN TWO, YOU'LL BE ABLE TO STAY WITH THE PERSON YOU LOVE FOREVER.
SHAAAA
ザザザ……
HAH...
SHE TALKS SO MUCH. IT'S LIKE SHE WAS BORN WITH HER MOUTH FLAPPING.
GASP
はん!!
S-SORRY IF I WENT TOO FAR.
UH...
ARE YOU MAD? I'M SURE YOU DIDN'T LIKE THAT...
TH-THAT'S NOT IT!
I DIDN'T MIND.
IT'S JUST...

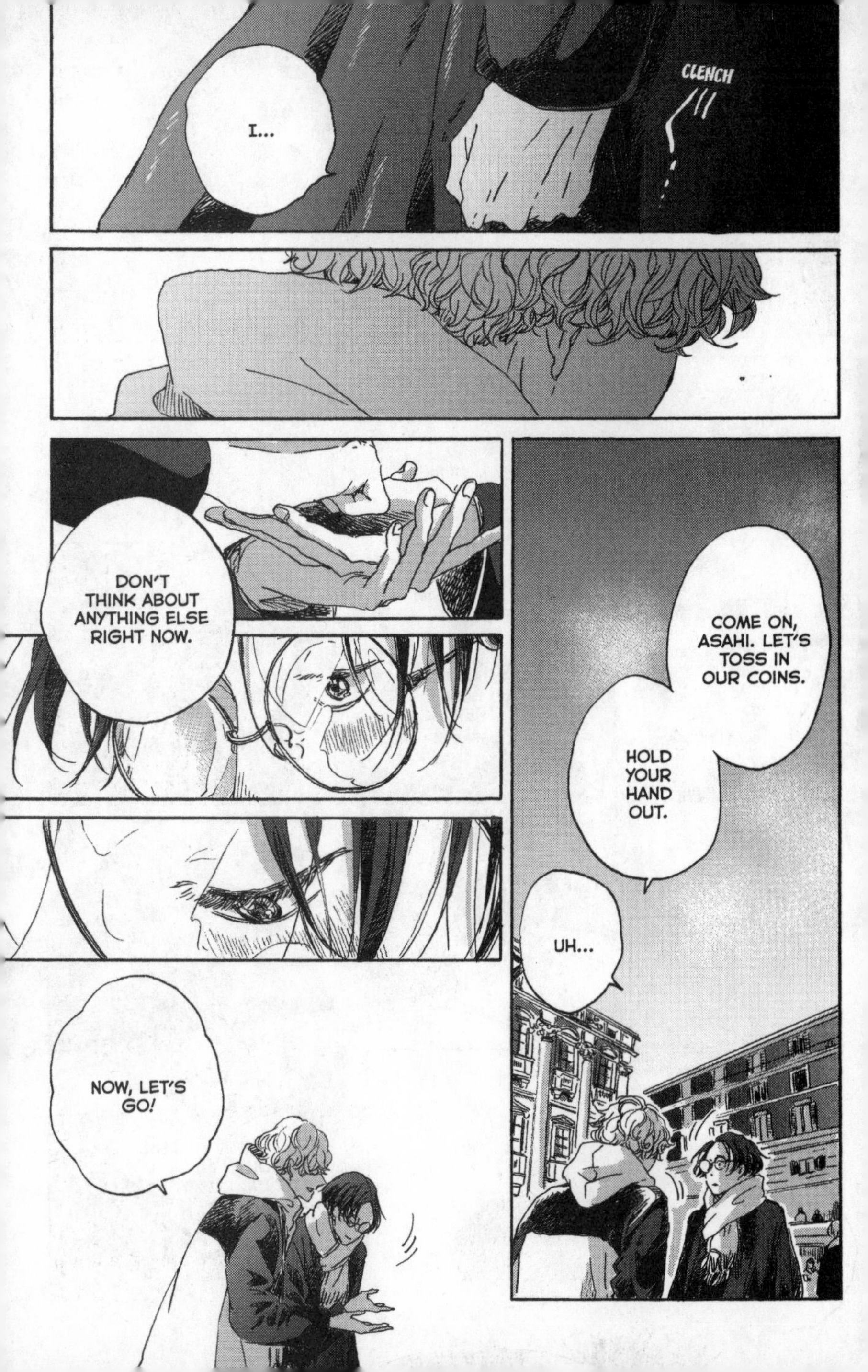
CLENCH
I...
COME ON, ASAHI. LET'S TOSS IN OUR COINS.
HOLD YOUR HAND OUT.
UH...
DON'T THINK ABOUT ANYTHING ELSE RIGHT NOW.
NOW, LET'S GO!

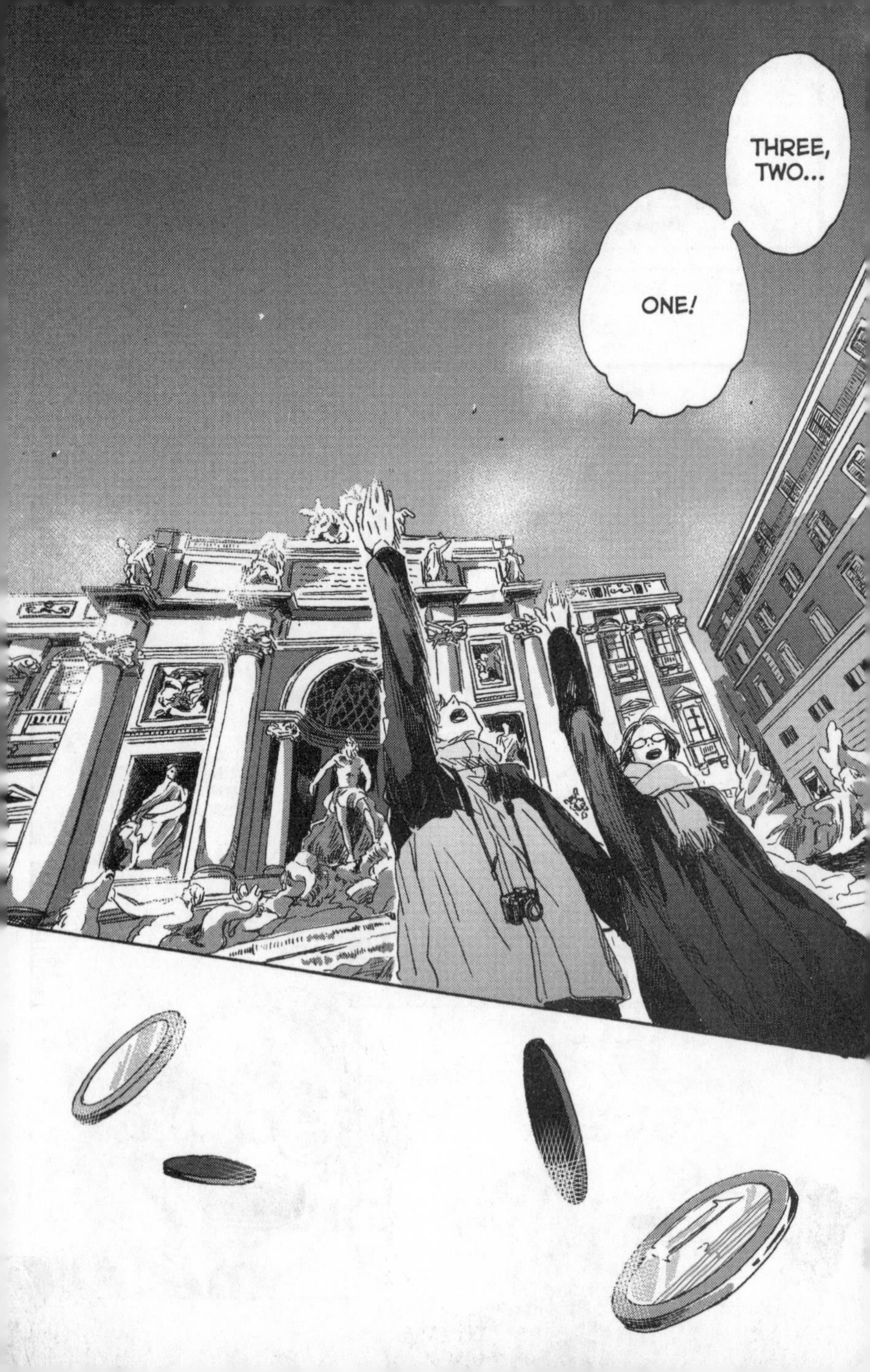
THREE, TWO...
ONE!

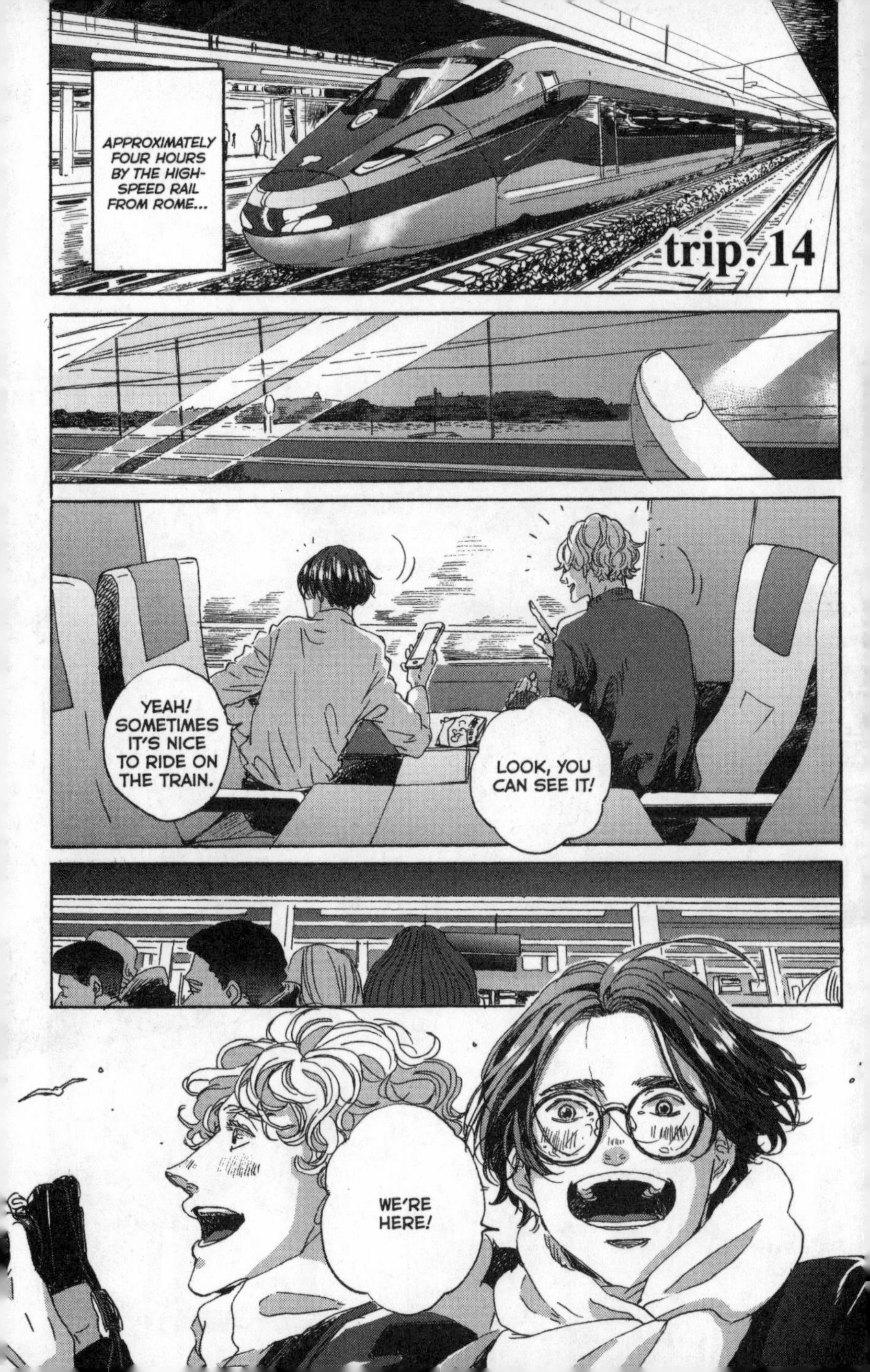
APPROXIMATELY FOUR HOURS BY THE HIGH-SPEED RAIL FROM ROME...
trip. 14
LOOK, YOU CAN SEE IT!
YEAH! SOMETIMES IT'S NICE TO RIDE ON THE TRAIN.
WE'RE HERE!

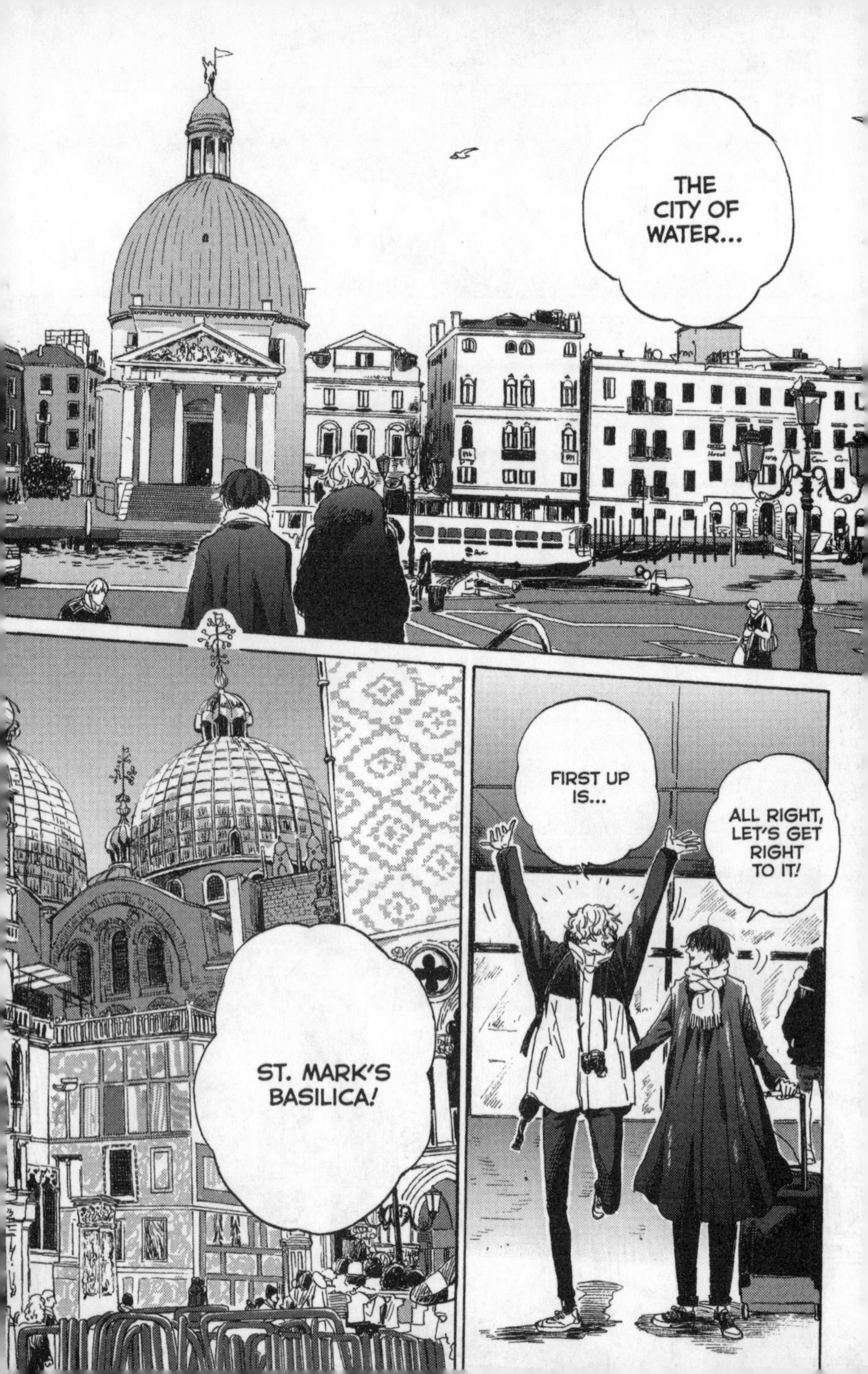
THE CITY OF WATER...
ALL RIGHT, LET'S GET RIGHT TO IT!
FIRST UP IS...
ST. MARK'S BASILICA!

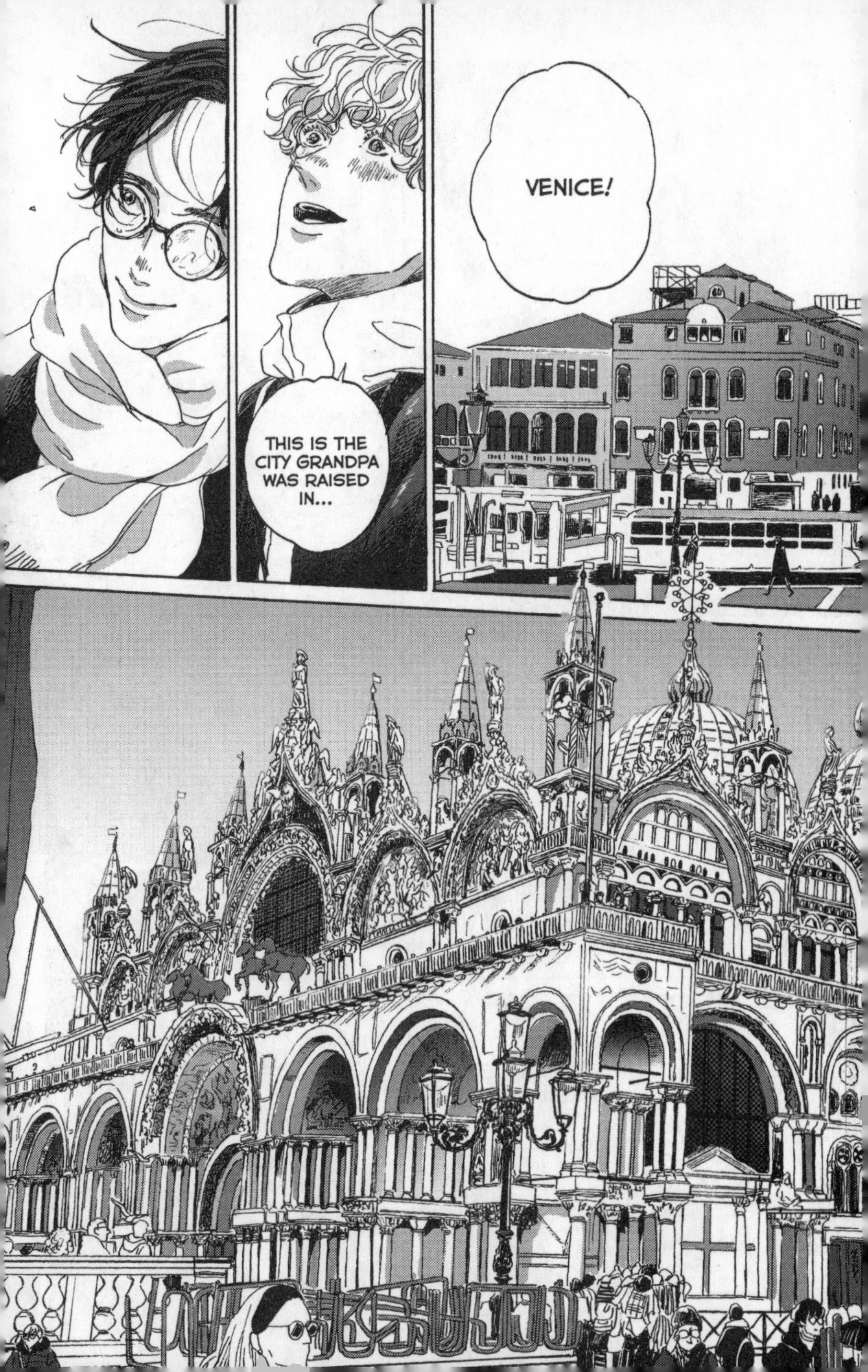
VENICE!
THIS IS THE CITY GRANDPA WAS RAISED IN...

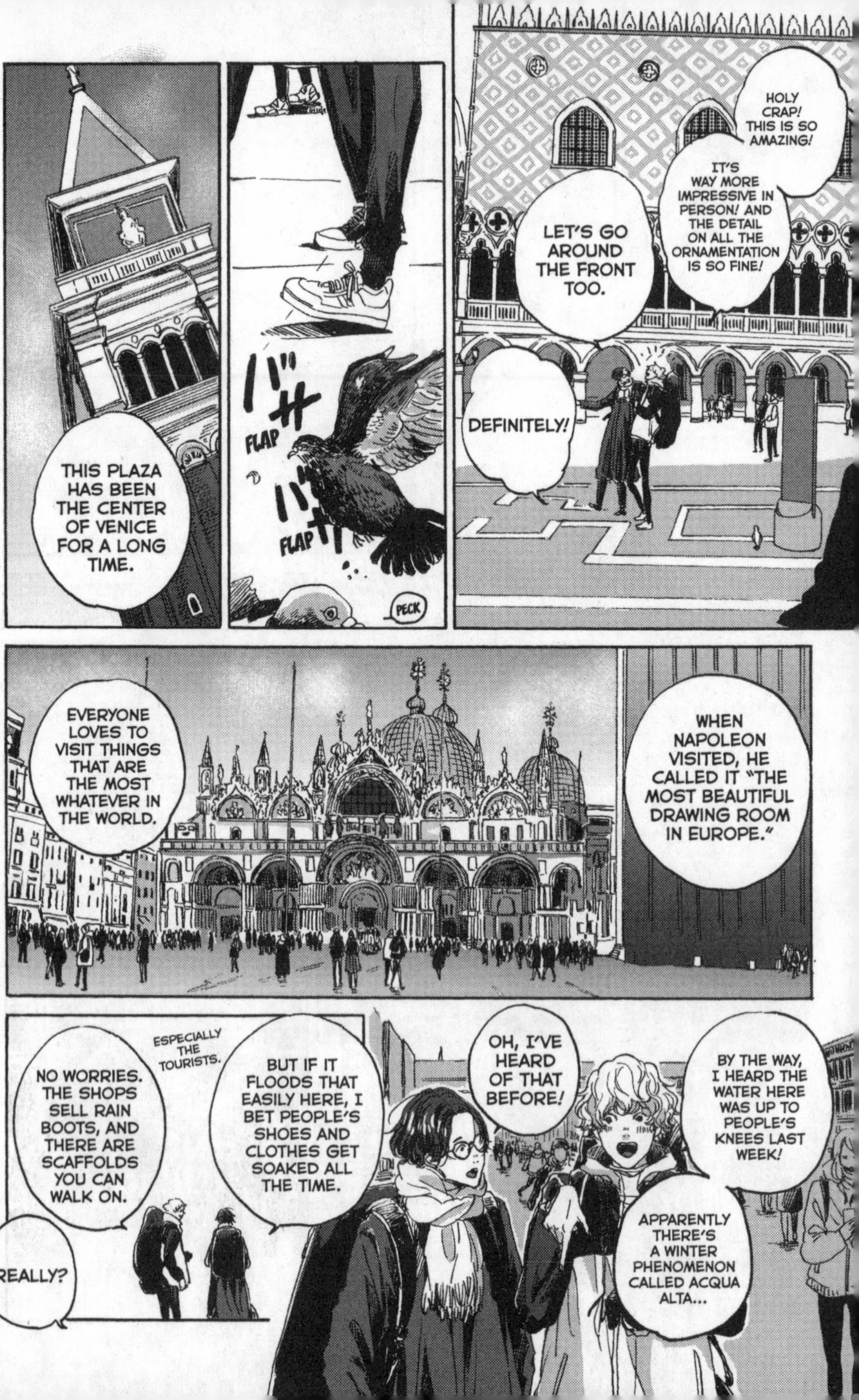
HOLY CRAP! THIS IS SO AMAZING!
IT'S WAY MORE IMPRESSIVE IN PERSON! AND THE DETAIL ON ALL THE ORNAMENTATION IS SO FINE!
LET'S GO AROUND THE FRONT TOO.
DEFINITELY!
FLAP
FLAP
PECK
THIS PLAZA HAS BEEN THE CENTER OF VENICE FOR A LONG TIME.
WHEN NAPOLEON VISITED, HE CALLED IT "THE MOST BEAUTIFUL DRAWING ROOM IN EUROPE."
EVERYONE LOVES TO VISIT THINGS THAT ARE THE MOST WHATEVER IN THE WORLD.
BY THE WAY, I HEARD THE WATER HERE WAS UP TO PEOPLE'S KNEES LAST WEEK!
APPARENTLY THERE'S A WINTER PHENOMENON CALLED ACQUA ALTA...
OH, I'VE HEARD OF THAT BEFORE!
BUT IF IT FLOODS THAT EASILY HERE, I BET PEOPLE'S SHOES AND CLOTHES GET SOAKED ALL THE TIME.
ESPECIALLY THE TOURISTS.
NO WORRIES. THE SHOPS SELL RAIN BOOTS, AND THERE ARE SCAFFOLDS YOU CAN WALK ON.
REALLY?

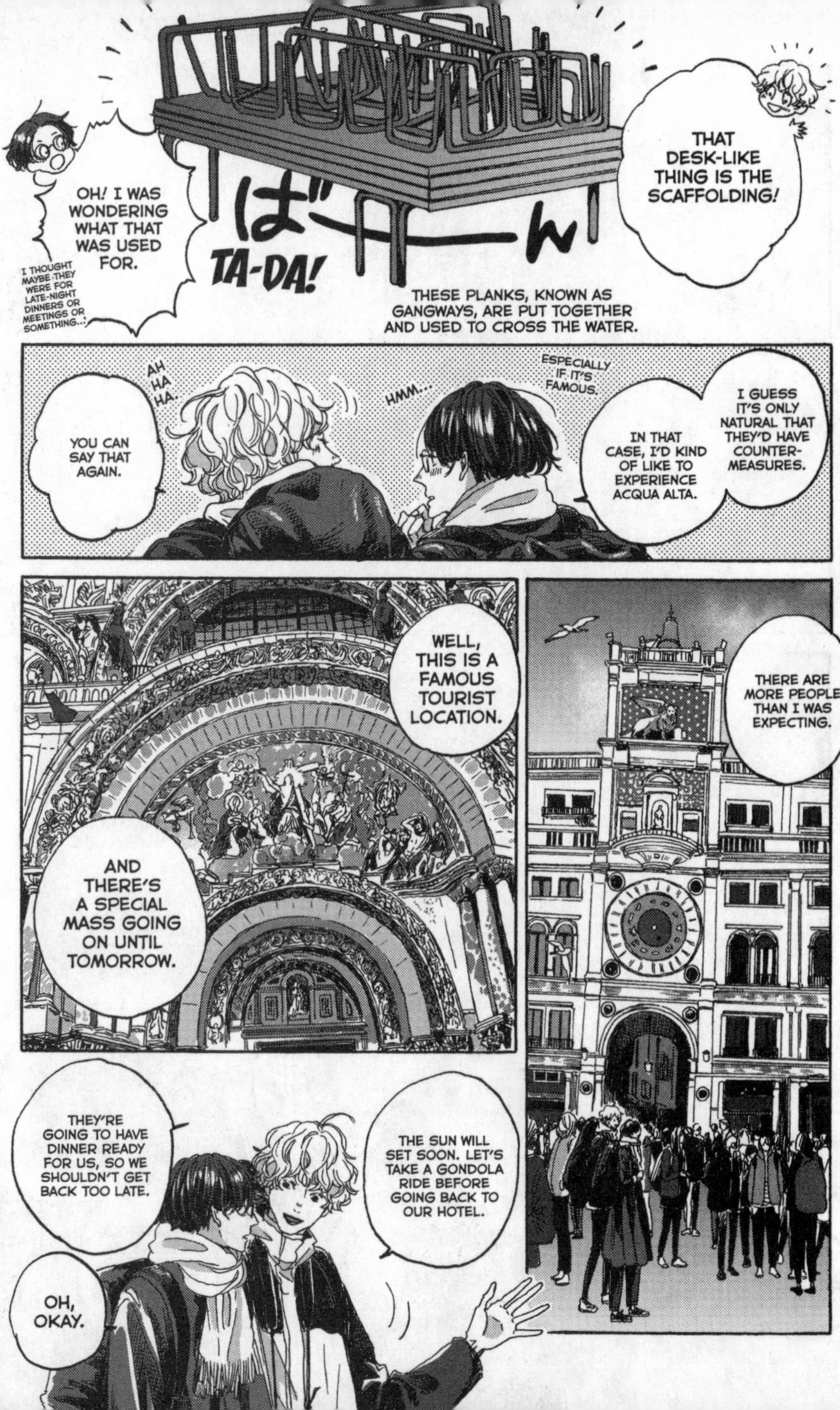
THAT DESK-LIKE THING IS THE SCAFFOLDING!
ばーん
TA-DA!
OH! I WAS WONDERING WHAT THAT WAS USED FOR.
I THOUGHT MAYBE THEY WERE FOR LATE-NIGHT DINNERS OR MEETINGS OR SOMETHING...
THESE PLANKS, KNOWN AS GANGWAYS, ARE PUT TOGETHER AND USED TO CROSS THE WATER.
I GUESS IT'S ONLY NATURAL THAT THEY'D HAVE COUNTER-MEASURES.
ESPECIALLY IF IT'S FAMOUS.
IN THAT CASE, I'D KIND OF LIKE TO EXPERIENCE ACQUA ALTA.
HMM...
AH HA HA.
YOU CAN SAY THAT AGAIN.
THERE ARE MORE PEOPLE THAN I WAS EXPECTING.
WELL, THIS IS A FAMOUS TOURIST LOCATION.
AND THERE'S A SPECIAL MASS GOING ON UNTIL TOMORROW.
THE SUN WILL SET SOON. LET'S TAKE A GONDOLA RIDE BEFORE GOING BACK TO OUR HOTEL.
THEY'RE GOING TO HAVE DINNER READY FOR US, SO WE SHOULDN'T GET BACK TOO LATE.
OH, OKAY.

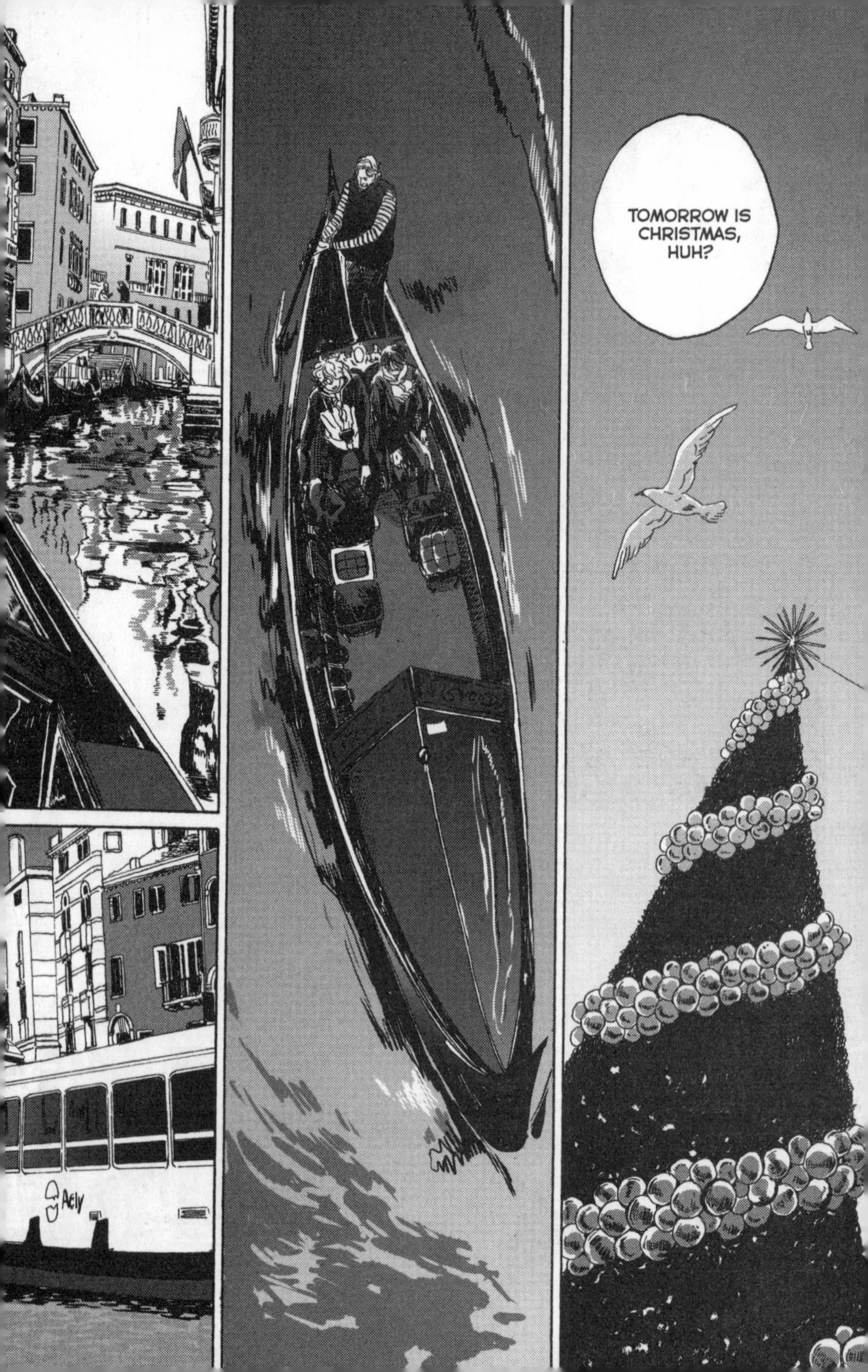
TOMORROW IS CHRISTMAS, HUH?

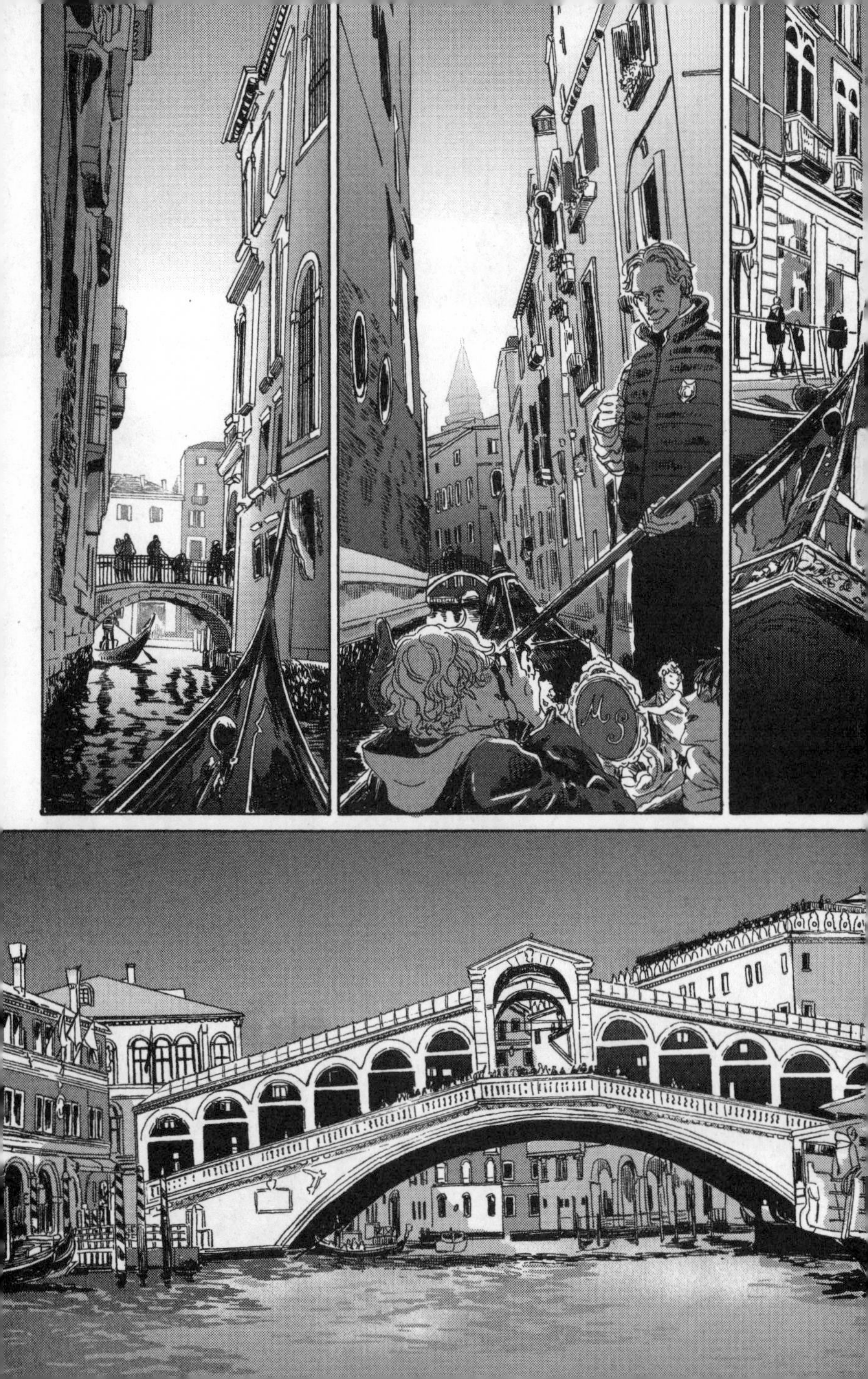

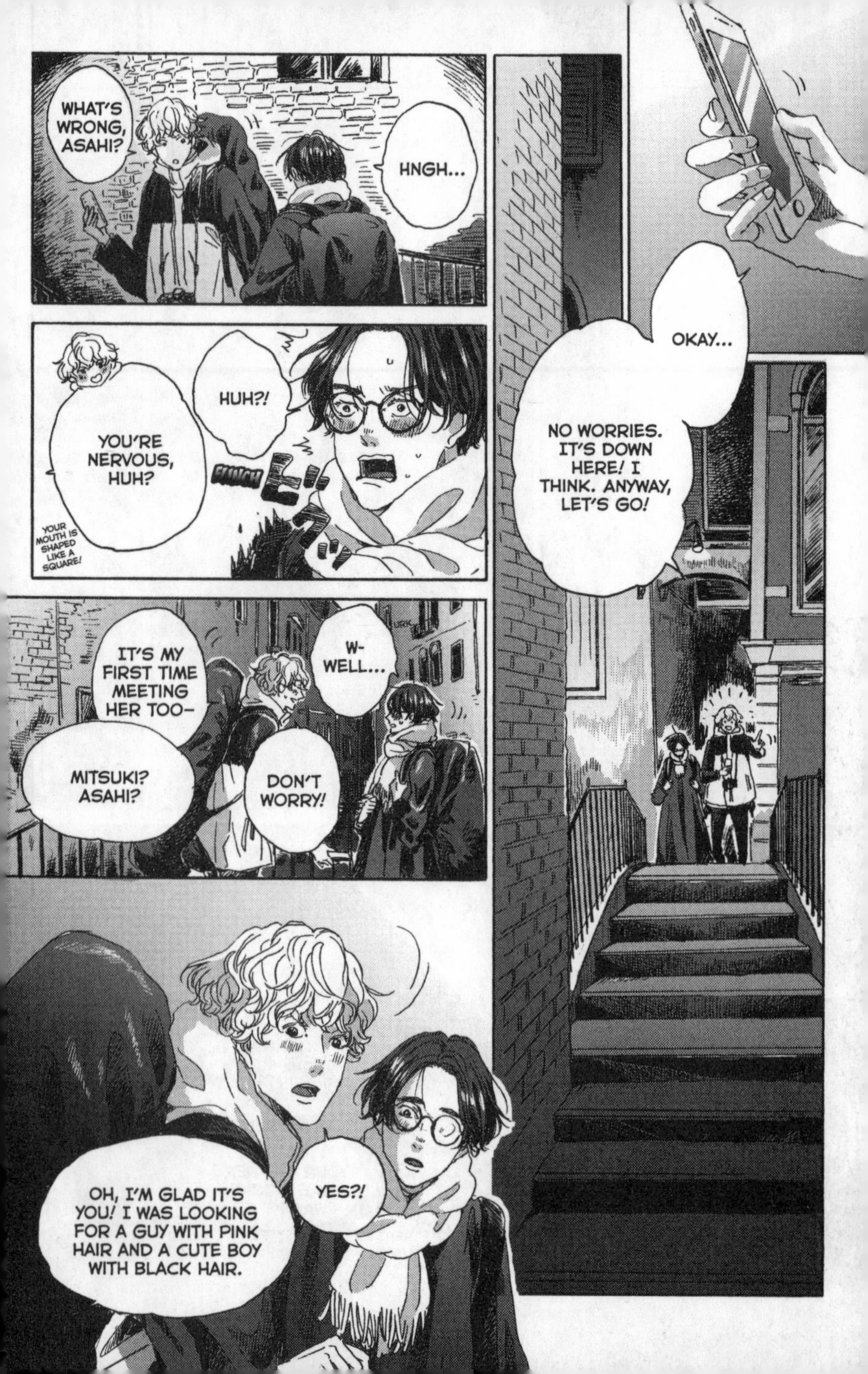
OKAY...
NO WORRIES. IT'S DOWN HERE! I THINK. ANYWAY, LET'S GO!
HNGH...
WHAT'S WRONG, ASAHI?
HUH?!
YOU'RE NERVOUS, HUH?
FLINCH
YOUR MOUTH IS SHAPED LIKE A SQUARE!
W-WELL...
URK
IT'S MY FIRST TIME MEETING HER TOO–
DON'T WORRY!
MITSUKI? ASAHI?
YES?!
OH, I'M GLAD IT'S YOU! I WAS LOOKING FOR A GUY WITH PINK HAIR AND A CUTE BOY WITH BLACK HAIR.

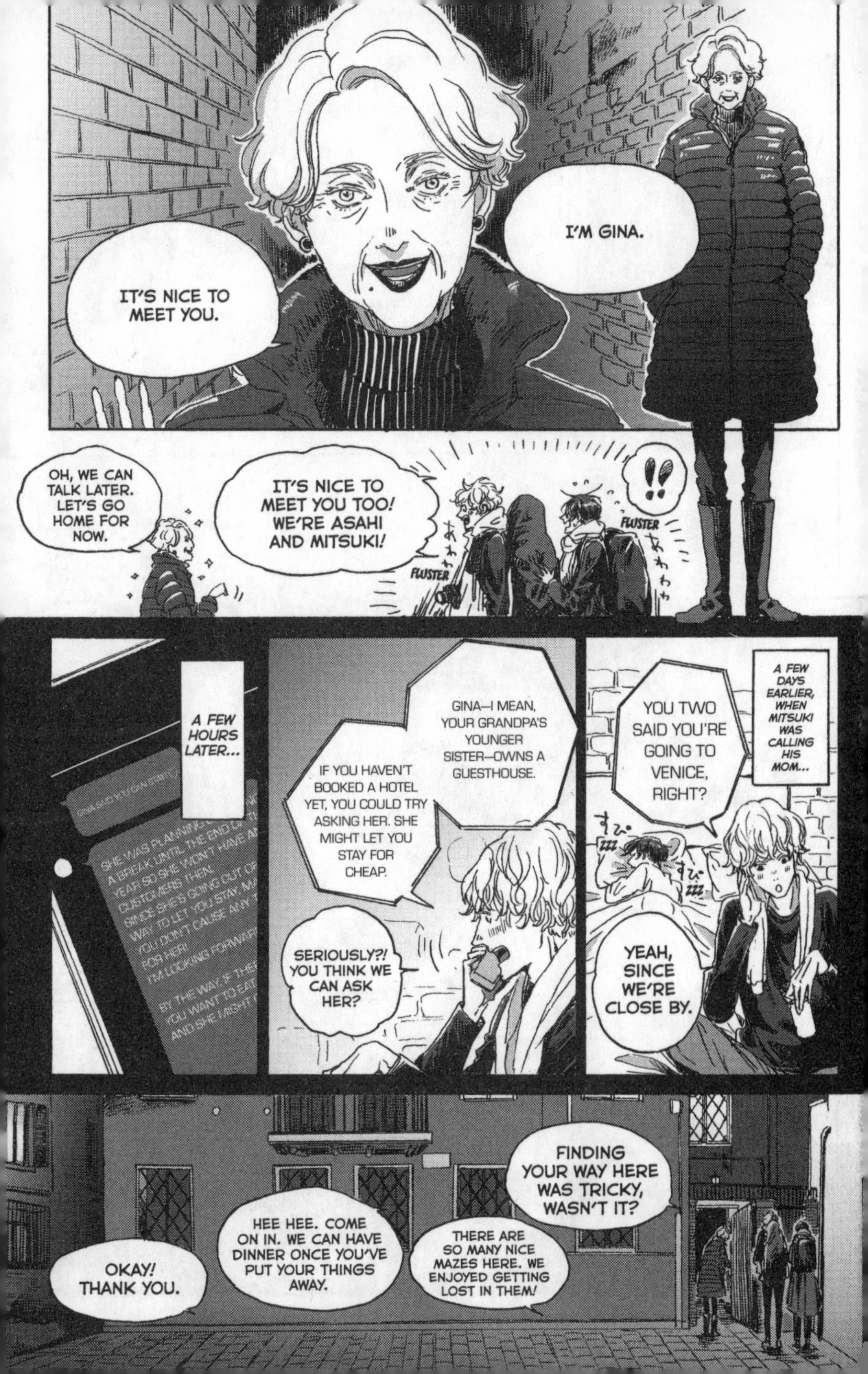
I'M GINA.
IT'S NICE TO MEET YOU.
!!
FLUSTER
IT'S NICE TO MEET YOU TOO! WE'RE ASAHI AND MITSUKI!
FLUSTER
OH, WE CAN TALK LATER. LET'S GO HOME FOR NOW.
A FEW DAYS EARLIER, WHEN MITSUKI WAS CALLING HIS MOM...
YOU TWO SAID YOU'RE GOING TO VENICE, RIGHT?
ZZZ
ZZZ
YEAH, SINCE WE'RE CLOSE BY.
GINA—I MEAN, YOUR GRANDPA'S YOUNGER SISTER—OWNS A GUESTHOUSE.
IF YOU HAVEN'T BOOKED A HOTEL YET, YOU COULD TRY ASKING HER. SHE MIGHT LET YOU STAY FOR CHEAP.
SERIOUSLY?! YOU THINK WE CAN ASK HER?
A FEW HOURS LATER...
FINDING YOUR WAY HERE WAS TRICKY, WASN'T IT?
THERE ARE SO MANY NICE MAZES HERE. WE ENJOYED GETTING LOST IN THEM!
HEE HEE. COME ON IN. WE CAN HAVE DINNER ONCE YOU'VE PUT YOUR THINGS AWAY.
OKAY! THANK YOU.

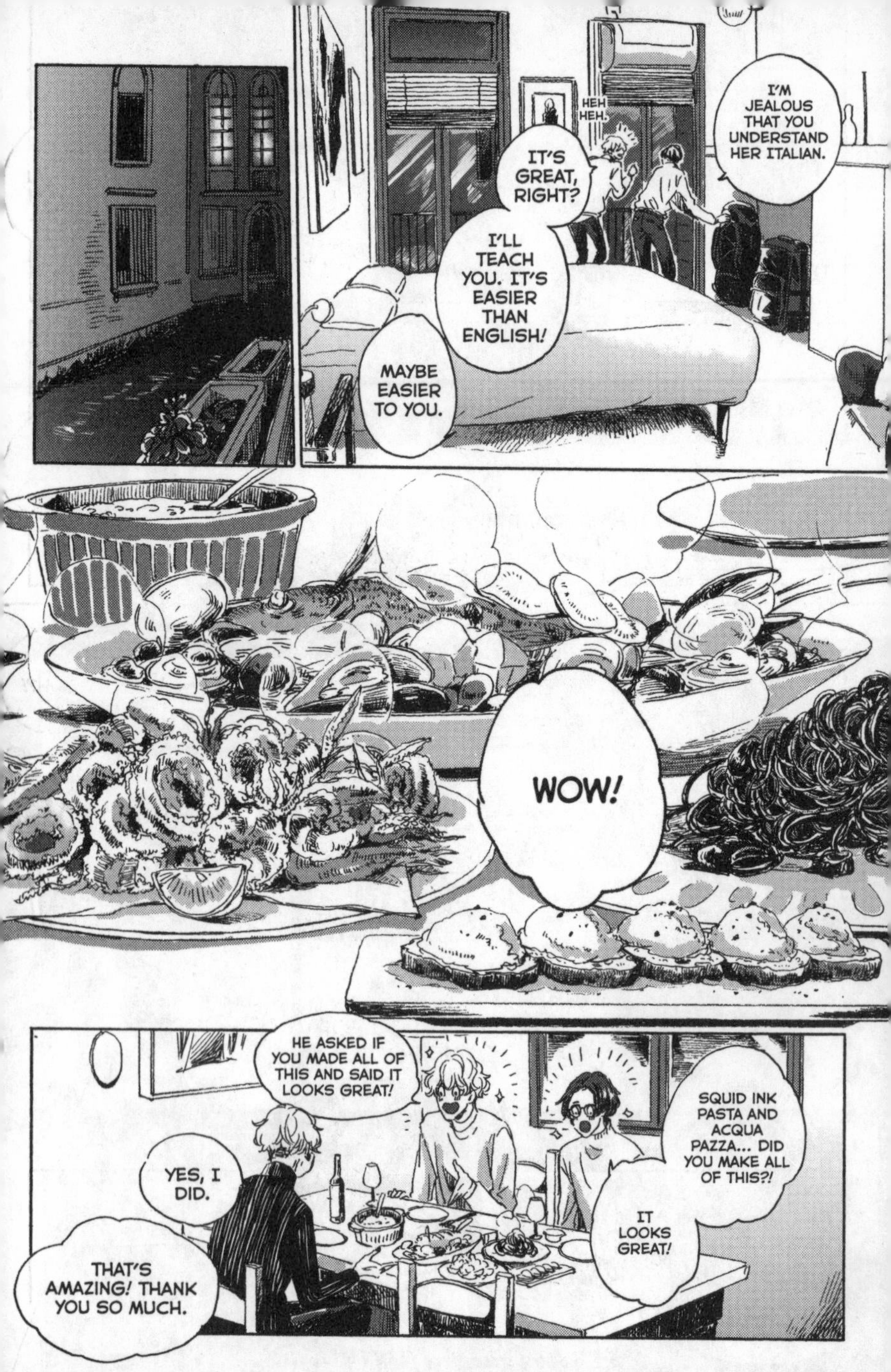
I'M JEALOUS THAT YOU UNDERSTAND HER ITALIAN.
HEH HEH.
IT'S GREAT, RIGHT?
I'LL TEACH YOU. IT'S EASIER THAN ENGLISH!
MAYBE EASIER TO YOU.
WOW!
SQUID INK PASTA AND ACQUA PAZZA... DID YOU MAKE ALL OF THIS?!
IT LOOKS GREAT!
HE ASKED IF YOU MADE ALL OF THIS AND SAID IT LOOKS GREAT!
YES, I DID.
THAT'S AMAZING! THANK YOU SO MUCH.

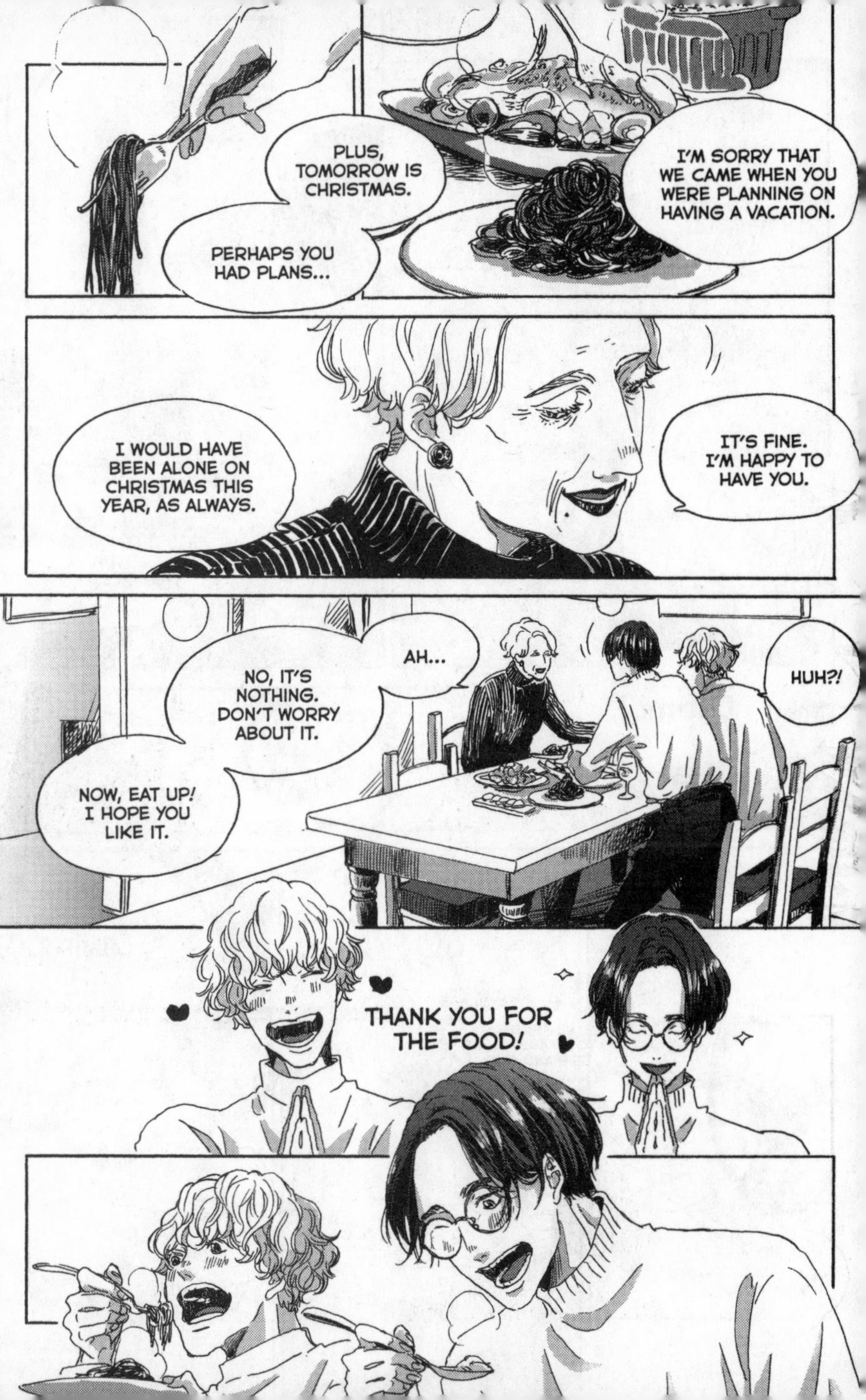
I'M SORRY THAT WE CAME WHEN YOU WERE PLANNING ON HAVING A VACATION.
PLUS, TOMORROW IS CHRISTMAS.
PERHAPS YOU HAD PLANS...
IT'S FINE. I'M HAPPY TO HAVE YOU.
I WOULD HAVE BEEN ALONE ON CHRISTMAS THIS YEAR, AS ALWAYS.
HUH?!
AH...
NO, IT'S NOTHING. DON'T WORRY ABOUT IT.
NOW, EAT UP! I HOPE YOU LIKE IT.
THANK YOU FOR THE FOOD!

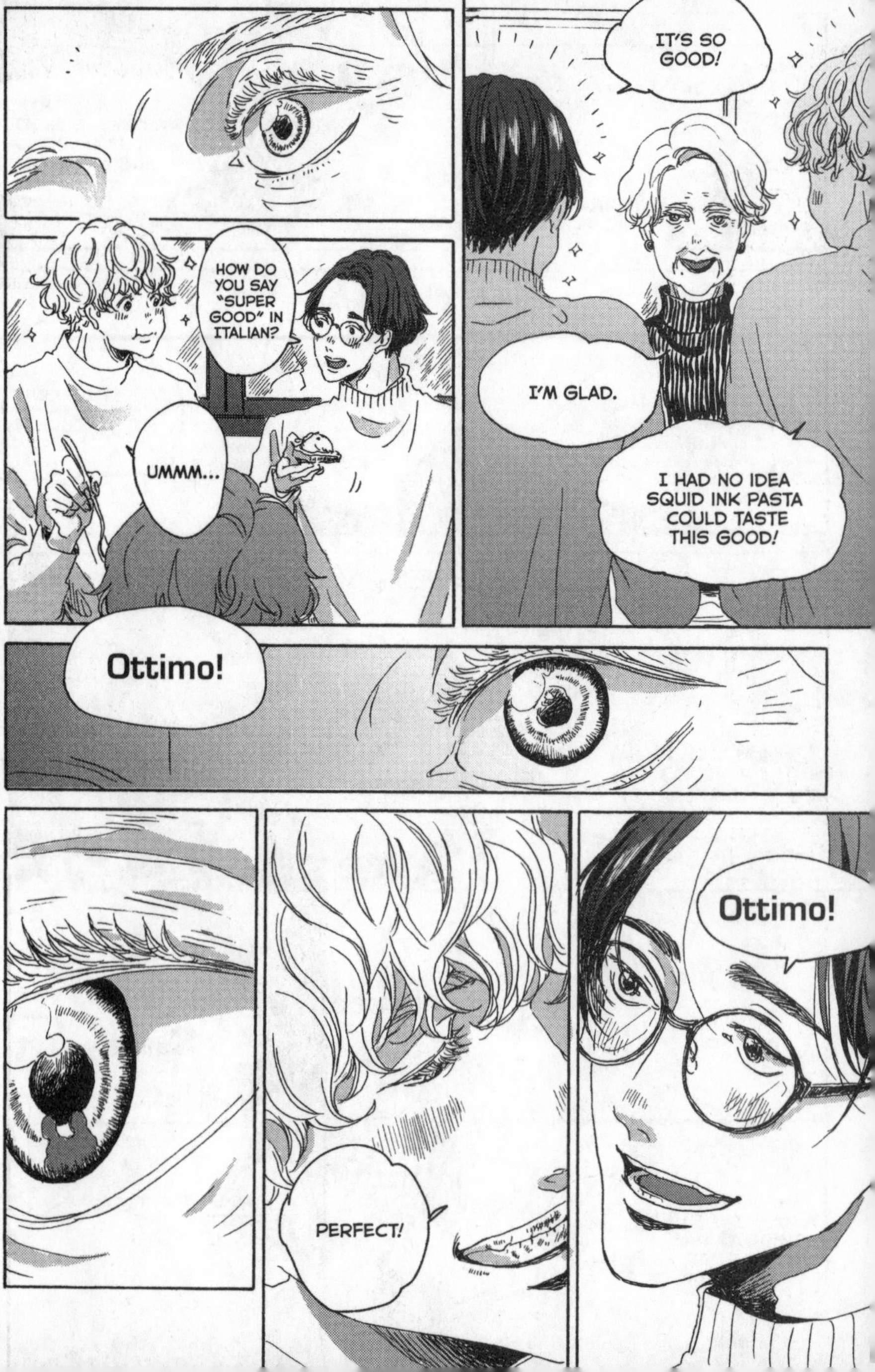
IT'S SO GOOD!
I'M GLAD.
I HAD NO IDEA SQUID INK PASTA COULD TASTE THIS GOOD!
HOW DO YOU SAY "SUPER GOOD" IN ITALIAN?
UMMM...
Ottimo!
Ottimo!
PERFECT!

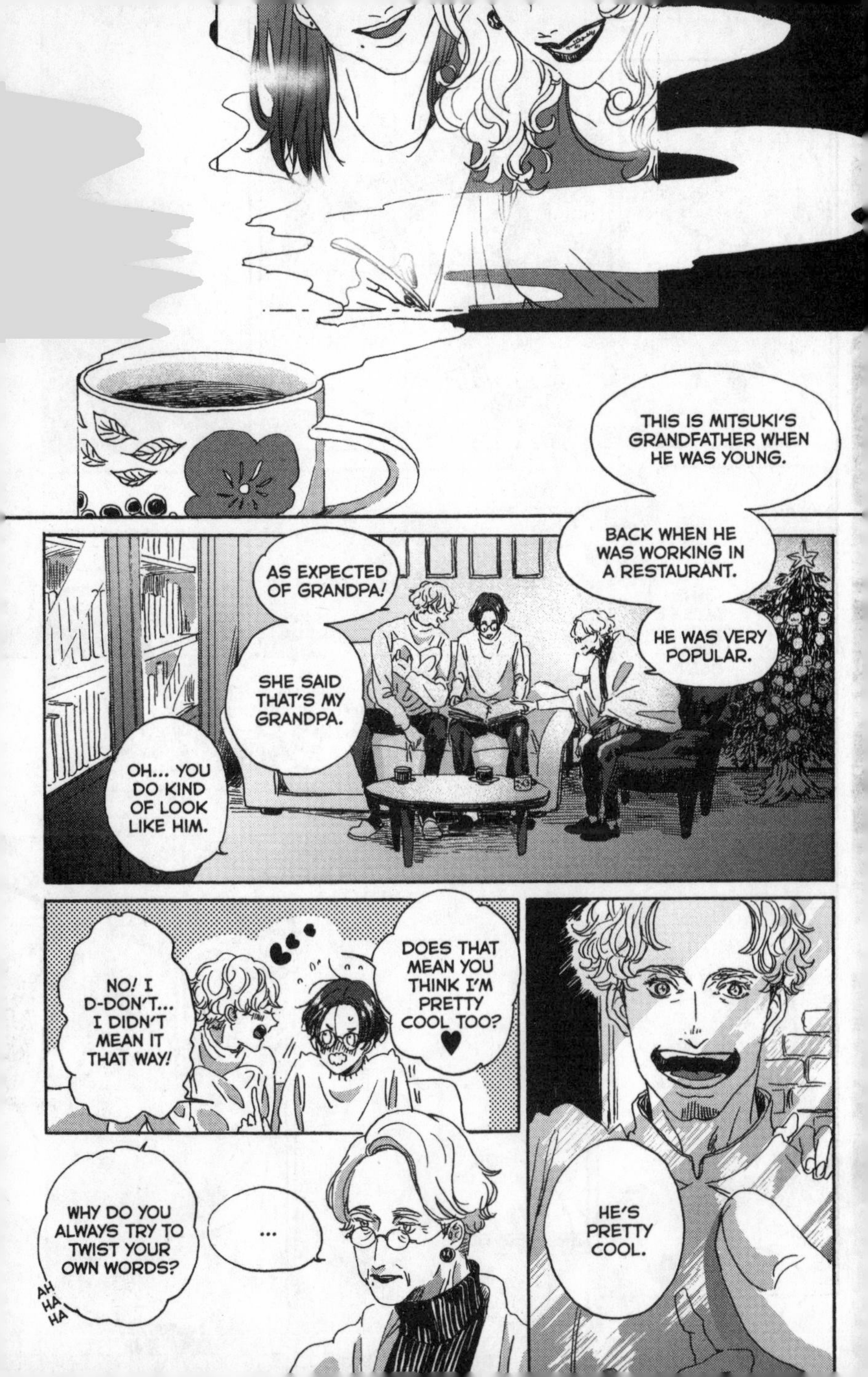
THIS IS MITSUKI'S GRANDFATHER WHEN HE WAS YOUNG.
BACK WHEN HE WAS WORKING IN A RESTAURANT.
HE WAS VERY POPULAR.
AS EXPECTED OF GRANDPA!
SHE SAID THAT'S MY GRANDPA.
OH... YOU DO KIND OF LOOK LIKE HIM.
HE'S PRETTY COOL.
DOES THAT MEAN YOU THINK I'M PRETTY COOL TOO? ♥
NO! I D-DON'T... I DIDN'T MEAN IT THAT WAY!
...
WHY DO YOU ALWAYS TRY TO TWIST YOUR OWN WORDS?
AH HA HA

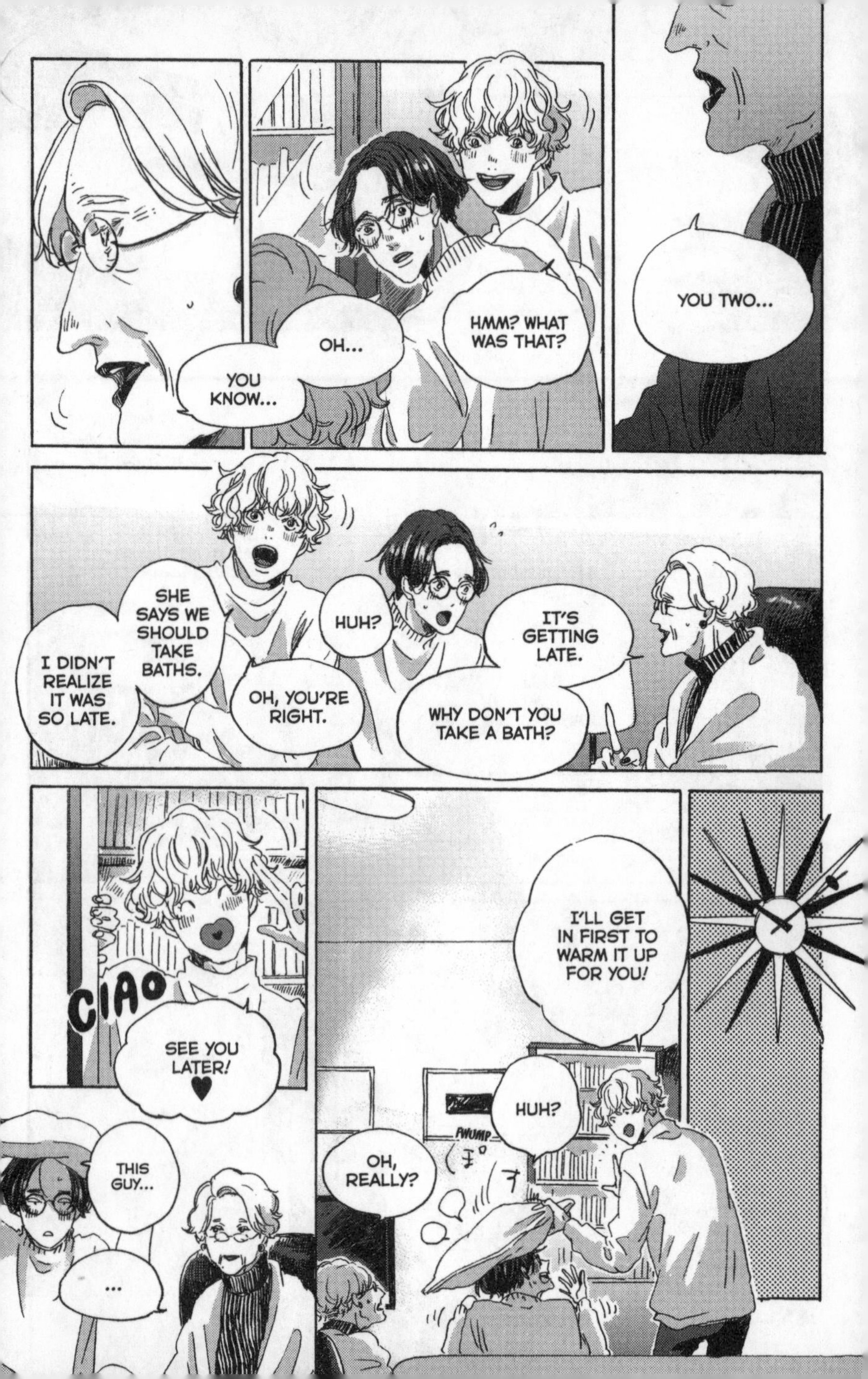
YOU TWO...
HMM? WHAT WAS THAT?
OH...
YOU KNOW...
IT'S GETTING LATE.
WHY DON'T YOU TAKE A BATH?
HUH?
OH, YOU'RE RIGHT.
SHE SAYS WE SHOULD TAKE BATHS.
I DIDN'T REALIZE IT WAS SO LATE.
I'LL GET IN FIRST TO WARM IT UP FOR YOU!
HUH?
FWUMP
OH, REALLY?
CIAO
SEE YOU LATER! ♥
THIS GUY...
...

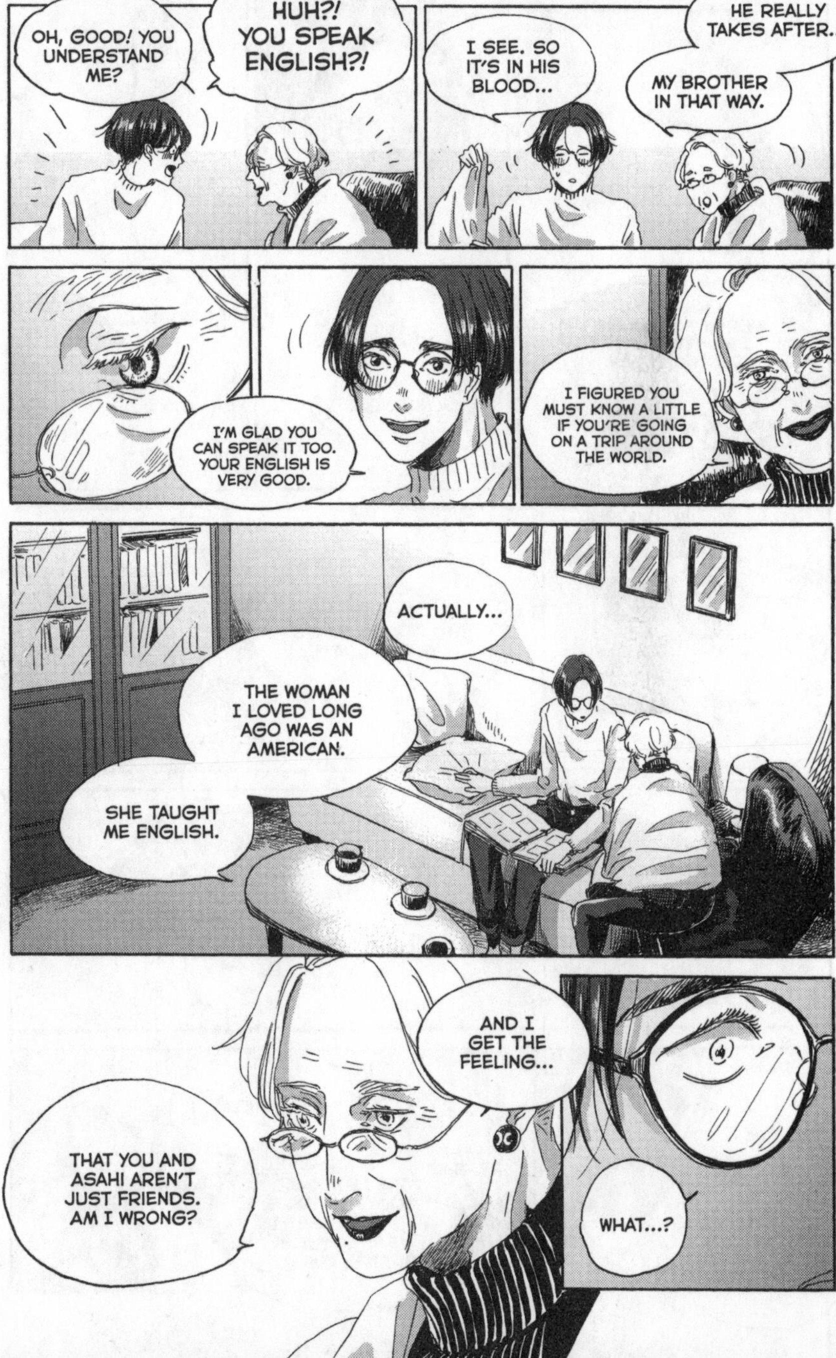
OH, GOOD! YOU UNDERSTAND ME?
HUH?! YOU SPEAK ENGLISH?!
I SEE. SO IT'S IN HIS BLOOD...
HE REALLY TAKES AFTER...
MY BROTHER IN THAT WAY.
I'M GLAD YOU CAN SPEAK IT TOO. YOUR ENGLISH IS VERY GOOD.
I FIGURED YOU MUST KNOW A LITTLE IF YOU'RE GOING ON A TRIP AROUND THE WORLD.
ACTUALLY...
THE WOMAN I LOVED LONG AGO WAS AN AMERICAN.
SHE TAUGHT ME ENGLISH.
AND I GET THE FEELING...
THAT YOU AND ASAHI AREN'T JUST FRIENDS. AM I WRONG?
WHAT...?

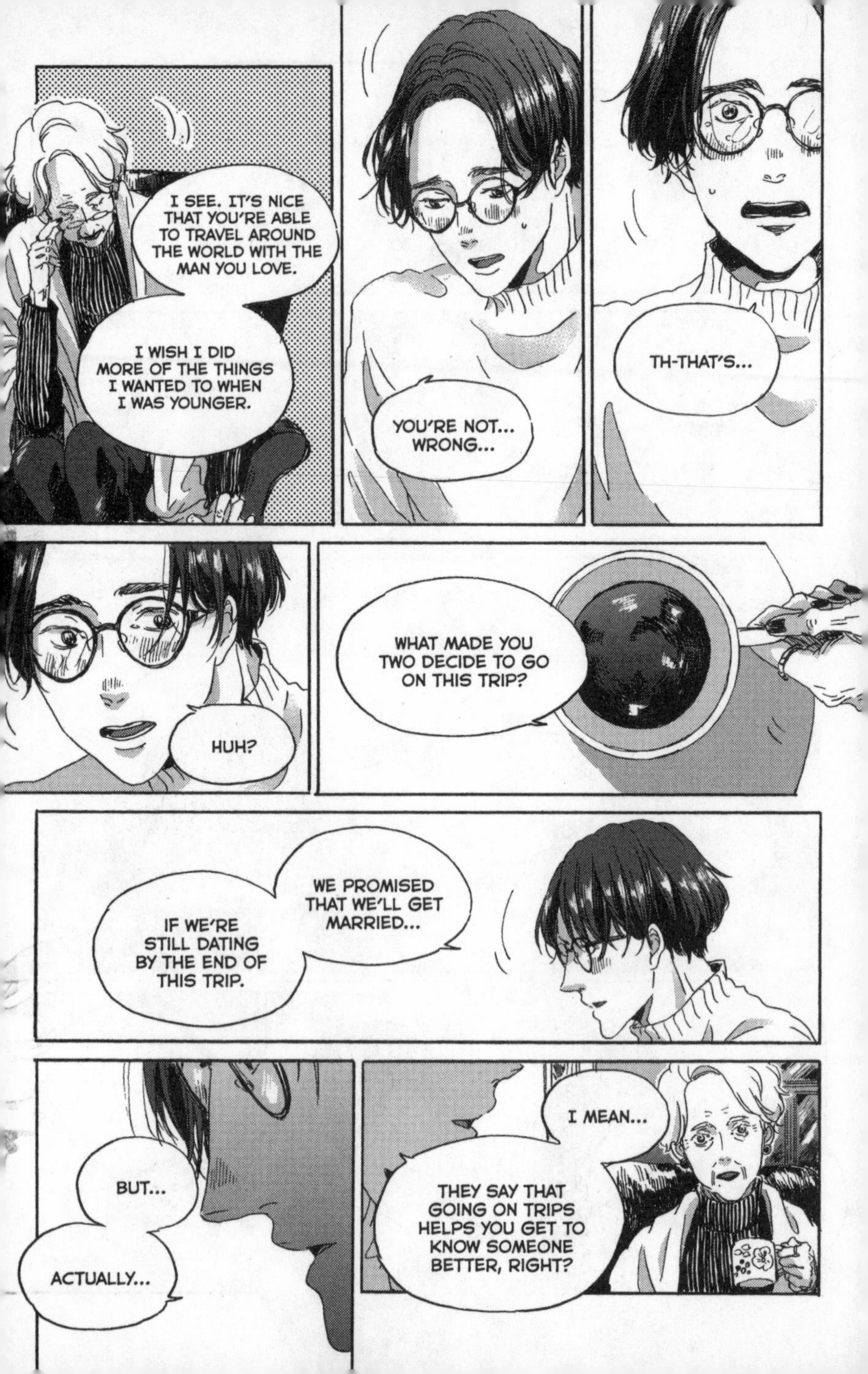
TH-THAT'S...
YOU'RE NOT... WRONG...
I SEE. IT'S NICE THAT YOU'RE ABLE TO TRAVEL AROUND THE WORLD WITH THE MAN YOU LOVE.
I WISH I DID MORE OF THE THINGS I WANTED TO WHEN I WAS YOUNGER.
WHAT MADE YOU TWO DECIDE TO GO ON THIS TRIP?
HUH?
WE PROMISED THAT WE'LL GET MARRIED...
IF WE'RE STILL DATING BY THE END OF THIS TRIP.
I MEAN...
THEY SAY THAT GOING ON TRIPS HELPS YOU GET TO KNOW SOMEONE BETTER, RIGHT?
BUT...
ACTUALLY...

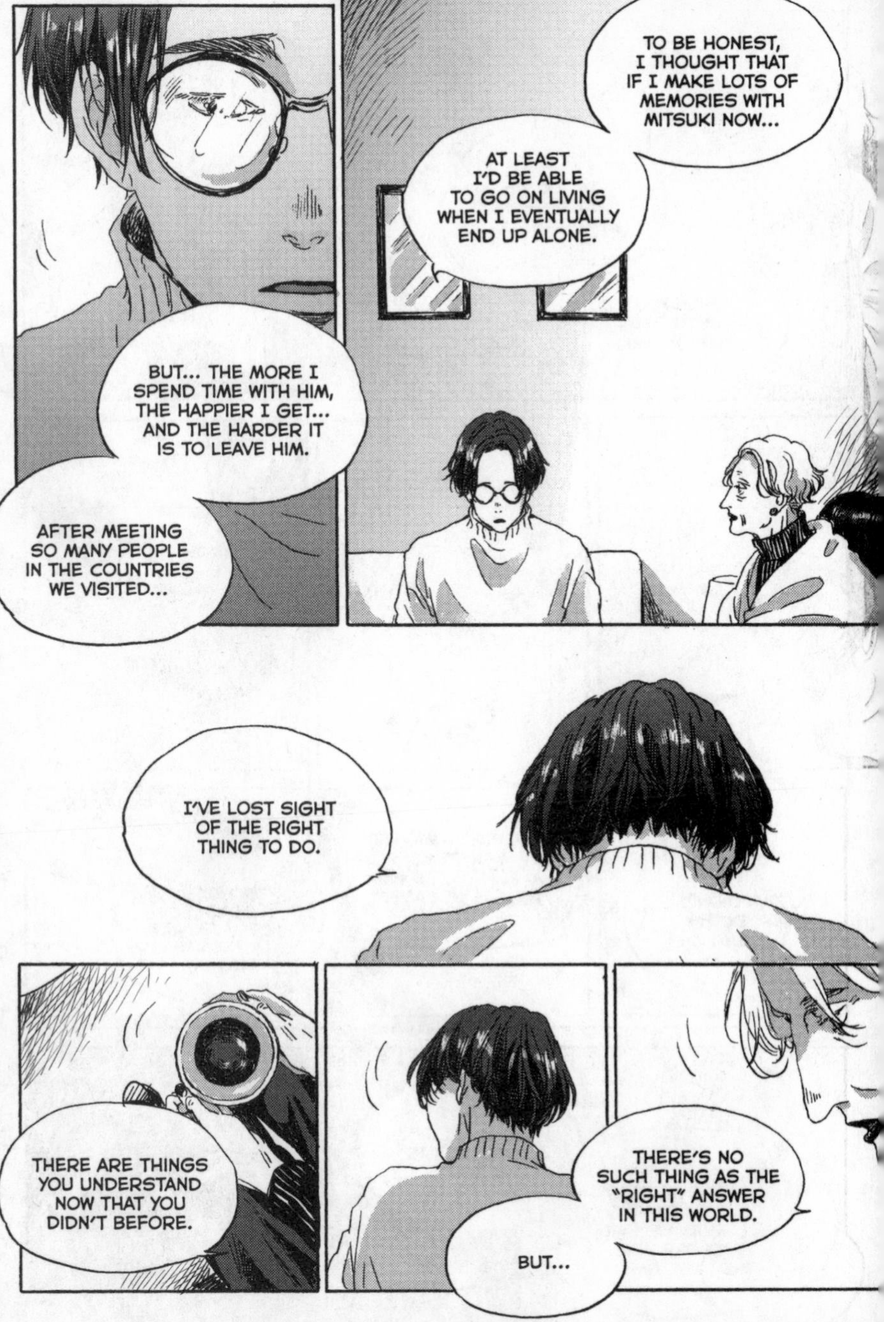
TO BE HONEST, I THOUGHT THAT IF I MAKE LOTS OF MEMORIES WITH MITSUKI NOW...
AT LEAST I'D BE ABLE TO GO ON LIVING WHEN I EVENTUALLY END UP ALONE.
BUT... THE MORE I SPEND TIME WITH HIM, THE HAPPIER I GET... AND THE HARDER IT IS TO LEAVE HIM.
AFTER MEETING SO MANY PEOPLE IN THE COUNTRIES WE VISITED...
I'VE LOST SIGHT OF THE RIGHT THING TO DO.
THERE'S NO SUCH THING AS THE "RIGHT" ANSWER IN THIS WORLD.
BUT...
THERE ARE THINGS YOU UNDERSTAND NOW THAT YOU DIDN'T BEFORE.

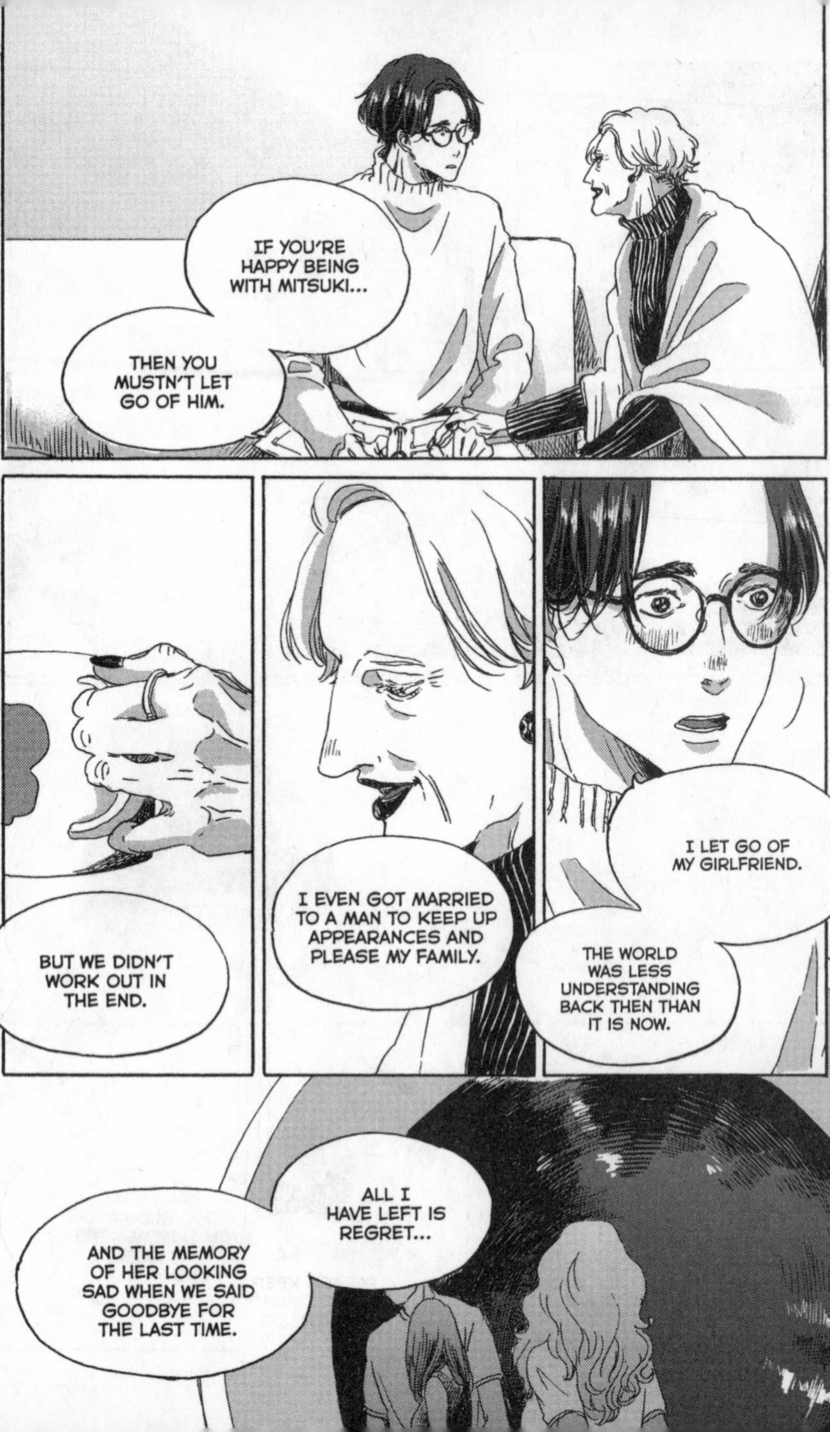
IF YOU'RE HAPPY BEING WITH MITSUKI...
THEN YOU MUSTN'T LET GO OF HIM.
I LET GO OF MY GIRLFRIEND.
THE WORLD WAS LESS UNDERSTANDING BACK THEN THAN IT IS NOW.
I EVEN GOT MARRIED TO A MAN TO KEEP UP APPEARANCES AND PLEASE MY FAMILY.
BUT WE DIDN'T WORK OUT IN THE END.
ALL I HAVE LEFT IS REGRET...
AND THE MEMORY OF HER LOOKING SAD WHEN WE SAID GOODBYE FOR THE LAST TIME.

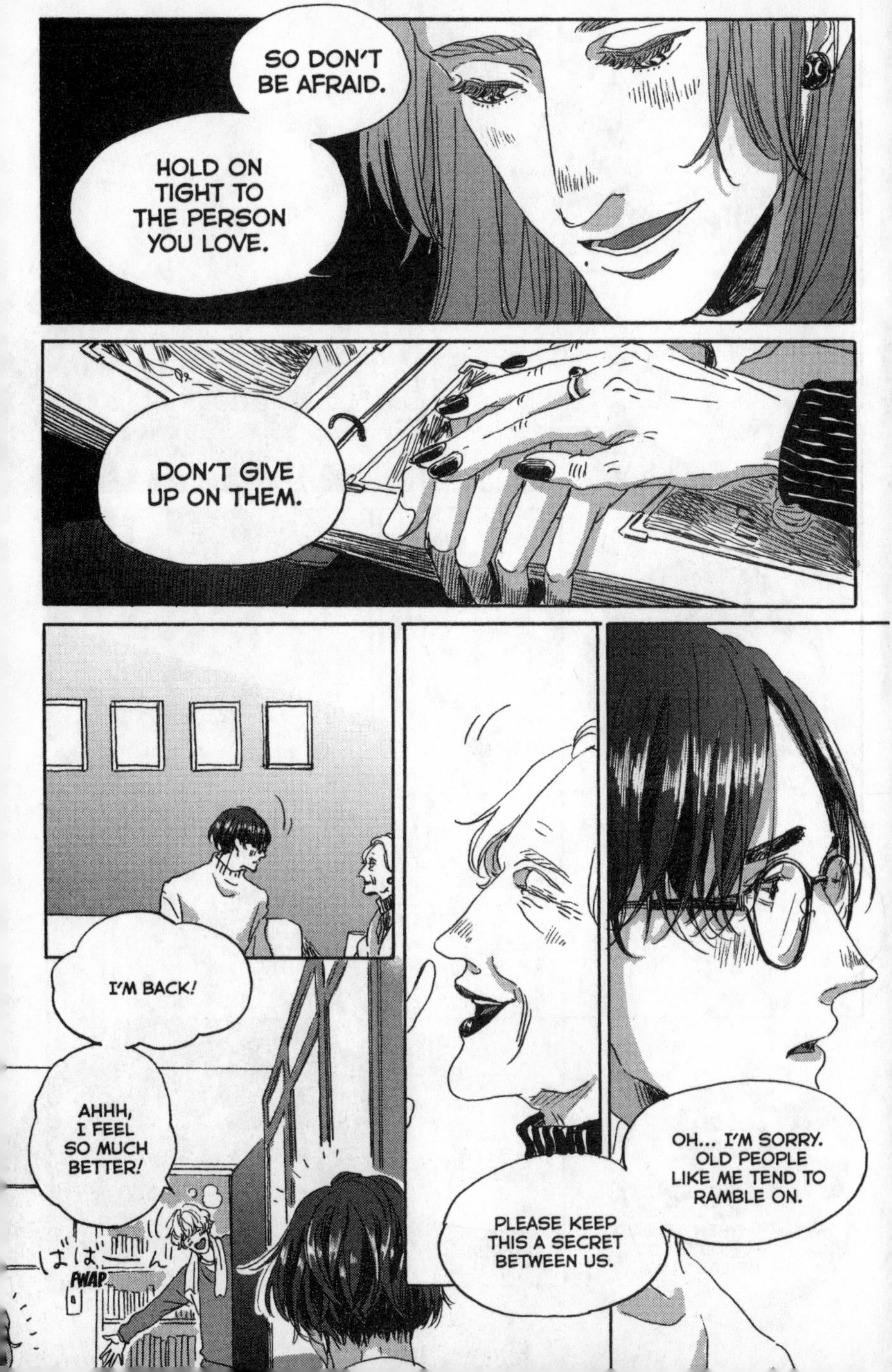
SO DON'T BE AFRAID.
HOLD ON TIGHT TO THE PERSON YOU LOVE.
DON'T GIVE UP ON THEM.
OH... I'M SORRY. OLD PEOPLE LIKE ME TEND TO RAMBLE ON.
PLEASE KEEP THIS A SECRET BETWEEN US.
I'M BACK!
AHHH, I FEEL SO MUCH BETTER!
ばばーん
FWAP

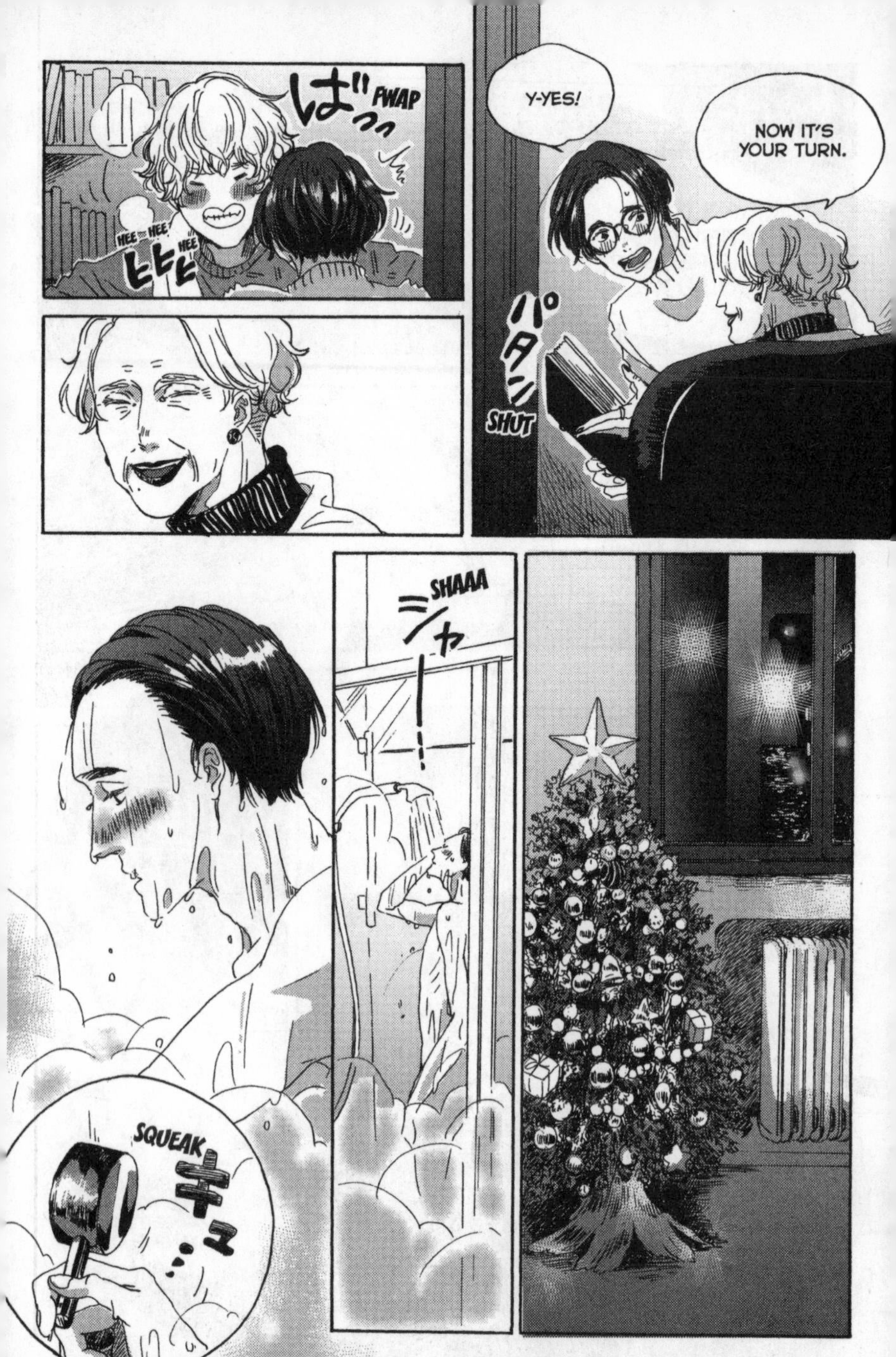
NOW IT'S YOUR TURN.
Y-YES!
パタン
SHUT
ばっ
FWAP
ヒヒヒ
HEE HEE HEE
シャー
SHAAA
キュ…
SQUEAK

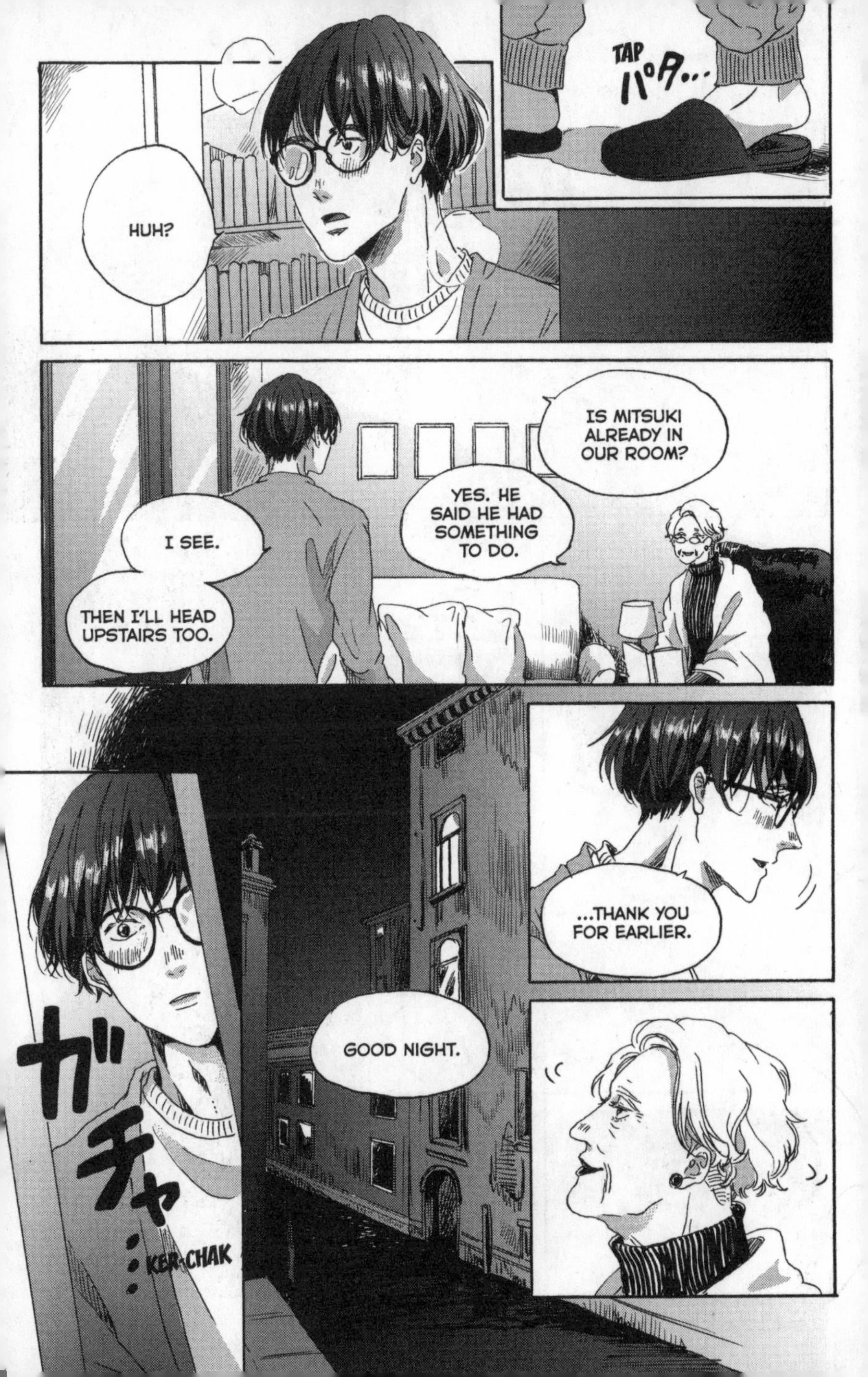
TAP
パタ...
HUH?
IS MITSUKI ALREADY IN OUR ROOM?
YES. HE SAID HE HAD SOMETHING TO DO.
I SEE.
THEN I'LL HEAD UPSTAIRS TOO.
...THANK YOU FOR EARLIER.
GOOD NIGHT.
ガチャ...
KER-CHAK

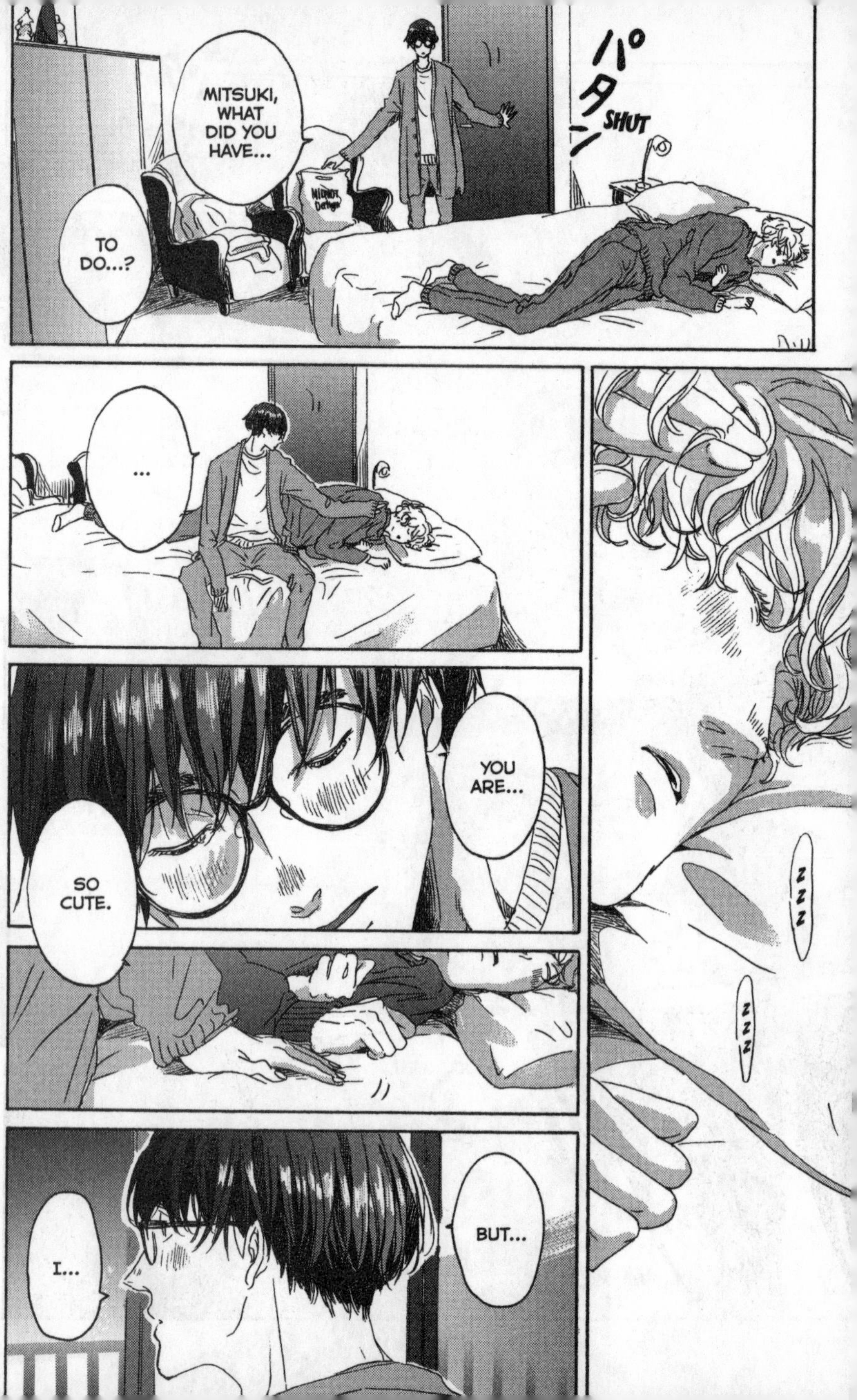
パタン
SHUT
MITSUKI, WHAT DID YOU HAVE...
TO DO...?
ZZZ
ZZZ
...
YOU ARE...
SO CUTE.
BUT...
I...

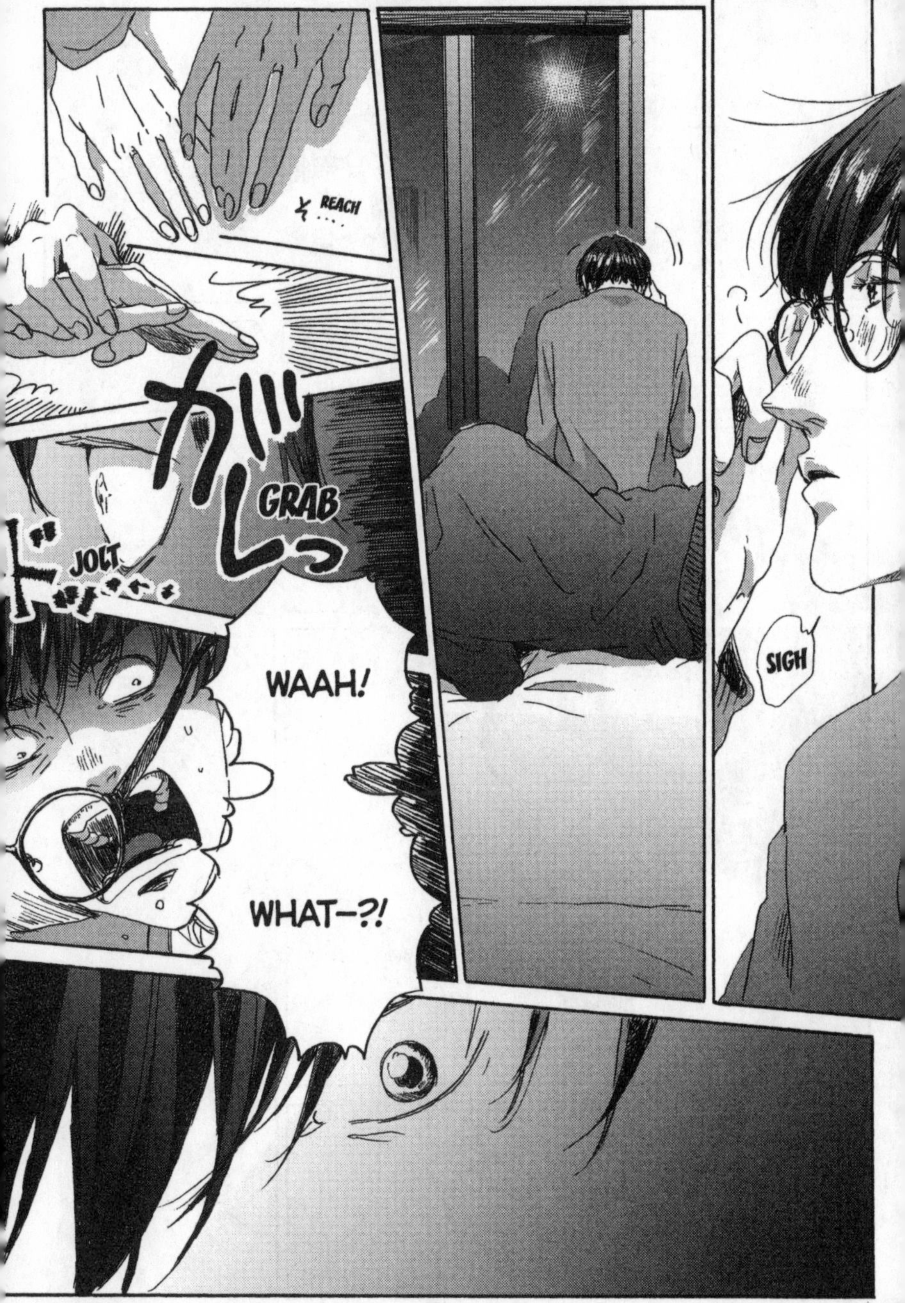
SIGH
REACH
がしっ
GRAB
JOLT
WAAH!
WHAT-?!

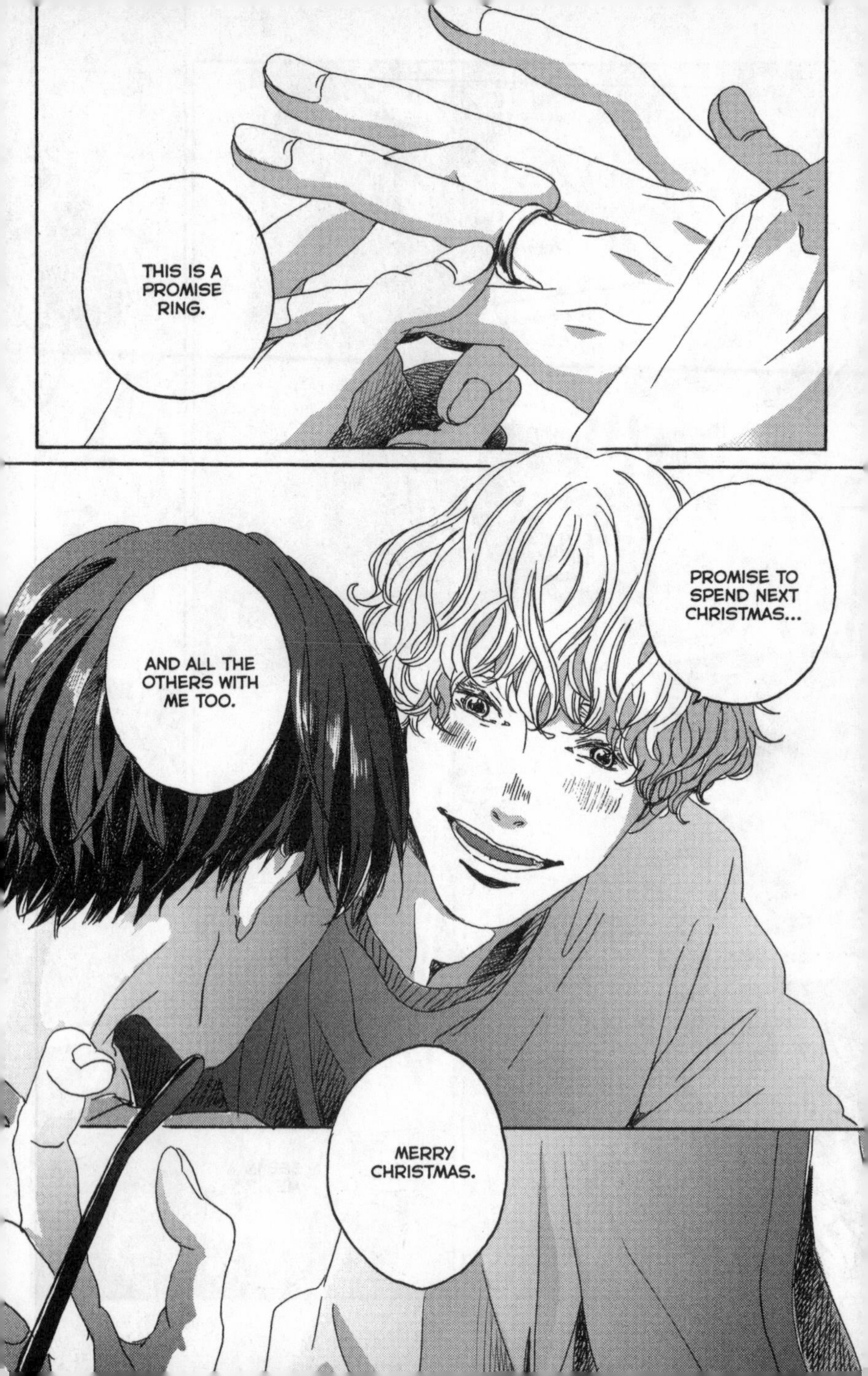
THIS IS A PROMISE RING.
PROMISE TO SPEND NEXT CHRISTMAS...
AND ALL THE OTHERS WITH ME TOO.
MERRY CHRISTMAS.

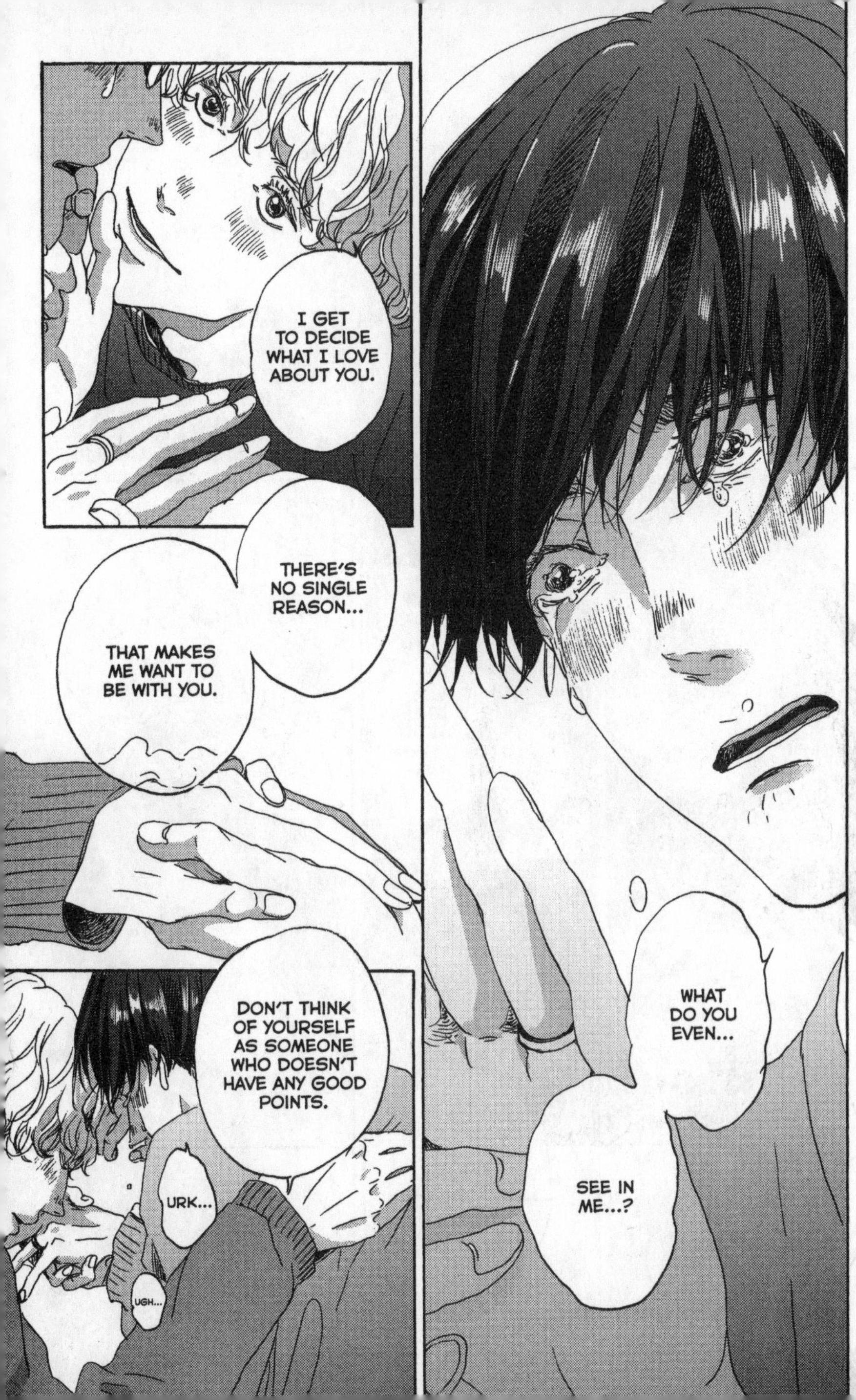
WHAT DO YOU EVEN...
SEE IN ME...?
I GET TO DECIDE WHAT I LOVE ABOUT YOU.
THERE'S NO SINGLE REASON...
THAT MAKES ME WANT TO BE WITH YOU.
DON'T THINK OF YOURSELF AS SOMEONE WHO DOESN'T HAVE ANY GOOD POINTS.
URK...
UGH...

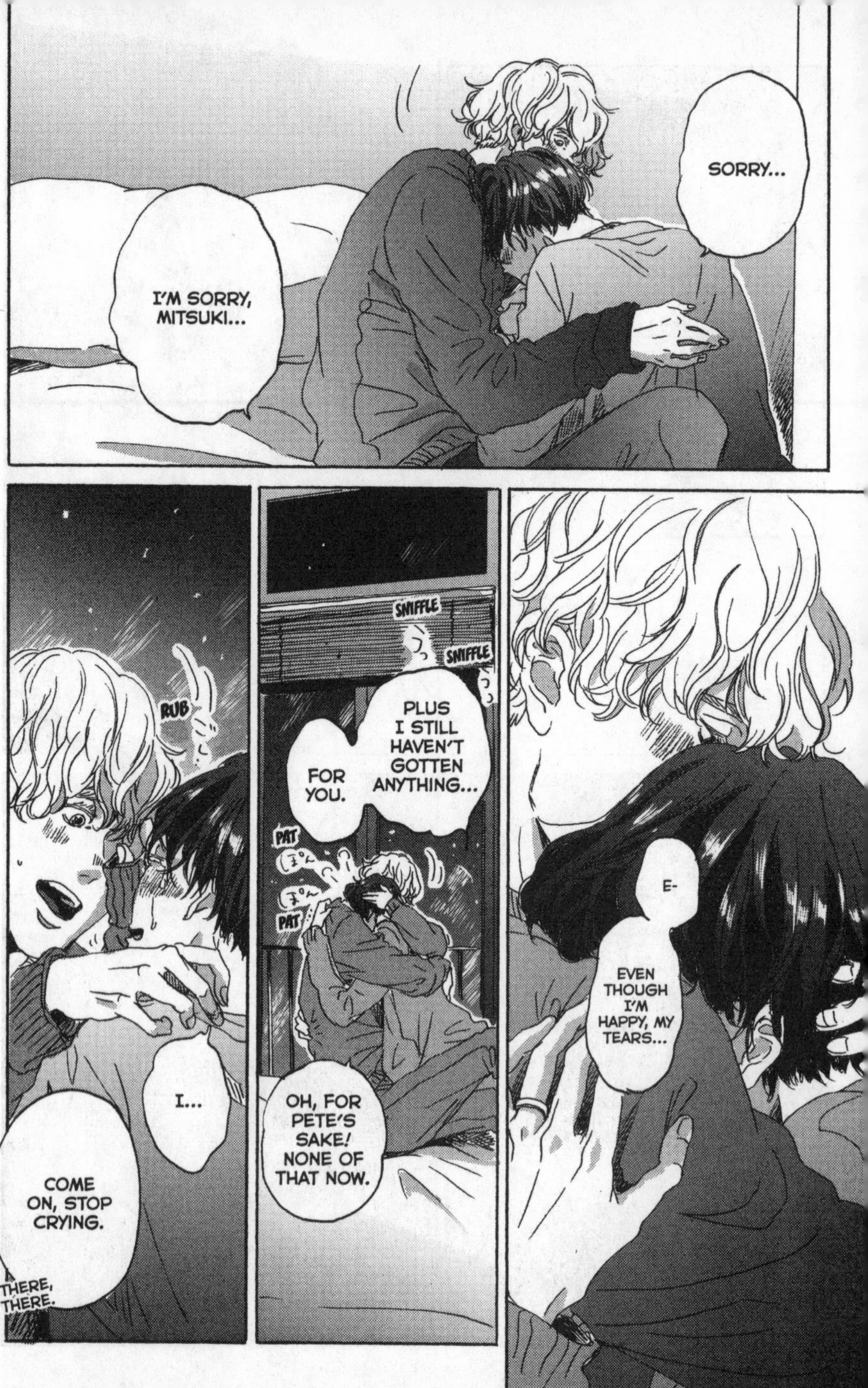
SORRY...
I'M SORRY, MITSUKI...
E-
EVEN THOUGH I'M HAPPY, MY TEARS...
SNIFFLE
SNIFFLE
PLUS I STILL HAVEN'T GOTTEN ANYTHING...
FOR YOU.
PAT
ぽん
ぽん
PAT
OH, FOR PETE'S SAKE! NONE OF THAT NOW.
RUB
I...
COME ON, STOP CRYING.
THERE, THERE.

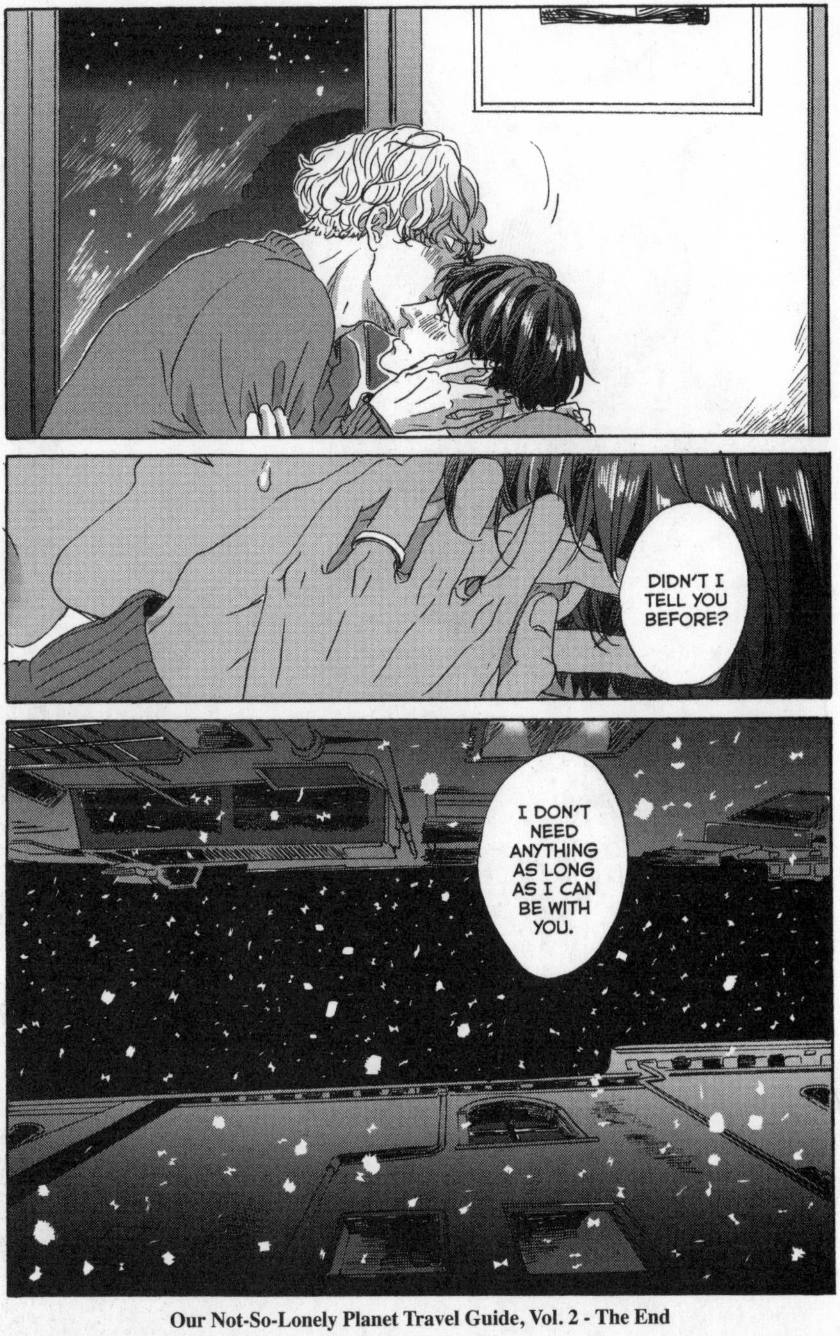
DIDN'T I TELL YOU BEFORE?
I DON'T NEED ANYTHING AS LONG AS I CAN BE WITH YOU.

Our Not-So-Lonely Planet Travel Guide, Vol. 2 - The End

Shoko Rakuta

I'M LOOKING FOR SERIOUS LOVE!

δ LOVE-x-LOVE δ   MATURE 18+

Born and raised in the countryside, Kyouhei immediately clashes with his next door neighbor, an outgoing playboy called Takara, when he moves to Tokyo. As someone who's always been teased for being a country bumpkin, he doesn't exactly have much in common with an extroverted city boy. But when Takara makes a move on him one day, Kyouhei can't get it out of his mind. Even though he can barely stand Takara, he can't help finding himself strangely drawn to him. But Kyouhei's not looking for a one night stand; he's looking for serious love!

DEKOBOKO BITTERSWEET DAYS

Atsuko Yusen

DEKO-BOKO BITTERSWEET DAYS

ATSUKO YUSEN

MATURE 18+ ♂LOVE-x-LOVE♂

Tiny and adorable when they first met, Rui – still just as adorable – now looms over his boyfriend, Yuujirou. Though they were little more than best friends at first, the confusion over their true feelings for one another smoldered until they confessed. Now every day passes with such overwhelming sweetness it's all they can do not to ask themselves, "am I allowed to be this happy?"

A slow-burn love story between a diminutive, athletic teen and his towering, kind-hearted best friend as they journey the slightly bitter road to adulthood towards sweeter days.

TOKYOPOP

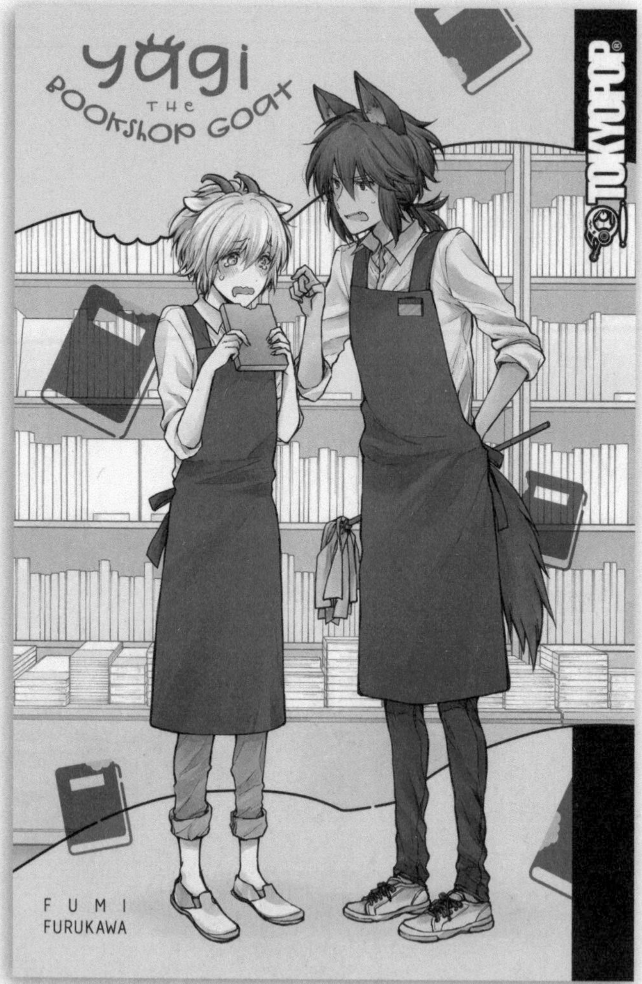
Yagi the Bookshop Goat
TOKYOPOP
FUMI
FURUKAWA

YAGI THE BOOKSHOP GOAT

Fumi Furukawa

LOVE-x-LOVE MATURE 18+

In this tranquil world where all animals live in peace, carnivores and herbivores have an agreement to live amicably. Yagi is a goat who loves reading (and eating!) books; his dream is to become a bookstore clerk, but goats who eat paper aren't exactly welcomed at places that sell books! But maybe he can charm Ookami, the scary wolf store manager into giving him a job...

TOKYOPOP

KOIMONOGATARI: LOVE STORIES, VOL 2

Tohru Tagura

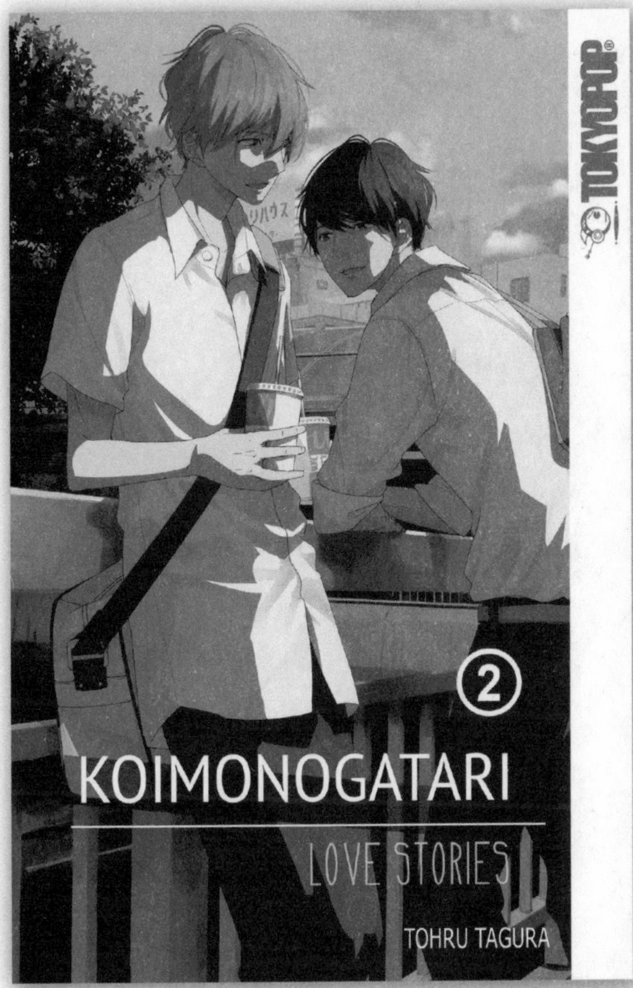
TOKYOPOP
2
KOIMONOGATARI
LOVE STORIES
TOHRU TAGURA

LOVE-x-LOVE

TOKYOPOP

When Yuiji accidentally finds out his classmate Yamato is gay and has a crush on his best friend, he doesn't know how to react at first. But after spending more time together, the two of them become close friends. While Yamato struggles with his sexuality, Yuiji supports him and keeps his secret, hoping that Yamato can find a way to accept himself and be happy. Meanwhile, Yuiji is having trouble feeling connected to his long-time girlfriend, realizing that although he still cares about her, the spark in their relationship has faded.

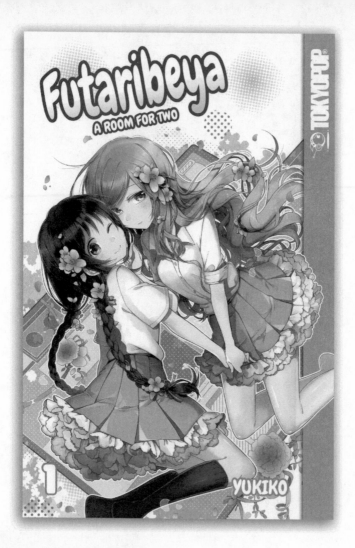

Futaribeya
A ROOM FOR TWO
TOKYOPOP
1
YUKIKO

FUTARIBEYA: A ROOM FOR TWO, VOL 1
Yukiko

LOVE x LOVE

As her exciting first year of high school begins, Sakurako Kawawa settles into her new lodgings. There, she meets her roommate — the stunningly beautiful Kasumi Yamabuki, who lives life at her own pace. From day one, responsible, level-headed Sakurako and lazy, easygoing Kasumi find themselves at odds with one another... But with their matching mugs and one bed to share, Sakurako and Kasumi's friendship is just beginning!

TOKYOPOP

ALICE IN KYOTO FOREST, VOLUME 1

Mai Mochizuki

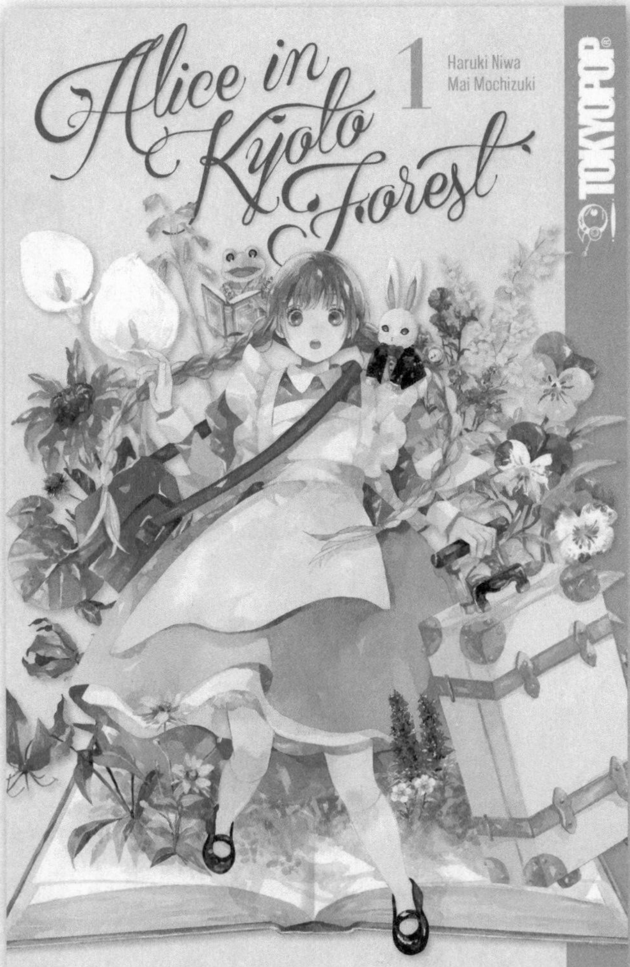
Alice in Kyoto Forest
1
Haruki Niwa
Mai Mochizuki
TOKYOPOP

FANTASY

TOKYOPOP

Orphaned at a young age, Alice has lived with her aunt for most of her childhood. But her uncle is abusive and resentful, and at fifteen years old, Alice decides to return home to Kyoto and train as a maiko, eventually hoping to become a geisha.
But when she arrives back to the city where she was born, she finds that Kyoto has changed quite a bit in the eight years since she left it. Almost as if it's a completely different world...

THE FOX & LITTLE TANUKI, VOLUME 1

Mi Tagawa

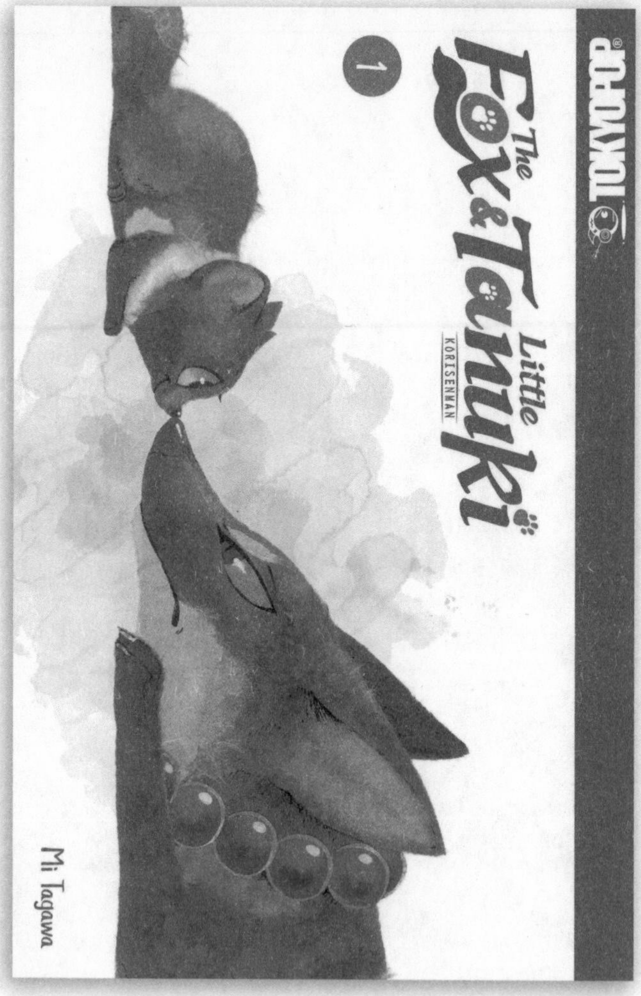
TOKYOPOP
The Fox & Little Tanuki
KORISENMAN
1
Mi Tagawa

FANTASY

It is said that there are some special animals occasionally born with great powers. Senzou the black fox is one of those... but instead of using his powers for good, he abused his strength until the Sun Goddess imprisoned him for his bad behavior. Three hundred years later, he's finally been released, but only on one condition — he can't have any of his abilities back until he successfully helps a tanuki cub named Manpachi become an assistant to the gods. Unfortunately for Senzou, there's no cheating when it comes to completing his task! The magic beads around his neck make sure he can't wander too far from his charge or ignore his duties, and so... Senzou the once-great Fox Spirit must figure out how to be an actually-great babysitter to an innocent little tanuki or risk being stuck without his powers forever!

TOKYOPOP

MAME COORDINATE, VOLUME 1

Sachi Miyabe

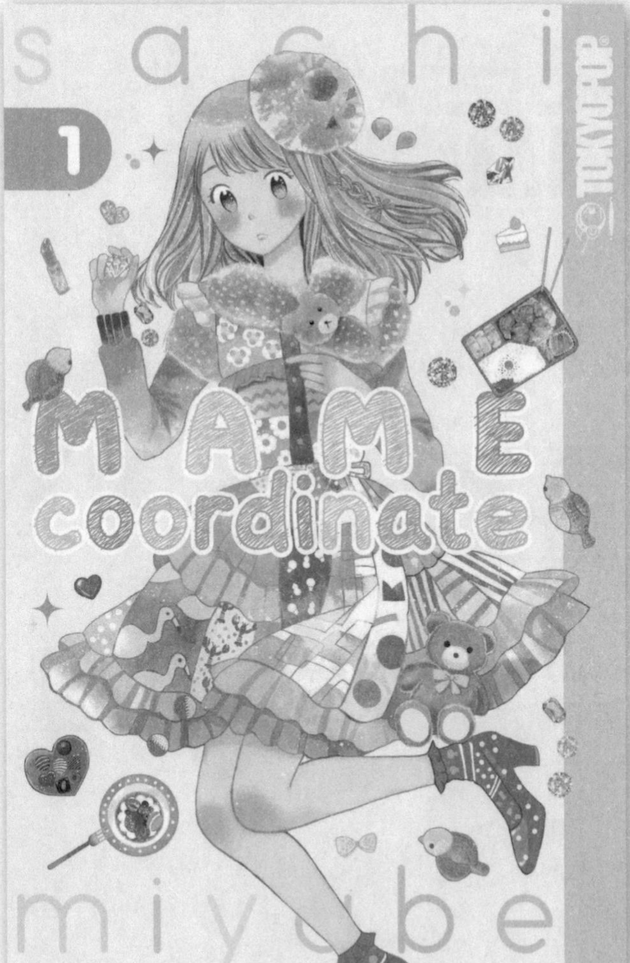

sachi
1
TOKYOPOP
MAME coordinate
miyabe

SLICE-OF-LIFE

She loves meat and fried foods, and eats only karaage bento. Wearing exclusively clothes with weird characters printed on them, her fashion sense is practically non-existent. No confidence in her own looks. Extreme social anxiety. She speaks with a country drawl, and even her name is unusual. But then Mame (born in Tottori prefecture) was discovered by an intimidating, bespectacled rookie manager, and now begins the arduous task of getting her ready for auditions! The road to Top Model looks awfully steep from here.

OSSAN IDOL! VOLUME 1

Mochiko Mochida & Ichika Kino

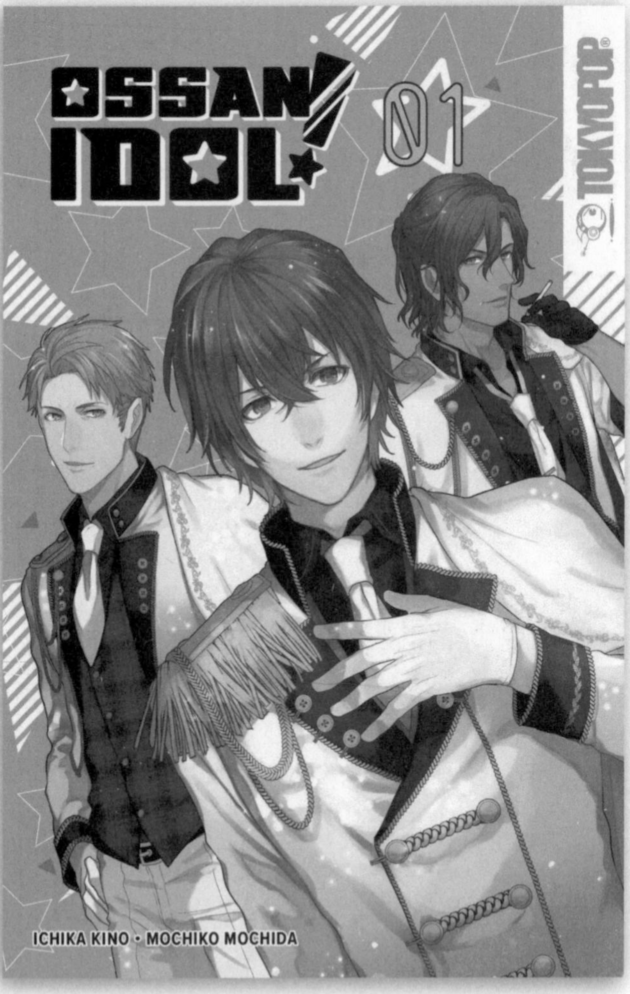
TOKYOPOP
OSSAN IDOL!
01
ICHIKA KINO • MOCHIKO MOCHIDA

IDOL

Miroku Osaki is 36 years old, unemployed, and unhappy. Having been bullied in his childhood and even into his adult life, he became a shut-in after being unfairly laid off. For a long time, the only thing that brought him joy was online gaming. Then, he tried the popular "Let's Try Dancing!" karaoke style. It was addicting... and transformative! Inspired by his new hobby, Miroku decides to turn his life around. He begins singing karaoke and going to the gym, where he meets Yoichi, the director of an entertainment company who encourages Miroku to pursue his dreams. Miroku only wanted to be good at the game he loves, but when he accidentally uploads a clip of himself singing and dancing, it goes viral! Can he really become an idol, even at his age? Suddenly, it doesn't seem so impossible!

DOUBLE, VOLUME 1

Ayako Noda

AYAKO NODA

D
O
U
B
L
E

01

TOKYOPOP®

DRAMA

TOKYOPOP®

Yuujin Kamoshima and Takara Takarada are fellow actors in the same theater troupe who live next door to one another, with similar day to day lives. Though they aren't exactly close friends, when Yuujin is cast as Takara's double, he sees first hand his extraordinary acting skills and is blown away. From that moment on, he's determined to help him succeed and support him in his dream of becoming a world renowned actor, even if Yuujin has to be in his shadow. But as the acting world begins to take notice, that's easier said than done...

© Ayako Noda 2019 / HERO'S

ALICE in BISHOUNEN-LAND
TOKYOPOP
1
Yushi Kawata & Yukito

ALICE IN BISHOUNEN-LAND, VOLUME 1

Yushi Kawata

LOVE-x-LOVE

Alice Kagami is an ordinary high school girl who doesn't really get her friend Tamami's obsession with idol games. There's more to life than handsome digital boys, dating sims, and mini-games, right? But then, Tamami is "chosen" as one of the top idol fangirls in the country and gets drawn into the game — and hapless Alice gets pulled in too! Between dealing with the mismatched members of her idol group to intense pressure to spend real money on gachas, how is a total idol game newbie supposed to take them to the top?

I WAS REINCARNATED AS THE VILLAINESS IN AN OTOME GAME BUT THE BOYS LOVE ME ANYWAY! VOLUME 1

Ataka, Sou Inaida & Hachipisu Wan

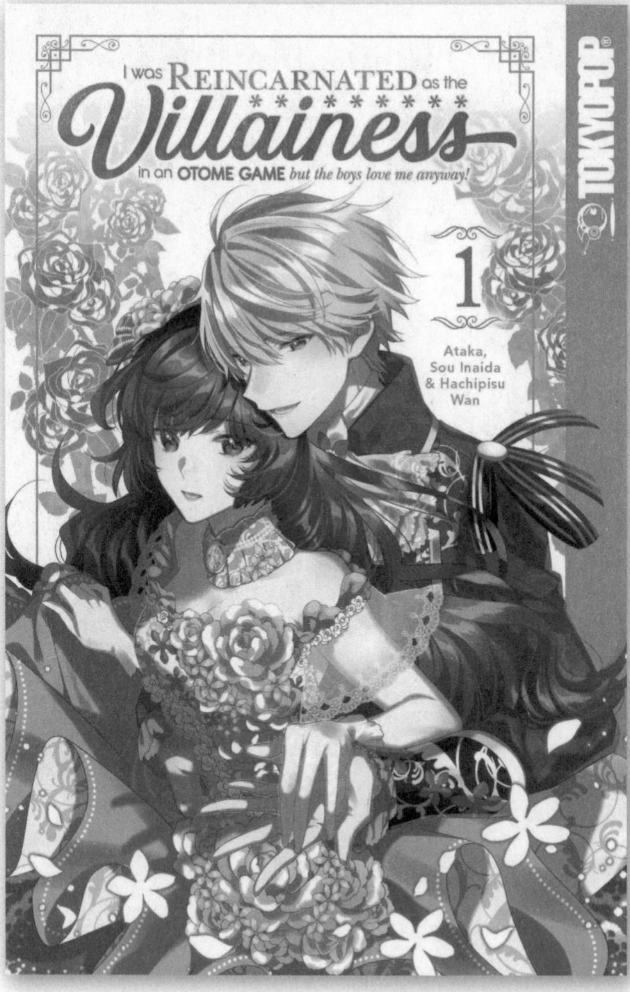
I was REINCARNATED as the
Villainess
in an OTOME GAME but the boys love me anyway!
1
Ataka,
Sou Inaida
& Hachipisu
Wan
TOKYOPOP

LOVE-x-LOVE

TOKYOPOP

Fated to die as the villainess of an otome game, Mystia sets out to change her own unhappy ending! Mystia Aren is the daughter of a noble family, and she just started high school. She's surrounded by a group of adoring classmates and her charming fiancé. Everything seems perfect. Except that this world is actually a dating sim called Kyun-Love, and Mystia knows she's been reincarnated into the role of the main character's evil rival! Mystia is determined to do everything she can to avoid her fate, but it's not as easy as it sounds. Especially when all the boys keep falling in love with her!

Would you like to be a family?

Koyama

WOULD YOU LIKE TO BE A FAMILY?

TOKYOPOP

KOYAMA

⚨LOVE-x-LOVE⚨

Families come in many shapes and sizes, and these three are no different! Takemura is a loner with little interest in socializing with others. Bullied in high school for being gay, he prefers to spend time by himself so he won't get hurt again. When he runs into his bright, friendly coworker Natsui in the supermarket, he's surprised to find out that he's a single father... and even more surprised to be invited to dinner, with no room to decline! Kuma is a good guy, but due to his constant scowl and rough appearance is often dismissed as a deadbeat. When he oversees his friend's older brother break up with his boyfriend, Yagi, Kuma becomes intrigued with this attractive stranger and slowly, his curiosity begins to blossom into a crush. Kodama is a reserved psychology major who is approached by the loud, outgoing Harada when he falls ill on his way home. It turns out the two of them study at the same university, and Harada insists the two become friends. But as they spend more time with one another, Kodama begins to question how he truly feels. Follow three very different relationships in this intimate collection of short Boys Love stories.

TOKYOPOP

STOP

THIS IS THE BACK OF THE BOOK!

How do you read manga-style? It's simple! Let's practice -- just start in the top right panel and follow the numbers below!

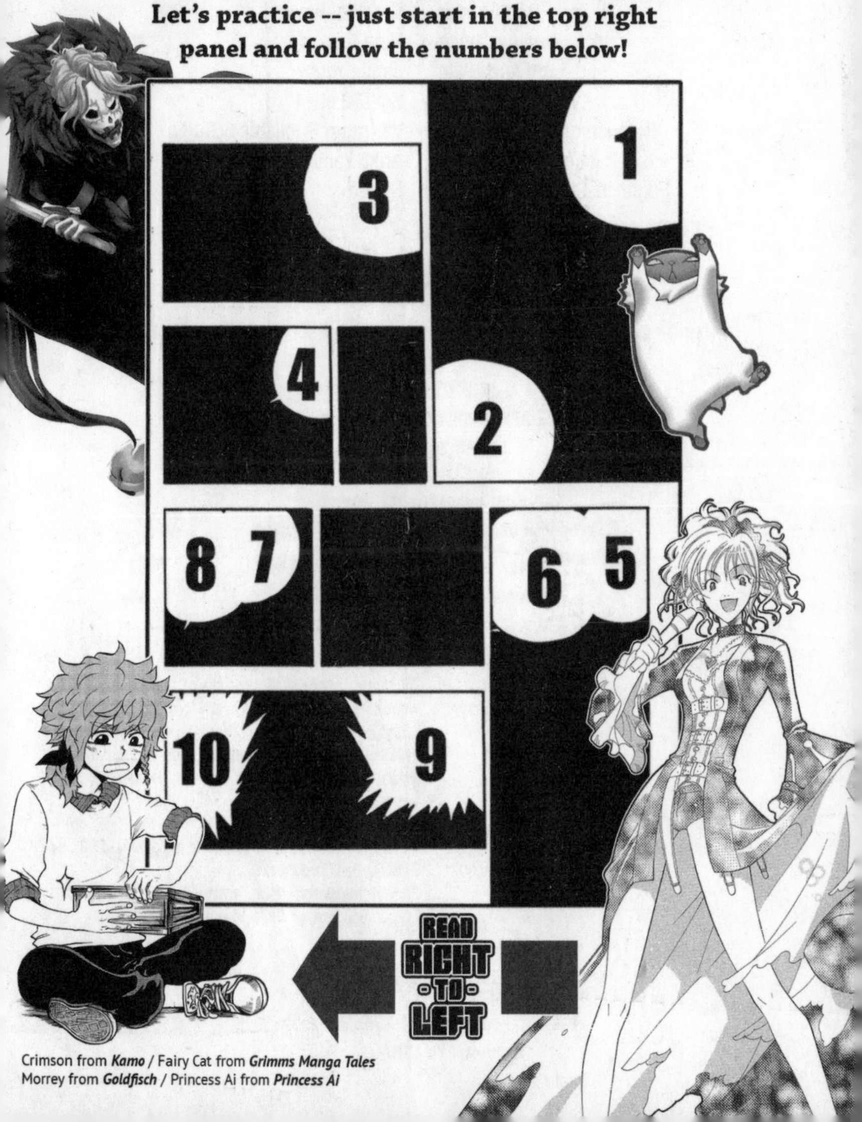
1
2
3
4
5
6
7
8
9
10
READ
RIGHT
-TO-
LEFT

Crimson from ***Kamo*** / Fairy Cat from ***Grimms Manga Tales***
Morrey from ***Goldfisch*** / Princess Ai from ***Princess Ai***

Our Not-So-Lonely Planet Travel Guide, Volume 2
Manga by Mone Sorai

Editor	- Lena Atanassova
Marketing Associate	- Kae Winters
Translator	- Katie Kimura
Copy Editor	- M. Cara Carper
Proofreader	- Caroline Wong
Quality Check	- Nina Sawada
Editorial Associate	- Janae Young
Graphic Designer	- Sol DeLeo
Retouching and Lettering	- Vibrraant Publishing Studio
Licensing Specialist	- Arika Yanaka
Editor-in-Chief & Publisher	- Stu Levy

A  Manga

TOKYOPOP and 👁 are trademarks or registered trademarks of TOKYOPOP Inc.

TOKYOPOP Inc.
5200 W. Century Blvd. Suite 705
Los Angeles, 90045

E-mail: info@TOKYOPOP.com
Come visit us online at www.TOKYOPOP.com

f www.facebook.com/TOKYOPOP
🐦 www.twitter.com/TOKYOPOP
📷 www.instagram.com/TOKYOPOP

ISBN: 978-1-4278-6850-3
First TOKYOPOP Printing: February 2022
Printed in CANADA